incisive account of an immigrant group whose impact has been profound. This lively and clearly written contribution to a full understanding of how the Irish have changed America (and vice versa) deserves the widest possible audience." —**Peter Quinn, author of** *Looking for Jimmy: A Search for Irish America*

"Jay Dolan has achieved a remarkable feat: He has told the sweeping story of the Irish in America with a great appreciation for its complexity, its tragedies, and its triumphs. The Irish have transformed the United States, and have been transformed themselves into something we call Irish America. Dolan explains how that process worked and why the story of Irish America remains relevant at a time when we continue to argue about immigration and assimilation."

—**Terry Golway, author of** *The Irish in America*

The Irish Americans

A History

JAY P. DOLAN

BLOOMSBURY PRESS
New York   Berlin   London

Published by Bloomsbury Press, New York

All papers used by Bloomsbury Press are natural, recyclable products made from wood grown in well-managed forests. The manufacturing processes conform to the environmental regulations of the country of origin.

LIBRARY OF CONGRESS CATALOGING-IN-PUBLICATION DATA

Dolan, Jay P., 1936–
The Irish Americans : a history / Jay P. Dolan.—1st U.S. ed.
p.   cm.
Includes bibliographical references and index.
ISBN-13: 978-1-59691-419-3 (alk. paper hardcover)
ISBN-10: 1-59691-419-X (alk. paper hardcover)
1. Irish Americans—History. I. Title.

E184.I6D59 2008
973'.049162—dc22   2008004476

First published by Bloomsbury Press in 2008
This paperback edition published in 2010

Paperback ISBN: 978-1-60819-010-2

1 3 5 7 9 10 8 6 4 2

Typeset by Westchester Book Group
Printed in the United States of America by Quebecor World Fairfield

For Patricia

Contents

Contents

Preface

For eighteen years I taught a course in Irish American history at the University of Notre Dame, home of the Fighting Irish. For much of my career I had focused on the history of American Catholicism. But teaching this course on Irish America kindled in me a desire to learn more about the history of Irish America. In many ways it was a love affair that intensified over the years. This experience inspired me to begin writing this book. William Shannon's book *The American Irish*, published in 1963, was the last history written for the general reader. Clearly a new history of the American Irish was needed that would incorporate the work historians had done since the 1960s. The time also seemed right given the renewed interest in Irish culture and history both in Ireland and in the United States. So once I retired from teaching in 2004, I undertook the writing of this book.

I have organized the book in much the same way that I structured my undergraduate course by focusing on four major themes that have dominated Irish American history—politics, religion, labor, and nationalism. But in one area these themes do not work so well: the eighteenth century. Until recently this has been the forgotten area of Irish American history. When thinking about the Irish in America, the Great Famine of the 1840s immediately comes to mind. For most people, this is when the story begins. Moreover, it was a Catholic story since the vast majority of the famine immigrants and those who followed them were Roman Catholics. But the history of Irish America begins in the eighteenth century, not the nineteenth, and it is not only a Catholic narrative but an Irish one that includes both Protestants and Catholics. The first two chapters cover this period, from

1700 to 1840. This remarkable history follows the Irish who settled along the rural frontier, where, as struggling farmers, they eked out a living by trading with Native Americans. By the late eighteenth century Philadelphia had become the capital of Irish America—the gateway for many Irish immigrants who were traveling west to the frontier as well as the home of numerous merchants who had established a prosperous trading network with Ireland.

After the American Revolution and the birth of a new nation, the Irish continued to immigrate, but their numbers were not very great. Included among them were a number of political radicals who were forced into exile because of their outspoken opposition to England's rule over Ireland. Mostly members of the middle class, they settled along the Eastern seaboard, where they kept alive the dream of Irish independence. Casting aside the bitter sectarianism that had plagued Ireland for so long, they dreamed of an Ireland where Irishmen and Irishwomen of all religious denominations were united in a common bond of nationhood. But the vast majority of immigrants in this prefamine period were not so irenic. Many of them were Catholics who brought with them a more sectarian, less inclusive attitude that contrasted sharply with the nonsectarian viewpoint of the middle-class political exiles.

Symptomatic of this change in attitude was the introduction of the term *Scotch-Irish* into the Irish American vocabulary. The term had been in use during the eighteenth century to designate the Ulster Presbyterians who had emigrated to the United States. From the mid-1700s through the early 1800s, however, the term *Irish* was more widely used to identify both Catholic and Protestant Irish. As long as the Protestants comprised the majority of the emigrants, as they did until the 1830s, they were happy to be known simply as Irish. But as political and religious conflict between Catholics and Protestants both in Ireland and the United States became more frequent, and as Catholic emigrants began to outnumber Protestants, the term *Irish* became synonymous with Irish Catholics. As a result, *Scotch-Irish* became the customary term to describe Protestants of Irish descent. By adopting this new identity, Irish Protestants in America dissociated themselves from Irish Catholics. The broader meaning of *Irish*, so prevalent in the colonial era, faded from memory. The famine migration of the 1840s and '50s that sent waves of poor Irish Catholics to the United States together with the rise in anti-Catholicism intensified this attitude. In no way did Irish Protestants want to be identified with these ragged newcomers. So they took on a new identity—an identity, some boasted, that did not include a drop of blood of the old Celtic (i.e., Catholic) Irish.

This major transformation took place between the 1790s and the mid-1840s. As Irish identity changed, so did Irish American history. Henceforth, the label *Irish* would identify Irish Catholics exclusively. These are the people who occupy center stage in this book after the Great Famine, when 1.5 million Irish, the majority of whom were Catholic, immigrated to the United States.

The nickels and dimes of these immigrants helped to transform the Catholic Church into the largest and most feared religious denomination in the country. "The Irish were born to rule," as one pundit put it, and they soon built powerful political machines in many cities. They were also in the forefront of the labor movement, leading the struggle for decent wages and humane working conditions. As Ireland strove to break free of English domination, its most ardent supporters were the Irish exiles in America. Each of these topics—religion, politics, labor, nationalism—is so vast that I dedicate a chapter to each one. Most of the book focuses on major American cities where the majority of the Irish settled. By the mid-nineteenth century, New York had replaced Philadelphia as the capital of the Irish. The Irish also traveled west to Chicago and San Francisco. Others moved to western mining towns such as Butte, Montana. As the narrative moves into the twentieth century, I continue the focus on the four major themes and the transformations that occur in each area. The final chapter discusses what I call the "triumph of the Irish." By the 1960s they had become one of the best educated and most prosperous ethnic groups in the nation. They had come a long way since the famine era, when their ancestors had arrived with little more than the clothes on their backs, working as ditchdiggers, porters, and maids. What is equally remarkable is that Irish Americans have stayed Irish even while embracing their adoptive land—an achievement that I seek to explain in the conclusion of the book.

I have to acknowledge that this history of the Irish in America is incomplete. I do not discuss their achievements in literature, which have been extraordinary. Nor do I examine the fields of music or sports, where they had a notable presence. I leave this to another day and another historian. Nonetheless, my hope is that the readers of this book will enjoy one of the great success stories in American history. The story deserves to be told once again.

PART ONE

A Forgotten Era, 1700–1840

CHAPTER I

Here Come the Irish

The Battle of the Boyne was the most famous of all Irish battles. It took place in July 1690 along the Boyne River, two miles west of Drogheda, where two kings, the Protestant William of Orange and the Catholic James II, fought the decisive battle that would crown the victor king of England and determine who would rule Ireland, Catholics or Protestants.

James had become king of England, Scotland, and Ireland in 1685, but three years later, leading English Protestants, fearful of a Catholic dynasty, urged the Dutchman William of Orange to invade England and seize the throne. After fleeing to France, James rallied his forces in Ireland, where he challenged William to fight for the right to be the king of the three kingdoms.

The troops were up at dawn on the first day of July, with William's forces, numbering about thirty-five thousand, controlling the north side of the river, while James's troops, about twenty-five thousand, defended the south bank of the river. At around ten in the morning, after a heavy bombardment of the Irish position from William's artillery, the Dutch Guard, an elite group of infantrymen, marched to the banks of the river with drums beating their cadence. Line after line of soldiers, marching eight to ten abreast, descended into the river, wading in water up to their armpits. Holding their muskets and powder high above their heads, they were eager to take on the best that the Irish and French forces had to offer. By the time they reached the middle of the river, the Irish forces let loose with a hail of shot from behind the hedges and houses and all about. When they reached the riverbanks, the Dutch Guard blazed away with musket fire and slashed furiously with their bayonets. James's Irish cavalry charged, slashing and stabbing whatever was in their way.

For almost an hour fierce fighting raged along the riverbank. Irish musketeers and pikemen supported the charging cavalry. Artillery fire from William's cannons filled the air with dense smoke, creating chaos and forcing the Irish soldiers to retreat and regroup. Counterattacks followed as more of William's troops crossed the river. The firepower of William's Dutch soldiers overwhelmed James's forces. As one regiment leader said, "The truth is that the enemy was stronger and their firepower heavier."[1] More troops followed, forging the river at various points, outflanking and outsmarting James's forces. The rout was on. William's cavalry carried the day, their swords stabbing a path through the Irish forces. King William himself, though wounded, with sword in hand, led several charges during the battle.

By the early afternoon the black smoke and dust began to disappear, and an eerie silence covered the battlefield. William of Orange could claim victory as the Irish troops, disorganized and outnumbered, retreated to the safety of the hills beyond the Boyne. James fled south to Kinsale, where he boarded a ship to France. It was hardly a fight to the bitter end: the number of soldiers killed was comparatively light, about a thousand of James's forces and five hundred of William's soldiers. But the war would continue for another year, laying waste to the countryside of Ireland, leaving death and destruction in its path. When a truce was finally declared in October 1691, the Protestant triumph was complete. A Protestant minority would rule Ireland for the next one hundred years. To this day Protestants in Northern Ireland still celebrate the triumph at the Battle of the Boyne.

The Protestant victory not only shaped the modern history of Ireland, but also laid the groundwork for the emigration of thousands of Irish to North America. The first wave of emigration occurred during the eighteenth century, when, prior to the American Revolution, as many as 250,000 emigrated from Ireland, most from the province of Ulster, in the north of Ireland.

Ulster had long been a citadel of Gaelic Catholic culture, but the English government wanted to change that. To accomplish their goal they began establishing plantations in the province by having loyal Protestants from Scotland and England settle on land confiscated from the native Catholic Irish. In this manner they hoped to civilize the province by establishing in Ulster what they believed to be the true religion. From the early seventeenth century to 1640, as many as one hundred thousand Scots settled in Ulster. They continued to arrive throughout the rest of the seventeenth century, settling mostly in the eastern half of Ulster, carrying with them a distinctive brand of Protestantism, Scottish Presbyterianism.

By 1715 about six hundred thousand people lived in Ulster. About half of them were Catholic, one third were Presbyterian, and the rest belonged to the Church of Ireland (Anglican) or other Protestant denominations. Nevertheless, the Church of Ireland, made up primarily of the elite landowning class, ruled the province. By law the Church of Ireland was the established church in Ireland. All Irish, Protestants as well as Catholics, had to pay taxes to support the Church of Ireland. To curb the growth and power of both Presbyterians and Catholics, the English government also passed a series of laws, known as the Penal Laws, that victimized Catholics as well as those Protestants who did not belong to the Anglican Church.

One such law, the Sacramental Test Act of 1704, required government officials to receive Communion in the Church of Ireland. This barred all Protestant dissenters, those who were not members of the Anglican Church of Ireland, as well as Catholics, from civil and military offices, effectively excluding them from public life. To curb the growth of the Presbyterian Church, the government closed their churches and schools and prohibited their clergy from officiating at weddings or funerals.[2] Such religious intolerance, a bone in the throat for many Ulster Irish, would become a major catalyst propelling thousands of them to leave Ireland for North America.

A group of Protestant ministers, addressing the king, underscored the deep sense of oppression that many Presbyterians felt: "Because of 'hardship and oppressions which the Protestant Dissenters laboured under . . . they have in great numbers transported themselves to the American Plantations' where they hoped to enjoy 'that liberty and ease which they are denied in their native country.' "[3] Though religious toleration increased by midcentury, dissenting Protestants and Catholics still remained second-class citizens in a land ruled by the Anglican elite.

The Penal Laws aimed at Roman Catholics were even more draconian. To prevent the growth of the Catholic Church, Parliament passed laws that banned priests and bishops from Ireland, outlawed Catholic schools in Ireland, prohibited Irish Catholics from studying at Catholic schools in Europe, prohibited marriages between Protestants and Catholics, excluded

Catholics from the professions (except medicine), and did not allow them to vote. In 1719 Irish legislators, frustrated at their inability to stem the growth of the clergy, sought to have them branded on the cheek. Others even sought to have outlawed priests castrated, though this legislation was never enacted.

To weaken the power of Catholic landowners, Parliament also enacted laws forbidding Catholics to purchase land and forcing those who owned land to divide it up at their death among their sons. In this manner the English sought to destroy the wealth of Catholics, since in those days land was the major source of a person's wealth. In this endeavor they were fairly successful. By the end of the eighteenth century Irish Catholics only owned 5 percent of Ireland's land, whereas in 1703 they had owned 14 percent.

Since the Penal Laws were too difficult to enforce, the Catholic Church survived. In the 1780s and '90s the Irish parliament repealed most of the Penal Laws. Nonetheless, they did have a psychological impact by reminding Catholics of their inferior status in the land of their birth, where they comprised the majority of the population. The Protestant triumph at the Battle of the Boyne had sealed their fate.

As powerful as religious oppression was in persuading thousands of people to leave Ireland, the main reason for emigration still remained economic. The first sizable exodus began in 1718 and ended in 1729, the chief reason being crop failure. This occurred in 1717 through 1719; the harvest failed again in 1726–28. Such misfortunes led the lord primate of Ireland, Archbishop Hugh Boulter, to remark that "Ireland experienced little less than a famine every other year."[4] The number of starving beggars increased while hard winters killed much of the cattle. Famine was especially acute in 1740–41, when as many as 480,000 people died. Among the Irish this period is still remembered as the Year of the Slaughter, a time when one of every five Irish died, a ratio that was much higher than in the Great Famine of the 1840s.

Adding to the misery of hunger, rents were rising. In the early years of the century people could lease land at bargain prices. But over time land became more scarce and thus more valuable. Leases also began to expire. As this occurred, Anglican landowners, many of whom were absentee landlords who seldom visited Ireland, raised the rents on their land. Rents were rising as crops were failing. One Irishman, writing to his sister in New Jersey, complained about the hard times: "This hath been avery hard yeere amongst the poore people, for Corn failed very much and now wheat is at twenty shillings abarell and other Corne pro-porsianable lands is got to an Extrame Rate heree so that any person who rents land [at these high rates] will likely be ruined financially." As their standard of living declined, many Irish considered emigration to Amer-ica, where, as one put it, "there are no Rents, no Tithes,"[5] and no lack of affordable land.

The decline of the linen industry was another major catalyst for emi-gration. The manufacturing of linen had replaced farming as the main-stay of the economy. So complete was this that linen made up one half of all the exports from Ireland to England by 1720. Entire families grew the flax, spun the yarn, and bleached the cloth. They rented the land they lived on, doing just enough farming to sustain themselves while concen-trating on the production of linen. As the English demand for linen less-ened and competition from European manufacturers increased, trade weakened.

In 1729 a slump in the linen trade along with a poor harvest sparked a rush to America. In this one year "between five and seven thousand men, women, and children—most from Ulster and most Presbyterian—headed for America, the vast majority to Pennsylvania." From 1730 to the eve of the French and Indian War in 1754, another fifty thousand Ulster Irish sailed for America.[6] Then, in the 1770s the linen industry collapsed, sparking a major exodus.

One Irishman, writing in 1773 to his brother who had emigrated to Pennsylvania, described these woeful times. Your family and "all your Acquaintance in this place," he wrote, "are very happy to hear of your safe Arrival with your Family out of A Land of Slavery into A Land of Liberty and freedom, and the more so as this Kingdom is much worse than it was even when you left it; Trading of all sorts and in all Branches Growing worse; and every day opens a new prospect of woe and misery; I need not tell you that Land is out of measure in high Rents and Tyths." He also noted that when "the Linnen Manafacture" was flour-ishing, rents would rise. "While Trade flourished the poor would Easily pay." The landlords came to expect these rents. But "Trade is now Sunk to A Very Low Ebb."[7] Nonetheless, rents remained high. Thus, squeezed by high rents and a meager income, many Irish chose to emigrate to what one Irishman described as "a land of peace and plenty, . . . the garden spot of the world: a happy asylum for the banished children of oppression."[8]

Failed harvests and economic depression were not new to Ireland.

Such misfortunes plagued Ulster in the seventeenth century. But they did not result in a massive exodus. Migration took place in the early eighteenth century, however, because by this time Ireland and America were closely linked. Though an ocean apart, America was well-known to Ulster's Irish. The major link was through a lively transatlantic trade between Ulster and the American colonies. The trading of flaxseed from America for linen from Ulster had transformed the river town of Derry into a major center of trade. Another connection between the two colonies was the work of Presbyterian missionaries who traveled back and forth across the Atlantic. By establishing religious ties between Ulster and America, they promoted the idea of emigration from a "Land of tireney" to "a land of Liberty" where people could worship freely.[9]

A third reason for the attraction of the American colonies was that the colonies promoted emigration. South Carolina and Georgia offered "cheap land, free tools and seed" to entice Irish Protestants to settle in their colony. As one Irishman put it in a letter to his American cousin, "The good bargains of your land in that country doe greatly encourage me to 'pluck up my spirits and make redie for the journey.'" Shipping agents also promoted travel to America by advertising it as the "garden spot of the world." Letters back home to Ulster singing the praises of America, where there were "noe Tythes nor Tythe mongers," were especially instrumental in influencing people's decisions to abandon Ulster. A government official noted that in their letters the emigrants often described America as "a good poor mans country where there are noe oppressions of any kind whatsoever."[10]

Although Irish emigration in the eighteenth century was heavily Presbyterian, a good number of Catholics did leave Ireland for North America. They were part of an Irish exodus to British colonies in the Caribbean and North America that had begun in the seventeenth century. As much as one fifth of the population of Barbados by 1666 was Irish, and throughout the West Indies their numbers continued to grow. In North America, Irish settlers could be found in "every mainland colony, particularly Virginia and Maryland, where tracts of land named 'New Ireland' and 'New Munster' were set aside for Irish settlers and their servants." But as a slave-based economy took hold in the West Indies, these colonies provided fewer opportunities for Irish workers with the result that during the 1700s most Irish Catholic emigrants went to the North American colonies. They comprised about one fourth to one fifth of the Irish migration prior to the American Revolution. Many came as indentured servants from Ulster as well as from the south of Ireland, where large numbers of Catholics lived. Mired in a life of poverty in Ireland because of rent gouging, victims of poor harvests as well as famine, thousands of Irish Catholics abandoned the land of their birth. Like their Presbyterian countrymen, they dreamed of a better life across the sea.

Nonetheless, despite harsh Penal Laws and severe economic distress, relatively few Catholics chose to emigrate. The historian Kerby Miller attributes this anomaly to their Gaelic tradition. As he put it, "Throughout this period the great majority of Catholics were Irish-speakers, largely insulated from the impulse to emigrate by the provincialism of Gaelic culture; by its secular, religious, and linguistic biases against individual initiative and innovation; and by literary modes which stigmatized emigration as *deorai*, or involuntary exile." This tradition of viewing emigration as exile "scarcely predisposed Irish-speakers to regard emigration with favor, especially if they enjoyed at least a subsistence living in traditional communities which remained intensely localistic and family oriented."[11] In addition, the Catholic Irish traditionally tended to be more oriented to Catholic Europe than to Protestant America. Irish merchants were scattered across Europe, and thousands of Irish served in the armies of Catholic countries on the Continent.

A final reason why so relatively few Catholics emigrated was the unwillingness of most North American colonies to welcome Catholics. Being Irish was bad enough. Being Catholic only intensified the discrimination since English Protestants had no love at all for Catholic papists who worshipped God in the wrong way. In Puritan New England an Irish Catholic was as rare as snow in July. In South Carolina the legislature passed laws banning the immigration of people "commonly called native Irish, or persons of scandalous character or Roman Catholics."[12] To prevent the immigration of Irish servants, Maryland, Pennsylvania, and Georgia passed laws that levied a tax on such servants. In Maryland, where the bulk of the Catholic Irish settled, penal legislation aimed at Catholics endured for much of the eighteenth century. Such laws denied Catholics the right to vote, worship publicly, hold office, practice law, and establish Catholic schools. During the French and Indian War of the 1750s, when anti-Catholic sentiment was riding high, the Maryland legislature passed a land tax to fund supplies for the war. Symptomatic of the strong feelings against Catholics, whom they judged to be allies of the French, the lawmakers doubled the tax on lands owned by Catholics.

Despite such discriminating legislation, Maryland became the center of Catholicism during the colonial period. A major reason for this was that an English Catholic, Cecil Calvert, had founded Maryland in 1634. The Catholic Calvert family ruled the colony for more than fifty years, until the Glorious Revolution of 1689 when William of Orange ascended to the throne of England. Within two years the rule of the Calverts was overthrown, and Maryland became a royal colony with a governor appointed by the Crown. In addition, the Anglican Church became the official state religion. Being Catholic in Maryland was no longer an asset, but a liability.

Maryland was a colony of slaves dominated by the gentry in the eighteenth century, a society, as one historian put it, "that kept most of its laborers in perpetual bondage and offered others a choice between permanent poverty and exile."[13] Even though those Irish who ventured to Maryland as indentured servants faced a harsh life, they still came in sizable numbers. In fact, so many were arriving that the Maryland legislature passed a law in 1699 imposing a tax on every Irish servant coming into the colony. Nonetheless, the Irish kept coming. A principal reason was that the Catholic gentry recruited Irishmen to come to Maryland as indentured servants with the promise of land after their time of service expired.[14] But as the century progressed, slaves increasingly became the bulk of the laboring class and the number of Irish servants emigrating to Maryland declined. The Irish were also numbered among the small farmer class that rented its land from the gentry landowners.

However, a few Irish Catholics achieved remarkable success. Even though Catholics made up less than 10 percent of Maryland's population, a considerable number of them belonged to the large landowning gentry. In fact, of the twenty wealthiest families in Maryland, ten were Catholic. At least three of these were Irish. The rest were of English heritage. Given the English roots of Maryland Catholicism, this was not surprising. What was extraordinary was the prominence of the Carroll family, whose fortune was one of the largest in Maryland.[15]

The Carroll family had lost much of their landed wealth in Ireland with the confiscation of land that took place after Oliver Cromwell's invasion in 1649. Nonetheless, Daniel Carroll of Ballymooney obtained a lease on a tract of land called Aghagurty that enabled him and his family to survive the turmoil of the Cromwellian era. His grandson Daniel, who later became the head tenant at Aghagurty, had four sons. Thomas died fighting William of Orange at the Battle of the Boyne. Anthony remained in Ireland, poor and illiterate the rest of his life. The other two brothers, John and Charles, emigrated to Maryland, where John passed into obscurity. Charles, however, acquired a remarkable fortune and founded a family of extraordinary fame.

With the help of a well-connected kinsman, Charles was sent to France at a young age, where he acquired a solid education, studying at Jesuit schools in Douai and Lille. Then, at twenty-five, he went off to study law in London. Three years later he obtained a commission from the ruling Calvert family as attorney general of Maryland. Abandoning London, he set sail for America, where he landed in October 1688 in St. Mary's City. Twenty-eight years old, he took up the post as attorney general of the colony. Ambitious and well educated, he was determined to succeed in Maryland, where Catholics were in control. But no sooner had he unpacked his bags, when news of the Glorious Revolution arrived in Maryland. Within a few months the Protestant takeover occurred and Carroll was out of a job. The victory at the Boyne River had claimed another victim. Then, with the passage of the Penal Laws, the Catholic Carroll found himself an outsider once again. In Ireland his family had been robbed of their land, but this time the young lawyer was determined that in Maryland the Carroll family would do better.

A staunch Catholic and a proud Irishman, Charles Carroll built a fortune, becoming the wealthiest man in Maryland by the time of his death in 1720. One of the keys to his success was that he married well. His first wife, Martha Ridgely Underwood, was an indentured servant who had married a successful landowner. When her husband Robert Ridgely died, she inherited thousands of acres of land. Shortly afterward she married Anthony Underwood. Then, on November 9, 1689, six months after the death of her second husband, she married Charles Carroll, who was the executor of Underwood's estate. Within a year Martha died in childbirth, followed by her infant son a few days later, leaving Carroll a sizable fortune. Just some two years after his arrival in Maryland, Carroll had become a wealthy landowner. Then, a few years later, he married Mary Darnall, a young woman half his age, and the daughter of one of the colony's richest and most powerful planters. Such good fortune enabled him to increase his wealth. When he died in 1720, he owned close to forty-eight thousand acres of land and 112 slaves. His wardrobe included eight suits, one trimmed with gold; five wigs; and an assortment of clothes appropriate for all occasions. His home in Annapolis had eleven rooms, all of which were well furnished. In addition, as was the custom with the

Catholic gentry, it housed a chapel where Annapolis Catholics could attend Mass. Not bad for a man who had started out herding sheep in Ireland.

Because of his wealth as well as his connections with the colony's power brokers, Carroll became an influential citizen. He was especially active on behalf of his fellow Catholics, who were continually challenging the royal government's efforts to proscribe their political and civil rights. Armed with a combative personality, he crossed swords with the colony's governor whenever he sought to gain more liberties for Catholics. He even spent time in jail because of insults hurled against the new colonial government. But Carroll and his coreligionists gained little from these struggles. The final defeat came in 1718, when the Maryland Assembly passed a law depriving Catholics of the right to vote. Politically powerless, they would remain disenfranchised until 1776.

Shortly before he died, and after the death of his eldest son, Carroll chose his second son, Charles, as his heir. In a letter to his son, he offered some fatherly advice on how Charles should identify himself: "I would have you Stile your Self in your Thesis Marylando-Hibernus."[16] In other words, he should always be known as a Maryland Irishman, proud of his heritage and steadfast in his faith.

Known as Charles Carroll of Annapolis, he expanded his father's fortune by developing the lands he had inherited and renting them out to tenant farmers. Included among these farmers were Irishmen Carroll recruited from Ireland as well as some Germans. He also was involved in banking, becoming the chief moneylender in Maryland. Unlike his father, he was not active in politics. His chief interest was to make money and build the family fortune. Resigned to political impotence because of his religion, he enjoyed the life of the wealthy gentleman. Nonetheless, he deeply resented the inferior social status conferred on him because of his religion. He also carried the bitter memory of his family's loss of land in Ireland and the many injustices they had suffered because of their religion. At one time he even thought of leaving Maryland when the assembly passed the double land tax on Catholics in 1756. Like his father, he was proud of his Irish heritage and loyal to his Catholic faith.

The most significant achievement of Carroll's life was the education and grooming of his one child, Charles Carroll of Carrollton, to become one of the new nation's premier citizens. Born on September 19, 1737, Charles was the illegitimate son of Charles Carroll of Annapolis and his cousin Elizabeth Brooke. Twenty years would pass before Carroll and Elizabeth were officially married. The reasons for the common law marriage most likely were Carroll's concern about protecting his fortune lest if he died, his widow, who would inherit a sizable portion of the estate, might, upon remarriage, transfer the Carroll legacy into another family that might even be Protestant. The other reason seems to have been his desire to compel his son to behave appropriately and prove himself a worthy heir since a son born out of wedlock could inherit nothing, because legally he was "looked upon as the son of nobody."[17] Such thinking on the part of Carroll reveals a calculating and domineering side of his personality. Soon after his official marriage to Elizabeth, Charles drew up his will, naming his one and only son as his heir since the young man had lived up to his expectations.

Like most sons in the gentry class, young Charles was sent to Europe for his education when he was only ten years old. Accompanying him on the journey was another youngster, his cousin John Carroll, who would later become the first Roman Catholic bishop in the United States. For the next sixteen years Charles pursued his education in St. Omer, Paris, and London. During these years father and son exchanged letters weekly. Through this correspondence Charles's father sought to control every aspect of his son's life, while the young boy earnestly sought to please his father in everything he did. In 1758, at age twenty, the son assured his father, whom he called Papa, that "I shall endeavor to manage my little affairs with all the care and attention I am capable of by avoiding the extremes of affectation and meanness. I keep strict accounts and shall send them to you at the end of the year so you will be able to Judge yourself whether I have spent foolishly or no."[18] Later that year Charley, as his father called him, met a "young, pretty, witty" woman while vacationing in France. This prompted more advice from Papa—"avoid any intimacy," he wrote, "or familiarity with ye fair Sex, especially Visits or Conversations without Witnesses."[19]

Charley was of medium height, with flowing, thick hair and a prominent nose. He had strikingly long legs and arms that contrasted visibly with his torso. Physically he was not an imposing figure, no more than five feet five inches tall, possessing, as he put it, a "puny constitution." He described himself as "naturally timid and bashful," as well as "stiff and reserved."[20] But such traits, noticeable in his early manhood, would recede into the background once he became a political activist during the revolutionary period.

When he returned to Annapolis in the winter of 1765, he was ready to turn his attention to managing the family's fortune. Three years later he married his cousin Mary Darnall. Together they had seven children, three of them living into adulthood. Papa knew Mary well since she and her mother had been living in his house for several years. Needless to say, for Papa, Charley's marriage was, as the domineering father put it, "entirely to my Satisfaction."[21]

A businessman and a planter, Charley managed the 12,500-acre family plantation, Doohoragen Manor, as well supervising the tenants at their other major plantation, Carrollton. Nonetheless, his dear Papa was still dominating his life, making sure that Charley lived up to his expectations. What Charles Carroll of Carrollton is most remembered for, and what finally liberated him from his father's controlling influence, are his political achievements. More like his grandfather than his father, Charles became a political activist who achieved a level of fame unimagined by either his father or grandfather.

When he first arrived in Maryland after so many years in Europe, where he had lived the life of an aristocrat, he was uncomfortable with the egalitarian tone of Maryland society. He particularly did not like the rising spirit of democratic protest that was surfacing in the colonies, which he attributed to the people's "ignorance, prejudice, and passion."[22] But he did support opposition to Great Britain, whose Parliament's policies he judged to be poorly conceived. He soon entered the political arena by challenging an old family nemesis, Daniel Dulany, in a debate waged in the newspapers for five months. They argued over whether the governor had the authority to raise fees on his own. Dulany defended the unilateral action of the governor, while Carroll warned against the abuse of executive power. Carroll's arguments proved to be more persuasive and gained him celebrity in the colony. Thrust into the political battle raging in the colonies, Carroll became a leading advocate in Maryland for independence. He went to the First Continental Congress in Philadelphia, but because of his religion he was not an official member of the Maryland delegation. This led him to conclude that such exclusion "is not less absurd than my bilief and I will serve them in a private capacity notwithstanding."[23] He later served in the Continental Congress in 1776, where he signed the Declaration of Independence, one of several Irishmen to achieve that distinction and the only Roman Catholic.

Carroll remained in public life until 1800, serving in both the Maryland Senate and the U.S. Senate. True to his aristocratic background,

Carroll supported the Constitution because he viewed it as the best means to restrain the excesses of democracy. A conservative revolutionary, he favored the interests of the propertied class of men over the democratic ideal of popular rule. He also feared the democratic tendencies of Thomas Jefferson, whose election as president in 1800 signaled the end of Carroll's political career. Jefferson's victory cost Carroll his seat in the Maryland Senate, where he had served from 1777. Never again did he hold political office. As he entered the twilight of his career, he devoted himself to managing his fortune and providing for his adult children. With the death of John Adams and Thomas Jefferson on July 4, 1826, Carroll became the last surviving signer of the Declaration of Independence. When he died in 1832 at the age of ninety-five, his estate included thirty thousand acres of land in Maryland, forty-five thousand acres in Pennsylvania, and personal property worth nearly $1.5 million.[24]

One of Carroll's biographers described him as "far less Irish in the way he defined himself than either his father or his grandfather."[25] But he was as firm in his faith. Shaped by the eighteenth-century Enlightenment, he was a devoted Catholic and an enlightened aristocrat. He stressed the personal experience of religion, the reasonableness of religion, and the spirit of toleration. Describing himself as a "warm friend to Toleration," he disapproved of what he called "the intollerating spirit of the Church of Rome, and of other Churches." Reflecting on his signing of the Declaration of Independence, he "had in view not only our independence of England but the toleration of all sects professing the Christian religion and communicating to them all equal rights." Like the rest of his family, he had "an unwavering, though sorely tested commitment to freedom of conscience." This was an integral part of the colonial Catholic tradition and fit in with the spirit of toleration fostered by the Enlightenment.[26]

From the bogs of Ireland's midlands to the banks of the Potomac River, the achievement of the Carroll family is a remarkable chapter in the history of Irish America.

A key reason for the Carroll family's continued commitment to Catholicism was the presence of a vibrant Catholic community in Maryland. In 1785 there were an estimated 15,800 Catholics in the colony or about 5 percent of the total population. Despite its small size the Church prospered. The gentry class provided the leadership for this community as it navigated its way through the obstacles put in place by the Penal Laws. Since public worship was forbidden, the Catholic gentry set up a network of private chapels throughout the colony where Catholics could worship. By 1760 there were fifty such chapels. Almost half of them were located in the three counties (St. Mary's, Charles, and Prince George's) where the bulk of Catholics lived. The gentry also provided the political leadership needed to protect the civil rights of Catholics.

English Jesuit priests had ministered to this community from the first days of the founding of the colony. Along with the gentry, the vast majority of whom were of English descent, the Jesuits fashioned an English style of Catholicism in Maryland. This meant the adoption of a survivor's mentality in an environment where their religion branded them as social and political outcasts. The English Catholic tradition also nurtured the piety of the Marylanders. Their religion manifested the qualities of personalism, discipline, and sobriety—qualities that were hallmarks of English Catholicism. The gentry also provided vocations to religious life, a visible sign of a community's religious vitality. As many as forty Maryland-born Catholics became priests in the eighteenth century. A similar number of women, thirty-six, entered the convent. Few Irish were included in these groups. One obvious reason was that the bulk of the Maryland Irish were poor farmers or servants and could not afford the high cost of a European education necessary for an aspiring priest or the sizable dowry required to enter the convent.

By the mid-eighteenth century as many as twenty priests, most English-born as well as some Maryland-born, were working in the colony. Over the years they had established sizable farms, and these had become active parish centers for the surrounding communities of Catholics. In addition, as itinerant missionaries, these priests visited Catholic settlers scattered throughout Maryland, where they would celebrate Mass in a local house chapel and minister to the needs of the people. Most Catholics were able to attend Mass once a month, but for those along Maryland's Eastern Shore, where few Catholics lived, Mass was more infrequent, perhaps once every two months.[27]

What happened to the fifty to sixty thousand Irish Catholics who migrated to the colonies? Every indication suggests that the vast majority never set foot in a Catholic chapel or had the blessings of a Catholic priest. In Maryland, for example, the Irish population in 1790 was 53,287, or one sixth of the state population. Catholics, many of whom were of English descent as well as German or Irish descent, numbered only around 16,000. The numbers tell the story. Despite the existence of an active Catholic community, most Irish Catholics in Maryland remained unchurched. Even though Maryland had its share of Ulster Presbyterians, especially in the western part of the colony, Irish Catholics still comprised a significant number of the 1790 population. But they did not show up as members of the Catholic Church. Kerby Miller concluded that those "Catholics who did leave Ireland during the colonial period seem to have been rootless, restless men . . . They emigrated, settled and often disappeared as solitary individuals. Since the great majority were single males, marriage usually entailed absorption into colonial Protestant family and networks."[28]

Another plausible reason why so few Irish remained associated with the religion of their ancestors was the decidedly English tone to Maryland Catholicism. Unlike their counterparts in England, Catholics in Ireland were the majority, not the minority. They became known for their militant resistance to religious discrimination, a style of resistance alien to English Catholics, who sought to survive by adopting a low profile. In Maryland Irish Catholics would have to adopt the more discreet English attitude in a setting where they were members of a minority religion. In addition, a distinctive ethnic Irish community did not exist in rural Maryland. The gentry landowning class of English descent, not the struggling Irish farmer or poor laborer, defined the Catholic community along the Chesapeake. Even more significant, Catholics in Ireland at this time were strongly attracted to folk religious practices. Much of these practices centered around holy wells or sacred places that were popular pilgrimage sites. Emigration meant abandoning this folk religion since they could not bring the wells or other sacred sites with them. This left a void that Maryland Catholicism could never fill. Finally, the number of priests in Maryland was never large enough to enable them to minister to all the Irish, who were widely scattered throughout the colony, living and working as small farmers or laborers. All of these factors suggest that the vast majority of Irish Catholics in colonial Maryland as well as elsewhere either remained unchurched or joined Protestant denominations.

The Irish Presbyterians, not the Irish Catholics, comprised the bulk of the Irish exodus in the eighteenth century. Coming from the northern and eastern counties of Ulster (Antrim, Derry, and Down), most of them, as many as 80 percent, paid their own way to America during the first wave of emigration in the 1720s. They traveled as families, raising money for passage by selling the unexpired leases that they held on their land.

After 1741, as famine and a failing economy plagued the countryside, most emigrants traveled as indentured servants because they were unable or unwilling to pay the cost of passage. This meant they were bound by contract to serve their colonial masters for four years for their passage to the New World. Most of these servants were single men or women who worked on farms; some had skills needed in an urban economy. So common was this practice among the Irish that nine out of ten indentured servants in Pennsylvania in the 1740s were Irish.[29]

Generally the captain of the ship signed up the men and women who wanted to sell their labor for the cost of travel to America. If he worked with an agent of an American master who needed such laborers, he would deliver the workers to the master at the dock in America. If he acted on his own, upon his arrival in the colonies he would auction off the servants "like cattle in a market," as one of them put it. A notice in a newspaper said it all: "Just imported from Dublin in the Brig Darby, A Parcel of Irish Servants both men and women, to be Sold Cheap by Israel Boardman."[30]

The commerce of indentured servants was a big business that responded to the labor shortage in the colonies. The entire process was formalized in written contracts, signed by the servant and the indentor, usually the ship captain, and witnessed by two people. By signing the contract the servant and the master pledged themselves to honor the terms of the contract. For the master this meant providing clothes, food, and lodging, while the servant promised to serve his or her master for the agreed-upon term. It was a form of contract labor in which the American purchaser owned the servant's labor.

Indentured servitude was for the young, who could adjust to the climate and, as one Irishman wrote, cope with "the pressure upon their minds on being rank'd and deemed as slaves."[31] Some servants ran away rather than suffer at the hands of cruel masters. In Pennsylvania newspapers ran notices with rewards for Irish runaways. Most, however, honored the terms of the contract. Then they were released from all obligations and collected their freedom dues, usually a small sum of money or tools and some clothes. Sometimes the master would refuse to pay the freedom dues. This is what happened to Philip Rorey, a servant in Chester, Pennsylvania, who "faithfully and honestly served such service as his Master was pleased to exercise him." Rorey took his master to court, petitioning the judge "to allow him all such necessaries as he may justly require by the Law made and provided for securing the Rights and

Properties of Servants." Rorey's petition was successful, and the court ordered his master to provide him with "a new and Compleat Suite of apparel."[32]

Most emigrant ships sailed from Derry or Belfast, though some did sail from the ports of Dublin or Cork in the south of Ireland. The journey across the Atlantic could take as many as nine weeks during the spring or as few as seven weeks during the summer months. Of course, some trips could last longer, even as long as fifteen weeks, depending on the weather. Since these ships were not designed to carry passengers, accommodations were rather grim. Most passengers lived in steerage or between the decks, in areas less than five feet high, sleeping two to a bed in eighteen inches of space. Overcrowding was common. Passengers complained most often about the lack of decent drinking water and poor food. Having scores of people huddled together in cramped living conditions for several weeks was a recipe for widespread disease. Dysentery, typhus, and smallpox were the most common. Occasionally sickness would reach epidemic proportions, causing a number of deaths.

One emigrant, whose voyage took nearly fifteen weeks under a ruthless captain, described some of the horrors of his journey in a letter to his father in Ireland: "Hunger and Thirst had now reduced our Crew to the last Extremity, nothing was now to be heard aboard our Ship but the Cries of distressed Children, and of their distressed Mothers, unable to relieve them. Our Ship now was truly a real Spectacle of Horror! Never a Day passed without one or two of our Crew put over Board; many kill'd themselves by drinking Salt Water, and their own Urine was a common Drink. Yet in the midst of all our Miseries, our Captain shewed not the least Remorse or Pity." When the ship finally reached the port of New Castle on the Delaware River, sixty-four of the emigrants and crew members had died.[33]

With the sea voyage completed, the next major decision was where to settle. A small number, no more than 10 percent of Ulster's emigrants, settled in New England. Few chose New England because the Puritan Yankees, largely of English stock, were not welcoming to the Irish, whom they derisively called "St. Patrick's Vermin." Londonderry, New Hampshire, named after the famed city in Ulster that symbolized the loyalty of Irish Protestants to the English Crown, was the most successful Irish settlement in New England. Free land and the opportunity to worship as Presbyterians attracted the Irish to Londonderry in the 1720s.

Some Irish also settled in New York. Though their number was not large, several men among them gained prominence. At least five royal governors had Irish roots, including William Cosby (1732–36) and George Clinton (1743–53). Another Irishman who had strong ties to New York was Peter Warren. A naval hero as well as one of the wealthiest men in Britain, he owned considerable land in New York, including a three-hundred-acre estate in Greenwich Village where a street is named after him. He also owned a large tract of land about 180 miles north of the city along the Mohawk River. He hired his nephew William Johnson to manage this estate and turn it into a profitable enterprise. Johnson not only succeeded in taming this wild frontier, but also became one of the wealthiest men in British America.

William Johnson was born in county Meath, Ireland, around 1715. William's mother, Anne Warren, was a member of an old English Catholic family that kept some of their land despite the massive expropriation that took place when the forces of Oliver Cromwell ravaged Ireland. His father, Christopher, was descended from the O'Neill family, who, unlike the Warren clan, lost their land in the aftermath of Cromwell's victory. Christopher's wife provided the family connection that enabled him to rent land and live a comfortable life as a tenant farmer and land agent.

William's uncle Peter Warren thought highly of his nephew, whom he affectionately called Billy, and asked him to manage his estate in northern New York. But there was one problem. Billy was Catholic. Peter had already converted to the Anglican Church and realized that he could not afford "to risk his rising status in American colonial society by entrusting a large estate on the sensitive frontier between Catholic France and Protestant Britain to a Catholic."[34] So young Billy converted as much for pragmatic reasons as for religious since he did not have a great interest in religion. Such conversions were not unusual in eighteenth-century Ireland, where the Penal Laws punished Roman Catholics. Becoming Protestant was the only way many Catholic landowners could keep their land and avoid descending into poverty. Neither Peter Warren nor William Johnson would have gained the stature they did if they had remained Catholic. But, for them, as for many such "converts," Catholicism still remained a part of their private life. As one writer put it, "Protestantism was a means to an end, but the continuity of the old Catholic culture was an end in itself." An Irish "convert" summed up this attitude when he wrote, "I would rather at any time entrust God with my soul than the laws of Ireland with my lands."[35]

Once he landed in New York, William Johnson soon made his mark. The young twenty-year-old was in charge of an estate located in the midst of the Mohawk nation. He soon gained the friendship and confidence of the Mohawks by learning their language and customs, even joining in their war dances and sitting in on tribal councils. They thought so highly of him that they would eventually initiate him into the Mohawk nation as a sachem, an honor reserved for their tribal leaders. His role as a mediator between the Indians and the British government was of such value that the British government appointed him superintendent of Indian affairs for the Northern Department. He made his fortune as a fur trader and landowner, amassing one of the largest estates in the colonies.

Shortly after his arrival in New York, Johnson entered into a common-law marriage with his German housekeeper, Catherine Weisenberg. Though they never formally married, he referred to her affectionately as "my beloved wife." They had three children. When Catherine died in 1759, Johnson took as his companion a young Mohawk woman, Mary Brant. He had eight children with Mary. Having, as his biographer put it, "an immense sexual appetite," he had romantic relationships with many other women during his life.[36]

Johnson's life on the estate was not unlike that of an Irish landlord in county Meath. He built a Georgian-style stone mansion, Johnson Hall, maintaining it in grand style. He hosted parties for high-class guests at this frontier mansion, an exotic locale where he wined and dined them with the finest the colonies had to offer in a setting that included the best Chinese porcelain and "plates of hand-painted Delft." He lived the life of an Irish country gentleman, surrounding himself with his close friends, all of whom were Irish. He imported most of his servants and tenants from Ireland. A lover of Irish music, he also imported Irish musicians, including a blind harpist, to play at his gala events. In addition, he sponsored festivities "for the villagers and tenants. St. Patrick's Day was, of course, a great occasion for revelry" with games and competitions and lots of beer.[37]

Johnson also enjoyed a successful military career, leading forces of provincial soldiers and Indians in several important battles against the French, who were challenging the supremacy of the British along the borders of the American colonies. After one such skirmish at Lake George in 1755 where his forces battled the French to a draw, it was still good enough to turn him into a hero in Britain, where Parliament voted him a reward of five thousand pounds. He also received the honor of being named a baronet of Great Britain. Henceforth, he was known as Sir William Johnson, First Baronet of New York.[38]

Johnson died in 1774 at his estate near Johnstown, the town that he founded, being spared the need to declare his allegiance to the Crown or the colonists as his countrymen prepared for the American Revolution. His heirs, loyal to the Crown, would not be so fortunate. They were forced to flee to Canada, while the victorious Americans confiscated Johnson's vast land holdings.

In becoming loyalists, Johnson's heirs were the exception among the Irish, most of whom were loyal patriots who supported the American Revolution. In fact, as many as one third of the Continental Army was Irish. A key reason for this was their resentment against the British government and the elitist Anglican Church, which had discriminated against them in Ulster. In Philadelphia some Irish did join the loyalist cause and fought together as a regiment throughout the war. But, in the rest of the middle colonies the Irish rallied to the patriot cause. In the Southern colonies, their response was more complex. In North Carolina, the eastern elite were the patriots, while the backcountry Irish, Presbyterians resentful of the eastern Anglican elite, formed a loyalist regiment. In other parts of the Carolinas the Irish were definitely anti-British. Large numbers of them joined the revolutionary army, not for especially patriotic reasons, but because of the opportunities their service offered, such as possible land grants and termination of their bondage as indentured servants.

Though New York was home to a number of prominent Irish settlers, the largest number of Irish had settled in Pennsylvania, with about one hundred thousand, or one quarter of all the Irish in the new nation in 1790, calling Pennsylvania home.[39]

Founded by the Quaker William Penn in 1681, Pennsylvania prided itself on its policy of religious toleration. For Irish Presbyterians, who had suffered under the yoke of Anglican intolerance, this was especially appealing. Furthermore, a lively trade existed between Philadelphia and Ulster. Most ships from Ulster landed at ports along the Delaware River. From here scores of newcomers journeyed about seventy miles west of Philadelphia to a region along the Susquehanna River where favorable land grants were available. This frontier country was the heartland of the Irish settlement, inhabited by Indians and traders who traveled back and forth between Philadelphia and the Ohio River valley. Life was harsh on the frontier. The settlers had to clear the land, build a cabin, plant the crops, and learn to survive. Historian Patrick Griffin wrote, "In such conditions, the earliest settlers scratched out a precarious living. While migrants may have had land, they had little else aside from livestock, Indian corn, and crude farming implements."[40]

This region could aptly be described as the Wild West. Violence and drunkenness permeated the settlements in the early years. Relations with the Indians were tense since some of the settlers squatted on land claimed by the Indians. Disputes over land were common. One institution that attempted to bring order to this frontier wilderness was the church.

In Ireland the church was the mainstay of the community. Their dissenting Presbyterian faith had given these Irish a distinctive identity that set them apart from the established Anglican Church. Presbyterians adhered to the Westminster Confession of faith, a profession of belief and church government different from that of the Anglican Church, where an episcopal hierarchy and an elaborate liturgy were the norm. As a minority religious community Presbyterians suffered discrimination at the hands of the ruling Anglican elite. Thus, they were not about to abandon a religion preserved at great personal sacrifice when they emigrated to the New World. Because of their isolation on the frontier they seldom enjoyed the benefits of a minister during the early years of settlement. Finally, in 1727 the community of Donegal obtained a resident minister. A meetinghouse soon followed, and then the settlers established a presbytery to supervise and promote religion in that region. The church became the guardian of order in these isolated frontier communities by disciplining those guilty of violent or unruly behavior. As a result some semblance of stability and discipline developed. Additional ministers, recruited from Ireland, followed as the number of congregations increased.[41]

During the 1730s a religious revival was beginning to take hold in the colonies. This was especially visible in the Connecticut Valley, where Jonathan Edwards, a young Congregational pastor, was urging his parishioners to turn over a new leaf by completely surrendering themselves to God's will. The famed English preacher George Whitefield came to the colonies in 1739, his second of seven visits to America. This was to be his most memorable. He traveled up and down the seaboard preaching a gospel of repentance and conversion. His travels took him to Philadelphia and then to the Pennsylvania frontier, where he promoted this new brand of religion. The revival took hold as scores of people embraced this new religion that emphasized the need for a heartfelt conversion. Later known as the Great Awakening, the movement not only succeeded in gaining many converts to the church, but it also sowed conflict in just about every community it touched. This was surely the case along the Pennsylvania frontier.

For the Ulster Irish, the Presbyterian Church and its badge of faith, the Westminster Confession, were essential to their identity. The enthusiasm generated by the religious revival of the 1730s and '40s challenged the centrality of this creed by deemphasizing its importance and stressing the need for a personal conversion, most often described as a new birth in the spirit. The Ulster-born Gilbert Tennent was the minister most responsible for promoting this new understanding of religion among the frontier communities. Along with his father, Gilbert Tennent had founded a Log College in Neshaminy, Pennsylvania, to train ministers for an evangelical ministry. The Tennents preached the need for a converted ministry, preachers who were distinguished for their piety rather than their theology. This challenge to the old-time religion identified with the Westminster Confession sparked a bitter debate within the churches. For some, the Old Lights, the key to their faith was adherence to the Westminster Confession. For others, the New Lights, the key was a new birth in the spirit, a religious conversion. This required preachers who had themselves experienced a religious conversion. As Gilbert Tennent noted in one of his most famous sermons, the real danger to religion was an "unconverted ministry." Ministers, even ones educated at the finest universities in Scotland, came under fire if they could not testify to their conversion. Itinerant preachers, educated at the Log College, traveled the frontier preaching this new gospel. They sparked conflict at just about every stop along their itinerary. This debate between the Old Lights and the New Lights split the church.

Other changes were taking place along the frontier as more and more settlers, many of whom were German, moved into the area. Land was becoming more scarce and thus more costly. The younger generation, hungry for land and more opportunity, became restless. The new revival religion appealed to these restless spirits. The founding generation of Irish settlers had to adjust to these changes. Many resisted leaving behind the old-style religion, which caused serious divisions within the community.

By the 1750s Pennsylvania's western frontier, Lancaster County, was more settled. The younger, more ambitious men and women moved south to a new frontier along Virginia's Shenandoah Valley. Such movement characterized the Ulster Irish. These mobile people seemed to thrive among the wilds of the frontier. Once one frontier became settled, a new generation moved on. After Virginia, the migration spilled over into the Carolinas and Georgia, where Presbyterian ministers rarely set foot. "As a result thousands of Ulster-Americans, 'burned over' by the evangelical fires of the first Great Awakening, turned to the Methodists, Baptists, and other denominations for inspiration and solace; by 1800 only 15,000 adult Americans were members of Presbyterian churches, although during the preceding century perhaps twenty times that number had emigrated from Ireland alone."[42]

Eventually the Ulster Irish could be found throughout the Appalachian region that stretched from Pennsylvania to Georgia and west to Kentucky and Tennessee. They comprised as much as 50 percent of the white population by 1790, planting in this area a distinctive Irish culture.

Irish settlements were not limited to the rural frontier. Irish also settled in the cities of colonial America, most notably Philadelphia and New York. These cities were home to a growing number of Irish merchants, lawyers, and professionals as well as a middle class of artisans and shopkeepers.

The population of the major city in the colonies, Philadelphia, numbered 42,520 by 1790. The eighteenth century was Philadelphia's golden age. The Declaration of Independence was written there, followed by the new nation's Constitution. In the 1790s it served as the nation's capital. Ideally situated along the Delaware River, Philadelphia was a major seaport and the center of Irish American trade. Beef, pork, and butter as well as linen were the principal goods imported from Ireland. In return, Philadelphia merchants shipped flaxseed, wheat, and flour to Ireland. In one year alone, 1769, forty-nine ships sailed for Ireland.[43] In addition, Philadelphia was the destination of thousands of Irish immigrants during the eighteenth century. Most of them moved into the interior of Pennsylvania, but a sizable number found employment in the city as artisans and tradesmen. By 1800, when the city's population numbered 61,559, at least 12 percent (7,387) of these city dwellers were Irish-born.[44]

The Irish were heavily numbered among the city's poor. Living in Northern Liberties, Kensington, and Southwark, a northern part of the city known as Irish Town, they comprised an "estimated 10 to 15 percent of Philadelphia's white population."[45] Benjamin Franklin described them as "extremely poor, living in the most sordid wretchedness, in dirty hovels of mud and straw, and clothed only in rags." They filled the city jail, accounting for almost 40 percent of all the convictions in the mayor's court in 1796.[46]

The leaders of Philadelphia's Irish community came from the merchant class. Numbering about sixty men by the late 1760s, these merchants gained their stature as a result of a trading network that fostered close affiliations among ship captains, firms in Ireland, and Philadelphia's merchants. Among these merchants were men of wealth and prestige who traded throughout the North Atlantic world. Some had interests in as many as twelve or more vessels. Below them were merchants who were not as wealthy or well connected, yet still engaged in overseas trade and invested in ships and property. At the base of the merchant class was a group of men who possessed enough capital needed to engage in intercolonial trade. Some from this group would eventually prosper, achieving considerable wealth.

These merchants came from different religious traditions—Quaker, Presbyterian, and Roman Catholic. The key to their success was kinship ties with merchants in Ireland. Though religion may have had a role in these links, family ties were crucial. In Cork, for example, the prominent Roman Catholic firm of John and David Moylan had family ties with Stephen Moylan, an important Philadelphia merchant. Philadelphia's Quaker merchants were related to prominent Quaker merchants in Dublin. As historian Thomas Truxes noted, "Kinship, reputation, and religion, perhaps in that order, determined the choice of partners and correspondents." Ship-owning partnerships often "crossed lines of religion," and "there is little evidence of deep sectarian divisions among" Philadelphia's Irish merchants.[47]

Philadelphia had several organizations that served the major ethnic groups in the city (German, English, Welsh, Scots, and Irish). Members of the merchant class played a leading role in founding these societies, especially in the case of the Irish. The Irish Club, founded in the mid-1760s, was primarily a gentlemen's eating and drinking club that met weekly. From this club emerged the Society of the Friendly Sons of St. Patrick. Founded in 1771, it is still in existence. In the eighteenth century it was more of a gentleman's club whose members were wealthy merchants. To be eligible for membership, one had to be descended "from Irish parents by either side in the first degree." Business connections as well as family links were important for gaining admittance into the society. Each year on St. Patrick's Day the Friendly Sons held a dinner at a city tavern. By 1784 they sponsored a parade on St. Patrick's Day in which "upwards of one thousand people" marched.

The Irish also founded the Hibernia Fire Company. Established in 1752, its purpose was to preserve "our own and our neighbours' houses from fire." Still in existence in 1799, it was one of the oldest of the city's fire companies with forty members.[48] Then in the 1790s a group of civic-minded Irishmen, some of whom belonged to the Friendly Sons, founded the Hibernian Society for the Relief of the Emigrants, whose purpose was to protect and assist the immigrants who were coming to Philadelphia in large numbers during this decade. Its membership, numbering 219 in 1790, came from various strata of society—innkeepers, grocers, schoolmasters—and included a sizable number of well-to-do merchants who also belonged to the Friendly Sons.

Some of Philadelphia's finest citizens came from the Irish community. Mathew Carey was a successful publisher of books and journals, known for his philanthropy. Stephen Moylan, of the merchant class, was the first president of the Society of the Friendly Sons of St. Patrick. He also served with distinction under General George Washington during the Revolutionary War. Another merchant, Thomas Fitzsimons, was a member of Congress in the 1790s and is remembered as the only Irish Catholic to sign the U.S. Constitution. John Barry, from county Wexford in Ireland, had a distinguished career as a naval officer in the Revolutionary War. Some of the city's first mayors were Irish-born Quakers. George Bryan, a merchant from Dublin, was a prominent member of the Presbyterian Church. He helped to write Pennsylvania's new state constitution in 1776. The successes of these and many other Philadelphia Irish established this city along the Delaware as a favorite destination of thousands of Irish emigrants. Soon, however, New York would challenge Philadelphia's prominence.

New York's strategic location along the Hudson River with easy access to the Atlantic Ocean made it an ideal port. During the eighteenth century it was second only to Philadelphia in population, as well as being an important center of trade with Ireland, with about one quarter to one third of its transatlantic exports bound for Ireland. The principal cargo on these ships was flaxseed, which was grown in Connecticut and the region bordering Long Island Sound. At its peak in the 1760s, New York's annual flaxseed fleets numbered as many as forty ships.[49] This flaxseed was the backbone of the linen industry in Ulster. The Irish merchant community in New York was smaller than that of Philadelphia, numbering only about thirty. Only a few of the firms became large, wealthy enterprises trading throughout the Atlantic world.

Prior to the mid-eighteenth century the Irish presence was not very noticeable in the city. But as trade with Ireland increased so did immigration. The ships that sailed for Ireland returned to New York with human cargo, so that by the 1770s the Irish had become a sizable presence in the city. In addition to the small merchant community, the Irish were scattered about in a diversity of occupations. Some owned clothing stores, others had established taverns. There were also Irish physicians associated with Kings College. The Irish artisan class included bookbinders, printers, tailors, weavers, and coachmakers. The city also had its Irish sailors and laborers.

Only about one third of the Irish newcomers came from Ulster, with the largest number coming from Dublin. The Anglo-Irish rather than the Ulster Irish were the dominant group in New York. This meant that the Anglican Church rather than the Presbyterian Church was more prominent. Worshipping at Trinity Church, they were the upper crust of New York's Irish immigrant community. The Catholic Irish were not numerous until late in the century. A visitor to the city in 1759 remarked that "there are some few Roman Catholics," whereas the Anglicans and Presbyterians were rather numerous. Those few Catholics most likely joined other established churches or remained unchurched. The first Catholic church in the city, St. Peter's, was not organized until 1785. Predominantly Irish, it included a few wealthy merchants. The majority of the parishioners, however, were poor artisans, cartmen, and laborers.[50]

The Irish also made their mark in politics. George Clinton won election as the first governor of New York in 1777 and served for six successive terms. In 1784 he appointed the lawyer James Duane, the son of an Irish-born merchant, as the mayor of New York. William Mooney was the founder of the Tammany Society in 1787, a social organization named after a Delaware Indian chief, and its first grand sachem. In the nineteenth century it would become a powerful political organization.[51] The New York Irish also had their fraternal organizations that never failed to celebrate St. Patrick's Day. As early as 1741 the Irish gathered to celebrate the holiday. In the 1760s the celebration began to include a parade complete with fife and drums. This would eventually develop into one of the largest St. Patrick's Day parades in the nation.

When the new nation conducted its first census in 1790, the Irish were one of the more prominent ethnic groups. Settling along the rural Appalachian frontier as well as in cities such as Philadelphia and New

York, they had made their mark on colonial America. Merchants and lawyers, farmers and laborers, Catholics and Protestants, they were a diverse people. Throughout this period they had an irenic spirit. Whether Catholic or Presbyterian, from Belfast or Dublin, they were all proud to be Irish. This would dramatically change in the next century when religious sectarianism created a great divide in the Irish community in the United States.

CHAPTER 2

A Time of Transition

On September 7, 1784, the ship *America* sailed from Dublin bound for Philadelphia. As the passengers boarded the ship, a young man, dressed as a woman and with the help of some friends, sneaked onto the ship, where he hid until the *America* was out at sea. At the tender age of twenty-four, Mathew Carey had become a wanted man. The police were searching for him, but for the second time in his young life, Carey fled into exile, avoiding a certain jail sentence. The first time France had become his haven. This time it would be the United States. Carey was an Irish nationalist who strongly opposed England's political control of Ireland. His fiery temperament had gotten him into trouble previously when he wrote a pamphlet advocating the repeal of the penal codes against Roman Catholics. Rather than have his son face certain jail because of the seditious tone of the essay, Carey's father sent him off to Paris, where he stayed for two years. After returning to Dublin, he founded a newspaper, the *Volunteer's Journal*, in which he published more of his essays denouncing the government.

In these essays Carey urged a total reform of Ireland's parliamentary government and a complete political separation from England, by force if necessary. The authorities thought he may even have been conspiring with French radicals to overthrow the government. This amounted to high treason, and as the attorney general said, there was "very little doubt of his conviction, which will give a more effectual check to the licentious spirit of the press."[1] But Carey eluded the dragnet, sailing for America along with other Irish who hoped to find a better life in the United States. "Behold me now landed in Philadelphia," wrote Carey, after seven weeks crossing the Atlantic, "with about a dozen guineas in my pocket, without relation or friend, and even without an acquaintance."[2]

When Carey arrived in Philadelphia, close to four hundred thousand Irish lived in the United States. In the 1790s another estimated sixty thousand arrived.[3] The bulk of these immigrants, about 60 percent, were Irish Presbyterians. Catholics made up about 20 percent, and the rest came from other denominations. The majority of these Irish settled in the Appalachian Trail region, a rural frontier that had become home to the eighteenth-century Ulster Irish. A noticeable change, however, was the large numbers of Irish newcomers who chose to settle in such cities as New York, Philadelphia, Baltimore, and Charleston. This migration to the cities would become more pronounced with each passing decade as the center of the Irish population shifted from the rural frontier to the network of cities that lined the Atlantic coast. Included among the 1790 emigrants was a sizable number of political radicals who were, like Carey, forced into exile because of their outspoken opposition to England's rule over Ireland—chief among them the United Irish exiles.

The Society of United Irishmen was founded in Belfast in 1791. Inspired by the radicalism of the American and French revolutions as well as Irish patriotism, its original goal was constitutional reform in Ireland. But it soon became more radical, adopting Irish independence as its goal and revolutionary tactics as its means. It sought to unite Irishmen of all denominations, casting aside the bitter sectarianism that had plagued Ireland for so long. Attracting mostly members of the middle class, it spread beyond Belfast to Dublin and regions in southeast Ireland, gaining a substantial following of both Catholics and Protestants. Finally, in 1798 the anticipated rebellion took place. It was a bloody failure, put down brutally by British troops. Facing death or jail, hundreds of United Irish supporters left Ireland for the United States. Mainly young men of a high socioeconomic background, they traveled with family or alone. About half of them were Presbyterians, with Catholics numbering about 28 percent.[4]

"There were, in effect, two main phases of radical Irish immigration," wrote historian David Wilson. "The first occurred between 1795 and early 1798, in response to the repression of the emerging revolutionary movement in Ireland; it included some who saw America as a temporary base in their continuing struggle for Irish independence, and others who regarded the United States as their new home." The second phase "began after the failure of the Rising in 1798, when the boats were packed with political refugees, and continued right up to 1805 and 1806."[5]

In the 1790s the U.S. Congress was divided between Federalists and Republicans, organized groups of politicians who had different views about the national government. The Republicans, whose leader was Thomas Jefferson, tended to be optimistic about politics and the economy and favored an increase in the participation of the people in the government, using democratic rhetoric to gain the allegiance of the people. The Federalist faction, led by John Adams, stressed the need for order and authority in government, putting little emphasis on involving ordinary people in government. They also thought the nation was under threat by enemies, both within and outside the United States. The major threat was France, which was at war with Great Britain at this time. For this reason they wanted to maintain a close alliance with Great Britain, while the Republicans were more sympathetic to France. Because the U.S. government supported England, France retaliated, seizing American merchant ships. War with France seemed imminent. As a result, anti-French feelings intensified among the Federalists. Anyone of Republican sympathies was suspected of being pro-French, possibly even a traitor. The Federalists saw this as an opportunity to weaken their Republican opponents, whom they believed were too pro-French. Since they controlled Congress, the Federalists passed the Alien and Sedition Acts in 1798. In urging the passing of these laws Congressman Harrison Gray Otis spoke for many of his Federalist colleagues when he "declared that he did not wish to invite hordes of wild Irishmen, nor the turbulent and disorderly of all parts of the world to come here with a view to disturb our tranquility."[6] This legislation not only sought to suppress dissent, but also to weaken the Jefferson Republicans, the Irish radicals' party of choice. With the election of Jefferson to the presidency in 1800 and Republicans in control, Congress let the Alien and Sedition laws expire and repealed the Naturalization Law of 1798, which had required fourteen years of residency for citizenship. Having survived this period of nativist paranoia, the Irish exiles proceeded to make their mark in American society.

Historian David Wilson described the United Irish exiles as "egalitarian democrats whose social attitudes spanned the spectrum of American life but whose center of gravity was somewhat to the left of center." Concentrated in New York, Philadelphia, and Baltimore, they formed a United Irish network along the Eastern seaboard that kept alive the dream of Irish independence. A talented group of exiles, they founded at least seventeen newspapers by 1812. In addition, some authored histories of Ireland, while others made their mark as gifted lawyers or educators. By

1812 they had become important figures in the nation's political, religious, and cultural life. Representative of this group of Irish radicals were two individuals who came from very different backgrounds.[7]

One was the fugitive Mathew Carey. Born in Dublin in 1760, he was raised in an upper-class Catholic family. His father was a baker who, Carey claimed, "by inflexible honesty, unceasing industry, and rigid economy . . . made a handsome fortune."[8] Having done so well in his business, Carey's father was able to provide his five sons with excellent educations. While an infant, a nurse dropped Mathew, injuring his feet so severely that he walked with a limp the rest of his life. This meant that young Mathew was not able to participate in games or sports. He also suffered from the jeers and taunts of his schoolmates. Timid and shy as a young boy, he found refuge in reading, developing a love of books that he nourished for the rest of his life. In his teens, he became involved in the radical politics of the day, and eventually his political radicalism forced him to flee to Philadelphia. Though not a member of the United Irishmen when he lived in Ireland, he did support their cause. He later joined the American Society of United Irishmen, whose goal was "to promote the emancipation of Ireland from the tyranny of the British government."[9]

Soon after his arrival in America, Carey embarked on a career in publishing and bookselling. By 1821 he had published eleven hundred books, and his Philadelphia bookstore became one of the largest in the country. A tireless worker, for twenty-five years he was present every day at his small store. Carey published such American works as Mason Locke Weems's bestseller, *The Life of Washington*. Carey employed Weems, who was a colorful, itinerant bookseller, to promote Carey's books in the Philadelphia region. Carey also distributed books from foreign presses as well as domestic presses. Historian Michael Carter noted that Carey "was friend and correspondent to virtually all of the major American literary, political, religious and economic figures of his time, from Benjamin Franklin, Thomas Jefferson, and the Marquis de Lafayette, to Noah Webster, Henry Clay and Sarah Josepha Hale."[10] One of Carey's most successful ventures was the publication of a family edition of the King James Bible. He also published the first Catholic Bible in the United States. He founded a journal, *The American Museum*, to foster the development of American literature. Though it only lasted for five years, the journal featured a large amount of American poetry. A trustee of St. Mary's parish, he also became a recognized leader of Philadelphia Catholicism. The most significant event in his personal life was his marriage to Bridget Flahavan on February 24, 1791. He wrote that they "lived together happily for nearly thirty nine years. We had nine children, of whom three have died, two in infancy and one, a daughter, of the most angelic character, at about seventeen years."[11]

An Enlightenment Catholic, Carey had a deep concern for others less fortunate. In his diary he wrote that he always wanted "to do good." This was an "overwhelming passion" in his life, which, he claimed, "I cannot resist." He wrote, "I have never seen distress without commiseration," and he always sought to provide "relief, as far as my circumstances permit."[12] This concern led him to become involved in numerous activities on behalf of Philadelphia's poor. In 1792, moved by the poverty of many recent Irish immigrants, he gathered together some of the more influential members of the Irish community to found the Hibernian Society for the Relief of Emigrants from Ireland. Not only did this society seek to assist the immigrants, but it also became a recruiting agency for the Jeffersonian Republican movement. Like his United Irish colleagues, Carey denounced the sectarianism that had for so long plagued Ireland. He promoted goodwill among Catholics and Protestants and joined with others in 1796 to form the Sunday School Society, serving as an officer for many years. An inveterate pamphlet writer, he wrote essays defending the poor and the need for public charity. He penned pamphlets on behalf of working women and was known throughout the city for his generosity. His private acts of charity were so numerous that he eventually ran out of money. As a result, his son had to provide him with additional income. When he died, a newspaper described him as an "esteemed philanthropist" and noted that "the cry of the poor, the widow, and the orphan, was never in vain at his door." His funeral procession in 1839 was one of the largest that Philadelphia had ever seen.[13]

Another noteworthy Irish radical was Thomas Addis Emmet. Born in Cork, Ireland, and raised in a prominent Church of Ireland family, Thomas Emmet attended Trinity College. After his graduation in 1782 he studied medicine in Scotland. But he changed careers from medicine to law and was admitted to the bar in Dublin in 1790. A successful lawyer in Dublin, he earned "more than 1000 pounds a year from his law practice." As one historian noted, "The world of Dublin was his oyster . . . but he preferred to risk all in the pursuit of a united and independent Ireland."[14] Like Carey, Emmet was an Enlightenment liberal who favored self-government for Ireland. Having joined the Dublin Society of United Irishmen in 1792, he soon became one of its key leaders.

When the British government cracked down on the society in 1798, Emmet, along with other United Irishmen, was imprisoned. He spent three years in jail. After his release he traveled to Germany and France hoping to gain support for Ireland's freedom from British rule. In 1803 his brother Robert was executed after a failed rebellion to gain Irish independence. Disillusioned with conditions in Ireland, Thomas sailed for New York in 1804 with his wife and family.

In New York he took up the practice of law. Emmet's reputation as a lawyer gained him distinction in the city, where he became one of the most admired citizens of his generation. A successful lawyer who earned more than $10,000 a year, he worked alongside other United Irish exiles, such as the lawyer William Sampson and the physician William J. Mac-Neven, to aid the many Irish immigrants who were coming to New York. In 1817 he became the first president of the Irish Emigrant Society. Emmet lived up to Enlightenment ideals of toleration and the United Irishmen's antisectarian goals. The Episcopalian Emmet did not hesitate to defend Catholic rioters who were arrested for fighting with Irish Protestants, gaining their release from jail. When he died in November of 1827, his funeral was one of the largest ever seen in New York. The entire city council attended; businesses throughout the city closed for the day; the flags of ships in the harbor flew at half-mast in his honor; and De Witt Clinton and Martin Van Buren along with other notable citizens served as pallbearers. He was held in such esteem that the New York Irish erected a thirty-foot-tall white marble obelisk in his honor in St. Paul's churchyard where he was buried. The inscription on the monument, written in Irish, read, "He contemplated great good for the land of his birth. He shed luster, and received commendation in the land of his decease." For years afterward Irish Catholics as well as Protestants would bring flowers to his grave to honor the memory of this Irish exile who had found a new homeland in the United States.[15]

Emmet was one of the last United Irish exiles to emigrate to the United States. Other Irish continued to come, but the War of 1812 brought a halt to emigration. Once peace was restored in 1815, the Irish resumed their emigration to the United States. In the thirty years prior to the Great Famine of 1845–50, over a million people left Ireland, primarily for economic reasons. During the Napoleonic wars agricultural prices were on the rise as the demand for food increased. But once the wars ended in 1815, agricultural prices declined, depressing the economy. Landlords began to convert their holdings from tillage to the grazing of cattle. This shift from "corn to horn" pushed people off the land, and there was little industry for them to turn to. Furthermore, Ireland's population was dramatically increasing as the mortality rate declined; contributing to this exceptional growth was an improved diet and a high fertility rate in an agrarian population marrying at a young age. From 4.7 million in 1791 the population ballooned to over 8 million by 1841. Such a massive increase intensified the depth of poverty in Ireland. By the 1820s over two million people could be described as living below the poverty line, making Ireland one of the poorest countries in Europe. Contemporary travelers never failed to notice the poverty of Ireland's people. One English observer reported what he found near the town of Midleton in county Cork:

> I went into several hovels . . . They all consisted of mud walls, with a covering of rafters and straw. None of them so good as the place where you keep your little horse. I took a particular account of the first place that I went into. It was twenty-one feet long and nine feet wide. The floor, the bare ground. No fireplace, no chimney, the fire (made of potato-haulm) [i.e., potato stems] made on one side against the wall, and the smoke going out of a hole in the roof. No table, no chair; I sat to write upon a block of wood. Some stones for seats. No goods but a pot, and a shallow tub, for the pig and the family both to eat out of. There was one window, nine inches by five, and the glass broken half out.[16]

By 1841 more than 40 percent of Irish families lived in such one-room mud cabins "where furniture was sparse, many lacking even bedsteads."[17] Another 37 percent lived in cabins with only two to four rooms. The people who lived in these cabins typically worked less than half a year, given the limited job opportunities available. Periodic famines (five between 1815 and 1844) only added to the their distress. Given these conditions, massive emigration was inevitable.

In Dublin, "there were handbills placarded on every corner, tree, pump ~ublic place in the city . . . and for 40 or 50 miles in the surrounding stating in substance that the people were fools not to leave the ꞏere there was nothing but poverty staring them in the face . . . here is one or more agents in every principal town in Ireland ꞏommission for collecting and forwarding emigrants to

Liverpool, where they take ship for America."[18] Small-town "newspapers carried notices of forthcoming sailings to the New World." Even in the poorest cabins printed notices of ships bound for Canada were "stuck upon the wall." Emigration fever was spreading throughout the country, so much so that by 1840, well before the Great Famine, emigration was becoming "an integral aspect of Irish life."[19]

Most of the emigrants came from Ulster in the north, where the mechanization of the linen industry resulted in a large number of unemployed workers. A sizable number of emigrants also came from Leinster, in the southeast of Ireland, where a similar technological change led to an increase in rural poverty as machine production in factories and mills displaced domestic spinning and weaving of linen. At first Protestants outnumbered Catholics, but by the 1830s the migration of Catholics surpassed that of Protestants. As a result, about one half of all the emigrants in this period were Catholic. This was a significant shift from the colonial period, when Protestants far outnumbered Catholics. Unlike migrations from other European countries, Irish emigrants were not inclined to travel as a family. In the twenty-five years before the Great Famine "only about half of the Irish emigrants landing at Boston and New York traveled in family groups."[20] Mostly young single folks, those under thirty-five, left Ireland; they were the redundant population in a rural economy for whom there was no future in Ireland. Women made up as much as 40 percent of these emigrants. Most of those who emigrated, as high as 60 percent by the 1840s, were unskilled laborers. The others were better-off farmers.

The first leg of the emigrant's journey was from a port in Ireland to Liverpool, England. Most of the shipping lanes in the Irish Sea led to Liverpool, the seaport that had become the main center of the Atlantic passenger trade. The journey took less than a day and the ships had no amenities. Most often they carried cattle, pigs, sheep, and horses along with the emigrants, who stayed on the top deck for the relatively brief journey. Once they arrived in Liverpool, they had to wait for a ship bound for North America. This could mean days of waiting in run-down flophouses. They purchased their own tickets or had them prepaid by relatives or friends in North America. When the time came, they boarded a ship destined for Canada or the United States. A sizable number of Irish, as many as 60 percent of all Irish emigrants, chose to sail to Canada. The primary reason was cheaper fares. From there they would then travel south to the United States; some settled permanently in Canada. New York was the harbor of choice for those who sailed for the United States, since by this time New York was supplanting Philadelphia as the Irish capital of the United States.

Sailing to North America took about five to six weeks. The sailing ships that carried the emigrants were built to carry timber or grain, not human cargo. Having delivered their cargo to Liverpool, they returned to North America with emigrants filling their empty holds. Accommodations were primitive, with poor ventilation amid crowded conditions where four people slept in a space six feet by six feet, in an area between the decks that was only five to six feet in height. Such an overcrowded environment enabled contagious diseases to spread easily. For a rural people who had most likely never been on a ship before, the long voyage across the Atlantic, where heavy storms were common, was frightening.

Ulster Irish emigrants followed the pattern of settlement that their eighteenth-century ancestors had established, settling in western Maryland, Virginia, and the Carolinas. Charleston, Savannah, Mobile, and New Orleans were the Southern cities where sizable numbers of Irish settled. But the presence of the Irish, from Ulster or elsewhere, south of the Mason-Dixon Line was limited. In fact, only about 7 percent of the Irish immigrant community in the United States in 1860 lived in the South. This represented less than 1 percent of the South's total population.[21] For Irish Catholics, who began to arrive in sizable numbers in the 1830s and '40s, the South was not appealing. The principal reason was that the slave-based cotton economy of the South did not provide enough job opportunities to attract large numbers of unskilled laborers. Unlike the East and the Midwest, the South did not develop a large urban-industrial market base to attract Irish laborers. Moreover, the major immigration ports were located in the North, not the South, with New Orleans being the lone exception. The Irish pattern of settlement began to become concentrated in the port cities along the Northeastern seaboard, where the Irish had already established strong communities. Three cities in particular were especially key destinations for the arriving multitudes.

Because of its port and its commercial links with Ireland, Philadelphia had been the Irish capital of colonial America, with a well-established and distinguished Irish community that attracted the newcomers. By 1850 as many as 72,312 Irish had chosen to live in the city; this represented about 18 percent of the city's population. Boston also attracted the Irish in this period. But their numbers were never large, only about thirty-five thousand by midcentury. Nonetheless, this represented about one fourth of the city's population. As appealing as Boston and Philadelphia may have been at this time, New York City was where the majority of Irish emigrants chose to settle. As early as the 1830s it had replaced Philadelphia as the Irish capital of the United States.

In the early nineteenth century New York was not only becoming a major industrial center, but was also undergoing a population explosion, reaching over three hundred thousand people by 1840, an increase of more than 500 percent in forty years. At this time about one of every four New Yorkers was a foreign-born Irishman or Irishwoman.[22] As the city expanded, new streets had to be constructed, more housing was needed, and laborers were in demand. The growing city had an expanding economy offering numerous jobs. The completion of the Erie Canal in 1825 established a transportation link between New York and the sprawling interior of the Midwest. Because of its huge harbor, which could accommodate a large number of sizable ships, as well as its ready access to the newly completed canal, New York emerged as the nation's leading center of trade with a large percentage of the nation's imports and exports passing through its harbor. Furthermore, a substantial Irish community, already in place in the city, served as an unofficial welcoming committee to the newcomers. New York had also become the primary destination for the emigrant ships sailing from Liverpool. All of these factors made New York the favored destination for large numbers of Ireland's emigrants.

New York's Irish settled in distinct neighborhoods, chiefly the Fourth, Fifth, and Sixth Wards, located south of Chambers Street at the lower end of Manhattan. The Sixth Ward was the epicenter of the city's Irish community. By the 1830s it was reputed to be the largest Irish community in the nation. It was also home to the Five Points, a neighborhood that became one of the country's most notorious slums. Visitors to New York never failed to comment on the squalidness of the neighborhood. As one New York fireman recalled, "No decent person walked through it; all shunned the locality." A recent study concluded that it was a "neighborhood rife with vice, crime, and misery." People were packed into wooden tenements "two or two and a half stories tall."[23] These buildings were some of the city's worst tenements with families often living, sleeping, and eating in a single room.

The majority of the Irish who lived in this neighborhood worked as day laborers, work described as "the hardest, most dangerous, and most financially precarious in Five Points."[24] They worked at laying sewer lines, digging foundations for new buildings, paving streets with cobblestones, or loading and unloading cargo from the many ships docked along the city's wharves. Their background in Ireland did not really qualify Irish emigrants for any other type of work. "Uneducated, accustomed to a marginal existence, a stranger to the refinements, thankful for a job at cash wages, [the immigrant] entered into the lowest stratum of free white labor as the hewer of wood and drawer of water, with his sole capital a brawny back and two strong hands." It was rough work, but for a poor Irish immigrant, it was better than his native land could offer. As one of them put it, America "is the best poor-man's country in the world."[25]

Most of the women who worked were employed in the neighborhood's garment industry doing needlework of some type, either at home or in one of the workshops. Seamstresses were not only poorly paid, but they also experienced periodic unemployment throughout the year.

The Five Points represented just one slice of New York's Irish. Other streets and neighborhoods housed an Irish middle class. A study of the Sixth Ward's Catholic church, Transfiguration, suggested that in 1840 the majority of its parishioners were skilled workers. These included tailors, carpenters, masons, and blacksmiths. In addition, a sizable number of petty entrepreneurs lived in the area. They were engaged in small neighborhood trades, such as groceries, porterhouses, and saloons. The trustees of Transfiguration parish included doctors, merchants, and neighborhood grocers. A number of the émigrés of 1798 were also distinguished doctors, lawyers, and journalists. This diversity of class manifested itself with the inauguration of the first Erina Ball on St. Patrick's eve in 1831, where the high price of admission guaranteed a select attendance.[26]

The diversity of class evident in New York in the 1830s and '40s had been present among New York's Irish since the late eighteenth century, but with one significant difference. With the new waves of immigration after 1815, more lower-class Catholics had settled in the city. As their numbers increased, they began to reshape the nature of New York's Irish community. In the late eighteenth century and early nineteenth century the Irish community was fairly egalitarian and inclusive. Class may have divided the community, but not religion. Religion did not define Irish identity. Catholics and Protestants joined the same organizations, such as the Friendly Sons of St. Patrick, the Irish Emigrant Society, and the Shamrock Friendly Association. For the émigrés of 1798, most of whom were Protestant, religious toleration was central to their value system. But as the number of lower-class Irish Catholic immigrants increased, the inclusive, middle-class values of the early republican period became less influential in shaping the Irish community. The expansion of the city's

Catholic Church gives some indication of how sizable this increase was. New York's first Catholic church, St. Peter's, was organized in 1785. It was twenty years before another church, St. Patrick's, opened its doors. Then in the next thirty years the increase in the number of Catholic immigrants was so substantial that fourteen parishes were organized. Eleven of these could be described as Irish parishes.

These Catholic immigrants brought with them a more sectarian, less inclusive attitude that contrasted sharply with the nonsectarian viewpoint of the middle-class émigrés. The increase in religious and political conflict in Ireland itself in the early nineteenth century was now being reflected in America. The difference could be seen in New York's two Irish American newspapers, the *Shamrock* and the *Truth Teller*. The *Shamrock*, edited by the United Irish émigré Thomas O'Connor, reflected the values of middle-class émigrés. The *Truth Teller*, which in 1825 succeeded the *Shamrock* as New York's leading Irish newspaper, appealed to the lower-class Irish. Its founding editor was an Irish-born priest, John Powers. The "mouthpiece of the Catholic Irish American community," it adopted a sectarian, militant tone when discussing Protestantism. Irish organizations also mirrored this shift. The Hibernian Universal Benevolent Society contrasted sharply with the more exclusive Friendly Sons of St. Patrick. Its members came from the working class, and included in their holiday parades "were painters, coopers, tailors, and cordwainers." The Ancient Order of Hibernians, founded in New York in 1836, also identified with the lower classes. Class divisions among the Irish even showed up in church when, in 1820, lower-class Irish clashed with the upper-class trustees of St. Peter's parish over the renting of pews in church—a practice that discriminated against the poor members of the parish.[27]

Symptomatic of this change in attitude among the Irish was the introduction of the term *Scotch-Irish* into the Irish American vocabulary. The term had been in use during the eighteenth century to designate the Ulster Presbyterians who emigrated to the United States. From the mid-1700s through the early 1800s, however, the term *Irish* was more widely used to identify both Catholic and Protestant Irish. As long as the Protestants comprised the majority of the emigrants, as they did until the 1830s, they were happy to be known simply as Irish. But as political and religious conflict between Catholics and Protestants both in Ireland and the United States became more frequent, and as Catholic emigrants began to outnumber Protestants, the term *Irish* became synonymous with Irish Catholics. For most Protestants, *Irish* now was a word filled with negative stereotypes such as superstitious papists and illiterate ditchdiggers.[28] As a result *Scotch-Irish* became the customary term to describe Protestants of Irish descent. By adopting this new identity, Irish Protestants in America dissociated themselves from Irish Catholics. The broader meaning of *Irish* faded from memory. The famine migration of the 1840s and '50s that sent waves of poor Irish Catholics to the United States, together with the rise in anti-Catholicism, intensified this attitude. In no way did Irish Protestants want to be identified with these ragged newcomers. So they took on a new identity, an identity, some boasted, that did not include a drop of blood of the old Celtic (i.e., Catholic) Irish.

WORK

During the 1820s the nation had fallen in love with canals. Every part of the country, or so it seemed, sought to build a canal. As many as forty major canals were built between 1785 and 1850. They stretched from Boston to Richmond and as far west as Chicago. Promoted as the path to a region's economic prosperity, most did not last long once the railroad made its debut. But one in particular did endure well beyond the arrival of the railroad. This was the Erie Canal. Begun in 1817, it was finally completed in 1825. An Irish American, De Witt Clinton, the governor of New York, spearheaded this project to its successful conclusion. Stretching from Albany to Buffalo, it linked the Great Lakes with the port of New York. It was ridiculed as "Clinton's Folly" or "Clinton's Ditch" because, to many, building a 363-mile canal stretching from the Hudson River to Lake Erie seemed preposterous. But it was so successful that within a few years it transformed the nation's economy by opening up a new transportation route to the Midwest. Without Irish ditchdiggers the Erie Canal could never have been built. A saying at the time was, "To dig a canal, at least four things are necessary, a shovel, a pick, a wheelbarrow, and an Irishman."

By 1830, when canal building was at its high point, thirty-five thousand people worked in the industry. The bulk of these workers were unskilled canallers, men who did the physically demanding and dangerous work of digging the ditches, blasting the rock, and building the locks. Most of them were Irish, and a large number were Irish speakers, how many it is difficult to know. In 1850, 432 people were working on the Chesapeake and Ohio Canal. Of them, 393 were Irish, 97 percent of whom were unskilled. The second-largest ethnic group was the Germans with 24 workers, most of whom were also unskilled. The Erie Canal employed as many as nine thousand workers. Again, the Irish ditchdiggers outnumbered everyone else. People complained that "there is thousands of Irish" in Albany in 1823. A young woman reported that the Irish came to Lockport in the 1820s "by hundreds." Mathew Carey wrote, "The Irish labourers are found uncommonly handy and active, and for years have a large portion of the work on canals and turnpikes." In a condescending manner, Charles Dickens said, "Who else would dig and delve, and drudge, and do domestic work, and make canals and roads, and execute great lines of Internal Improvement." "The poor Irishman, the wheelbarrow is his country," observed Ralph Waldo Emerson. Wherever there was hard, dirty work, there you would find the Irish.[29]

Some of them had worked as canallers in Ireland and later in England. Hoping to take advantage of a depressed economy in England, recruiters from New York traveled to Britain to hire these workers. Notices were also placed in Irish newspapers promising good wages. The president of the Chesapeake and Ohio Canal wrote, "Meat, three times a day, a plenty of bread and vegetables, with a reasonable allowance of liquor, and light, ten, or twelve dollars a month for wages would . . . prove a powerful attraction to those . . . who have at this moment a year of scarcity presented to them."[30] Such promises persuaded a large number of canallers to emigrate to America. This was one way contractors were able to meet the labor demand.

The canallers were migrant workers who moved from job to job. Once they finished their work on the Erie Canal, most moved on to other projects. Some went to New England, often traveling in construction gangs with one worker serving as their leader and job broker. They found work in such places as Lowell and Worcester, Massachusetts, where the canal fever sparked the building of these water highways. Others headed for the Midwest, to Ohio or Indiana, where canals were also being built. Some were recruited to work in New Orleans, where they would build the New Basin Canal.

The job of the canaller was physically demanding as well as dangerous. Young boys did the light work of hauling water and driving the horses that hauled the rock and dirt to and from the work sites. The older men did the hard work of wading through muck, clearing the ground of rocks and trees. Then they had to break up the ground with their picks or horse-drawn plows, removing the dirt with their wheelbarrows and horse-drawn wagons. They were the human machines that built the canals. Along the

Erie Canal near Syracuse, Irish laborers worked in knee-deep water, with legs swollen from dampness, with leeches and mosquitoes attacking their bodies. This led to a ditty that the canallers sang as they cut their way through the earth:

We are digging the ditch through the mire;
Through the mud and the slime and the mire, by heck!
And the mud is our principal hire;
Up our pants, in our shirts, down our neck, by heck![31]

When they came to hard rock, they had to blast their way through. Drilling holes and filling them with powder, they lit the fuse and ran for cover. At Lockport, New York, along the Erie Canal, they had to blast through two miles of solid rock. This was dangerous work that often had dire consequences if the laborer was not proficient when it came to lighting the fuse. But it paid more, so few Irish turned down the opportunity to risk life or limb.

The job of the canaller was not only physically demanding, but it also paid poorly. Most often hired by the month, the ditchdiggers earned about eight to ten dollars a month in the 1820s. The contractor provided room and board. The work was never steady due to bad weather, illness, or injury. On a good day these men worked from dawn to dusk. Unemployment was chronic, forcing many to travel to find other jobs where they could work. As bad as the pay was and as demanding the job, these workers still fared better than their counterparts in Ireland or England. Women also worked at these construction sites. Though their numbers were small, they cooked and cleaned while caring for the men in the shanty camps.

Life in these shanty camps was raucous and violent. Numerous strikes and riots took place, with the 1830s being especially violent. The Irish were particularly inclined toward faction fighting. These were feuds between groups identified as Corkonians (from county Cork in the southwestern province of Munster) and Connaughtmen, also known as Fardowners (from the province of Connaught on the west coast). Workers would live and work with their own kind. For the Irish this meant staying with men from their own region in Ireland. One worker described this intense regionalism among the Irish: "The Irish on the public works in this country are divided into two great parties, viz. Fardowns & Corconians, & bear a deadly hatred towards each other. One of an opposite party dare not seek employment on a contract where the other party were in employ."[32]

These disputes could become deadly. One such riot took place along the Chesapeake and Ohio Canal in 1834 between the Fardowners and the Corkonians. A fight between the two groups ended with the death of one of the Fardowners. That began a war that lasted a few days and resulted in a number of deaths and many injuries. Witnesses "observed five men in the agonies of death, who had been shot through the head; several dead bodies were seen in the woods, and a number wounded in every direction." Federal troops had to be summoned from Baltimore to quell the riot. On the surface this appeared to be just another ethnic brawl. But it was more than that. The riot was precipitated by a dispute over the nonpayment of wages for work done as well as the prospect of unemployment. To the winners of the war would go the spoils of future employment.[33]

The canallers lived in wooden shacks. These barrackslike bunkhouses varied in size—some held as many as one hundred workers while others housed fifteen to twenty. But regardless of size, they shared the same spartan features—open windows welcoming flies and mosquitoes, a cooking pot and hearth in the middle of the building with a hole in the roof as a chimney. They slept on wooden planks covered with straw. Those not so fortunate slept on the floor. Dozens of these shanties lined the canals, housing hundreds of workers. Some shanties housed families where husband and wife and children lived along with a few boarders. This domestic shanty became more common after the 1830s as more and more married men became dependent on canal work.[34]

Disease added to the dangers of the worker's life. Typhoid thrived in the work camps. Malaria and yellow fever flourished in the swampy terrain of a canal. Cholera took on epidemic proportions in the antebellum period, claiming its victims in the tenements of the city as well as in the Paddy camps that sprang up along the canals. The cholera epidemic of 1832 devastated Irish neighborhoods in New Orleans. In addition, Irish canallers working on the New Basin Canal in New Orleans died by the hundreds, victims of malaria and yellow fever. At least three thousand, and perhaps as many as twenty thousand, died while working on the canal. Popular folklore memorialized their deaths in song:

> Ten thousand Micks, they swung their picks,
> To dig the New Canal
> But the choleray was stronger 'n they,
> An' twice it killed them awl.[35]

As historian Peter Way put it, "Injury or death was part of the job, ordinary, unavoidable, indiscriminate, a danger assumed when one picked up a shovel."[36] But for these Irish workers there really was no choice. Working on the canals was better than no work at all. Nor were they afraid to speak out when they believed their employers were exploiting them. Protests and strikes were common along the canals, with the Irish in the forefront of such demonstrations. The Irish would continue this tradition throughout the second half of the nineteenth century, when they took on a leading role in the American labor movement.

This first wave of nineteenth-century immigrants helped to develop industrial America. They provided the muscle and brawn needed to build and expand the nation's cities in this era of unprecedented urban growth. The nation's first transportation network could not have been built without the efforts of thousands of Irish ditchdiggers. When their work on the canals was done, many of them chose to settle in the cities along the canals. Many went into the construction industry in such places as Buffalo, Albany, Rochester, Chicago, Worcester, and dozens of other cities where Irish communities were beginning to form. The ditchdiggers settled down, married, and became the founding generation of these urban Irish communities. Some became landowners, such as Padraig Cundun, who emigrated in the mid-1820s to work on the Erie Canal. By 1834 he was the owner of a farm. Others became shopkeepers or worked on the docks in New Orleans or worked in the quarries near Syracuse.[37] Little did they know that within a few years a new tidal wave of Irish immigrants would land on America's shores. Their presence would strengthen and expand the modest Irish communities that these laborers had established.

POLITICS

The Irish who immigrated to the United States in this prefamine period carried with them a long tradition of political involvement. The émigrés of the 1798 rebellion possessed an acute sense of politics developed during their struggle to gain independence for Ireland. They carried this radical democratic tradition to America. Indeed, one congressman described these United Irishmen as "the most God-provoking Democrats on this side of Hell." At a time when the new nation was still struggling to establish itself as a democratic republic, the 1798 émigrés made an important contribution toward this goal. According to historian David Wilson, the basis for this influence was their commitment to "the rights of man, freedom of thought, equality of opportunity and economic expansion"—values that were central to the American experiment.[38]

Radicalized by their experience in Ireland, the United Irishmen brought this tradition to the party of Jefferson and Madison. Realizing this, their Federalist opponents sought to curb their influence by passing the Alien and Sedition laws in 1798. Through this legislation they hoped to weaken the political influence of these "most God-provoking Democrats."

Jefferson's victory in the presidential election of 1800 not only spelled the defeat of the Federalists and their anti-Irish legislation, but it also helped to cement the bond between the Irish and the democratic political tradition. Indeed, Jefferson's victory encouraged many more Irish to emigrate to the United States, where they strengthened the radical wing of Jeffersonian Republicanism. Through the newspapers they founded as well as their organizations, they promoted Jeffersonian Republicanism. It was chiefly their leadership and example that persuaded the new Irish immigrants to align themselves with Jefferson. Assessing their political influence, David Wilson wrote:

> In the period between Jefferson's inauguration and the outbreak of war with Britain, the United Irishmen attempted to implement in America the political program that had been denied them in Ireland. Viewing the Federalists as an American version of the aristocrats and Orangemen who had defeated democracy in the Old Country, the United Irishmen were determined to give them no quarter in the United States. In the process, they frequently displayed the same kind of intolerance that they denounced in their enemies. On the radical edge of the American Republican movement, they pushed for liberalized naturalization laws, a more democratic and rational judicial system, constitutional revision in Pennsylvania, and the extension of full religious freedom for Catholics throughout the country; a militant minority also worked for a religious revolution that would turn the United States into a deist democracy.[39]

The political involvement of the United Irishmen exiles was only one aspect of Irish political activity in this prefamine period. Other Irishmen, both Irish-born and American-born, were also involved in politics. New York's Sixth Ward offers a classic example of the Irish affinity for politics. The Irish were introduced to politics at the neighborhood level, where one of the key institutions was the saloon. More than a watering hole for thirsty customers, the saloon was also a gathering place where deals were made and jobs obtained. Commenting on the saloonkeeper's influence in the neighborhood, one contemporary wrote, "The liquor dealer is their guide, philosopher, and creditor. He sees them more frequently and familiarly than anybody else, and is more trusted by them than anybody else, and is the person through whom the news and meaning of what passes in the upper regions of city politics reaches them." Another avenue to political power was the volunteer fire company. These organizations were famous not just for their heroism but also their pugilism. Election-day brawls that could escalate into large-scale riots were common in the antebellum period. Candidates would call on their supporters in the local fire company to intimidate their opponent's supporters at the polls. The outcome of an election was often determined by who had the best pugilists. Many of the ward's political leaders first gained recognition and respect through their leadership in a volunteer fire company. The police force was another avenue to political standing. The Irish were particularly attracted to the police force because of the prestige and security it provided. But jobs on the police force were also political plums, to be reserved for those who were most loyal to the party. Once on the force they could help the party in numerous ways. As historian Tyler Anbinder noted, "Such service enabled many a Five Points policeman to rise out of the ranks to both party leadership and elective office."[40]

The career of Constantine J. Donoho exemplified how politics worked in the neighborhood. A liquor dealer, he operated a grocery at 17 Orange Street that featured a well-stocked bar. He not only sold food and drink but also lobbied his customers to vote for the candidate that he and his party were supporting. He was known as "a zealous, firm, hard-fisted Democrat of the old school" who became "king of the politicians of the sixth ward" in the 1840s. His real power came from his position as a street inspector. In this capacity he hired "men to clean, pave, and repair the ward's streets, giving him more patronage power than any other man in the ward." On election day, Con, as he was known, and his men were ready to do battle on behalf of their candidate. Black eyes and broken noses were badges of victory as well as defeat. "Fighting and toughness were prerequisites to political power," noted Anbinder.[41] Con Donoho possessed enough of these skills to be acknowledged as a leader. After the fighting, Con would retreat to his pulpit at the grocery, ready to campaign for the next election.

In those days, the Irish were often in the forefront of election-day riots either as victims or perpetrators of mob violence. They were involved in a notorious riot during the 1834 municipal election. The Whigs, who opposed the policies of Andrew Jackson's Democratic Party, wanted to oust the Democrats—predominantly Irish—from power in the Sixth Ward. Their strategy was to prevent the Democrats from intimidating voters at the polls. The Whigs, mostly non-Irish, said the Democrats, mostly Irish, started the riot. The Democrats claimed that it was the fault of the Whigs. For two days, hundreds of men were engaged in fistfights and rioting. Anarchy reigned in the city. The pleading of the mayor to stop the fighting prevailed and order was restored.

Another election riot took place in the Sixth Ward in 1842. This time the fighting took place among the supporters of rival candidates in the Democratic Party seeking to be elected as alderman of the Irish Sixth Ward. The issue of public funds for Catholic schools had become entangled in the election. The state legislature had passed a bill in April, the Maclay Act, that weakened the city's Protestant Public School Society but refused to finance Catholic schools. The city's Democrats split over this issue, with Protestants supporting the Public School Society and Catholics endorsing the Maclay Act. The passage of the Maclay Act, two days before the election, intensified the hostility between the political rivals. Local gangs fought one another outside the polling places. The violence escalated as rioters pursued their victims into their homes and wherever they sought refuge. Rioters even attacked the home of Bishop John Hughes, whom they singled out because of his support of public aid to Catholic schools and his fierce opposition to the Public School Society. They broke his windows, doors, and furniture. Learning of this, Walt Whitman, who called the Maclay Act "a statute for the fostering and teaching of Catholic superstition," commented, "Had it been the reverend hypocrite's head that had been smashed . . . instead of his windows, we could hardly find it in our soul to be sorrowful."[42]

By the 1830s the Irish working class had taken political control of the Sixth Ward. But, at this time, the best they could hope for was to become a ward alderman. Felix O'Neil, a grocer from county Sligo and a trustee of the Transfiguration Catholic parish, was one immigrant who gained this prize in the 1840s. But the next generation was more ambitious. They wanted to change city politics, not just ward politics. Eventually they would gain control of Tammany Hall, the political machine of the Democratic Party. Once they achieved this, New York politics would never be the same.

NATIONALISM

Closely allied to the Irish love of politics was their strong sense of Irish nationalism. This was a spirit of peoplehood that permeated nineteenth-century Ireland and was transplanted to Irish America. Fundamental to this was a sense of identity. The Irish viewed themselves as a people set apart with their own unique language, culture, and history. From this history they created their own heroes, such as St. Patrick and Brian Boru, as well as such sacred places as Croagh Patrick and the Hill of Tara. This sense of identity was especially heightened in the modern period as it acquired a more political meaning expressed in the people's desire to gain their rightful place as a nation among nations. By the late eighteenth century this seemed to be a reachable goal under the leadership of the United Irishmen. But their demise and the passage of the Act of Union in 1800, which dissolved the Irish parliament and created the United Kingdom of Great Britain and Ireland, put that goal out of reach. Losing what little political independence it had, Ireland was once again under the thumb of England. The Act of Union became a bone in the throat of the Irish people throughout the nineteenth century, continually encouraging in them an intense desire to be free of British rule.

This nationalism was entwined with a deep-seated hatred of England. A contributor to the *Edinburgh Review* in 1825 put it succinctly. "Centuries of oppression and misgovernment have generated a deep-rooted and cordial hatred of the English name and nation in the minds of the vast majority of the Irish," he wrote, infecting them with "a strong nationality." Daniel O'Connell, Ireland's most famous politician of the nineteenth century, believed that the Irish not only had "vivid contempt" for the English parliament, which ruled Ireland, but they also "felt only hatred of England." Such hatred would endure for decades throughout the Irish diaspora.[43]

The United Irishmen planted the seeds of nationalism in Irish America in the early nineteenth century. Both Protestant and Catholic émigrés shared a commitment to Irish independence that transcended religious and political differences. Thomas Addis Emmet spoke for many when he asserted, "The highest aspiration and most fervent aspiration of the United Irishmen was to make Ireland what America is—politically free." The clubs they founded to assist the emigrants became political clubs as well, where they promoted the cause of Irish nationalism. Their newspapers carried news from the old country, keeping their readers informed of events in Ireland and cementing the bonds between the emigrants and Ireland. The songs and poems of this era contributed to this sense of Irish consciousness. A number of United Irishmen wrote histories of Ireland "that were intended to raise the reputation of their countrymen in America and provide intellectual ammunition for the struggle back home."[44] Mathew Carey's work *Vindiciae Hibernica*, published in 1819, not only sought to correct the role played by Catholics in the uprising of 1641, but also sought to strengthen the pride of the Irish people. These émigrés also pursued more radical measures. They sent money and ammunition to Ireland in the hopes of encouraging an uprising. A pattern of Irish American support developed among the more radical wing of the community and would remain constant throughout the nineteenth and twentieth centuries. In the 1820s, as the political activity among Ireland's Catholics increased, Irish American nationalism intensified.

By the early nineteenth century Catholics in Ireland enjoyed numerous civil rights. They could vote, hold some political offices, own land, and practice the professions. But they could still not sit in Parliament, the legislative body that controlled Ireland's affairs, or hold other senior political positions. In other words, they were still second-class citizens in their own country, where a Protestant minority controlled the Catholic majority. Onto the stage stepped the lawyer Daniel O'Connell, who would lead a massive Catholic civil rights campaign, known as Catholic Emancipation, to abolish these last vestiges of discrimination.

Born in county Kerry in 1775 and educated in France and London, O'Connell began his legal career in Ireland during the late 1790s. A successful lawyer, he became active in the Catholic Emancipation movement in the early 1800s, helping to found the Catholic Association in 1823, a political organization of merchants and professional men. O'Connell transformed this organization into a mass political movement when he suggested that anyone who could pay a penny a month could become a member. Known as the Catholic rent, this contribution of a penny a month gave thousands of people a chance to participate in the Catholic Emancipation campaign. By enlisting the support of the masses, O'Connell launched a crusade that taught the people the importance of grass-roots democracy. A gifted orator, O'Connell gained national notoriety as the chief spokesman for Catholic Emancipation.

The Irish in the United States enthusiastically supported this campaign. United Irishmen émigrés were the catalyst for organizing the New York Irish. William Sampson, Protestant lawyer and émigré, electrified the crowd at a rally in July 1825 when he linked the crusade for Catholic Emancipation with the American struggle for political freedom, saying, "It is that terror, tyranny and persecution that has made the population of Ireland so truly Catholic, and it is the knowledge of that sacrilege that places an honest man, particularly an American, on the side of Catholic Ireland."[45] Meetings took place in Boston, Baltimore, Washington, and many other cities where the Irish had settled. By 1829 as many as twenty-four branches of the Friends of Ireland had organized to support O'Connell's campaign. The New York paper the *Truth Teller* promoted the cause by keeping its readers informed of events in Ireland, as well as printing accounts of the meetings sponsored by Irish American nationalists. The Irish sent money, perhaps as much as five thousand dollars, as well as letters of encouragement to O'Connell. When O'Connell was elected to Parliament in April 1829, Catholic Emancipation was achieved as Parliament finally abolished the last vestiges of discrimination against Catholics. Throughout the United States, Irish Americans celebrated the victory with solemn Masses, the ringing of bells, and fireworks.[46]

Another campaign of O'Connell's, the effort to repeal the Act of Union, further inflamed the fires of Irish American nationalism. O'Connell launched this campaign in Dublin in April 1840. By October the Boston Irish had gathered to form a Repeal organization. More than fifteen hundred Irish showed up for a public rally. A fish packer, a hack driver, a coal and wood dealer, and a newspaper editor ran the meeting. They formed a Friends of Ireland society, issued an address to the Irish of New England, then solicited members and funds from numerous cities and towns. They raised over one hundred pounds for O'Connell's campaign. In the next year the Repeal campaign expanded beyond New England with Repeal organizations being formed in towns and cities along the East Coast. A national convention took place in Philadelphia in 1842. New York hosted another convention a year later. By reporting on O'Connell's campaign, Irish newspapers raised the level of nationalist sentiment. Following a familiar pattern, money, called Repeal Rent, was collected and sent to Ireland along with letters and testimonials encouraging O'Connell in his struggle.[47]

But O'Connell lost the support of most Irish Americans when he condemned the American institution of slavery. O'Connell's strong stance against slavery made him "a hero of the antislavery movement." Allied with William Lloyd Garrison, who spearheaded the American abolition movement, O'Connell made numerous speeches condemning slavery. He vowed never to visit the United States as long as it was a slaveholding country, even refusing to shake the hand of a proslavery advocate. His speeches inspired African Americans to the extent that they held a meeting in New York City to honor O'Connell, whom they celebrated as their friend and advocate.[48] While traveling in Ireland, an American abolitionist and ardent admirer of O'Connell, Charles Lenox Remond, composed "An Address of the People of Ireland to Their Countrymen and Countrywomen in America." He and his allies in the Hibernian Anti-Slavery Society gathered seventy thousand signatures, headed by the names of O'Connell and Father Theobald Mathew, the renowned Irish temperance preacher. Remond's essay inspired abolitionists in Ireland and the United States for the next twenty-five years. Addressing both men and women, it urged them to "treat the colored people as your equals, as brethren. By all your memories of Ireland, continue to love liberty—hate slavery—*cling by the abolitionists*, and in America you will do honor to the name of Ireland."[49]

The address, however, failed to persuade the immigrant Irish to join the American abolition movement. First of all, by the 1840s the Irish had aligned themselves with the Democratic Party, which was proslavery. To advocate abolition not only meant abandoning their political home, but it would also have allied them with the radical wing of American politics: abolitionists willing to divide the nation over the issue of slavery. For these newcomers, whose Americanism was always suspect, this was too radical a step to take. Also, by this time religion had divided the Irish community into the rising majority of Roman Catholic Irish and the outnumbered Presbyterian Scotch Irish. Most Roman Catholics, including the Irish, supported slavery at this time. Furthermore, the antislavery movement had a strong anti-Catholic bias. In fact, "by the late 1840s," wrote historian John McGreevy, "antislavery activists frequently denounced slavery and Catholicism as parallel despotic systems." As a result few Catholics were inclined to join the abolitionist crusade.[50] In addition, African Americans and Irish often competed for the same jobs. To free the slaves would only mean more competition for jobs. In the end, the Irish chose to support slavery rather than Daniel O'Connell.

Nor did O'Connell help the situation. He issued a number of histrionic addresses to Irish American Repealers rebuking them for their reluctance to join the abolitionist crusade. "Over the broad Atlantic I pour forth my voice," he wrote, "saying—Come out of such a land, you Irishmen, or if you remain, and dare countenance the system of slavery . . . we will recognize you as Irishmen no longer."[51] Such harsh words doomed the Repeal movement in Irish America. Clubs collapsed and contributions dried up. When O'Connell died in 1847, the Repeal campaign also expired.

Their support of slavery and their opposition to O'Connell raises the issue of the racial attitudes of the Irish toward African Americans. In the 1830s Irish and African Americans coexisted quite peacefully, often living in the same neighborhoods in cities such as New York and Philadelphia. In the Five Points bars, men and women, black and Irish, drank, sang, and danced to tunes that blended Irish and African musical styles. Irish men and women made love with African Americans and some brave interracial couples defied social norms by entering into marriage. But as the debate over slavery heated up in the 1840s, relationships between the Irish and the African Americans so deteriorated that a British traveler observed, "The poorer class of Irish emigrants, are greater enemies to the negro population and greater advocates for the continuance of negro slavery, than any portion of the population in the free states."[52] What caused this shift, or as some historians have put it, how did the Irish become white?

When the Irish arrived in the United States, they were recognized as white with all the privileges of citizenship, including the right to vote, sit on juries, and move about the country without any restraints. Nonetheless, they suffered discrimination and prejudice and were often depicted with such terms as *savage*, *bestial*, and *simian*—terms also used to describe blacks. They were even referred to as "niggers turned inside out," while blacks were called "smoked Irish."[53] But did this racial description of the Irish in terms similar to blacks mean that to escape such identification they had to choose to create a new racial identity by becoming "white"? As historian Kevin Kenny has argued, for the Irish such an option of choosing whiteness, "deliberately distancing themselves from African Americans in order to advance themselves socially, seems unnecessarily abstract and tends to overestimate the degree of conscious agency involved in the process."[54]

Rather than adopting a racial identity of whiteness to set them apart from blacks, a more straightforward explanation for their shift to a hostile, and at times violent, relationship with blacks would be their allegiance to the Democratic Party and the competition between blacks and Irish for similar jobs. The Democratic Party welcomed the Irish upon their arrival in the United States by providing them with jobs, registering them as voters, and in general looking after their welfare. The Irish gladly accepted such tangible benefits and entered into an alliance with the Democratic Party that would endure for over a century. In the antebellum period the Democratic Party, in defending slavery, became the party of white supremacy. Rather than being oppressed and discriminated against, the Irish, as the foot soldiers of the party, now adopted the role of the oppressor in their relationships with African Americans. The proslavery attitude of most Catholic Church leaders made this alliance with the party of white supremacy all the easier. Furthermore, in Boston, New York, and Philadelphia the Irish and the blacks often competed for the same jobs since they were both at the bottom of the occupational hierarchy. Though the extent of this competition is disputed, there is no question that it took place. As Frederick Douglass, the escaped slave and noted abolitionist, wrote, "Every hour sees us elbowed out of some employment to make room for some newly arrived emigrant from the Emerald Isle, whose hunger and color entitle him to special favor. These white men are becoming house servants, cooks, stewards, waiters and flunkies."[55]

African Americans held most of the jobs along New York's waterfront in the late eighteenth and early nineteenth centuries, but by the 1850s the Irish had pushed them off the docks, where they would dominate the workforce into the twentieth century. A similar development took place as increasing numbers of Irish "elbowed out" African Americans in such unskilled jobs as laborers or porters; Irish women replaced black women as maids and domestic servants. When black workers were used as strikebreakers, Irish workers retaliated violently. The Irish feared that the blacks might push them out of the workforce, and if slavery was abolished, then they would overpower them for sure. To defend themselves against such possibilities, they set up boundaries between themselves and African Americans that fostered racial hostility. Such hostility would develop into one of the worst intergroup hatreds ever seen in the United States.[56]

RELIGION

By the 1840s the Catholic religion became the most prominent feature of Irish America and, in the eyes of many, its most objectionable feature. Prior to 1800 Roman Catholicism was a small sect, centered in Maryland and Pennsylvania and numbering about 35,000. By 1840 the Catholic population had increased to 663,000. The increase was due mainly to the large numbers of immigrants from Ireland and Germany. By this time the Church was present up and down the Northeast coast, stretching west to the Ohio Valley, and south to New Orleans and Mobile. The number of dioceses had increased from one in 1790 to twenty-two by 1844. But as one prelate noted, the Catholic Church in the United States "was the worst organized church" in the nation.[57] To remedy this, the bishops decided to gather together in a national council with the hope of bringing some order and uniformity to this expanding institution. Five such councils took place from 1829 to 1844. One of the persons most responsible for these national meetings was John England, the Irish-born bishop of Charleston, South Carolina. According to England, such gatherings would not only help to establish a "nationally-organized system within the church," but they would also be a visible manifestation of the unity and the strength of the Catholic Church.[58]

John England was one of the most remarkable prelates of this era. Born in 1786 in Cork, Ireland, he abandoned the study of law to pursue a calling to the priesthood. As a priest in Cork he acquired a reputation as an ardent defender of the civil rights of Irish Catholics at a time when they still had to endure religious discrimination. Like Daniel O'Connell, his contemporary in this struggle for civil rights, England embraced an understanding of Catholicism that was well ahead of its time, endorsing the concept of religious liberty as well as the separation of church and state, beliefs fairly common in the United States at this time, but quite uncommon within European Catholicism. In Cork he edited and managed the secular newspaper the *Cork Mercantile Chronicle*. He was also a chaplain at the city jail, where he worked with prisoners who were sentenced to the penal colony in Australia. Because of his exceptional talents, the Vatican appointed him to be the first bishop of Charleston, South Carolina, a diocese that stretched across Georgia and the Carolinas. This region was hardly a citadel of Catholicism, but the city of Charleston did house a number of Irish Catholics who were desperate for an Irish bishop.

As the bishop of Charleston from 1820 to his death in 1842, England promoted a model of Catholicism that was truly exceptional. Charleston's Catholics were riddled with dissension over the issue of authority in the local congregation. England brought peace to the community by fashioning a republican style of church government in which clergy and laity worked together. As he stated, he wanted to fashion a church in which "the laity are empowered to cooperate but not to dominate." The centerpiece of this arrangement was a written constitution that England presented to the clergy and laity in September 1823. Accepted by the assembly, the constitution endorsed the election of parish lay trustees and annual conventions of clergy and laity to discuss the needs of the church, as well as lay representatives chosen to participate in these meetings. These conventions met annually from 1823 until England's death in 1842. In seeking to adapt Catholicism to the American republican environment, England wanted to create something new in the Catholic world. Regrettably, most of the other bishops did not approve of his republican ideas. When he died, his vision died with him.

In addition to promoting a new model of Catholicism, England also founded the first Catholic newspaper in the United States, the *U.S. Catholic Miscellany*, and wrote many articles for the paper. In these essays he championed the idea of the compatibility between American democratic values and Roman Catholicism. A skilled orator, he was invited to speak in pulpits, both Catholic and Protestant, throughout the country. His reputation was such that he was asked to speak before the U.S. Congress in 1826, the first Catholic priest to have this honor. His theme on this occasion was once again the compatibility between American democratic values, as articulated in the nation's Constitution, and Catholicism. When this Irishman died in 1842, the Catholic Church lost its most ardent advocate for a model of Catholicism that was rooted in the democratic ethos of the American political tradition.

It is ironic that one of the most talented prelates of the time was the bishop of a diocese located in the hinterland of American Catholicism. The church in Charleston could never rival Catholicism in New York, a city that would eventually become, as one priest put it, "the Rome of our modern Republic."[59] Whereas the entire Diocese of Charleston, which comprised North and South Carolina as well as Georgia, had as few as seven thousand Catholics by 1842, New York City alone numbered fifteen thousand Catholics in 1815 and increased to an estimated ninety thousand by 1840.[60] As in Charleston, the Irish made up a sizable majority of New York's Catholics. The Irish flavor of New York Catholicism was especially evident among the clergy. Half of all the priests in the diocese were Irish in 1845, and the bishop, John Hughes, was Irish as well. Among those Catholic sisters working in the city, the Irish were also prominent. Though the city's Germans were reluctant to acknowledge it, the Irish ruled the Catholic Church in New York. In addition to sixteen parish churches in the city, eleven of which were Irish, Catholics were supporting a newspaper, two orphanages, a hospital, as well as two colleges for men and an academy for women.

Another Northeastern city that experienced significant Catholic growth was Philadelphia. Between 1808 and 1832 the number of Catholics increased from ten thousand to twenty-five thousand. As in New York, the clergy were overwhelmingly Irish, numbering twenty-five of the thirty-five priests working in the diocese. A number of them spoke Irish since many of the Irish laborers in the region preferred to hear their sermons in Irish rather than English.[61] In addition, the bishop of Philadelphia in 1844, Francis Kenrick, was, like Hughes, born in Ireland. At this time the city's Catholics were supporting eleven parishes, nine of which were Irish, along with a college for men and three orphanages.

The Church was in much better shape in the cities than it was in the rural countryside. In a tour of upper New York State in 1830 the bishop of New York, John Dubois, commented that "endless numbers of neglected souls" were scattered far and wide. Rarely, if ever, did they see a priest.[62] Half of the Catholics in New England lived in Boston. The others were spread throughout the rest of the region. As a result whole families were in danger of losing the faith. The challenge for the clergy was to restore the faith of the newcomers by introducing them to the practice of traditional Catholicism.

The Irish who arrived in these decades practiced a religion that was distinctively Irish. The vast majority of them were not Mass-and-sacraments Catholics. The trademark of this style of Catholicism was regular attendance at Mass and reception of the sacraments, principally confession and the Eucharist. But many Irish immigrants had not received the sacraments of confession or Communion for years, "some even 30 or 40 years," noted one missionary.[63] In addition, they were strikingly ignorant of basic Catholic beliefs. Such a low level of adherence to the official Mass-and-sacraments style of Catholicism was consistent with the type of religion popular in Ireland during these years.

In Ireland, the religious practices of the people, what can be described as popular Catholicism, were rooted in their Gaelic culture. This popular religion focused on such sacred sites as holy wells and participation in rituals, known as patterns, at these sites, as well as pilgrimages to such holy places as Croagh Patrick or Lough Derg. Many of these places had been considered sacred even in pre-Christian times. This type of popular religion coexisted with the more official rituals of Catholicism that took place in the parish church. But, for most Irish people participation in rituals at holy wells confirmed their identity as Catholics.[64] They were Catholic and religious, but in a distinctively Irish manner.

An Irish immigrant described these sacred sites: "Holy Wells were numerous to which people would make visits, there alone and in silence beg of the patron saint of the well to intercede for them to obtain relief from God and tie a piece of cloth on a limb or branch of a tree hanging often over the well as a token of a pilgrimage being made. Many miracles were made on the border of these wells. St. Brendan's in the County Galway had many."[65]

Ireland had as many as three thousand holy wells. People would gather at these shrines, sometimes thousands of the devout who had traveled long distances, to honor the saint associated with the sacred site. When the emigrants sailed for America, they left a big part of their religion behind since it was rooted in Ireland's landscape. For the Church in the United States, the challenge was to reintroduce these newcomers to the official brand of Catholicism that had always existed in Ireland, but at the margins of the people's practice of religion. For a Church that was experiencing a population explosion and a dire shortage of clergy, such a challenge was extremely difficult to meet. As a result, the practice of Catholicism among large numbers of the Irish was at a low level. These were the anonymous Catholics. Catholic by birth and heritage but not in practice, they lived on the fringe of parish life. They comprised anywhere from 40 to 60 percent of the Irish community in such places as New York and Philadelphia. The rest were regular churchgoers for whom the parish was a central institution in their lives. In the Irish Catholic hinterland, however, places such as southern Maryland, western Pennsylvania, and northern New England, the vast majority of Irish were Catholic in name only. Rarely did they meet a priest. For them their Catholic religion was largely a memory, left behind in Ireland along with the sacred sites they had once visited.

The extraordinary growth of the Catholic population in the early decades of the nineteenth century frightened many Americans. The United States had always been a Protestant nation, but now Catholics, most of whom were foreigners, seemed to be overrunning the country. At the same time that this was taking place, the United States was undergoing a religious revival, led by Protestant evangelists. Labeled by historians the Great Awakening, this revival endured throughout the 1820s and '30s. Centered in the cities, it unleashed a tide of religious enthusiasm that changed forever the face of American Protestantism. The impetus behind this revival was not only the need for individual conversion, but also the conversion of a nation. It was a crusade to build a Christian America. But in the minds of most Protestants, Catholics were not Christians. They were regarded as renegades, apostates who belonged to a church described by many as the biblical "whore of Babylon." Their allegiance to the pope in Rome and the apparent control of the clergy over the minds of the faithful flew in the face of the American values of freedom and democracy. As the inventor, and passionate nativist, Samuel F. B. Morse put it, "Popery is opposed in its very nature to Democratic Republicanism; and it is, therefore, as a political system, as well as religious, opposed to civil and religious liberty, and consequently to our form of government."[66]

This attitude toward Catholics was not new. It originated with the Protestant Reformation in the sixteenth century and was transplanted to colonial America. Such strong anti-Catholic feelings had subsided in the postrevolutionary era, when toleration rather than bigotry prevailed. It was easier to be tolerant of Catholics when they were a small minority. With the rise in immigration and the increase in the number of Catholics, anti-Catholicism reappeared with a vengeance, lasting for much of the nineteenth century. Newspapers, schoolbooks, and all types of fictional literature nurtured such feelings. In the words of a noted historian who wrote the definitive history of this Protestant crusade, "The average Protestant American of the 1850's had been trained from birth to hate Catholicism."[67]

The Protestant churches were united in their opposition to Catholicism as they sought "to make America the scene of a new Reformation in which Popery would be driven from the land and the work of Luther and Calvin brought to a successful end."[68] This was the atmosphere awaiting Irish Catholic newcomers. As a writer for the *North American Review* observed, "It must be admitted that the Irish have to encounter considerable prejudices in this country in almost every section of the Union, though in different degrees. In some places they are openly and even violently expressed."[69]

The violence surfaced with unusual intensity in August 1834, when an angry mob burned the Ursuline convent school in Charlestown, Massachusetts. Incited by the fiery, anti-Catholic rhetoric of the preacher Lyman Beecher, and under the impression that a nun was being held in the convent against her will, a mob of forty to fifty men torched the convent. A crowd of people, along with local fire companies, stood by and watched the building burn to the ground. Despite a public outcry at such violence, Boston's Irish Catholics continued to be harassed. Before long, mob violence against Catholics would break out again. As one observer noted, the prejudice against the Irish was particularly harsh among New England Yankees. As he put it, "New England is the hardest soil for an Irishman to take root and flourish."[70] Outbreaks of violence were not limited to Boston, however. New York witnessed a terrible riot in the summer of 1835 between "natives and Irish." Centered in the Irish enclave of Five Points, it involved several thousand people. After a few days of rioting the police were able to restore peace.[71] This was but one of several anti-Irish riots in New York during this era. But the worst riot to engulf the nation at this time took place in 1844 in Philadelphia, the City of Brotherly Love.

Feelings were tense between Irish and American workers because of competition over jobs made scarce by the depression of 1837–44. The growing antipathy toward Catholics made a bad situation worse. Bishop Francis Kenrick of Philadelphia fueled this hostility by requesting that Catholic students in public schools not be required to read from the Protestant King James Bible. Protestants looked upon this not only as an attack on the Bible, but also an assault on the religious ethos of the public school, which most Americans regarded as a sacred temple. The spark that ignited the riot was a nativist rally on May 6 in the Irish neighborhood of Kensington. Words were exchanged between the Irish locals and the nativists. Pushing and shoving followed, then shots were fired, fighting erupted, and Kensington went up in flames. During three days of rioting more than thirty homes, two Catholic churches, and the Catholic seminary were destroyed. At least six people were killed and many were seriously injured. Then in July, another riot between Irish and nativists took place. Before it was over, thirteen people "had been killed and more than fifty wounded in the three days of fighting."[72]

The Philadelphia riots appeared to be a decisive turning point in the perception of Irish Catholics. In the early years of the nineteenth century the popular image of the Irish focused on character traits. The stereotype of the Irish described Paddy and Bridget as clannish, ignorant, pugnacious, superstitious, and gloomy, though they could also be warm, hospitable, jovial, intelligent, and industrious.

Though the negative traits outweighed the positive, there was hope since such negative qualities, according to popular perception, were not innate. They were the result of the environment in Ireland. In a more salubrious setting, Paddy and Bridget could, despite all their flaws, become outstanding Americans. The well-known minister and president of Yale Timothy Dwight believed that "their defects and vices . . . are owing to the want of education, or to a bad one." Once they gained the advantages that other Americans had, the Irish would "stand upon a level with any of their neighbors." A young Harvard student, in a commencement address in 1840, articulated this point of view when he said, "The sin of the Irishman is ignorance—the cure is Liberty."[73] Such condescending thinking was prevalent at this time, not just toward the Irish, but to other immigrant groups as well as African Americans.

After the riots in Philadelphia, however, there was less optimism about reforming the Irish. The popular stereotype, evident in the literature of the day, now portrayed the Irish as innately ignorant and violent. Reflecting this change, another Protestant divine from New England, Theodore Parker, commenting on the number of crimes committed by the Irish in Boston, said, "The Irish are ignorant, and, as a consequence thereof, are idle, thriftless, poor, intemperate, and barbarian." The popular stereotype of the Irish had evolved from one that saw them shaped by the environment to one that said their failings were innate. By their very nature, even visible in their physical features, the Irish were inferior. They could no longer become Americans. As one New York patrician put it, "Our Celtic citizens are almost as remote from us in temperament and constitution as the Chinese."[74] Like the Chinese, they were now perceived as an inferior race, not just another immigrant group.

Dale Knoebel, who has studied this evolution of the popular stereotype of the Irish, concluded, "In the late antebellum years, to identify an individual or a group as 'Irish' was to mobilize a word image which portrayed its subjects as un-American, Catholic, violent in temper, politically tractable, and ideologically rigid. Conversely, to identify anyone as Roman Catholic was virtually . . . to label them Irish." Knoebel went on to write, "Because the verbal image of the Irish was so pejorative, because it connected its targets with so many unfavorable characteristics and made these seem permanent and innate, and—most of all—because this image was on almost everyone's lips, it was a source of hostility to the American Irish which might operate apart from any other."[75] This stereotype would become even more deeply ingrained in the popular imagination after the famine migration of the late 1840s brought more poor and desperate Irish to America's shores.

For the Irish, two major transformations had taken place between the 1790s and the mid-1840s. Irish identity changed significantly. From being an inclusive designation of identity for both Catholic and Protestant, the term *Irish* had been transformed into a sectarian label that was exclusively used to identify Irish Catholics. Henceforth, Irish Protestants came to be known as Scotch-Irish. Secondly, the Irish, most especially the new immigrants, who were once viewed as potential American citizens, had descended in the popular mind to an inferior race incompatible with the American nationality. To most Americans, being Irish and Catholic was a liability, not an asset. Such prejudice would follow the Irish throughout the rest of the nineteenth century.

On the eve of the Great Famine the major features of Irish America were already in place. The Irish, the vast majority of whom labored in menial jobs, exhibited an intense nationalism as well as an attraction to politics and a loyalty to Catholicism that was rooted in centuries of oppression in Ireland. These characteristics would intensify in the years ahead as millions of working-class Irish Catholics chose to settle in the United States. This period in Irish American history has too long existed in the shadow of the postfamine period. Nevertheless, these decades shaped the future of Irish America.

PART TWO

The Famine Generation and Beyond, 1840–1920

CHAPTER 3

The Great Hunger

In Ireland the summer of 1845 was unusually wet. August was so damp that crops of corn were "blighted and mildewed." An article in the *Dublin Evening Post* noted, "The new potatoes have suffered much from the heavy rains, any that have been dug out up to the present time were quite wet and unwholesome as food."[1] Then in September the first sign of a potato blight appeared. By early October the blight was more widespread, moving west across Ireland. The wet summer provided an ideal climate for the fungus to spread and wreak havoc on that fall's potato harvest. The blight had followed a mysterious journey, spreading either from Peru from potatoes shipped to Europe along with guano—bird excrement used as fertilizer—or from the United States, where ships sailing from Eastern ports could have carried diseased potatoes to Europe. After spreading through Europe the invisible plague finally reached Ireland, carried across the Irish Sea by wind and rain.

The failure of the potato crop in 1845 was only partial, since a large portion of the crop had been harvested before the blight struck. In 1846 there was total failure, with as much as 90 percent of the potato crop destroyed. The fear of misery and starvation spread across the land. The "death-sign," as an Irish land agent put it, was the "fearful stench" of rotting potatoes, which "became almost unbearable." This same agent, having planted more than a hundred acres of potatoes, sadly wrote that "it had all passed away like a dream."[2]

Another eyewitness left this description of what happened that fateful summer: "The leaves of the potato had been blighted, and from being green, parts of them were turned black and brown, and when these parts were felt between the fingers they would crumble into ashes . . . The air was laden with a sickly odor of decay, as if the hand of death had stricken the potato field."[3]

In 1847 the potato harvest was meager since little seed had been available for planting. Starvation and disease ravaged the land in that fateful year of Black '47, so named because of the magnitude of suffering. The winter of 1846–47 was especially bitter. In 1848 half the crop was lost. Cholera struck that year and into 1849, when the number of deaths rose to record levels. In 1849 and 1850 the potato crop failed again, prolonging Ireland's agony.

The history of Ireland and Irish America changed forever when famine struck in the mid-1840s. In the early nineteenth century Ireland had experienced several famines, but because it was so devastating, the famine of 1845–50 has become known as the Great Famine, or in Irish, *An Gorta Mor* (the Great Hunger). For five years, hunger and disease hounded victims across the fields and lanes of rural Ireland, eventually claiming more than a million lives. Ireland would never be the same. Such a vast tragedy, the famine has inspired numerous songs, poems, and stories. For years its memory shaped the attitudes of the Irish toward the English, whom many blamed for the famine. As John Mitchel, one of Ireland's most outspoken nationalists, put it, "The Almighty sent the potato blight, but the English created the famine."[4]

By the 1840s Ireland's population had skyrocketed to over eight million. One of the most densely populated countries in Europe, it was also one of the poorest. In addition, the Irish were dependent on a single crop, the potato. Such extraordinary reliance on the potato would prove devastating if the crop ever failed. That is exactly what happened in 1846, and again and again for the next four years. With too many mouths to feed and too poor to obtain food, an estimated 1.1 million people died from disease or starvation. Another million and more, having lost hope in Ireland, chose to emigrate. Ireland's reliance on the potato had spelled the country's doom.

The potato, having originated in Peru, was introduced to Ireland in the late sixteenth century. By the eighteenth century it had become the staple of the Irish diet, most especially for the poor. On the eve of the famine more than half of Ireland's population relied on the potato as their main source of food. Given the small plots of land that the Irish peasants lived on, the potato was the perfect subsistence food, since an abundance of potatoes could grow on a small plot of land, even in the poorest conditions, with little labor required. The average adult male consumed twelve to fourteen pounds of potatoes each day, with women and older children consuming as much as eleven pounds, and children under ten around five pounds. Even though they had a rather monotonous diet, the potato-fed Irish were better nourished than the poor in other European countries, enjoying a respectable life expectancy at that time of thirty-eight years.

The Irish had no other food that could supply their nutritional needs once the potato harvest failed. Another possible source of nourishment was fish, but though Ireland was surrounded by an ocean full of fish, its fishing industry was totally inadequate to harvest the rich fishing banks that were located twenty to twenty-five miles out to sea. Local fishermen did not have the proper boats to navigate the dangerous ocean waters, so they fished close to shore in currachs, small boats made of wood and canvas. Once the famine hit, however, some became so weak that they could not even row their boats, finally selling their boats and nets to buy food. As for fishing the many rivers in Ireland, these were on the property of the landlords, and poaching laws were enforced as strictly as ever during the famine.

The effects of the famine were felt most deeply in the west and southwest, where many people were subsistence farmers, living on tiny plots of land. In Mayo and Clare, two of the poorest counties, they died by the thousands. Facing starvation, "whole families walled themselves into their cabins and died." In the western part of county Cork, the suffering was just as bad. In the town of Kenmare in Kerry the local priest wrote, "They were dying by the dozens in the street."[5] A Cork magistrate left the following "account of a visit to the neighbourhood of Skibbereen in west Cork (perhaps the worst afflicted locality in the country) in late December 1846":

> I entered some of the hovels . . . and the scenes that presented themselves were such as no tongue or pen can convey the slightest idea. In the first six famished and ghastly skeletons, to all appearance dead, were huddled in a corner on some filthy straw, their sole covering what seemed a ragged horse-cloth, and their wretched legs hanging about, naked above the knees. I approached in horror, and found by a low moaning they were alive, they were in fever—four children, a woman and what had once been a man.[6]

A physician, visiting the village of Schull in southwest county Cork, "had met a man, a father tottering along the road—a rope was over his shoulder, and at the other end of the rope, streeling along the ground were two dead children whom he was with difficulty dragging to the grave."[7]

In Skibbereen they buried the poor in their rags, dropping them into a large pit outside the town, a mass grave still visible today as a memorial to Ireland's Great Hunger. People worked overtime making coffins for those who could afford them. The sliding coffin, called such because the bottom slid out, allowing the body to drop into the grave, became commonplace since it could be used again and again for those families who could not afford a coffin to bury their dead.

One eyewitness captured the tragedy in a memorable passage. Speaking of the horror wrought by the famine, he wrote:

> They died in their mountain glens, they died along the sea coast, they died on the roads, and they died in the fields; they wandered into the towns, and died on the streets; they closed their cabin doors, and lay down upon their beds, and died of actual starvation in their own homes.[8]

During the famine numerous evictions took place. A principal reason was the manner in which the British poor law operated. The poor law stipulated that landlords had to pay the rent of all holdings valued at four pounds or less. This proved to be an incentive for them to rid their estates of those poor tenants unable to pay the rent on these small holdings. As a Cork merchant commented, this clause in the poor law "almost forced the landlords to get rid of their poorer tenantry; in order that they should not have to pay for these small holdings, they destroyed the cottages in every direction."[9] Even more draconian was another clause in the poor law that was added in 1847. Known as the quarter-acre clause, it stipulated that anyone who held more than a quarter acre of land was not eligible for public assistance. For poor and starving tenants, the only way to gain assistance was to reduce their holdings to less than a quarter acre by turning over the land to their landlord. Once this took place, landlords cleared their estates by destroying the tenants' homes as well as taking what little land they still possessed. After the land was cleared, the landlord could turn it into a more commercially viable estate with cattle and sheep replacing the evicted tenants. Many tenants, already starving and destitute, refused to turn over their land, knowing that they would lose their houses as well. They would rather die as paupers at home than as homeless vagabonds in a ditch along the road.

To clear their estates of the poor, landlords became ruthless in evicting their tenants who could not pay the rent. With police standing guard, hired hands, known as the crowbar brigade, tore down the mud cabins, forcing their occupants to roam the countryside, begging for food. As many as fifty thousand families, an estimated 250,000 people, were permanently evicted from their homes from 1849 to 1854. Once again it was in the west and the southwest of Ireland where the bulk of these evictions took place.

People remembered these brutal evictions for years to come. One eyewitness described what happened to a family in Tipperary:

> The sheriff, a strong force of police, and above all the crowbar brigade, a body composed of the lowest and most debauched ruffians, were present. At a signal from the sheriff the work began. The miserable inmates of the cabins were dragged out upon the road; the thatched roofs were torn down and the earthen walls battered in by crowbars: . . . the screaming women, the half-naked children, the paralysed grandmother and tottering grandfather were hauled out. It was a sight I have never forgotten . . . The winter of 1848–49 dwells in my memory as one long night of sorrow.

After their homes were destroyed, "people live in banks and ditches," wrote one observer, "like animals, until starvation or weather drives them to the workhouse."[10]

The response of the British government to Ireland's tragedy was less than adequate, in large part due to the English attitude toward the Irish. For centuries the English looked upon the Irish as inferior people. Such cultural prejudice was widespread during the 1800s. The *Times* of London, in early 1847, spoke for many English when it declared that Ireland was a "nation of beggars" whose "leading defects were 'indolence, improvidence, disorder, and consequent destitution.' "[11] Many in the political elite believed that the famine was God's work, a providential intervention to force the Irish to become more self-reliant. Charles Trevelyan, the head of the English treasury and the person in charge of famine relief, bluntly said the famine was "a direct stroke of an all-wise and all-merciful Providence" that "laid bare the deep and inveterate root of social evil" plaguing Ireland. This was God's punishment of the Irish, and in this manner Ireland would be cleansed. Only then could it participate fully "in the social health and physical prosperity of Great Britain," as Trevelyan put it.[12] A firm belief in laissez-faire economics reinforced this attitude. This meant that the government's intervention in Ireland's economy would be limited. The famine became "a heaven-sent opportunity to stamp out Irish laziness, ingratitude, violence and ignorance, and to remake Ireland in the image of industrious, efficient, orderly England."[13] That more was not done to keep people alive was, in historian Peter Gray's words, "due to the triumph of ideological obsession over humanitarianism."[14] The Irish people deeply resented this bias. Such resentment would fuel the fires of Irish nationalism throughout the nineteenth century and into the twentieth.

Nonetheless, the extent of the famine was so great that the British government was forced to intervene, but its intervention was completely inadequate. The first responses were public works projects that provided employment and wages so that people could buy food. This took place in 1845–46 when Robert Peel was prime minister. Peel also encouraged the importation of grain to alleviate the people's hunger. John Russell succeeded Peel as prime minister in 1846 shortly before the situation deteriorated. During his tenure, the public works program continued as the Irish poor built docks where there were no ships and roads that went nowhere, paid for by the British government. But the wages were completely inadequate to feed a starving family. Russell, a firm believer in private enterprise as the solution to the problem, reluctantly introduced soup kitchens to "keep the people alive." Not surprisingly this effort was well received, proving "to be the most effective means of containing the ravages of the famine."[15] But the government viewed the soup kitchens as temporary, closing them down by the end of September 1847.

A primary form of relief from 1847 until the end of the famine was the workhouse, where people worked for food. Derided as "Bastilles of the poor," they housed the able-bodied poor, who worked at such tasks as grinding corn or breaking stones, for eight to ten hours a day. Breaking stones was so hated that some applicants for assistance declared that "they would rather die than break stones." Ireland had as many as 130 workhouses by 1847 that had been built to provide work and food for the poor. In normal times they were often crowded. When mass starvation gripped the countryside, they were inundated with hundreds of starving men, women, and children seeking relief. Some workhouses, built to accommodate eight hundred persons, were forced to house as many as twenty-eight hundred.[16] Mortality rates in these overcrowded, disease-infested refuges skyrocketed during the famine. Such relief efforts were no match for the overwhelming poverty and prolonged famine.

Ever since the famine, people have debated the culpability of the British government. The claim that during the famine more than enough food was produced in Ireland to feed all of its people still haunts the memory of the Irish to this day. Instead of remaining in Ireland, it was exported to Britain to "satisfy the inexorable demands of the Irish landlords . . . for their rents." As a result "of the forced export of all this food, a million people starved to death or died of disease." For this reason people still claim that the British government was guilty of genocide against the Irish people. Without question tons of food left Ireland for England during the famine, the shipments often guarded by the military to protect looting by the starving masses. But to set the record straight, as James Donnelly put it, it is imperative to acknowledge that more food was imported to Ireland in the years 1847 and 1848 than was exported. "Total imports (1,328,000 tons) exceeded total exports (460,000 tons) by a factor of almost three to one." In fact, in terms of calories in the Irish diet, "grain imports were worth almost three times as much as grain exports during the late 1840s." But the potato was such a central part of the Irish diet and its loss "so enormous" that "even if all the grain exported in those years had been retained in the country," it would still not have compensated for the loss of the potato.[17]

Though the claim of genocide is without merit, the government of the world's richest and most powerful nation could undeniably have done more to prevent the deaths of over a million people. By the Act of Union in 1800, Ireland had become part of the United Kingdom of Great Britain, but the government failed to provide for its people, causing ruin and starvation rather than prosperity. Though the government spent about seven million pounds on Irish relief, this represented "less than one-half of one percent of the British gross national product over five years."[18] Yet, the government spent more than seventy million pounds on the Crimean War of 1854–56. A fundamental reason for such an inadequate response to the famine was the cultural imperialism of the English toward the Irish. Rather than being an equal partner in the United Kingdom, Ireland was looked upon as an inferior colony whose people were in need of reform.

The Great Famine transformed the demography of Ireland by increasing the level of emigration. The Irish had been leaving home in large numbers since 1815, when the economy went into a downturn. But once the Great Hunger took hold, emigration became a flood. In 1847, one of the worst years of the famine, more than 230,000 people, fleeing disease and starvation, left Ireland. This was double the number of the previous year. Then, in 1848 when the potato crop failed again, another mass exodus took place. In 1849 and 1850 more than 200,000 left each year. The exodus reached its peak in 1851, when about 250,000 emigrated. It is estimated that during the famine, from 1846 to 1851, at least 1.5 million people left the country, more than had emigrated in the previous twenty-five years. In eleven years, from 1845 to 1855, more people left Ireland (2.1 million) than in the prior 250 years.[19] In other words, almost one quarter of the nation's population left the country at this time. Of these emigrants, 1.5 million sailed for the United States. The others traveled to Australia, Great Britain, and Canada. Such a mass exodus was unprecedented in Irish history and was never to be repeated, even though emigration from Ireland would continue throughout the nineteenth and twentieth centuries. Unlike emigrants from Italy or Greece, few Irish emigrants desired to return to the land of their birth. Once they left, they were gone forever.

Where famine struck the hardest, emigration was the heaviest, namely in Connacht and Munster, provinces in the west and southwest. In fact, Connacht lost half of its young population in the 1840s because of emigration or death.[20] Prior to the famine, emigration was heaviest in counties in Ulster and Leinster located in the north and east, but the famine changed the patterns. Henceforth, Ireland's emigrants would come from its poorest rural counties located in the west and southwest. But those who left were not the poorest of the poor, but people of "some means, because the cost of the passage required some accumulated savings or other assets that could be converted into ready cash." As historian Cormac O Grada noted, "In the hierarchy of suffering the poorest of the poor emigrated to the next world; those who emigrated to the New World had the resources to escape."[21]

During the famine a sizable family emigration did take place, but the proportion of single, young male emigrants increased, setting a pattern that continued in the postfamine period. And for the first time, large numbers of women were leaving Ireland. This was unusual in Europe, where the typical emigrant was a young, single male. The large number of female emigrants would become a trademark of Irish emigration through-out the rest of the nineteenth century.

Unskilled laborers comprised more than half of the emigrants during the famine. These emigrants were poorer and had fewer skills than those who had emigrated prior to the famine. While Protestants made up the majority of prefamine emigrants, as many as 90 percent of the famine emigrants were Catholic. Another feature of the famine emigration was the large number of Irish-speakers who left Ireland. One plausible esti-mate concluded that as many as half a million of them were Irish-speakers. Their presence in the United States strengthened the Gaelic character of Irish America, which was already very noticeable in the early nineteenth century.[22]

A key determinant to emigration was the correspondence of the emigrants themselves. Those who had already fled Ireland wrote back to their friends or relatives encouraging them to emigrate. Such letters, known in Ireland as the "Amerikay letter," had become common long be-fore the famine. It is estimated that "between 1833 and 1835 over 700,000 letters from New York passed through the Liverpool post office, eleven times the reverse correspondence; the bulk of these were probably letters from Irish settlers."[23] For those thinking about emigrating, these letters provided the best information about the United States. Comment-ing on this, the American correspondent of the *London Daily News* wrote:

> What brings such crowds to New York by every packetship is the letters which are written by the Irish already here to their relations in Ireland, accompanied, as they are in a majority of cases, by remittances to enable them to pay their passage out. It is from this source, and this mainly, if not only, that the Cork or Galway peasant learns all he knows about the United States, and he is not in the least likely to trust to any other.[24]

When the Amerikay letter arrived in the village, friends and family would gather together waiting for the letter to be read. Since many Irish were illiterate, they would seek the assistance of someone who could read the letter. Often known locally as the "scholar," this person would read the letter to a keenly interested audience. The scholar was often the parish priest. The priest in Schull in county Cork remarked, "When they write home, the friends come to me to read them. The accounts are very flattering. The general observation that they make in the letter to friends is, that there is no tyranny, no oppression from landlords, and no taxes."[25] The next day the letter would travel through the village so those who could not be present for the official reading could find out information about their relatives and friends in America. For days afterward the entire village would talk about the news in the letter.

Before the emigrants left home, their friends and neighbors would gather on the last night before the departure to celebrate a ritual known as the American wake. This developed from the traditional wake of the dead, when relatives and friends of the deceased would sit up all night in the company of the body, mourning the person's passage. The American wake was an Irish custom associated with the Irish-speaking regions of western Ireland. It was practiced as early as 1830, but perhaps was not widespread at that time. By the late nineteenth and early twentieth centuries, however, it had become common. In the 1850s and '60s the American wake was a somber affair with no dancing or singing. It was a true wake, recalled a native of county Mayo, "though not of a dead person, but a living one who next day would be sailing for the promised land." As time passed, however, the ritual became more convivial. The evening would be spent telling stories; singing songs, most often sad ballads; dancing to the music of the fiddle and the flute; and exchanging gifts. Then, in the early-morning hours after a night spent devouring large amounts of food and putting away liberal amounts of whiskey or beer, both provided by neighbors and friends, the emigrant's friends would accompany him or her to the train station, or if that was too distant, they would wave their last good-bye at a nearby crossroads or hill.

Like the Irish wake of the dead, this ritual was filled with both sadness and gaiety. But sadness was the prevailing emotion, for there was little chance that the emigrant would ever again return home. As one person put it, "It was as if you were going out to be buried." In fact, traditional Irish countrymen "made very little difference between going to America and going to the grave."[26]

Most emigrants sailed from Dublin or Queenstown, a port south of Cork. The next stop in the journey was Liverpool, the major port of embarkation in the prefamine period and remaining so through the famine. In Liverpool some emigrants bunked down in a flophouse to wait for the next ship sailing for North America. Others would look for work to pay for the next step in their journey.

The cost of the transatlantic trip at this time was less than three pounds, comparable to the cost of a young cow or the annual rent of a farm in Mayo. This was a substantial sum for one person. To help pay the cost, many emigrants relied on relatives or friends in Ireland and the United States. The case of a Donegal widow's son was not unusual. He borrowed money for his passage from an uncle in 1845. Then for two years he sent home money to support his family. Finally, in 1848 he was able to bring out his mother and his four brothers. This was known as chain migration, where one of the older children goes first and, after acquiring some money, sends it home to finance the journey of another member of the family; eventually the entire family emigrates. Such assisted emigration was common among the Irish long before the famine. But it increased substantially as the Great Hunger worsened. In 1848, family or friends sent as much as half a million pounds to those who wanted to follow them out of Ireland. By 1850 the amount of money sent had doubled. Some landlords, wanting to clear their estates of the poor to convert the land into more commercially viable areas for cattle and sheep raising, promoted the emigration of their tenants by paying for their journey. But only about twenty-two thousand emigrants were assisted in this manner.[27]

Sailing across the Atlantic to North America took about five to six weeks. In 1847 many small, poorly constructed ships were put into service to meet the needs of the thousands of people bound for North America. These ships were death traps, "coffin ships" as they became known. Their passengers were poorly provided with food and water and were forced to live in overcrowded conditions that became breeding grounds for fever and typhus. These coffin ships had terrible mortality rates.

Almost half of the emigrants in Black '47 chose to sail to Canada since the cost of a ticket was about half of that to New York. When bound for Quebec, ships were required to stop at Grosse Isle, a quarantine station located on the St. Lawrence. The first ship arrived in May. Out of a total of 241 emigrants, 9 had died during the journey, and 84 were victims of typhus.[28] As more ships arrived, their cargoes of sick and dead overwhelmed the hospital at Grosse Isle. By September, as the shipping season was ending, as many as fourteen thousand emigrants were still being held in quarantine on board ships in the river. It would be days before the dead could be removed, their bodies decomposing in the holds of the ships. As many as 5,424 of the dead were buried in a mass grave at Grosse Isle, where a monument memorializes this tragic chapter in the history of Irish emigration. Many more died at sea or soon after landing in Canada. Of the hundred thousand emigrants who sailed to Canada in 1847, an estimated thirty thousand died. But if you add those who died in the coffin ships while en route to the United States, then the total number of dead on these coffin ships was about fifty thousand.[29] But, as historian David Fitzpatrick noted, "The lingering nightmare of the coffin ships did not impede emigration, serving merely to divert it elsewhere and to instill a lasting distaste for Canada as a destination . . . Neither death nor discomfort could staunch the flow out of Ireland."[30] But as horrible as the journey to Canada was in Black '47, most emigrants survived the transatlantic journey during the famine years.[31]

As Fitzpatrick suggested, emigration scarcely slowed in the postfamine period. From 1851 to 1921 as many as 4.5 million people left Ireland, with about 3.7 million of them going to the United States. "No other country," wrote Fitzpatrick, "lost so large a proportion of its people" during the nineteenth century "or experienced such consistently heavy emigration over so long a period." Included among these emigrants were about one million Ulster Protestants, the vast majority of whom settled in the United States.[32]

The typical Irish emigrant in this period came from the poorest rural regions in the west of Ireland, especially Munster and Connacht. They were laborers and servants whose journey was financed by remittances from relatives in the United States. Most were young, under thirty, single, and about half were women.[33]

The journey out of Ireland changed dramatically in the postfamine period. Gone were the coffin ships and the perilous monthlong trip across the North Atlantic in sailing vessels. Replacing them by the 1860s were steamships that took no more than twelve to fourteen days to reach North America. By the early twentieth century bigger and better ships reduced the journey to less than a week. Emigration had become a big business as thousands of people from all over Europe journeyed to the United States as well as to other countries. New laws were put in place to regulate this transatlantic enterprise, resulting in fewer deaths, better food, and generally less crowded accommodations on board these ships. The largest number of ships sailed from Ireland in April and May. Another peak occurred in September and October before winter weather made ocean crossings uncomfortable and hazardous.[34] Rather than traveling to Liverpool, by the 1870s the vast majority of emigrants from Munster and Connacht sailed from Queenstown (Cobh), where today a museum and a sculpture honor the memory of the thousands of Irish men and women who left their homeland in search of a better life.

The flow of emigration to the United States was closely linked to the health of the American economy. When times were good in the United States, the opportunity for work was a powerful force. When the economy went sour, as in the late 1870s and the 1890s, emigration declined. In addition, crop failures in Ireland, along with agrarian unrest in the 1870s and 1880s, as well as economic recession, persuaded people to emigrate.

As critical as this link with the economy was, even more important was the changing structure of the family in postfamine Ireland. Prior to the famine land was transferred and divided up within the family among the sons with each succeeding generation. As a result the family farm diminished in size over time and was no longer able to support an entire family. To preserve the family farm, a system of land transfer developed whereby control of the property passed to a single inheritor, generally the eldest son. This practice became much more prevalent after the famine. From this developed the stem family, an arrangement in which the son inheriting the farm brought his wife into his parents' household prior to the death of one or both of the parents. Since the parents were often reluctant to give up control of their farm, the son had to wait for years before he could get married and inherit it. That explains why in Ireland by 1914 the average age of marriage for men was thirty-three years, one of the highest in Europe. Women also entered marriage at a later age, twenty-eight, than in most other countries at this time.[35] The parents of the prospective bride and groom almost invariably arranged these marriages.

Economics, not love, determined the choice of a spouse since a key issue was the value of the farm and the size of the bride's dowry. In Kerry, a familiar proverb, "Beauty didn't boil a pot," captured the insignificance of romance in these matches; the negotiations could be quite prolonged, even contentious. The dowry not only enhanced the wealth of the farm owner, but it also provided a dowry for one of the groom's sisters so she could enter into her own match. This meant that the inheritor's other siblings were left without any stake in the family property. As a result, only two children in a typical family of six children could expect to inherit or marry into land. The other two thirds were the family's "surplus off-spring." Since the possibility of employment was limited, and the opportunity for marriage for young women was also restricted, the surplus offspring had little choice but to emigrate. Emigration was a stage in a young person's life cycle. Being reared as potential emigrants, they knew that when they reached adulthood, they "must travel."[36] A ballad from Sligo captured this situation:

> My father was a farming man, used to industry,
> He had two sons to manhood grown, and lovely daughters three,
> Our acres few that would not do, so some of us must roam,
> With sisters two I bade adieu to Erin's lovely home.[37]

In the postfamine period about half of the emigrants were women—farmers' daughters displaced by the stem-family tradition. The inferior status of women in postfamine Ireland also encouraged many to emigrate. Living in a patriarchal society, women were denied economic opportunity and the independence that went along with it. Young, single men enjoyed a privileged position. The athletic pitch and the pub were the center of their lives, while young women were confined to the home, where they performed domestic chores. In addition, a young woman's chances of marriage were rather slim unless, as one observer put it, "she has a fortune."[38] If she did not have a fortune, chances were, as one woman put it, "I'd be stuck on a farm with some old geezer for the rest of my life."[39] The only other alternatives were either the convent or a life of spinsterhood in a society where men ruled the roost. This explains not only why a record number of young women emigrated, but also why an unusually high number entered the convent, where they could attain a measure of status and independence not available to them on the farm.

One of the most remarkable aspects of Irish emigration was the large amount of money sent back to Ireland by those who had left. It is estimated that between 1848 and 1900 as much as $260 million was sent back to Ireland from North America, 90 percent of this from the United States. A large portion of this money was in the form of prepaid tickets sent by emigrants to family members who could not afford the cost of the transatlantic journey.[40] Other remittances provided a valuable source of income for family left behind in Ireland, enabling them to maintain their small farms. With this newfound money they could add a new roof to the family home, make other improvements on the farm, and even buy more land. The extraordinary financial link between these transatlantic Irish communities underscored the close bonds that held these families together despite miles of separation—a bond reflected in the staggering number of letters sent to Ireland. The Irish post office distributed seven million letters in 1857; by 1914 the number had increased to twenty million. Families, an ocean apart, remained united in affection through the simple bond of letters sent to loved ones.[41]

When the emigrants set sail for the United States, the vast majority of them landed in New York. By the mid-nineteenth century, New York had monopolized the immigrant trade. Its fine harbor was a decided advantage over Philadelphia's, where the Delaware River was frozen much of the winter. In addition, the trip from Europe to Philadelphia was longer. The Erie Canal, which opened New York to the hinterland of the Midwest, was another advantage that other port cities such as Boston or Baltimore did not share. And New York's railroad lines enabled the newly arrived to travel to midwestern destinations. New Orleans was another major port for immigrants, especially those heading to the South and the Mississippi Valley, but it would never rival New York as a point of entry.

In the 1850s, the state government of New York, along with the federal government, sought to gain greater control of immigration. The arrival process had become chaotic: unscrupulous agents, known as runners, claimed to represent employers or boardinghouses and victimized the new arrivals. To remedy this situation and bring some order to the arrival process, a new immigration station, Castle Garden, was opened in 1855. A former concert hall located at the tip of Manhattan Island, Castle Garden became the gateway to America for millions of immigrants. Here they could register, be examined, and arrange for lodging or transportation without being preyed upon by the notorious runners. As many as eight million immigrants passed through Castle Garden before the federal government opened a new immigration station on Ellis Island in 1892.

The first person to pass through Ellis Island was Annie Moore, a fifteen-year-old Irish immigrant from county Cork. Her parents, along with her older brother, had emigrated to the United States in 1888 and were living in New York. In a typical chain-migration pattern, they now sent for the rest of the children. Annie, together with her two younger brothers, sailed from Queenstown (Cobh) on the SS *Nevada* in December 1891. After a journey of several days, they arrived at Ellis Island on January 1, 1892, and Annie was the first person processed at the newly opened facility. To mark the occasion she was presented with a ten-dollar gold piece. She settled in New York, where she met her husband, Joseph Schayer, a German immigrant who lived on the city's Lower East Side and worked as an engineer and a salesman at the Fulton Fish Market. Three years after her arrival in New York, she and Joseph were married in St. James Catholic Church. They had eleven children, five of whom survived to adulthood. Annie died in 1924 of heart failure and was buried in Calvary Cemetery. She is honored by sculptures at the Ellis Island Immigration Museum and the Cobh Heritage Center. For years the true identity of Annie Moore was unknown, until finally in 2006 genealogical research discovered who she really was. Prior to then it was believed that the Annie Moore of Ellis Island fame was a woman who died in Texas in 1923.[42]

Much like young Annie Moore and her family, when emigrants arrived in the United States, they preferred to settle in already established Irish communities. Most of these communities were along the East Coast, stretching from Boston to Baltimore. Already by 1850, 80 percent of the foreign-born Irish lived in New England and the Middle States. This pattern of regional concentration would continue throughout the nineteenth century. Some did travel inland to the Midwest and beyond. The Irish were the largest foreign-born group in California in the 1870s. St. Louis had a sizable Irish population by 1860, 29,926, as did Chicago, 19,889. But the Dublin of America was New York. By 1860 one in four New Yorkers was Irish; in fact, at that time more Irish lived in New York, 260,450, than in Dublin. Philadelphia, the capital of eighteenth-century Irish America, still had a sizable Irish population, 95,548, by 1860. But it would never rival New York. Boston was another favorite place of Irish settlement for the famine and postfamine immigrants, boasting an Irish-born population of 45,991 in 1860.[43]

In the postfamine era, Irish America entered a new chapter in its history. Stretching from the 1850s to the early years of the twentieth century, this era reshaped and intensified the features of prefamine Irish America. Young, unskilled men and women entered the workforce, and before long they became a powerful voice in the labor movement. Having a deep sense of loyalty to the land of their birth, they would join forces with Ireland's nationalists as, together, they waged a long and at times violent campaign to gain Ireland's independence. Settling in U.S. cities, the Irish would play a major role in shaping the politics of urban America. During these years the Irish attachment to Catholicism grew stronger, while their sons and daughters took on key leadership positions in the Church. This was the era that decisively shaped the future of Irish America.

CHAPTER 4

From Paddies to Patriots

I n telling her life story, an Irish domestic recalled her early years in a town close to Londonderry where she lived with her family in a peat cabin that had a good thatched roof. "When the potatoes rotted," she said, "that was the hard times." After typhus claimed one of her sisters, her mother said, "There's a curse on ould green Ireland and we'll get out of it." So they saved some money and sent her sister Tilly to America because, as she put it, "She always had more head than me." She went on to say, "Tilly came to Philadelphia and got a place for general housework at Mrs. Bent. Tilly got but $2 a week, bein' a greenhorn. But she larned hand over hand . . . and Mrs. Bent laid out to teach her. She larned her to cook and bake and to wash and do up shirts—all American fashion. Then Tilly axed $3 a week. Mother always said, Don't ax a penny more than you're worth. But know your own vally and ax that." Tilly saved enough money to bring her sister, the narrator of this story, to Philadelphia. The sister recalled, "When I got here Mrs. Bent let Tilly keep me for two months to teach me—me being such a greenhorn." Well trained, she went out on her own and got a position "for general housework with Mrs. Carr" where she earned two dollars until she "learned to cook good, and then $3 and then $4." Proudly she noted, "I was in that house as cook and nurse for twenty-two years." Her sister Tilly lived with the Bents "till she died, eighteen years."[1]

For the McNabb sisters, like so many other Irishwomen who emigrated to the United States, domestic work became the preferred occupation. The best place to find such work was in the city, where middle-class housewives were in desperate need of domestic servants.

The overwhelming majority of Irish emigrants headed for the cities rather than the rural frontier. Though most grew up in rural areas, by 1920 87 percent of the foreign-born Irish lived in cities. The only group with a higher percentage was Russian Jews. The reason was primarily financial. Most Irish just did not have the money that was necessary to travel to a rural area and take up farming. It cost about one thousand dollars in midcentury to start a farm—a sum beyond the reach of poor, unskilled immigrants. One bad harvest, drought, or locust plague could wipe out the investment overnight. Moreover, most were rural peasants, such as the McNabb family, whose idea of farming was digging potatoes. Lacking both the funds as well as the skills needed to settle on the rural frontier, they chose the city instead. Cities were already expanding at this time. Between 1830 and 1860 the U.S. urban population had increased nine times. Such an urban explosion meant that jobs for laborers were plentiful, especially in the Northeast, which was the economic core of the nation. The Irish male—young, strong, unskilled, and eager for work—fit the profile of the type of worker needed to build the streets and the housing in these expanding cities. What happened in New York was repeated in many cities from Boston to San Francisco.

In 1840 the line of settlement in New York City did not reach above Fourteenth Street. By 1865 it had expanded beyond Fifty-eighth Street. An entire new city was built on Manhattan Island during these years, and the Irish helped to build it. Moreover, the middle-class population was growing at this time in urban America. Many of these families wanted servants to work in their homes, and Irishwomen, whose lives were centered in the domestic sphere in Ireland, were well prepared to fill this demand. In addition, the Irish were a gregarious people drawn to city neighborhoods where there was a sense of community reminiscent of the rural villages where they grew up. But perhaps the most attractive element of the city was the presence of established Irish communities. A friendly face, a familiar voice, a recognizable church, and an Irish-run saloon—this is what appealed to the newcomers.

Subsequent waves of immigrants followed the pattern of settlement established by midcentury. The Northeast continued to be the favorite choice for the Irish newcomers. In fact, this pattern continued throughout the twentieth century, so that by 1970 three of four Irish immigrants lived along the East Coast. New York, Philadelphia, and Boston still remained choice destinations for Irish newcomers at the end of the twentieth century. Pittsburgh and Providence also had sizable numbers of

Irish-born, as did Newark and Jersey City. Nonetheless, as the nation's economic core moved west to Chicago and the industrial region surrounding the Great Lakes, the Irish moved west as well. Chicago was the capital of the Irish Midwest with 73,912 Irish-born residents in 1900. Many Irish pushed beyond the Mississippi, settling in the mining towns of Colorado, Nevada, and California, where there was a demand for unskilled laborers. The mining town of Butte, Montana, was a magnet for Irish moving west. By 1900 it had the largest proportion of Irish-born in any city in the nation (twelve thousand out of forty-seven thousand). San Francisco was another desired destination, with close to sixteen thousand Irish-born by 1900. The Irish presence in the South hardly grew at all. In fact, more Irish natives lived in New York City than in all of the Southern states combined in 1900.[2]

LABOR AND LODGING AT MIDCENTURY

The famine immigrants were some of the poorest people ever to set foot on North America's shores. New York bishop John Hughes described them as "the poorest and most wretched population that can be found in the world—the scattered debris of the Irish nation." In New York, two thirds of the people admitted to the poorhouse in 1858 were Irish. The New York Association for Improving the Condition of the Poor claimed that half the people it assisted in 1852 were Irish.[3] In Boston, too, they filled the city's poorhouse. In a letter to a colleague in Ireland, an Irish priest working in Newburyport, Massachusetts, described the plight of the famine immigrants in his congregation who were dependent on day wages: "Many cannot even find employment owing to the crowds that have come from Ireland this year and many of the latter arrive in such a needy helpless utterly destitute state that it requires the utmost effort which their friends or countrymen can make to keep them from starving even in this land of reputed plenty."[4]

In Philadelphia half of the people in the poorhouse were Irish immigrants. In Southern cities where they settled it was the same scenario. They filled the poorhouses, where disease and death were widespread.[5]

Given their poverty and lack of marketable skills, the Irish filled the ranks of the lowest-paying jobs. In New York nine out of ten laborers were Irishmen. But this represented only 20 percent of the Irish male workforce, whereas in Boston, San Francisco, and New Orleans almost half of all Irish workers worked as laborers. In Philadelphia about one fourth to one third of the Irish workforce were laborers. Among Irish-women, domestic work was preferred. Seven out of ten domestic servants in New York were Irishwomen.[6] Other Irishwomen worked as seam-stresses, doing piecework at home or in workshops. As one immigrant woman put it, "No female that can handle a needle may be idle."[7] In other cities the pattern for working women was similar, with domestic service the dominant occupation.

Of course, not all Irish immigrants were stuck at the bottom of the urban workforce. A good percentage of them were employed as skilled blue-collar workers such as carpenters, bricklayers, coopers, painters, or mechanics. In New Orleans as many as one third of Irish workers were employed in skilled or semiskilled jobs. In San Francisco the ratio was similar, whereas in New York about half of the Irish workforce had skilled or semiskilled occupations. Then there were the Irish-born bookkeepers, clerks, peddlers, lawyers, and merchants—white-collar positions that en-joyed a measure of prestige in the community.[8] Nevertheless, the Irish im-migrant community at midcentury was overwhelmingly blue-collar.

Burdened by poor education and victims of discrimination, the Irish experienced little occupational mobility. In fact, when compared with the British and the Germans, they fared poorly, having the highest percentage of workers slipping down the occupational scale and the lowest percentage moving up. When they did move out of unskilled work, they did so slowly. A rural, peasant background did not prepare them well for an emerging industrial economy.[9] Being Irish and Catholic at midcentury was clearly a handicap that kept most Irish stuck at the lower end of the occupational hierarchy.

The neighborhoods of the famine immigrants revealed the depth of their poverty. In midcentury New York, the Irish were still clustered in Lower Manhattan, in the Fourth, Fifth, and Sixth Wards. These neighbor-hoods had a mingling of tenements, factories, stables, slaughterhouses, sa-loons, and retail stores. By the 1860s, little had been done to improve the living conditions of New York's immigrant population. Some of the city's worst tenements were in these neighborhoods. These hovels had such names as Sweeney's Shambles, Folsom's Barracks, and the Baghdad Hotel, epithets that left little to the imagination. Even worse than tenement living were the cellars and shanties on these tenement lots where more than thirty thousand Irish men, women, and children lived.[10] The many families who lived in these dwellings shared the outhouses that decorated the backyards.

Large numbers of Irish also lived in the shantytowns that grew up on the periphery of the city.

Samuel Gompers, a famous labor leader who grew up in New York, described a tenement that was representative of most working-class homes in the mid-nineteenth century: "Our apartment . . . was a typical three-room home. The largest, the front room, was a combined kitchen, dining-room, and sitting room with two front windows. There were two small bedrooms back, which had windows opening into the hall. We got water from a common hydrant in the yard and carried it upstairs. The toilet was in the yard also." Living next door to a slaughterhouse, Gompers recalled that "all day long we could see the animals being driven into the slaughter-pens and could hear the turmoil and the cries of the animals. The neighborhood was filled with the penetrating, sickening odor. The suffering of the animals and the nauseating odor made it physically impossible for me to eat meat for many months."[11]

As the city expanded, the Irish moved out of lower Manhattan to neighborhoods farther uptown. By 1855 a large number of Irish lived in the Eighteenth Ward, located on the city's east side just above Fourteenth Street. Another Irish enclave was the Twentieth Ward, located north of Twenty-sixth Street on the city's west side. Housing appeared to be better in these neighborhoods where the more upwardly mobile Irish were settling.

The pattern of settlement in New York was duplicated in many other cities. In Boston the Irish clustered in the North End and Fort Hill, two of the most congested and depressed neighborhoods of the city. Overcrowding was notorious in the cellar apartments. Cool in the summer, these dwellings, built beneath street level, offered little light or air and were frequently flooded. The Irish chose these neighborhoods because the rents were cheap and they were located near the docks and factories where they could find work. A Boston health inspector left the following description of an Irish neighborhood:

> In Broad Street and all the surrounding neighborhood . . . the situation of the Irish is particularly wretched . . . This whole district is a perfect hive of human beings, without comforts and mostly without common necessaries; in many cases, huddled together like brutes, without regard to sex, or age, or sense of decency; grown men and women sleeping together in the

same apartment, and sometimes wife and husband, brothers and sisters, in the same bed.[12]

In Philadelphia the Irish settled along the Delaware and Schuylkill rivers in Kensington, Southwark, and Moyamensing. As in Boston these were the industrial neighborhoods where Irish laborers were in demand. Philadelphia was not as congested as New York or Boston, but the Irish neighborhoods still housed some of the city's worst tenements, described by one observer as "no better in any respect than pens of cattle."[13] In Moyamensing some of the Irish lived in shantytowns along the Schuylkill. In San Francisco the most heavily Irish neighborhoods bordered the waterfront. But as in New York and Boston the Irish were well dispersed throughout the city. This same pattern of concentration in certain neighborhoods as well as dispersal throughout the rest of the city could be found in such Southern cities as New Orleans, Charleston, and Mobile. There the Irish lived near the docks, where they could find work.

Irish immigrants had a remarkable "hunger for home ownership." Though this was not unique to the Irish, their level of property ownership compared favorably with that of other immigrant groups. Moreover, the longer they lived in the United States, the more they outperformed other groups in terms of property ownership. In Ireland, owning one's own home was but a dream for most Irish, especially for those who would emigrate. Driven from the land by famine and hard-hearted landlords, they hoped to realize that dream in the United States. This would provide them with the security that they so lacked in Ireland, where many had forcibly been evicted from their homes. As homeowners they could now congratulate themselves that "thank God, tis are own, anyhow, and nobody can take it from us."[14]

The key to home ownership was the building and loan association, an immigrant institution that enabled low-income families to acquire a mortgage at a reasonable rate. The Hibernia Savings and Loan Society was one such institution in San Francisco. By 1869 it had 14,544 depositers and assets of over ten million dollars.[15] Philadelphia had a number of these people's banks, many of which had a decidedly Irish clientele. One immigrant, writing home to his sisters in Ireland, noted that "a great many working people own the houses they live in." In Newburyport, Massachusetts, Irish workers were especially successful in acquiring property. Even the lowliest laborer could satisfy the desire to own property.[16] Similar patterns of home ownership among Irish laborers could be found in Poughkeepsie, Detroit, and Albany. Though the amount of property owned was not excessive, such small successes were a significant achievement for these immigrant families.

THE IRISH IN 1900

The profile of the Irish-born community at the turn of the century was in some ways strikingly similar to that of the immigrant community at mid-century. Those who arrived in the United States in the closing decades of the nineteenth century were just about as poor as their famine predecessors. The vast majority came from the poorest regions of Ireland, the western provinces of Munster and Connacht. Mired in poverty, these men and women were fleeing a homeland that offered them little hope for the future. Their future was in America, their land of opportunity. More than 91 percent of all the emigrants from Ireland in 1900 described themselves as laborers or servants. In other words, these emigrants were stuck at the rock bottom of Ireland's economy.[17]

Timothy Meagher's study of the Worcester Irish confirms this bleak picture. He concluded, "There was little substantial change in the economic status of Irish immigrants over the course of the nineteenth century."[18] There may have been a few success stories in business or politics, but the vast majority of the Irish-born remained blue-collar workers. Statistics tell the story clearly. By 1900, Meagher notes, "Nearly 70 percent of Worcester's Irish immigrant men were unskilled or semiskilled workers. In the same year, nearly half of all single immigrant women were servants, and the rest, unskilled or semiskilled factory or service workers."[19] The picture in Boston in 1890 was similar, with as many as two out of three immigrant Irish working as unskilled laborers.

Outside New England, the Irish tended to have greater success moving up the economic escalator. In Philadelphia, for example, in 1880 only about one half of Irish workers were unskilled laborers. In Detroit the number was even lower, whereas in Chicago 59 percent of Irishmen were manual laborers. In California the number was lower still with only three out of ten male workers employed as unskilled laborers. Women, who comprised 21 percent of the Irish workforce, remained stuck at the bottom of the occupational hierarchy. Wherever they lived and worked, the vast majority became domestic servants, while others worked as maids in hotels or boardinghouses.[20]

The reason for the poor occupational status of the immigrant Irish in New England was the stagnant economy of the area as well as the persistent discrimination the Irish experienced from the Yankee-dominated business community. Where you lived certainly made a difference in the opportunities for occupational mobility. If you moved west, chances were that you could do better. But regardless of where they settled, "there was no Irish heaven in the U.S.," as historian Patricia Kelleher put it.[21]

As late as 1904 the percentage of Irish paupers was higher than that for other immigrant groups.[22] Arriving at a time when the United States was experiencing severe economic depressions, 1873–77 and 1893–97, the Irish immigrants faced considerable hardships. Their living conditions were strikingly similar to the destitution of the famine immigrants. In Philadelphia, New York, and Worcester newly arrived immigrants settled in the poorest neighborhoods, where poor sewerage, overcrowded tenements, and widespread disease made life cruel.

Contemporary accounts of Irish slums in Boston, New York, Philadelphia, and Chicago revealed neighborhoods where unemployment, disease, and alcoholism were extensive. The mortality rate in these neighborhoods, as in Worcester, was exceptionally high, with tuberculosis running rampant, so much so that it gained the title "the Irish disease." Alcoholism was also widespread. Such excessive drinking, often because people "could not stand the work," as one Irishwoman said of her alcoholic husband, destroyed family life in these slums.[23] This led to mental illness as well as persistent poverty. As a result, a high percentage of Irishwomen ended up in mental institutions. Children, the innocent victims of this culture of poverty, were often left abandoned on the street, destined for a city orphanage.

Nonetheless, even as most newly arrived immigrants crowded into America's densely packed slums, many others were gainfully employed in jobs provided by an expanding industrial economy. In fact, the Irish-born could be found at every level of the occupational hierarchy. Some few arrived as professionals and continued their professional careers in the United States. Others came as shopkeepers and clerks and obtained similar positions in their new homeland. In 1900 as many as 10 percent of the Irish-born workers belonged to the professional or low white-collar class. A large number of them, 36 percent, were employed in skilled or semiskilled trades in construction, steel mills, mining, transportation, and railroads. Among the women only 5 percent were employed in professional occupations, chiefly teaching, or other low white-collar jobs such as bookkeeping or sales. A small number, about 15 percent, worked in skilled or semi-skilled jobs in textile mills or shops sewing or making clothes.[24] For this group of Irish men and women, a ledge separated them from the more prestigious white-collar occupations. Few were able to climb over this ledge. Most remained blue-collar workers throughout their lives. The occupational mobility of Irish immigrants in the late nineteenth century was almost as small as that of American blacks, and they slipped down the occupational scale more quickly than the native-born.[25] What was true for the famine immigrants remained true for those who followed them to the United States. In reality, it was a land of limited opportunity for most immigrants. Those who did prosper were not the immigrants, but their American-born children.

Raised in an immigrant household, the immigrants' American-born children were second-generation immigrants. They absorbed the Irish immigrant culture along with the American culture. The presence of this second generation radically changed Irish America. By 1900 American-born Irish numbered 3.37 million, while the number of foreign-born Irish had declined to 1.6 million from its 1890 peak of 1.87 million. In every major city where the Irish had settled, the second-generation Irish outnumbered the foreign-born Irish. By the turn of the century more Irish were living in the United States than in all of Ireland—half a million more![26]

One of the key differences between the foreign-born and American-born Irish of the late nineteenth century was work. While most immigrants were stuck at the bottom of the occupational hierarchy, the American-born Irish had obtained better-paying jobs. Stephan Thernstrom's study of Boston compared the occupational profile of the foreign-born and American-born Irish in 1890. Two out of three foreign-born were unskilled laborers, while among the American-born the number was only one out of three. As many as 38 percent of the second generation worked in white-collar occupations, such as law. In Worcester, Timothy Meagher found that the "occupational advance of American-born men and women over the immigrant generation was indisputable . . . Nearly a quarter of the American-born men had gained white collar positions by 1900, two and a half times the proportion of immigrant men, and one-third of the American-born men were skilled workers compared to one-fifth of the immigrant men." American-born Irishwomen in Worcester followed a similar pattern, even surpassing the men in terms of occupational advancement. Rather than pursue domestic service they chose white-collar work such as teaching. In Worcester, over half of the public-school teachers in 1910 were second-generation Irishwomen. This was one of the highest percentages of any school system in the United States.[27]

A national study done at the turn of the century painted a similar picture. Only 2 percent of Irish-born men belonged to the professional class, whereas as many as 16 percent of the American-born Irishmen were professionals. There was a major difference in the low white-collar occupations, such as bookkeepers, clerks, and salesmen. Fourteen percent of the American-born were so employed, but only 8 percent of the foreign-born. At the bottom of the pyramid were the unskilled laborers. This category claimed 26 percent of the foreign-born and 17 percent of the American-born. American-born Irishwomen were also moving up the occupational ladder. One of four of them was working in a white-collar job, many as teachers. Others worked as saleswomen in the large retail industry that was developing at this time, or as bookkeepers or clerks. A significant number, about three in ten, worked in skilled trades in textile mills or needle trades. The most striking advance was the decrease in the number working as domestic servants. Whereas more than half of their Irish-born sisters worked as servants, only 16 percent of the American-born were employed in domestic work.[28]

A profile of Chicago's Irish elite illustrated the occupations that attracted this segment of the community. Published in 1897, this biographical history contained the stories of 302 Irishmen. The very existence of an Irish version of Chicago's Social Register was an indication of how far the Chicago Irish had come by the late nineteenth century. Many of the men profiled had experienced significant occupational mobility over their careers. Eighty percent of them were American-born. As many as two thirds were either lawyers or businessmen. None was involved in banking, an area of the economy often controlled by Anglo-Saxon Protestants. All but a rare few were Catholic and members of the Democratic Party. Most of them came from working-class families. Many of the lawyers gained their degrees by studying at night while working at another job. Included in the group were a few priests as well as a number of prominent policemen and firemen. These members of the Irish elite had gained respectable positions in Chicago society, but few of them could be considered wealthy.[29]

With better jobs came better neighborhoods. The American-born Irish lived in what can be described as typical middle-class neighborhoods.

One such district was Washington Park in Chicago. Located on the city's South Side, near the University of Chicago, it featured wide boulevards, a beautiful park, restaurants, theaters, and shops. It was a step up from the blue-collar working-class neighborhoods located farther north. Apartments in Washington Park could boast of an inside bathroom, running hot and cold water, steam heat, gas, and electricity. This neighborhood was the focal point of James Farrell's classic Irish novel, *Studs Lonigan*. Patrick, Studs's father, was a painting contractor who had moved with his family several times before he became a "prosperous homeowner" in Washington Park. He was a "typical middle-class Chicagoan whose success and identity are embodied in his position and property in . . . Washington Park." Like his Irish Catholic neighbors' his world was centered around St. Patrick's, the neighborhood church. In many respects the Lonigan family was representative of the "steam heat" Irish who had made it to the middle class.[30]

Dorchester was a streetcar suburb of Boston. By 1900 about one fourth of its residents were middle-class Irish. They were clustered around Meeting House Hill, where St. Peter's Church was located. An active and prosperous parish, the church and its school attracted upper segments of the Irish middle class. The houses they lived in reflected the vast range of middle-class economic capabilities. Some resembled Newport-style mansions, built on an acre of land; others were more modest two-family homes. The classic New England three-decker homes, for the less prosperous, could even be found in Dorchester. This neighborhood was a world apart from Boston's North End and Fort Hill, where the foreign-born Irish had first settled. A Dorchester address in 1900 was a decisive sign that the Boston Irish had finally arrived.[31]

One quarter of the Philadelphia Irish in the early twentieth century lived in West Philadelphia. A streetcar suburb, it was home to numerous white-collar Irish who worked downtown. Another favorite address for the Irish was Northwest Philadelphia. Four out of ten of Philadelphia's Irish lived there in 1930. This was a mixture of lower-middle-class and working-class families. Though not as fashionable as West Philadelphia or Dorchester, it was a better neighborhood than South Philadelphia, where many of the newly arrived foreign-born Irish lived.[32]

Certain features existed in every Irish neighborhood. Most often it was the pathological nature of the lower-class neighborhood that captured the attention of observers. They never failed to mention the crime, poverty, disease, and alcoholism. Though such undesirable characteristics were certainly present, Irish neighborhoods had other features that were less noticed but surely more attractive. Indeed, in many ways these ethnic neighborhoods were reminiscent of the social milieu of rural Ireland.

One such quality was the tightly knit nature of the community. Most people's work and family life was known to the rest of the neighborhood. Many were related by marriage, and this further strengthened the social network, as did the lack of privacy in these urban villages. The open-door environment encouraged people to help one another in troubled times, be it from a death in the family or poverty. Mr. Dooley, the fictional Chicago bartender created by Finley Peter Dunne, captured this caring spirit in one of his monologues. In his typical Irish brogue, he commented:

> Afther all 'tis th' poor that keep th' poor. They ain't wan sthrugglin' fam'ly in this war-rd that ain't carryin' three others on its back. A pound iv tay in ye'er house means a hot cup f'r thim poor Schwartzs'... The man Clancy down th' sthreet that nobody likes, him bein' a notoryous infidel, be dead if it wasn't f'r th' poor iv a poor parish.[33]

In the working-class neighborhood the saloon was a central institution. It could be a stepping-stone to the middle class for the more successful proprietors. A commercial establishment, it was also a social center for men, as few women would set foot inside them. Mr. Dooley explained its popularity with the workingman:

> Th' unbenighted American wurrukin'-man likes his dhrinks— as who does not? But he wants to take it in peace. His varchues has been wrote about. But let him injye his few simple vices in his own way, says I. He goes to th' saloon an rich men go to th' club mos'ly f'r th' same reason. He don't want to go home.[34]

The spiritual center of the Irish neighborhood, be it working-class or middle-class, was the church. The neighborhood was so identified with the parish church that when people were asked where they lived, they would not say the east side or west side, but St. Patrick's or St. Bridget's; no further description was necessary. The parish complex typically included a large church richly decorated with stained glass imported from Europe and marble altars from Italy. The largest building in the neighborhood, it stood as a testament to the people's faith. In addition to the church there would be a school, a convent, and a rectory spread across one or more city blocks. These churches fostered more than just religion. They were also social and recreational centers where Irish men and women of all ages would gather for festivals, ball games, and dances. Life in the parish and the neighborhood was so encompassing that people seldom left the area. Their lives were centered in the neighborhood and its social and religious institutions. Of course, people from other ethnic and religious backgrounds lived nearby, since no neighborhood would be completely inhabited by the Irish. Nonetheless, the neighborhood's major social and cultural institutions were identified with the Irish. In this cultural enclave, Irish Catholics seldom mingled with people from other ethnic or religious backgrounds.

In addition to the church, the local Democratic club played a prominent role in these neighborhoods. From here emanated the patronage jobs linked to the local political boss. Frequently, this meant that the policeman patrolling the neighborhood was an Irish cop who most likely lived in the area and knew his constituents by reputation if not by sight. The local fire department was also loaded with Irishmen from the neighborhood. Patronage, whereby politicians rewarded their supporters with jobs, kept politicians in office and the neighborhood clientele satisfied.

"We Want No Micks Here"

A major reason for the lack of occupational mobility among the Irish, both foreign-born and American-born, was discrimination. It was commonplace for help-wanted advertisements either explicitly or implicitly to discourage Irish men and women from applying for certain types of work. Such notices became so commonplace that the phrase *No Irish need apply* became integrated into the oral tradition of Irish America. Families wanting to hire domestic servants discouraged Irish applicants either explicitly, by stating that no Irish need apply, or implicitly, by urging only women from ethnic groups other than Irish to apply. Some factories turned away Irish applicants with the stinging reply, "We want no micks here."[35] In Boston, Worcester, and in many other New England cities, the Yankees controlled the banks. This meant that the Irish would be excluded from this segment of the economy. In Worcester it was common knowledge that "no Yankee-owned bank . . . would hire an Irish Catholic."[36] Such exclusion from this and other types of employment significantly handicapped the Irish in their climb up the economic ladder.

Though discrimination against the Irish was hardly a myth, it was only one aspect of a more profound and widespread bigotry rooted in a long-standing British tradition. It was part of the cultural chauvinism that the English transplanted to colonial America. Coupled with the anti-Irish attitude was an anti-Catholic prejudice. Such hostility to all things Irish and Catholic had reappeared with a vengeance in the United States in the early nineteenth century. Then in the 1850s a political movement, identified with the Know-Nothing Party, was launched to curtail immigration and, specifically, the influence of Catholics.

The Know-Nothing Party had its origins in a nativist fraternal organization, the Order of the Star Spangled Banner, founded in 1850. In 1853 this organization became known as the Know-Nothings reportedly because its members would feign ignorance when asked about the organization. The ideology of the party was rooted in anti-Catholicism and a deep-seated hostility toward immigrants. Know-Nothings believed that Protestantism defined American society. From this flowed their fundamental belief that Catholicism was incompatible with basic American values. Because they believed that Catholics had too much political power, they wanted to limit the influence of political parties and their conniving politicians who were helping Catholics gain this clout. They were also against the extension of slavery and wanted to limit the sale of liquor. Finally, they wanted to curtail the political influence of immigrants by extending the five-year waiting period for naturalization and the subsequent privilege of voting to twenty-one years. They urged voters to vote only for native-born citizens. As their favorite motto put it, "Americans must rule America!"[37]

By the end of 1854 the Know-Nothing Party had soared to national prominence. As historian Tyler Anbinder wrote, "With more than 10,000 lodges and 1,000,000 members, the Know Nothings entered 1855 brimming with confidence."[38] Before long they would elect eight governors, more than one hundred congressmen, and thousands of other local officials, including the mayors of Boston, Philadelphia, San Francisco, and Chicago. Their most decisive victory was in Massachusetts, where two of every three voters in Massachusetts supported a Know-Nothing candidate in the 1854 state election. As a result, the entire congressional delegation, all 40 state senators, and all but 3 of the 379 state representatives, as well as the governor, won election as candidates of the Know-Nothing Party. Once in office they passed a series of laws aimed specifically at the Irish Catholics of Massachusetts. These included the mandatory reading of the

King James Bible in the public schools, disbanding Irish militia units and confiscating their weapons, dismissing Irish state workers, and deporting as many as 295 poor Irish back to Liverpool because they were a drain on the public treasury. In addition, they voted to deprive Catholics of their right to hold public office.[39]

The bigotry of the Know-Nothings was so oppressive that in 1855 it prompted Abraham Lincoln, a rising Illinois politician, to declare in a letter to a friend:

> Our progress in degeneracy appears to me to be pretty rapid. As a nation we began by declaring that *"all men are created equal."* We now practically read it "all men are created equal, *except negroes.*" When the Know-Nothings get control, it will read "all men are created equal except negroes, *and foreigners, and Catholics.*"[40]

The decline of the Know-Nothing Party was almost as swift as its rise to prominence. The debate over slavery destroyed the Know-Nothings by dividing the proslavery and antislavery factions within the party. In their June 1855 convention the Know-Nothing Party supported the Kansas-Nebraska Act, which allowed the extension of slavery in the western territories. Northern Know-Nothings, who opposed such an endorsement of slavery, then began to abandon the Know-Nothing Party for the antislavery Republican Party. Their departure marked the end of the Know-Nothing movement.[41] Slavery, the "fire bell in the night" that Thomas Jefferson warned would be the "knell of the nation," had trumped the issues of nativism and anti-Catholicism. In time, the question of slavery would plunge the entire nation into a bloody civil war.

THE FIGHTING IRISH

Once the Civil War began, the Irish joined the armies of both the North and the South. As many as 140,000 Irishmen fought under the Union flag. Another 30,000 wore the colors of the Confederacy. In terms of their proportion of the general population, the Irish were also the most underrepresented immigrant group fighting for the Union. A major reason for this was their allegiance to the Democratic Party and their opposition to Republican support for emancipation.[42] Those in the North, where the bulk of the Irish lived, would fight to preserve the Union, but their ardor cooled considerably once President Lincoln emancipated the slaves. This coolness, if not outright opposition, to the abolition of slavery was not only a trademark of the Democratic Party, but also a distinctive characteristic of the American Catholic Church, which claimed the allegiance of the Irish.

During the war many regiments in both the North and the South were predominantly Irish. One of the most famous was the Irish Brigade, led by the charismatic Thomas Francis Meagher. Meagher was an Irish rebel whom the British had imprisoned because of his involvement in the movement for Irish independence. After doing time in an English prison, Meagher was sent off to a penal colony in Australia in 1849, banished for life from Ireland. Three years later he escaped to the United States, where he found success in New York as a noted orator and lawyer. Once the Civil War broke out, he joined the Union army. Before long he organized a brigade made up of Irish recruits whom he persuaded to join the battle with him to preserve the Union. Known as the Irish Brigade, they fought in several bloody battles. At Antietam, where the casualties were the worst for any single day of the war—some twenty-three thousand men—the Irish Brigade lost as many as 60 percent of its soldiers.[43]

Next was Fredericksburg, where Meagher led the Irish Brigade against Irish Confederate soldiers, one of whom was Willy Mitchel, son of John Mitchel, a renowned Irish nationalist. In the 1840s John Mitchel had abandoned a career in law to join Meagher and other young Irishmen in a campaign to gain independence for Ireland. A fierce nationalist, Michel discovered a new career as a publicist, writing for the *Nation*, the voice of Young Ireland, the name given to this band of nationalists. Mitchell wrote, "The people's sovereignty—the land and sea and air of Ireland for the people of Ireland—this is the gospel that the heavens and earth are preaching, and all hearts are secretly burning to embrace . . . It is the mighty, passionate struggle of a nation hastening to be born into new national life."[44] Such language was too much for the authorities, who arrested Mitchel for treason. Found guilty, he was transported to Australia in 1848. Five years later he escaped, fleeing to the United States. Eventually he settled in Tennessee, where he became a staunch defender of slavery, believing "negro slavery the best state of existence for the negro, and the best for his master."[45] Supporting the Confederacy, he wrote dispatches on the war for a Richmond newspaper. All three of his sons joined the Confederate army; two of them, John and Willy, died in battle, and their brother, James, was wounded. One of the ironies of Irish history is that Meagher and Mitchel, two renowned Irish nationalists joined in a common struggle for Ireland's independence, ended up in the United States on opposite sides during the Civil War.

At Fredericksburg the Union army suffered a disastrous defeat. As at Antietam, the Irish Brigade endured heavy losses. One soldier described the scene:

> The Irish Brigade . . . comes out from the city in glorious file, their green sunbursts waving . . . every man has a sprig of green in his cap . . . They passed just to our left, poor fellows, poor, glorious fellows, shaking good-bye to us with their hats! They reach a point within a stone's throw of the stone wall. No farther. They try to go beyond, but are slaughtered.[46]

The Confederate soldiers who did the slaughtering belonged to the Georgia Irish brigade.

At Gettysburg the tide turned as the Union army was victorious in the largest battle ever fought during the Civil War. The human cost was, once again, terribly heavy, with as many as fifty-one thousand killed, wounded, or missing during the three days of battle. John Mitchel's youngest son, Willy, died fighting at Gettysburg. According to one report, his body was "buried with a note attached: Private Mitchel, son of an Irish patriot."[47] Many other Irish, from both the North and the South, died at Gettysburg. Today a number of monuments at the Gettysburg National Military Park display the Irish shamrock, reminding visitors of the sacrifice these young men made on the field of battle.

Not long after Gettysburg the Irish were involved in another bloody battle. This time it was on the streets of New York, where the infamous Draft Riot of 1863 took place. By the spring of 1863 the Union army was facing a manpower shortage. To overcome this, Congress passed a conscription law to enforce a military draft. If a man's name was drawn in the lottery, he could avoid military service by hiring a substitute or paying a fee of three hundred dollars. The Democrats vehemently opposed the draft, viewing it as "an unconstitutional means to achieve the unconstitutional end of freeing the slaves."[48] They inflamed the debate by framing it as a "rich man's war/poor man's fight" since all a man needed was three hundred dollars to avoid military service. Such a sum was far beyond the reach of an Irish laborer. Opposition among the Irish surfaced in the

Pennsylvania mining region and in Boston as well. But the most virulent opposition erupted in New York City.

Irish workers in New York were particularly hostile to black laborers because of their competition in the labor market. This resentment was heightened when black strikebreakers were used to counteract a strike by Irish longshoremen in June. This hostility, as well as opposition to Lincoln, was simmering below the surface by the time the draft lottery took place in early July. On Saturday, July 11, the first day of the lottery passed peacefully. Much discussion took place in the saloons of the working-class neighborhoods on Sunday, especially of the unfairness of the three-hundred-dollar waiver. Workers threatened to attack the draft office when it opened on Monday. When Monday came, they not only attacked the draft office, burning it to the ground, but they roamed the city burning, looting, and killing. For four days rioters, most of whom were Irish, went about the city attacking the homes and businesses of prominent Republicans. The Colored Orphan Asylum was destroyed and at least eleven blacks were murdered, some savagely lynched. The mob even turned on Irish cops and soldiers who tried to quell the riot. One such victim was Colonel Henry O'Brien, who was brutally murdered and his body dragged through the streets. When it was all over, as many as 105 people were dead. The New York draft riot has gone down in history as one of the nation's bloodiest urban riots. Moreover, the behavior of the Irish during these fateful days and the racism they exhibited reinforced their reputation for violence. In the aftermath of the riots, a number of the Northern elite produced "some of the most sustained and virulent anti-Irish sentiment in American history." The *New York Times* condemned the Irish as "brutish" and " 'animal' while the *New York Tribune* called the rioters a 'savage mob,' a 'pack of savages,' and a mob of 'incarnate devils.' In this way, the racist Irish were themselves racially reduced to the level of the animal kingdom."[49]

Before long, the New York Irish were rioting again. These were the Orange Day riots, which occurred in 1870 and 1871. This time it was Irish Catholics against Irish Protestants. Both riots occurred on July 12, the traditional marching day for Irish Protestants, known as the Orangemen, to celebrate the victory of Prince William of Orange over King James II at the Battle of the Boyne in 1690. More than a commemoration, it was a celebration of the supremacy of Protestantism over Catholicism. But more than religion was involved in these civil disturbances. Irish

Protestants were carrying on the American nativist tradition that believed the Catholic Irish were a threat to American republican values. On the other hand, Irish Catholics looked upon the Orangemen as a symbol of the oppression they had experienced in Ireland as well as the hardships they were enduring as members of an exploited working class. On July 12, 1870, as the Orangemen paraded through the city north to Elm Park just above West Ninetieth Street, they sang songs that mocked Catholics and their religion. One of the more provocative songs celebrated the 1798 rebellion when the Crown's military tortured Catholics to gain information about the United Irishmen. Part of a verse warned Catholics:

> Oh, Croppies, ye'd better be quiet and still
> Ye shan't have your liberty, do what ye will,
> As long as salt water is found in the deep
> Our foot on the neck of the Croppie we'll keep.[50]

Irish workers along the parade route cursed the marchers and vowed revenge. Revenge took place in Elm Park after the parade where the police had to intervene to stop the fighting. When the fighting ended, eight people were dead. The following year the parade proceeded as planned despite the police commissioner's objection. It took place with an escort of several hundred policemen and members of the National Guard. Crowds along the parade route "pelted parading Orangemen and their guards with bricks and paving stones."[51] The soldiers panicked and opened fire on the crowd. By the time the fighting ended, sixty-seven people were dead and more than one hundred were injured. The Orangemen never marched in New York again.

The Irish involvement in the draft riots and the Orange riots strengthened the popular stereotype of the Irish as an inferior race that was innately ignorant and violent. This stereotype, solidified after the Philadelphia Bible riots of 1844, was still prevalent in the 1870s. The popular science of the day, known as physiognomy, reinforced this image of the Irish. A pseudoscience, it sought to judge the character and temperament of humans "from features of the head and face, the body, and the extremities."[52] By examining the size of a person's head and the features of the face, the physiognomist could determine where this person would rank in the human hierarchy.

A noted scientist described the Gaelic physiognomy as follows: "Bulging forward of lower part of face—most extreme in upper jaw. Chin more or less retreating . . . (In Ireland the chin is often absent). Retreating forehead. Large mouth and thick lips. Great distance between nose and mouth. Nose short, upturned, frequently concave, with yawning nostrils."[53] That was hardly a description that would win a beauty contest. Certain mental traits were supposed to accompany such facial features and they were not complimentary either.

This was the age of Darwin and Huxley, a time when there was great interest in human evolution. L. Perry Curtis, who has studied the link between the science of physiognomy and the Irish, observed that "the net effect of Victorian ethnology was to undermine the environmentalist view that Englishmen and Irishmen were fundamentally alike and equally educable. Instead of narrowing the gap between Anglo-Saxons and Celts, the newer forms of evolutionary thought associated with Darwin, Wallace, Huxley, and their disciples, tended to polarize Englishmen and Irishmen by providing *a scientific basis* [italics mine] for assuming that such characteristics as violence, poverty, improvidence, political volatility, and drunkenness were inherently Irish and only Irish."[54] In ranking the races of the world these scientists placed the Irish, often referred to as the "white negro," below the Anglo-Saxon and just above the Negro.

This was also the era of the penny press. New technology, a rising population, and increasing literacy stimulated the growth of newspapers and magazines. Illustrated magazines became especially popular, with the cartoon being a standard feature. Paddy, as a monstrous Celtic beast, was a favorite object of these artists. "By the 1860s no respectable reader of comic weeklies," wrote L. Perry Curtis, ". . . could possibly mistake the simous nose, long upper lip, huge, projecting mouth, and jutting lower jaw as well as sloping forehead for any other category of undesirable or dangerous human being than that known as the Irish."[55] The congenial Paddy had become a monster in the popular press.

This image of the Irish ape-man, prevalent in Victorian England, also became popular among American cartoonists. New York's greatest cartoonist was Thomas Nast. He published frequently in *Harper's Weekly* during the 1860s and '70s, sketching cartoons that reinforced the racial image of the Irish. L. Perry Curtis stated that whenever Nast "drew an Irish-American, he invariably produced a cross between a professional boxer and an orangutan."[56] Nast was strongly anti-Catholic and a fierce opponent of New York's Democratic political machine. Some of his most famous cartoons depicted Catholics as a menace to American society. In his cartoons satirizing either Catholics or Democrats, the simian Irishman was always a featured figure.

The cartoons of Nast as well as others were a powerful force in shaping the popular stereotype of the Irish. In these cartoons the medium provided the message. You did not have to be literate to understand that the Irishman was a threat to society. Moreover, the science of physiognomy validated such pejorative images of the Irish as monsters.

THE EMERGENCE OF THE AMERICAN IRISH

With the passage of time the brutish image of the Irish began to change. A key reason for this was the success of the American-born Irish in moving into the middle class by the turn of the century. By 1900, not only did the American-born Irish outnumber the foreign-born, but they also began to define what it meant to be Irish in the United States.

While the Irish were gaining stature in American society, the nation was trying to adjust to the influx of the new immigrants from Southern and Eastern Europe, who were arriving in large numbers in the 1880s and '90s. Before long the nativist spirit that had singled out the Irish in the 1840s and 1850s reappeared, but this time it was directed against these newcomers. Fueling this nativism was a new form of racialism that celebrated the Anglo-Saxon heritage and denigrated the presumed inferior people from Southern and Eastern Europe. The specific targets of this racism were Italians, Jews, and Slavs. Being from the British Isles, the Irish were now considered acceptable and assimilable to the American way of life. The cartoonist's Paddy, that monstrous Celtic brute, was replaced by the caricature of the Jew as a greedy Shylock or the Italian as a crafty crook.

As the Irish left their old immigrant neighborhoods, turning them over to the newcomers from Southern and Eastern Europe, they moved to new streetcar suburbs. They moved up to white-collar jobs and adopted a middle-class lifestyle symbolized by lace curtains in their windows and steam heat in their homes. Before long they were referred to, derisively in most instances, as "steam-heat Irish" or "lace-curtain Irish."

The Irish had come a long way since the days of the famine. As second-generation Irish were assimilated into American society and achieved success in a variety of areas, the Irish took on a new self-identity. This could most visibly be seen in the parades they sponsored in the early years of the twentieth century. St. Patrick's Day had always been a day for the Irish to parade. In 1919 such a parade took place in Providence, Rhode Island. During the World War the Irish in Providence had gone to great lengths to prove their loyalty to the nation. On St. Patrick's Day they continued to manifest this patriotism by ending the parade "on the State House lawn where two thousand children assembled in the shape of an American flag." The Irish wanted to be accepted as 100 percent Americans. They were patriots, not Paddies. Such patriotism was one major element in their self-identity. But the parade also celebrated their ethnic heritage. The eight thousand marchers and the thousands of spectators who lined the parade route proudly displayed the Irish green and cheered for Irish independence at a time when their ancestral homeland was at war with the British. Though their nationalism would wane after the establishment of the Irish Free State in 1922, loyalty to their Irish heritage remained strong among the American-born Irish. This allegiance was another key element of their self-identity. The final element, which blended these two loyalties together, was religion. Another parade, a public ritual filled with meaning, illustrated how strong this commitment was.[57]

This parade also took place in Providence. Sponsored by the Holy Name Society, forty thousand priests and laymen marched, and thousands of spectators lined the parade route. These Catholic displays of power were a regular event in Providence and in many other cities. At this particular time, 1922, when anti-Catholicism was once again surfacing with the Ku Klux Klan, such public militancy was judged necessary. Fueling this militancy was a self-confidence that was not so evident in the mid-nineteenth century when anti-Catholicism was also riding high. To a degree the Irish had made it by the 1920s. With one foot firmly planted in American society, they proudly manifested a high degree of self-confidence as American Irish. Their religion still labeled them as outsiders in the predominantly Protestant America of the 1920s. Nevertheless, they were not about to remain passive in the face of the Ku Klux Klan. This militant and self-confident attitude shaped the self-identity of the Irish. Buoyed by this spirit, they were not at all hesitant to manifest it in such public spectacles as a parade.

As historian Timothy Meagher argued, "Most Irish American Catholics began to define themselves as militant American Catholics."[58] Religion had trumped ethnicity by the early years of the twentieth century. Though they would never cease to be Irish—or as the writer John O'Hara put it, "once a Mick, always a Mick"—their Catholicism, more than anything else, defined who they were.

Over centuries Catholicism had become, as historian Kerby Miller put it, "the central institution of Irish life and the primary source and expression of Irish identity."[59] In the United States it had gained a similar stature by the turn of the century. Irish Catholic Americans had become Catholic American Irish. This self-identity would become even more pronounced during the first half of the twentieth century, when the American Catholic Church acquired unusual power and prestige. How the Church was able to gain such a prominent place in the Irish community is a remarkable chapter in the history of Irish America.

CHAPTER 5

The Catholic Irish

On a sunny Sunday, May 25, 1879, thousands of New Yorkers filled the streets surrounding St. Patrick's Cathedral. The fair weather had attracted an unusually large crowd, and "a dense mass of people in holiday attire crowded the sidewalks." Ushers in formal dress did their best to seat the ticket holders, and Irish policemen held back the crowds, as city and state politicians arrived in force. Among them were William Grace, who would soon become the first Catholic mayor of New York, and "Honest John" Kelly, the head of Tammany Hall, the city's Democratic political machine. Over four hundred priests and forty-one bishops marched in procession to the church, where an estimated seven thousand people awaited the arrival of the clerical entourage and the dedication and blessing of the new cathedral performed by John Mc-Closkey, the cardinal archbishop of New York. On this day Catholics were filled with feelings of pride. They had come a long way in the last half century. It was a dramatic change from earlier years when nativist New Yorkers threatened to burn down the old cathedral. Times had changed as Protestants mingled with Catholics inside and outside the church and such prominent families as the Vanderbilts rubbed shoulders with papist priests and prelates.[1]

Hailed as "the noblest temple ever raised to the memory of St. Patrick," St. Patrick's Cathedral would become the most famous Catholic church in the United States.[2] Not only was it an enduring icon of Catholicism, but it was a testament to the powerful presence of the Irish in the Catholic Church in the United States. Though American Catholicism had acquired an ethnically diverse character during the nineteenth century, the Irish—who had arrived first, in such large numbers, with their own priests and women religious (i.e., sisters/nuns) following close behind—had by 1879 gained control over the Church in the United States. Their dominance increased over time, so much so that the Irish would soon define what it meant to be Catholic in America.

In New York, the Rome of American Catholicism, twenty-three of the city's thirty-two parishes were Irish by 1865. For every German Catholic there were as many as seven Irish Catholics in the city. As other immigrant groups arrived, the Irish still remained a dominant presence, claiming more than half of the city's parishes even into the 1880s. Boston Catholicism was even more Irish with over 90 percent of the parishes in the diocese having an Irish clientele. The Irish had a virtual monopoly on the priesthood with nearly 80 percent of the priests ordained between 1875 and 1924 coming from Irish families. Chicago Catholicism was not much different. Of all the parishes established between 1833 and 1915, almost half were Irish (89 of 202). The Germans and Polish trailed far behind with only thirty and thirty-three parishes respectively. In Philadelphia, San Francisco, and many other cities Catholicism was also overwhelmingly Irish. Even though they never accounted for more than half of the nation's Catholics, the Irish dominated the hierarchy with two of three bishops in 1900 having Irish roots. Such major dioceses as Boston, Philadelphia, Chicago, and San Francisco had an Irish bishop in 1900. Ever since the days of John Hughes in the 1840s, New York has always had an archbishop of Irish descent.[3] Irish hegemony in the Church caused a great deal of unease among other ethnic groups, especially the Germans and the Polish, who constantly challenged it during the late nineteenth century. But, the Irish had such a strong grip on the seats of power that they were able to fend off such challenges.

The Irish who arrived prior to the Great Famine carried with them a religion grounded in the Celtic past where devotions at holy wells and pilgrimages to sacred sites were how they expressed their Catholic faith. Regular attendance at Mass and participation in the sacraments was not yet an Irish tradition. The Great Famine changed this as the Gaelic culture began to disappear under the pressures of emigration and population decline. The Irish took on a new identity in the postfamine era, an identity rooted in their Catholic religion. The key to this transformation was what historian Emmet Larkin labeled a "devotional revolution."[4]

The architect of this revolution was Paul Cullen, the archbishop of Dublin from 1852 to 1878. Trained in Rome, he shared the vision of Pope

Pius IX to revitalize Catholicism by strengthening the institutional Church. In 1850 at the Synod of Thurles, Ireland passed a body of legislation that would shape Irish Catholicism for the next one hundred years. The parish church, not the holy well, became the center of religious practice. No more baptisms at home or wakes and burials of the dead without a Mass at church. Regular attendance at Mass, and at least the annual reception of the sacraments, now became the norm for anyone who wanted to be a *practicing Catholic*, a phrase that now became the coin of the realm.

As the unofficial head of Irish Catholicism, Cullen ruled with an iron fist. He forced the clergy to shape up by focusing on a clerical education that stressed a disciplined life rooted in prayer and a commitment to pastoral work. His influence in Rome enabled him to appoint as bishops men who shared his rigorist brand of Catholicism. The number of priests increased as did the number of sisters and brothers. New churches were built and old ones restored, modeled on the ornate churches of Rome with their marble statues and baroque art. Sunday Mass became the centerpiece of Catholic piety. Parish missions, or what can be described as Catholic revivals aimed at revitalizing the faith of the people, became annual events. The clergy took control of the popular pilgrimages to holy wells and other sacred sites. All religious practices were now under their supervision as the Church widened its circle of influence over the people. The transformation was so complete that by the end of the century Ireland was one of the most religiously observant countries in the Catholic world, with more than 90 percent of the people regularly attending Sunday Mass. Ireland's devotional revolution was part of a larger religious renaissance in the Roman Catholic world during the pontificate of Pius IX. In the United States, the Irish clergy would be the architects of this renaissance.[5]

Ever since the Act of Union in 1800 dissolved the Irish parliament, a wave of nationalism had engulfed Ireland. Daniel O'Connell's campaign for Catholic Emancipation linked Ireland's national identity with Catholicism so tightly that it defined what it meant to be Irish. Being Irish also took on a sectarian quality once it became synonymous with being Catholic. Allegiance to Catholicism, in defiance of centuries of prejudice and discrimination from English Protestants, became a badge of identity, a historical grudge that has persisted to the present. This sectarian mentality would follow the Irish to the United States, where it would be reinforced as they encountered discrimination because of who they were and how they worshipped.

Irish hegemony in the American Church meant that the Irish brand of Catholicism would become the standard for others to follow. The post-famine immigrants were a new breed of Catholic, quite different from those who emigrated in the prefamine period. This was especially true of those who came of age when Paul Cullen ruled the Irish Church. They were not simply Roman Catholics but Irish ones who were passionate in their beliefs and practices. The arena where this was best displayed was the parish church.

In the 1840s and '50s, the Church in America was still trying to cope with an unprecedented expansion of the Catholic population, most of whom were poor Irish refugees of the Great Famine. In general, parishes were poor. In New York some were even forced into bankruptcy, auctioning off the church building to the highest bidder. Many congregations worshipped in old churches purchased from Protestant congregations who were fleeing the Irish invasions of their neighborhoods. These second-hand churches were spartan wooden buildings or plain stone structures. Transfiguration parish in New York City's Sixth Ward fit this profile exactly. Founded in 1836, its first house of worship was an old Presbyterian church purchased by the founding pastor, Felix Varela, a Cuban national-ist who had sought refuge in New York. Pastor of a poor Irish parish, he was never able to get it out of debt. After years of struggling, the church building was auctioned off in 1853. The parish then moved to Mott Street, to an old Episcopal church that became the new home for the Sixth Ward's Irish Catholics.

In the 1840s the parish church was not much more than a Mass house. Since the devotional revolution had not yet taken hold in Ireland or the United States, a plain style of Catholicism was still practiced. The church buildings reflected this simplicity—they lacked the stained glass and religious art that would eventually become commonplace. Their primary function was religious—Mass on Sundays and during the week, one or two spiritual confraternities, celebrations of major religious feast days such as Easter and Christmas, along with the celebrations of marriages, baptisms, and burials. If the parish had a school, it was generally housed in the church basement with few resources and few students.[6]

The 1850s was a key transitional period for the American Catholic Church. By midcentury it had become the largest denomination in the country with a population of 1.6 million, principally because of immigra-tion. Within ten years the Church would almost double in size, reaching a population of 3.1 million. No longer a small sect located on the periphery of the American religious landscape, the Catholic Church, in the words of Philip Schaff, a noted historian of Christianity, was beginning "to make its influence felt in the public life of the United States."[7] The number of clergy increased, as did the number of parish churches. Chicago had only three Irish parishes in 1853. By 1869, sixteen of the city's twenty-five Catholic parishes were Irish. In New York it was much the same, with eight new Irish parishes founded in the 1850s. Other cities experienced similar expansion as Irish immigrants flooded the nation's cities and towns.[8]

Fueling this expansion, similar to the one occurring in Ireland, was a buoyant optimism about the future place of the Catholic Church in the United States. The boldest expression of this confidence was New York's Archbishop John Hughes's decision to build a cathedral church whose grandeur would rival that of the churches of Europe. He chose a location on the outskirts of the city, where, in an open field in the summer of 1858, surrounded by a crowd of more than one hundred thousand cheering Catholics, mostly Irish, he laid the cornerstone of St. Patrick's Cathedral. Ridiculed as "Hughes's Folly," it would take more than twenty years before the church would open for worship. Still unfinished when it was dedicated in 1879, its Gothic magnificence soared high above Fifth Avenue, by then one of the nation's most fashionable boulevards, reminding all who passed that Irish Catholics were a force to be reckoned with in the nation's leading city.[9]

By the 1870s Catholics across the country were building their own churches modeled on the grand churches of Europe—no more Protestant hand-me-downs. The expansion continued throughout the remaining decades of the century as the number of Catholics, both clergy and laity, as well as the number of churches, grew exponentially. These grandiose churches were a source of pride to the Irish as they had built them with their own money. A study done of parish finances in New York in the 1880–1920 period concluded that "about half the parish income typically came from the dimes and nickels collected as seat money at mass, with most of the rest coming from special collections and parish fairs, and only relatively small proportions from large donations by wealthy individuals."[10] This pattern of Church financing was typical in Catholic America, where working-class Catholics financed the expansion of a working-class Church. In many respects this was one of the most remarkable achievements of the Irish people.

By the 1880s a new type of Irish parish was emerging. Up until then the Catholic parish was primarily a religious institution. But as the city expanded and immigrant neighborhoods developed, the parish was transformed into a community institution, not just a religious one. In a new homeland where people were searching for a sense of social place and community, many Irish immigrants found this in the parish. As the parish became a community institution, numerous societies were founded with a greater diversity of purpose. These societies or organizations had explicit social, recreational, charitable, and educational goals. Spiritual confraternities were still present, but they were far outnumbered by all the other organizations. This trend continued into the twentieth century with the most notable shift being the establishment of more societies for young people. By the 1920s the Irish parish had reached its golden age. Along with all its organizations it had a full calendar of events: dances, plays, minstrel shows, card parties, fairs, and picnics. As one New York priest put it, this network of organizations was "aimed to meet every need of the parishioner and to deal with every condition."[11] Irish parishioners may physically have left the neighborhood for work or on other occasions, but for many the parish remained the center of their world. The manifest purpose of the parish was clearly religious, but it had also become a key social institution that enabled its parishioners to establish some semblance of a community life. Holy Family parish, located on the Near West Side of Chicago, was an excellent example of this type of all-inclusive parish that developed in the closing decades of the nineteenth century.

Historian Nick Salvatore described Holy Family as "the quintessential Irish, working class parish of late nineteenth century Chicago." It was the pride of the Jesuits, the religious order that founded the parish in 1857.[12] Located in an ethnically diverse area, it was the designated Irish parish. Other churches in the area ministered to the needs of German and Bohemian Catholics. Parishes serving distinct ethnic groups had become the accepted pattern of parish formation since the early years of the nineteenth century. It was not unusual for several Catholic churches to be located within an urban neighborhood, each serving a specific ethnic group. On Sunday mornings German, Irish, and Bohemian Catholics would pass each other on the street as they walked to their own churches for Sunday Mass. Though they were all Catholic, they seldom intermingled, staying within their own cultural enclaves, marrying their own kind.

Holy Family's founding pastor, Arnold Damen, S.J., was born in Holland in 1815. Recruited to the Jesuits by the missionary Pierre De Smet, Damen traveled to the United States in 1837, where he entered the Jesuit seminary in Florissant, Missouri. Shortly after his ordination to the priesthood, he took on the challenge of founding a new parish in Chicago, where he had recently given a successful parish mission. Damen is remembered not only as the founding pastor of Holy Family, but also as a gifted preacher who throughout his life traveled across the United States preaching parish missions. Quite popular during the nineteenth century, these missions were the Catholic version of the religious revivals so common among American Protestants. Described "as a preacher of rugged eloquence and remarkable driving power," Damen was known as the Catholic Beecher, a reference to his more famous contemporary Henry Ward Beecher.[13]

Damen acknowledged that the people in the parish "are almost all very poor." Nonetheless, they were willing to contribute "as far as they are able to build the new church." Damen himself went door-to-door throughout the neighborhood soliciting funds for the church. He even auctioned off his horse and buggy, forcing him to travel the neighborhood on foot. Damen also recruited volunteers who canvassed the parish soliciting funds for the new church. Though Chicago and the rest of the nation were in the midst of a severe depression, the campaign was so successful that within just three years the large stone church, which still stands on Roosevelt Avenue, was opened for services. Three years later another fund-raising drive took place to expand the church. Reflecting the working-class character of the congregation, most of the contributors gave five dollars or less. Only 15 of the 539 who contributed gave more than twenty-five dollars. One of the contributors was the grandmother of the novelist James T. Farrell. He recalled that she "contributed 25 cents toward a stained glass window in [Holy Family church]. She was proud of this," he wrote, "all her life."[14]

Damen wanted nothing but the best for his people, a church they could be proud of and that would favorably compare with the Protestant churches. He hired one of Chicago's best architects and stipulated that the stained-glass windows "be equal to that of the windows in St. James church," the pride of Chicago's Episcopalians. Shortly before Holy Family's dedication in 1860 the *Chicago Tribune* praised "its interior as one of the finest by far in the city, if indeed it has a superior in the United States." The writer went on to predict that Holy Family "will ever be one of the most marked and prominent objects of interest in our city, for its size and costliness."[15]

The Gothic magnificence of Holy Family church stood as a landmark on the city's West Side. Like a magnet, it attracted scores of people to the neighborhood. Damen wrote in 1865 that "almost two thousand new houses have been built in our parish." As the neighborhood developed, the number of parishioners grew from two thousand in the late 1850s to over nineteen thousand by the 1880s. "Pride in the parish," wrote historian Nick Salvatore, "became interwoven with pride in one's residence" as families sought to create "a world for themselves within the protective shadow of the sacred building."[16]

One reason the parish was so popular was its commitment to education. By the 1860s the Catholic Church in the United States was committed to the establishment of the parish school as an alternative to the public school. John Hughes spoke for many when he said, "Build the schoolhouse first, and the church afterwards." Some ethnic groups, the Germans being a prime example, were much more committed than others. A key reason for this was language. German parish schools were critical in preserving the language and culture of the immigrants. The English-speaking Irish, on the other hand, did not have to struggle with language preservation, and therefore their commitment to the parish school was not as strong. But there was no question about Holy Family's commitment to a Catholic education for its young people. From the beginning the parish supported separate schools for boys and girls. By the 1870s five schools in the parish offered an education from grade school to college to over thirty-five hundred students. One of these schools, St. Ignatius College, was the forerunner of Loyola University. The Madames of the Sacred Heart established an academy for women that would eventually evolve into Barat College. By fostering middle-class aspirations, these schools became the primary economic escalator that carried the children of Irish blue-collar workers into the white-collar middle class.[17]

Like many parishes at this time Holy Family sought to meet every need of its parishioners. It sponsored as many as twenty-five different organizations, spiritual, recreational, educational, and charitable. Most likely as many as ten thousand people belonged to one or more of these organizations. Appealing to every age group, they sponsored numerous events and activities: bands, baseball clubs, dramatic groups, picnics, and bazaars. A highlight of the year was the parish fair. "Part highbrow entertainment and bazaar, Holy Family's fairs featured drama and music as well as the sale of domestic goods, everything from fancy needlework and homemade delicacies to rosaries, paintings, and statues." A significant source of revenue, these fairs also "contributed to Holy Family's growing reputation as a center of neighborhood life and refinement."[18]

In its heyday in the 1890s the Holy Family complex occupied an entire city block, where the church, schools, convents, and athletic fields stood as a proud testament to the faith and generosity of Chicago's West Side Irish. Solidifying Holy Family's central place in the area were the annual processions on the occasion of the archbishop's visit to administer the sacrament of confirmation to the young people of the parish. Newspapers carried detailed accounts of hundreds of girls and boys decked out in their finest outfits marching in formation to meet the archbishop. Irish policemen led the parade, followed by more than a thousand children and adults representing various parish organizations. Thousands of parishioners lined the streets, proudly admiring all who passed. On this day the Holy Family Irish were making a statement that this was their piece of earth, their neighborhood where they could parade, proudly displaying the symbols of their faith.

Holy Family was remarkable, but not unique. Every city and town where the Irish settled could boast of an Irish Catholic parish. St. Peter's in San Francisco was another excellent example of an Irish parish that was the center of the people's universe. As one parishioner put it, "The parish was the center of activity, and all our lives were tied up in the things that happened there. The families were very close. You knew everyone who went to church regularly." As historian Jeffrey Burns wrote, "St. Peter's reveled in its Irishness, celebrating Irish culture and nationalism and reflecting an unmistakably Irish ethos." They celebrated St. Patrick's Day with Mass, a sermon in Irish, a parade, and an evening dinner featuring Irish music. Like Holy Family, St. Peter's sponsored elementary and high schools for both boys and girls. Parishioners considered these schools "the pride of St. Peter's." With its buildings filling an entire city block, St. Peter's stood as a Catholic citadel in the midst of the city's Mission District.[19]

The engine that drove the religious life of these parishes was a new style of Catholicism that had emerged in the second half of the nineteenth century. Best described as devotional Catholicism, it sought to bind Catholics to the institutional Church by providing them with a demonstrative, emotion-packed religion distinguished by its emphasis on the practice of religious rituals, communion with a heavenly host of saintly relatives, and devotion to a suffering savior, all of which was mediated through a sacramental system controlled by the clergy. These rituals centered around a particular person—Jesus, Mary, St. Patrick—and they could be performed privately or in public in a church ceremony presided over by the priest. Since they required the recitation of many prayers, they were adaptable to such public communal ritual. Before long these public celebrations surpassed the Sunday Mass in terms of popular response.

A key to the popularity of devotional Catholicism was the spiritual confraternity, or what was more commonly known as the sodality. As one priest acknowledged, "Sodalities are the life of my parish." Holy Family had as many as sixteen sodalities, numbering more than seven thousand members, each with a specific focus, aimed at different age groups. They promoted "devotion to the Sacred Heart of Jesus, the Blessed Virgin, St. Ann (for married women), St. Agnes (for working girls), and St. Joseph (for working boys). In addition, there were groups for altar boys who assisted the priest at Mass, the Sanctuary Society, separate sodalities for married and single men, a group devoted to spiritually preparing members for death and a sodality devoted to encouraging the daily practice of saying the rosary, a particular Catholic devotion to the Virgin." So central was the sodality to parish life that Holy Family "parishioners raised over $40,000 to build Sodality Hall, which quickly became the nerve center" for the parish. It housed offices for the various organizations, a large auditorium, a reading room with more than three thousand books, and "smoking rooms and gymnasiums (for men only)." As the diverse functions of Sodality Hall suggest, the sodality had a social function as well as an explicitly religious purpose. It not only nourished the culture of Catholic piety, but as a social organization it bound Irish Catholics together, giving them an increased sense of identity in an ethnically and religiously diverse environment.[20]

The interior of Holy Family church housed a museum of artistic splendor, a place of mystery and wonder appealing to the senses and the imagination of worshippers. A huge, beautifully carved wooden altar dominated the interior. Surrounding the altar were "statues of Faith, Hope and Charity, the cardinal virtues to which all Catholics aspired." Statues of favorite saints transfixed the eye of the believer. One side altar featured St. Joseph wearing an Irish derby as he escorted his wife and holy child on their flight to Egypt. The stained-glass windows, depicting scenes from the lives of the saints, were visual aids for prayer and meditation. A local newspaper, celebrating the beauty of the church's interior, noted that Catholicism was "a religion of symbols . . . it appeals to the soul through the senses . . . employ[ing] poetry and music, sculpture and painting, and the symbols of color to reach the feelings, and connect them with the divine by a bridge of beauty."[21] This appeal to the senses and imagination reinforced the culture of devotional Catholicism by strengthening the personal bonds between the devout and their favorite saints.

Many Irish Catholics decorated their homes with the religious symbols of devotional Catholicism. These symbols—crucifixes, statues, holy pictures, and candles—were advertised in the Catholic press and readily available in the local religious-goods store. A social worker's description of an Irish Catholic home on New York's West Side highlighted the family shrine, featuring an image of the Virgin with a rosary wrapped about her neck. In addition, the home had a family Bible, a picture of Saint Anthony on the bureau, and on the walls pictures of Christ healing the sick, Saint Benedict, and other saints. Parish schools also promoted the culture of devotional Catholicism. Not only did children learn the religion of the catechism, they were also introduced to the celestial community of the saints and the elaborate network of devotions that brought these heavenly relatives into their lives. Statues and pictures of the saints as well as biblical scenes decorated the rooms and corridors of the school. One young girl remarked that in such an environment you "really did begin to live all day long in the presence of the Court of Heaven."[22]

The practice of devotional Catholicism had a special appeal to women. A 1902 study of church attendance in New York found that 73 percent of all Catholic adult churchgoers were women. They also were prominent participants in the annual parish revivals. Without a doubt the church was a major sphere of activity for women. As one priest recalled about his work in an Irish parish, "Life for all the women centered about the parish churches." They ran the parish bazaars and socials. Pillars of the church, they faithfully dropped their nickels and dimes into the collection basket. They made sure that the children went to church, decorated their homes with appropriate religious artifacts, and urged their husbands to attend Mass and the parish revivals. Reminiscences often noted their heroism as they struggled to survive in a working-class culture and a fickle economy. Jack Callahan, a Boston Irishman, who later became a noted criminal, fondly recalled his mother as "a great Catholic. The Pope of Rome," he wrote, "never had a more devout follower than my mother. Religion was everything in the world to her. I've seen her go to church when she could hardly walk. I've seen her give money to the church when there wasn't food in the joint to feed a canary. Whenever I complained that I didn't want to go to church because I was either poorly shod or poorly dressed, she would come back at me with: 'God don't look at your shoes and your clothes, son, he only looks at your soul.'" Willie Sutton, a notorious bank robber, who grew up in an Irish neighborhood in Brooklyn, recalled that his mother "filled the house with religious paintings and artifacts and was always stuffing rosary beads and religious medals into my pockets." She also saw to it that Willie went to church regularly. Once these young men left home, they also left the Church. But when it came time to write their memoirs, they fondly acknowledged the powerful religious presence of their mothers as they were growing up.[23]

A study of parish histories in the nineteenth century leaves no doubt about the central place of women in the devotional life of the parish. Devotional societies were overwhelmingly the domain of women, single women in particular. This seemed to be because unmarried Catholic career women, most likely schoolteachers, had few organizational activities in which they could participate. Single women gravitated to the church and its devotional societies, where they could establish their own separate world.

On the other hand, mutual aid and charitable societies were the domain of men. The St. Vincent de Paul Society was a prominent parish organization. Men from all walks of life joined the organization with the hope of ministering to the needs of poor families by providing them with food, clothing, and fuel. In Holy Family parish the men's sodalities were active in promoting both the religious and social lives of their members. They also sponsored an evening school, "which held classes in bookkeeping, commercial law, and penmanship," and "an employment bureau opened in evenings at Sodality Hall." Another major organization was the Holy Name Society, which appeared in the early twentieth century. This society was for men only, and its purpose, to defend and uphold the holy name of Jesus, reflected the more militant, muscular version of Catholicism that was beginning to surface at this time. In Holy Family parish the men's sodalities merged into the Holy Name Society in 1918. One of their tasks was to care for young Catholic boys whom the city's criminal courts had granted parole by assigning them to the care of individual members of the society. In just one year's time the courts assigned almost six thousand youths to the society; at the same time the society obtained jobs for more than fifty-five hundred young boys.[24]

Most visible in the parish community were the values of middle-class respectability. Patrick Ford, a prominent Irish journalist, described the ideal Irish American as one who was "respectable, well to do, cultural, and devoutly religious."[25] Though few Irish could claim to possess all these attributes, they did express their religion in a restrained, respectable manner. They dressed up for church on Sunday, to the point that those who lacked the proper dress were oftentimes too embarrassed to attend. Siblings even shared their good clothes so that one could attend Mass while the other waited at home for his or her turn. Etiquette books were available that sought to educate Catholics in the proper behavior both in and outside of church. Photos of parish processions at Holy Family church captured well-dressed parishioners who lined the street watching the children march. These processions expressed the proud, confident brand of Catholicism that was surfacing by the turn of the century. A triumphant spirit was on display that said, "We Catholics are the one true church." In promoting this model Catholics were building a strong fortress community that encouraged a cultural enclave, separate from other ethnic and religious groups.

But how many people endorsed this model? A study of the New York Irish in 1902 concluded that "the great majority of Irish New Yorkers had at least some connection with a Catholic parish. Approximately 91 percent of the Irish-born said they were Catholic; of these, 90 percent claimed membership in a specific parish."[26] But claiming church membership did not mean that these people attended church. The percentage of Catholics who did attend church regularly stayed fairly consistent throughout the postfamine era, never getting any higher than 50 percent, and in some places such as San Francisco it was even lower. Not surprisingly, the percentage of women attending church was higher than that of men. About one half of the school-age population attended the parish school. The number who could be considered core Catholics—regular churchgoers as well as active in parish societies—was most likely in the 30 percent range, maybe lower but not any higher.[27] The parish, then, represented a microcosm of the Catholic community. Some people were active Catholics, core members of the parish, whereas others, the majority, were marginal members who identified with the parish but did not regularly attend church. According to Church law these lukewarm Catholics were living in sin, the lost sheep whom the clergy hoped to reclaim.

Was the postfamine Irish Catholic community any more religious than the prefamine Irish who had emigrated to the United States? That is difficult to say. Most likely they were not. But by the early twentieth century Irish Catholics were clearly more assiduous in practicing the rituals of Mass-and-sacraments Catholicism than their predecessors by attending Mass more regularly, receiving Communion more frequently, and performing a greater variety of devotions. Moreover, it was a new style of religion, devotional Catholicism, which was quite different from the folk religion of the prefamine Irish. This new culture of piety not only influenced how the Irish practiced their religion, but it also shaped their religious beliefs.

Devotional Catholicism was theology in practice. Though expressed in a manner different from the dry, intellectual style of the catechism, it arose out of a specific theology. The four main concepts emphasized in this theology were authority, sin, ritual, and the miraculous. Such concepts are found in other religious traditions as well, since they are so fundamental to the Christian system of belief. Yet within the Roman Catholic tradition they took on a special meaning, setting Catholics apart from other Christians, and among the Irish they acquired a distinct quality that was grounded in the Irish historical experience.

A belief in the miraculous was deeply rooted in the Irish landscape. Wherever you turned in Ireland, there was a holy well or shrine. Flocking to these holy sites on special days, people prayed for favors or blessings for themselves and their families. This tradition has remained a distinct characteristic of Irish Catholicism to the present. Though they could not bring the wells or holy mountains with them when they emigrated, the Irish did bring their attachment to folk religion. This existed alongside the official brand of Mass-and-sacraments Catholicism, and it would be difficult to determine which was more popular. Many Irish believed in the supernatural powers of scapulars, charms, and relics, as well as certain practices associated with birth and marriage. The festive wake, an unusual mixture of mourning and gaiety, was a remnant of Irish folk religion. The custom persisted in the United States despite the opposition of Church authorities.

Another indication of the Irish fascination with the miraculous was the widespread belief in healings. At Irish parish missions, the blessing of the sick often took place, sometimes with apparently miraculous results. The use of holy water obtained from the Marian shrine in Lourdes, France, was also popular. Priests at the University of Notre Dame promoted this devotion through their magazine, *Ave Maria*. They had water from the shrine shipped to Notre Dame, then mailed it to people who requested the water. Those who used the water believed in its healing powers, recounting the cures in letters to the priests at Notre Dame that were published in *Ave Maria*.

Closely allied to the miraculous was the need for ritual. The Mass and the celebration of the various sacraments such as baptism and marriage were the most sacred rituals in the Catholic liturgy. But there was much more. A major aspect of this ritual dimension was devotion to the saints. The Irish carried this with them, be it a loyalty to Patrick, Bridget, Columba, or Gobnet. Some of these rituals took place publicly in church, such as the celebration of St. Patrick's feast day. Others were performed privately. Without a doubt the recitation of the rosary, a Marian devotion, was widespread, as was the novena, nine days of prayer to honor a particular saint or to obtain a particular request.

Devotional Catholicism put a great deal of emphasis on sin. Catholicism was a religion of dos and don'ts. In emphasizing sin, it fashioned a multitude of rules and regulations that helped to discipline and strengthen Catholics in their battle against evil. The confession of sins to a priest in the sacrament of penance was a ritual that any devout Catholic had to undergo. It was so fundamental that a priest's popularity might depend on his performance in the confessional. If he sat there for long hours, hearing confessions in a kind and understanding manner, then he ranked right up there with the saints. If he failed to meet these expectations, then he was just an ordinary priest and the lines at his confessional would be short.

Prayer books also put great emphasis on sin and confession. Devotional guides, prayer books associated with a particular devotion, also reinforced the culture of sin. The Sacred Heart devotion, popular with the Irish, stressed human sinfulness and the need for reparation for past sins. The parish mission, a Catholic revival meeting, also stressed the horror of sin. Groups of religious-order preachers toured the country conducting revivals in parishes where for a week or more the preacher would hammer home the saving truths of Catholicism, urging people to repent and do penance for their sins. The success or failure of a parish mission depended on the number of sinners the preacher could persuade to repent and reform. Like so much of devotional Catholicism, the emphasis at these revivals was on individual sins and individual sanctification.

The Irish had a strong penitential tradition. Dating to the medieval monastic era, it exhibited a severity that has persisted into modern times. People would walk barefoot up the rocky, rugged terrain of the holy mountain of Croagh Patrick in reparation for past sins. Deprivation of food and sleep were common practices at Lough Derg, where Irish Catholics annually flocked to do penance and gain forgiveness of their sins. Nurturing this need for penance was a strong feeling of guilt. In stressing the enormity of sin so much, preachers seldom failed to plant a profound sense of guilt in the conscience of the sinner. This guilt would hound sinners until repentance cleansed their conscience. Even then, for an Irish Catholic guilt could linger.

Some sins appeared to be more serious than others. One was intemperance. One priest went so far as to say that in Ireland "intemperance formed part of the national character." A major reason for the high incidence of intemperance in Ireland among young men was the stem family tradition, which forced those sons who would not inherit the farm to spend much of their spare time drinking with other young males. They carried this tradition to the United States, where the ubiquitous saloon became a drinking club for young men. In some parishes "drunkenness was said to run wild among the men—young and old."[28] To combat the scourge of the saloon and the evil of drink, Irish clergy launched a temperance crusade.

The Irish temperance advocate Father Theobald Mathew arrived in the United States in 1849 to launch the first phase of this crusade. For two and a half years he traveled across the country visiting all the major cities where Catholics had settled, promoting temperance and administering the pledge of total abstinence to over five hundred thousand people.[29] The crusade continued during the second half of the century as the tide of reform and the movement toward prohibition gained strength. Parish missions always featured a sermon on intemperance, aimed at young male bachelors as well as their fathers. Drunkenness was portrayed as the worst of all sins since it takes away the individual's rational faculties. As the preacher put it, "It is the only sin which deprives God of his power to forgive." Its evil effects were always highlighted in vivid and sentimental detail. According to the preacher, the most prominent "tenant of hell" was the drunkard father, and its "doorkeepers" were the liquor dealers, who lived off the "blood money" exchanged for a "glass of poison."[30] Both men and women took the total-abstinence pledge in large numbers, which the preachers proudly recorded in their mission reports. Temperance societies were also popular in Irish parishes among both men and women, their goal being to curb the influence of the saloon and "return the husband—immigrant workingmen in particular—to the home."[31]

According to the clergy, the other vice bedeviling the Irish was sins of the flesh. When it came to sex, the Irish were prudes. Unlike temperance, sex was taboo for the preacher. When it was discussed, most often in the context of chastity, it was done cautiously and briefly. In Ireland the system of marriage and the stem family tradition shaped the Irish attitude toward sex. Those sons and daughters who could not marry were, according to Catholic moral teaching, obliged to live a life of permanent celibacy. The opportunity for marriage and a family was one of the major reasons why so many young Irishwomen emigrated. No doubt many single men chose emigration for the same reason. When they arrived in the United States, the Irish tradition of promoting celibacy as a noble way of life followed them. But this was not an easy option for young men and women who would remain single into their thirties.

Prescriptive literature enshrined the single woman's vocation to celibacy. This was an easier road to salvation than marriage. According to the theology of the day, wrote historian Leslie Tentler, "sexuality was not integral" to a person's moral identity "in any remotely positive way but evidence of our nature's fallenness. Thus, the perfect mode of existence was consecrated virginity." Since "the great majority of people were not called to this state, for them marriage was necessarily the better part."[32] In school the nuns daily extolled the virtue of chastity and offered their celibate lives as examples to their young students. The single woman won praise because she remained celibate, supported her family in Ireland with frequent remittances, and supported the Church. Guidebooks portrayed the life of a domestic servant as a vocation that resembled that of a nun—hard work, obedience, celibacy, and prayer. This was the path to salvation.

Of course, not all Irish maidens were able to live up to these ideals. A considerable number turned to prostitution, but their numbers were relatively low in comparison with those of other ethnic groups. For those women who had turned to prostitution as a way of life, the Church established institutions that sought to reform them. The catalyst in this endeavor was Catholic women, both religious and lay. Many cities had a House of the Good Shepherd, an institution managed by the Sisters of the Good Shepherd, whose apostolate was to aid abandoned women, many of whom had become prostitutes. The clients in these institutions were overwhelmingly Irish, as were the nuns who cared for them. These institutions were never large enough to accommodate all those who sought their assistance.

Celibacy was also urged on young bachelors. When it came to sex, the Irish clergy were moral rigorists. Popular literature, especially the lives of the saints, sought to persuade young men of the importance of purity and the evils of lust because, as one prayer book warned, "nothing can injure or dishonor you more than the sin of impurity." One mission preacher described lust as the "seven-headed monster" that, since it wreaks "terrible havoc amongst souls . . . should be strongly attacked in all its manifold forms." A guidebook for young men described "the vice of Impurity" as "an abomination before God."[33] By condemning sins of the flesh in such extreme language as "this filth of iniquity," the Church ensured that any young man falling victim to this "vice of impurity" would suffer a heavy burden of guilt.

In warning young men to avoid sins of the flesh, the clergy depicted women as evil temptresses who could lead them down the path to perdition. One guidebook, when discussing morality, described the fate of Samson, who lost all his strength as soon as he "abandoned himself to a woman." In another place the author wrote, "In regard to women, do not trouble yourself about them until the time comes for a suitable marriage." Another popular writer counseled his male readers to be men of "pure hearts" whose "first and chief care is to seek the beautiful soul much more than the beautiful body."[34] Such admonitions strengthened the bachelor culture so prominent among the Irish by reinforcing the separation of the sexes and extolling the virtue of purity, a virtue that many young men would find difficult to practice.

Another major influence on the Catholic psyche was the concept of authority. During the nineteenth century new theologies and new philosophies transformed the meaning of God and ultimately of religion itself. Such ideas challenged the teaching authority of the Catholic Church. To counteract these influences the Church responded with excessive vigor. In 1870 the Vatican Council declared that the pope was infallible, claiming that his teaching authority was supreme. The attitude of infallibility filtered down to the local parishes, where the priest was regarded as God's oracle. Basking in the power of the pope and the local bishop, the pastor became the chief authority figure for the faithful. His word was gospel, not subject to challenge. As one Irish pastor put it, "By divine appointment the clergy rules."[35] The duty of the laity was to listen and obey. Of course, many Catholics questioned the wisdom and authority of their priests, but rarely did such challenges become public, especially among the Irish.

For the Irish the priest occupied a hallowed place in their history. During the penal days he was hunted down and persecuted. An object of scorn to his Protestant detractors, he became a revered figure in the Gaelic tradition, earning the title of *Sagart aroon* (the Dear Priest). This tradition of respect for the clergy was also quite evident in Irish America. Put on a pedestal by history and tradition, the priest enjoyed a position of prestige in the community.

In the nineteenth century the need for priests was so great that it was common for bishops to travel to Ireland to recruit them. One source of new recruits was All Hallows College in Dublin. Founded in 1842, its graduates served as missionaries throughout the Irish diaspora. Over the nineteenth century, All Hallows sent more than six hundred of its graduates to the United States, where they worked in many different regions of the country, with California being the favorite destination for close to 30 percent of these Irish missionaries. Irish seminaries in Maynooth, Waterford, Kilkenny, and Wexford also sent their graduates to the United States. Irish religious orders sent some of their own as well. This tradition of Irish-born priests working in the United States was so strong that eventually they became known as the FBI (foreign-born Irish), a nickname bestowed by the American-born clergy that was not a term of endearment.[36]

One of the great blessings for an Irish mother was to have one of her sons ordained a priest. By giving her son to the Church, she stood apart and above other women in the parish. Most of those priests born in the United States came from lower-middle-class Irish families. Nonetheless, the Roman collar was a magical key that opened the door to many benefits reserved for the upper classes.

Some priests were both revered and feared. Others were revered and loved. One son recalled his father's relationship with the Church and the clergy. A hard-drinking longshoreman, the father, Dick Butler, went to Mass "every week because of the combined efforts of his wife and the priest." His son remarked that his father "was big enough to lick all the priests in the country but he feared them more than he feared God."[37] Those priests who became pastors of a parish often ruled like Irish landlords. One such priest was Maurice J. Dorney of Chicago.

Dorney was an American-born Irishman who was pastor of St. Gabriel's parish, in an Irish working-class community located on Chicago's South Side near the Union Stockyards. Pastor for thirty-four years, he gained a reputation as "King of the Yards" because of his influence in gaining jobs for his parishioners in the stockyards and arbitrating labor strikes. With a church, two schools, rectory, and convent, St. Gabriel's was a typical parish complex. An Irish nationalist, Dorney supported the Irish Land League and their efforts at land reform in Ireland. He was also a temperance advocate who sought to keep saloons off the residential streets of his parish. Those brave few who challenged him on this issue had to suffer the humiliation of Dorney chastising them by name from the pulpit. No one doubted for a moment who was boss in the parish. When he died, they lowered the flags to half-mast at the International Amphitheater and most of the big city plants in the stockyards. On the day of his funeral the stockyards suspended business for five minutes.[38]

Another Irish priest of even more renown was Edward McGlynn of New York. Born in New York of immigrant parents, he was sent to Rome at the age of thirteen to study for the priesthood. A gifted student, he received a doctorate in theology at the end of his Roman education. Back in New York in 1860, McGlynn had a few different pastoral assignments, the most notable as the spiritual caretaker for the African American squatters and Irish laborers living in Central Park's shantytown. This experience awakened in him a commitment of service to the poor as well as a realization of the need for social reform. In 1866 he became pastor of St. Stephen's parish, located on East Twenty-eighth Street, and remained there for the next twenty-one years. While at St. Stephen's, a huge parish of over twenty-five thousand members, he was revered as the poor people's priest. An advocate of social reform on behalf of the laboring classes, he was always ready to help the poor, even giving away his own clothes to those in need. He was an electrifying speaker, much in demand in New York and beyond to deliver addresses at key events, both religious and political. He was also a popular confessor who reportedly spent hours in the confessional, counseling and consoling those who came to him. He was beloved by his parishioners, and his portrait hung in the homes of many of them.

An ardent Irish nationalist, he supported the Irish Land League, believing that the land of Ireland belonged to the people of Ireland. McGlynn also became an enthusiastic supporter of Henry George, whose radical proposal for social reform, known as the single-tax theory, explained in his widely popular book, *Progress and Poverty*, inspired a legion of followers. His support of George and his theory of social reform got McGlynn in trouble with his archbishop, Michael Corrigan. This came to a head in 1886 when McGlynn, against the wishes of Corrigan, campaigned for George, who was running for mayor of New York. Corrigan lost patience with the rebel priest and suspended him. Several months later, in July 1887, church authorities in Rome excommunicated McGlynn for refusing to travel to Rome to explain his controversial ideas of social reform. Five years later he was reconciled with the Church, having been absolved by the pope's delegate of any alleged heretical teaching that grew out of his support for George and his social reform platform. Corrigan then exiled him to a parish in Newburgh, where he remained until his death in 1900. After a funeral service in Newburgh, another service took place in St. Stephen's in New York. His body lay in state well into the night, while forty-five thousand persons paid their final respects to their priest and friend. Years after his death his grave site continued to be the site of annual pilgrimages of his many supporters.[39]

Peter Yorke of San Francisco was another Irish priest who became a legend in his own lifetime. Born in Ireland, he was an ardent Irish patriot who made his parish, St. Peter's, into a center of nationalist fervor. The parish sponsored classes in Irish language, dancing and music, and Irish history. On St. Patrick's Day the parish celebration was extraordinary, with a parade, a solemn Mass with a sermon in Irish, and an evening celebration with dinner and dance complete with Irish music. When the Irish leader Eamon de Valera visited San Francisco in 1919, Father Yorke was his escort. Yorke was also an apologist for Catholicism, a journalist, an advocate for Catholic education and liturgical reform, as well as a champion of the labor movement. At his death he was eulogized as the "Father of the organized labor movement of San Francisco." Like McGlynn, his forceful advocacy for the poor got him in trouble with his superiors.

People fondly remembered Yorke's evening walks through the parish, greeting his parishioners by name. Children held him in awe. He was remembered as an inspiration to young men and women and as a "counselor to the old, and a messenger of mercy at the bed of death." For many years after his death, parishioners kept alive his memory with an annual Yorke Memorial Mass followed by a pilgrimage to the cemetery where he was buried. As with McGlynn and Dorney, "it is difficult to determine," wrote historian Jeffrey Burns, "where the man ends and the myth begins."[40]

Indispensable members of any Irish parish were the women religious, or sisters as they were best known in times past. Like the clergy they wielded extraordinary authority, especially in the parish schools, where their rule was legendary. They were the Church's infantry, the unsung heroes who undertook a wide variety of ministries including teaching and caring for the sick, the unemployed, and prostitutes. Of the more than forty-six thousand sisters working in the United States in 1900, it is safe to say that more than half were Irish. Suellen Hoy, who has studied the recruitment of Irish sisters during the nineteenth century, concluded that "a minimum of four or five thousand" Irishwomen emigrated to the United States "as sisters or intending to become sisters . . . It is certain that they all came in groups at the invitation of a bishop, priest, or nun, almost all of whom were also Irish." For these women, concluded Hoy, religious life offered "an exciting opportunity. They provided such women with an arena in which to use their education, develop their talents, and assert a measure of their independence." In those days entering the convent did not mean the end of a useful life.[41]

Some of the women recruited in Ireland as sisters were adults, while others were children who emigrated to the United States and later joined a religious congregation. Some belonged to orders in France or other European countries and were eventually assigned to American missions. An elaborate network established between convents in Ireland and the United States facilitated this migration. Like All Hallows College, which trained men to become missionaries, there were institutions in Ireland whose sole purpose was to train young women to become missionary sisters beyond Ireland. One such institution was St. Brigid's Missionary School in Callan, county Kilkenny. From its founding in 1884 until closing in 1958, it trained over nineteen hundred young women for convents overseas, primarily in Australia, New Zealand, and America. And, of course, thousands of American-born daughters of Irish immigrants attended parochial schools staffed by Irish nuns. Many of them decided to enter a religious congregation. Despite their different paths to religious life, they all shared an Irish Catholic heritage.[42]

Prior to the 1880s women religious were involved in a variety of ministries staffing orphanages, schools, hospitals, and shelters for women, as well as visiting the sick and those in prison. In New York City the Sisters of Mercy, recruited from Ireland by Archbishop Hughes, opened a House of Mercy in 1848 that became a refuge for women fleeing Irish famine and poverty. The sisters provided thousands of immigrant women with shelter, job training, and job placement.[43] The Sisters of Charity opened St. Vincent's Hospital in New York in 1849. Its founder was the Irish-born Ellen Hughes, the archbishop's sister, who was known as Sister Angela. Like his contemporary in New York, the archbishop of San Francisco traveled to Ireland to recruit the Mercy sisters to come to the city by the bay to minister to the needs of a growing Catholic community. After a two-month journey from the Irish port of Queenstown via New York and across the isthmus of Panama, seven Sisters of Mercy finally arrived in San Francisco in December of 1854. Led by Sister Mary Baptist Russell, an energetic twenty-five-year-old immigrant from county Down, the Mercy sisters began a ministry that continues to the present. They founded many institutions, including a House of Mercy, orphanages, and parish schools, but the most sparkling jewel in the crown of their work was St. Mary's Hospital. Founded in 1857, it is the oldest Catholic hospital west of the Rockies. Accompanying the Sisters of Mercy on their transatlantic, transcontinental journey was a group of Irish Presentation sisters whom Archbishop Alemany also recruited. Their ministry was principally teaching in parochial schools.

Another contingent of Irish Mercy sisters arrived in Chicago in 1846, beginning a ministry that included caring for the sick and injured, providing shelter for the homeless, and staffing schools for young women and children. The leader of this group of nuns was a twenty-four-year-old, Irish-born woman, Margaret O'Brien, one of seventeen children born to the wife of a barrelmaker. Mother Agatha, as she was known, was a dynamo who repeatedly complained that the needs were so great in Chicago's growing Catholic community that she "had not one moment to spare." In 1851 she undertook the running of what would become known as Mercy Hospital, an institution that still stands in the heart of the city. When cholera struck in the summer of 1854, it swept through the city claiming hundreds of victims. Mother Agatha, along with other Mercy nuns and some laywomen, went out to nurse the sick and dying. Then she herself became sick and died, a victim of cholera at the age of thirty-two. Three other Mercy sisters, along with the pastor of the Irish parish of St. Patrick, also died, as did more than fourteen hundred other people in that dreadful summer.[44]

A number of Irish Mercy sisters from Chicago also served as "soldiers of mercy" during the Civil War. They were part of a contingent of some six hundred nuns, many of whom were Irish, who worked as nurses during the war.[45] They staffed military hospitals and hospital ships. At first the soldiers viewed the sisters, dressed in their unusual religious garb, with suspicion and even hostility. But, by the war's end the sister nurses were not only accepted, but highly praised for their heroic work with the wounded and dying. Irish nuns also served as nurses during the Spanish-American War.

One of the more remarkable Irish nuns of this era was Mary Irene Fitzgibbon, a Sister of Charity who founded the Foundling Asylum in New York City in 1869 and supervised it for twenty-seven years. During those years Sister Mary Irene and her colleagues cared for thousands of infants and their mothers who were too poor to care for themselves. It also cared for infants abandoned by their mothers. These babies were left in a wicker basket placed at the asylum's entrance with a bell nearby to alert the attending nurse that the basket had an occupant. Often a note was attached to the infant. One mother wrote, "Guard this little one and if things turn out as I hope I shall repay you for your trouble." Another baby had the following note pinned to a blanket: "I am a poor woman . . . without means and without relatives to nurse my baby. Therefore I beg you for God's sake to take my child and keep it. I remain your humble servant."[46]

When Sister Mary Irene died in 1896, the city witnessed a tribute that one newspaper claimed was unprecedented in the history of New York. As the hearse carried her body through the city streets, thousands of mourners, estimated to number as many as twenty thousand, joined the procession to the church on the city's east side where the funeral Mass was to take place. In a front-page article the *New York Times* eulogized this daughter of Irish immigrants as "the most remarkable woman of her age in the sphere of philanthropy." At the time of her death the asylum "housed an average of six hundred women and 1,800 infants at a time and also provided day care of working mothers, a maternity hospital for poor women, a children's hospital and a shelter for unwed mothers." With a budget of $250,000 Sister Mary Irene was administering the largest institution of its kind in the country and the only one in New York "to guarantee care for all children and women . . . regardless of religion, race or ethnicity, marital status or ability to pay for care."[47] Known today as the New York Foundling, the agency founded by Sister Mary Irene is set to celebrate its 140th anniversary in 2009.

For Irish nuns a new era began when in 1884 the U.S. bishops mandated every parish in the country to establish a school. Though their wish of a school in every parish never materialized, this decision did transform the ministry of Catholic sisters, since they would staff the new schools. Henceforth, the ministry of women religious became more specialized. They still operated hospitals and orphanages, but with each passing year more and more sisters became teachers in parish schools, which increased in number by at least one hundred a year between 1884 and 1900. In Boston, for example, by 1920, 60 percent of women religious were in teaching. The schoolhouse had become "an extension of the convent." As historian Kevina Keating observed, many young women thought that "being a sister meant being a teacher."[48] Irish sisters also founded a number of academies as well as several of the Catholic women's colleges established pre-1920, such as Trinity College in Washington, D.C., St. Catherine's in St. Paul, Minnesota, and Marymount in New York.

Sisters, like priests, were held in high regard within the Catholic community. To be called to the service of God was the most esteemed privilege and honor a young Catholic woman could have. Moreover, the profession allowed these immigrant daughters to become school principals, administrators of hospitals and orphanages, college presidents, and university professors. But the vast majority of them became parochial-school teachers, the critical labor force that allowed the Church to build an educational system whose only rival was the public school. They were anonymous heroes, held in awe by their students and worked to death by an institutional empire of schools, hospitals, and orphanages that could not have existed without their cheap labor. Their discipline in the classroom has become legendary and even ridiculed, but these Irish sisters provided generations of Irish men and women with the basic education that enabled them to step onto the economic escalator that would take them to the middle class. That was no small achievement.

As powerful as Irish priests and sisters were, they could never challenge the authority of the bishop, who ruled like a king over the local church. Being a good administrator, rather than a successful pastor, was the necessary attribute for promotion to the hierarchy. In addition, whom you knew and not what you knew was paramount. For these reasons the nation's bishops were not very distinguished. An Irish bishop sent to the United States by the Vatican in 1878 to report on the state of the Church said as much when he reported that of sixty-eight bishops, he considered only ten as noteworthy. The rest were mediocre, and he believed, as far as theological understanding was concerned, they were even less than mediocre.[49] But, two Irish chieftains stood out as representatives of two different eras in the history of Irish America. One of these was John Hughes, the archbishop of New York.

Hughes was the recognized leader of the Catholic Church during the immigrant era of the mid-nineteenth century. An immigrant himself, he was the son of a farmer who had emigrated with his family to Maryland. Twenty years old when he arrived in the United States in 1817, Hughes worked for three years as a laborer prior to entering the seminary to study for the priesthood. As a parish priest in Philadelphia and later as the archbishop of New York, Hughes gained a reputation as an excellent speaker as well as a fierce apologist for the Catholic faith. In Philadelphia he achieved notoriety for publicly defending the Church against attacks by a well-known Protestant minister. As bishop in New York, he defended the rights of Catholics to have equal access to public funds to support their parish schools. Though he lost this battle, his forceful performance enhanced his reputation as a fighter for Catholic causes. When nativist mobs threatened to attack the city's Catholic churches, Hughes "stationed more than 3,000 Catholic men—'armed to the teeth'—to protect church property." Later, after nativist mobs had destroyed some Catholic churches in Philadelphia, Hughes bluntly told city authorities, "If a single Catholic church is burned in New York, the city will become a second Moscow."[50] This pugnacious Irishman was the personification of a militant Catholicism fighting to gain its rightful place in Protestant America. Like so many other priests, he was an Irish nationalist and an enthusiastic admirer of Daniel O'Connell, whom he had met on several occasions. He carried bitter memories of England's treatment of the Irish, referring to this often in his talks and correspondence. For him England was "an apostate nation" that had crushed the Irish people.[51]

He was an authoritarian ruler. One priest described him as a "tyrant but with feeling." When some priests in New York discussed the need for priests' rights, Hughes responded in his typical direct, blunt manner. He told them "he would teach them County Monaghan canon law; he would send them back to the bogs whence they came." When the Sisters of Charity refused to accept his control over their order, Hughes threw them out of the diocese and founded a new religious order that he could control. He would accept no authority other than his own in, as he put it, "my diocese." He also waged a war against the lay trustees of the city's parishes: he was the boss in the Church, not the lay trustees. "Episcopal authority came from above and not from below," he said, "and Catholics did their duty when they obeyed their bishop."[52]

Hughes, who died in 1864, was also a visionary who sought to build a Church that would stand apart from Protestant America, a fortress Church that was not anxious to win friends or influence public opinion. Such an attitude would serve the Church well during the immigrant era, when nativism was widespread. His grand cathedral, St. Patrick's, would eventually become the national symbol of American Catholicism. Hughes was one of the first, and surely one of the most energetic, champions of the parochial school, an institution that would become the bedrock of Catholic culture in the United States. Recognizing the growth of Catholic political power, presidents consulted him as the spokesman for Catholics, even sending him on diplomatic missions.

Another Irish Catholic prelate who also became a recognized national figure was James Gibbons, the cardinal archbishop of Baltimore. Gibbons was born in Baltimore in 1834 of immigrant parents. Three years later his family returned to Ireland, where they remained for sixteen years. This was not a happy time for them, however. James's father, Thomas, died of cholera during the famine of 1847. Two years later his younger sister died. Shortly afterward, James's mother, Bridget, along with her five children, emigrated to the United States for a second time, this time settling in New Orleans in 1853.

Ordained a priest in 1861, Gibbons was put on the fast track toward the episcopacy. A rising star, he was well liked as well as talented. Seven years after his ordination, he was made a bishop at the age of thirty-four—the youngest bishop in the entire Catholic world at the time. Nine years later he became the archbishop of Baltimore, and in 1886 the pope honored him with the cardinal's red hat. He remained the archbishop of Baltimore for more than forty-three years, until his death in 1921.

Though they were both Irish and raised by immigrant parents, Gibbons and Hughes were as different as night and day. Hughes was a militant, sectarian Catholic who used the anti-Catholic frenzy of the age to rally and unite his flock. His influence was mainly limited to his own diocese. Gibbons on the other hand was a national figure whose reputation spread far beyond Baltimore, and indeed beyond the United States. He was a polished statesman, the quintessential American who wanted all Catholics to become more American and less ethnic. He was not as colorful as the combative Hughes, who symbolized the fighting Irish of the immigrant era who had to struggle for their daily bread. Hughes's threat to torch the city of New York if any Catholic churches were attacked was a tactic the more moderate Gibbons would never even have contemplated. The Baltimore cardinal was the symbol of the American-born Irish who were anxious to gain a seat at the table of the American middle class. Though he had lived through experiences that made bitter nationalists of other Irishmen—the famine and the death of his father from cholera—Gibbons rarely spoke of his Irish background and shared no more than a lukewarm nationalism.

As the undisputed head of the American Catholic Church, Gibbons allied himself with three other Irish prelates, John Ireland, Denis O'Connell, and John Keane, to push for a more modern, American expression of Catholicism. They endorsed religious toleration, the separation of church and state, and the assimilation of Catholic immigrants. One of Gibbons's most notable achievements was his intervention at the Vatican to prevent the condemnation of the predominantly Catholic labor union the Knights of Labor because of their secrecy, which raised suspicions of anti-Catholicism among some clergy. This gained him acclaim as a champion of the working class. He was an American patriot devoted to American principles. A frequent visitor to the dining salons of Washington, he enjoyed warm relationships with Presidents Grover Cleveland, Theodore Roosevelt, and William Taft. Roosevelt said that Gibbons was "the most respected and venerated and useful citizen of our country." When he died, the national press eulogized him. The *New York Herald* wrote, "The death of Cardinal Gibbons is more than the passing of an old man and honored churchman. It is the ending of the life of a great American, a fine figure in the national scene." The paper described him as "everybody's Cardinal. No matter what their religious beliefs, Americans who knew him held him in the highest respect and esteem."[53]

By the time Gibbons died in 1921, the Roman Catholic Church—and Irish America—had achieved a stature and acceptance across the country that was unthinkable during the era of John Hughes. This did not happen by accident. It was the result of a conscious effort by the American-born Irish to become more American and thus as good a patriot as any blue-blooded Puritan. The American-born Irish, not the immigrant, would now define what it meant to be Irish and Catholic in America.

With the Irish leading the way, the twentieth century would be the age when Catholicism would become an American church—robust in defending its Catholicism and proud in affirming its Americanism.

CHAPTER 6

Born to Rule

In the rogues' gallery of Irish politicians, none was more cunning than the rascal king of Boston, James Michael Curley. When he was running against Thomas Joyce for the House of Representatives, he never hesitated to use "dirty tricks" in his campaign. After blasting Joyce from every street corner and platform, Curley turned some of Joyce's own adherents against him the night before the election. Curley sent his henchmen out to ring doorbells rather late at night at the homes of Joyce's supporters after they were settled in bed for the evening. When the angry voters answered the doorbell and "asked why in the hell they were being roused from slumber at such an unseasonable hour, my cohorts said," as Curley recollected, "they merely wanted to make sure they were going to vote for Thomas Joyce the next day." The response was something like "Why I wouldn't vote for that son-of-a-bitch if his opponent was an Orangeman." Curley won by seventy votes. As the rascal king often said, "Do others, or they will do you."[1]

Such tricks as that helped to gain Curley legendary status in Boston's political history. But he was hardly the exception among the Irish. Their prominence was such that the Irish, politics, and the Democratic Party have become synonymous. From the moment they set foot in the United States the Irish began to make their mark politically. As historian Thomas O'Connor observed, "politics was one path to success in the New World," and "it was a path the Irish chose with gusto and determination." As a New York Tammany politician and noted raconteur, George Washington Plunkitt, put it, "The Irish was born to rule."[2] They began by gaining leadership roles in the volunteer fire companies that were so prominent in the early years of the nineteenth century. From their neighborhood base they acquired access to political power. With the rise of machine politics in the post–Civil War period, they took control of city and state governments. Loyal to the Democratic Party, they nominated one of their own, Al Smith, to be their candidate in the presidential election of 1928. Though he lost, he blazed a trail for another Irish Catholic, John F. Kennedy, who would seek the presidency in 1960 and win. Kennedy's victory was the culmination of the Irish Catholic ascent from immigrant shantytowns to the most distinguished address in the country, 1600 Pennsylvania Avenue. The White House, designed by another Irishman, James Hoban of Charleston, South Carolina, finally had an occupant whom Irish Catholics could claim as one of their own. A great-grandson of an Irish immigrant who fled the famine had been elected to the highest office in the land. The key to this triumph was the skill the Irish possessed in the political arena.

Why were the Irish, more so than other immigrant groups, so attracted to politics? A major reason was their experience in Ireland. For years Irish Catholics had been denied access to the political process. By the end of the eighteenth century this had changed as the Penal Laws were gradually repealed. But full civil rights for Catholics did not arrive until Daniel O'Connell launched his Catholic Emancipation campaign in the 1820s. Leader of a political crusade that involved all levels of the population, O'Connell succeeded in gaining for Catholics the right to sit in the English parliament. The campaign in the 1840s to repeal the Act of Union was another political movement that mobilized the Irish. The activity of the Land League in the 1880s and the Home Rule campaign of the 1890s also organized the masses and exposed them to the need for political organization. Throughout the nineteenth century and into the twentieth century, political involvement had become a tradition for the people of Ireland. The immigrants arrived with these experiences fresh in their minds. These struggles had strengthened their loyalty to the nation, and such fierce loyalty would also become a main ingredient of Irish politics in the United States, especially in their allegiance to the Democratic Party.

Another cultural influence was their familiarity with Anglo-Saxon law and government, a tradition that had been transplanted to the United States. The Irish knew the way town or city government was supposed to work. They could understand the role of a policeman or judge, and the court was a familiar institution in a new setting. Their English language was also key. The school system in Ireland had increased the rate of literacy and sharpened the English-language skills of the people. Unlike the Germans or later the Italians, Irish immigrants did not face a language barrier upon their arrival. This not only speeded their naturalization, but it also gave them immediate access to political participation.

The Irish arrived in large numbers just when American party politics was taking off. In the mid-nineteenth century, when scores of Irish were arriving, modern city governments were beginning to take shape. This enabled the Irish to gain many of the new jobs created as cities formed police and fire departments. This was also a time when the political machine emerged. The machine was a political organization that operated outside of, but often controlled, the legally established government. The key to its success was its ability to organize the electorate and gain voter support by offering supporters the tangible benefits of public office—jobs, contracts, and franchises. The Irish became the leading practitioners of machine politics. Those who benefited from the machine's patronage became tied to the political machines that governed the cities, working on their behalf to see that Irish politicians stayed in power. The Democrats, having successfully gained the allegiance of the Irish during the Jefferson era, solidified this loyalty with their pro-immigration policy, while the Republican Party had little appeal to the Irish because of its nativist roots and its anti-slavery stance.

The saloon was an ethnic institution that could be found in German, Irish, Polish, and Italian neighborhoods. But among the Irish it was more than a watering hole. It often became the neighborhood base for the political machine, a gathering place where jobs were brokered and voters mobilized. "As a political headquarters," wrote historian Perry Duis, "it was an ideal 'store,' from which an ambitious proprietor could 'sell' services along with beer and whiskey in exchange for nickels and votes . . . It was perhaps the most open social institution in the neighborhood. By operating all hours of the day and night, the proprietor was accessible to thousands. In this position, he was known to everyone in the procession of hundreds who daily passed through his doorway, and in return he knew much of his clientele by their first name."[3] For many Irish saloonkeepers the saloon served as a stepping-stone to a political career.

The Church was another urban institution linked to politics. As a vital center of neighborhood life, it provided a model for aspiring politicians by illustrating the importance of the personal touch between the leader and his constituents. The Church also nurtured the sense of tribal loyalty as well as the value of hierarchical rule or what in politics was known as boss rule. Loyalty and discipline, key values in the Church, were necessary for the survival of the machine. In addition, parish clubs and organizations provided recruits for the political party. Most often the Catholic Church supported the Democrats, thus reinforcing the bond between the party and the people.

A final reason why the Irish gravitated toward politics was their own ambition. Discriminated against both because of their birth and their religion, politics became a way for them to make it. As Frank Skeffington, the fictional Irish mayor in Edwin O'Connor's classic, *The Last Hurrah*, explained to his nephew, "When I began it was long ago, and the situation around here was a bit different. I had no education to speak of, a good many roads were closed to our people, and politics seemed to be the easiest way out." As he put it later, the Irish "had arrived and they wanted in. Even worse than that, they got in."[4]

The Irish love for politics was visible on election day, when they turned out to vote in numbers that were higher than those of other ethnic groups. In San Francisco in 1900 "the proportion of Irish-born registered voters was nearly double that of the city's other foreign born . . . and nearly equaled the rate for the native-born."[5] A similar pattern was true in Boston, Chicago, and New York. Commenting in 1894 on "the Irish conquest of our cities," John Paul Bocock wrote, "the Irish American almost invariably becomes the father of voters, and it is safe to say that his sons never fail to vote on the first election day after their majority." He went on to note how widespread and successful the American-born Irish were in "securing such offices as those of alderman, councilman, policeman, municipal clerk, bureau chief, and mayor. They have entered the race with unflagging effort and unfailing success." He concluded by noting, "The Irish in America have a genius for municipal government—at least for getting municipal offices." A study of city bosses written in 1930 underscored this skill for gaining political office when it profiled the political careers of twenty bosses. All but three of them were of Irish descent.[6]

This genius was especially notable in the cities, where the Irish helped to build powerful political machines. Chief among these would be New York, Jersey City, and Albany, as well as San Francisco. In other cities, such as Chicago and Boston, Irish politicians fashioned local ward machines that controlled one or more neighborhoods rather than an entire city.

One of the earliest machines identified with the Irish was the Democratic political organization in New York City known as Tammany Hall. A powerful presence in New York, it ruled the city for eighty years, from the 1850s to the 1930s. For most of those years the Irish controlled Tammany Hall.

The most notorious boss of Tammany was William M. Tweed, who ruled the organization in the 1860s. Neither Irish nor Catholic, Tweed has become a symbol of the greed and corruption associated with machine politics. Starting out in a volunteer fireman's club on the city's Lower East Side, he built up a social network that enabled him to enter politics. He soon achieved elected office as an alderman from the city's Seventh Ward. Later he won a seat in Congress, but he got bored and returned to New York, where he gained powerful positions within the city government. By the time he was forty years old, he was elected chairman of Tammany Hall, and later that year, 1863, he became its grand sachem.

Six feet in height, Tweed weighed over three hundred pounds. With his graying beard and mustache along with his piercing blue eyes and his bulging stomach, he was an imposing sight. He boasted that he never drank nor smoked, but "being a man of large body," he confessed, "I am fond of eating." He carried himself with a certain swagger that went along with his arrogant personality, captured so well in a famous quotation attributed to him by the cartoonist Thomas Nast: "As long as I count the ballots, what are you going to do about it?" In his prime he was the third-largest landowner in New York. He also "owned two steam-powered yachts, a Fifth Avenue mansion, an estate in Greenwich, Connecticut and a shirtfront diamond pin valued at over $15,000 ($300,000 in today's money)." He drove around the city in a carriage drawn by four horses and traveled about the state in a private railroad car, playing poker with his friends along the way.[7]

Two of his closest associates were Peter Barr "Brains" Sweeney, a saloonkeeper and an American-born Irishman, and Richard "Slippery Dick" Connolly, a foreign-born Irishman. Along with Abraham Oakley Hall, who was the city's mayor at the height of Tweed's power, these four made up what became known as the Tweed Ring. They ran the city for several years, or, as one pundit put it, "The city was run by Oakley Hall, Tammany Hall and alcohol."[8]

Through bribes and kickbacks Tweed and his associates became wealthy, shamelessly robbing the city treasury of an estimated forty-five million dollars, almost one billion in today's dollars.[9] The famous Tweed courthouse, a historic landmark in the city, cost as much as thirteen million dollars to build, twice as much as the cost of Alaska, and after twelve years it was still not finished. The original appropriation from the state legislature in 1858 stated that it should not cost more than $250,000! With two thirds of the cost of the work going to the Tweed Ring as kickbacks and one third to the contractor, the bills submitted were monstrous. For three tables and forty chairs, the city paid $179,729! Lumber worth $48,000 cost the city $460,000.[10] This was only one of many projects that enriched Tweed and his associates.

Nonetheless, many of the city's poor Irish looked upon Tweed as a modern Robin Hood who provided them with food, fuel, and jobs. The machine had twelve thousand city jobs to give away, with a payroll of $12 million. If there were not enough jobs to go around, the machine created jobs—hiring twenty workers to inspect three water pumps. As many as four thousand laborers reportedly worked in Central Park, where the cost of maintenance skyrocketed to six million dollars over a year and a half from the normal $250,000 a year.[11] Such patronage, along with the personal touch of Boss Tweed, captivated the common people. He influenced the state legislature to appropriate funds to aid Catholic schools, orphanages, and hospitals. Irish Catholics certainly appreciated such kindness. The generosity of the machine is what enabled the Tweed Ring to stay in power for so long. As corrupt as they were, they looked after the little people. On election day no one could tell how many votes they could bring for the machine. As George Washington Plunkitt put it, "The poor are the most grateful people in the world, and let me tell you, they have more friends in their neighborhood than the rich have in theirs."[12]

The Tweed Ring met its demise when its corruption became too public. The cartoons of Thomas Nast that attacked Tweed's thievery helped to shape public opinion against the Ring. Then Tweed's enemies released records that documented his thefts from the city treasury. He was indicted, charged with fraud, and eventually convicted. He died in jail in 1878. Connolly escaped jail by fleeing the country with millions of dollars; Sweeney settled out of court; Hall went to trial and was acquitted. The Tweed Ring was crushed, but the political machine known as Tammany Hall survived and indeed prospered under new leadership.

The next boss of Tammany was John Kelly, the first of ten successive Irish Tammany bosses. Known as Honest John, he was one of seven children born in New York to Irish immigrant parents. He got his start in politics with a volunteer fire organization, where he displayed a talent with his fists. An alderman, then twice elected to Congress, he resigned to become sheriff of New York County. Party reformers selected him, untouched by the Tweed scandal, in 1874 to head Tammany Hall, where he remained until his death in 1886. Under Kelly's leadership Tammany Hall became a well-oiled machine.

The political machine adopted a hierarchical model that resembled that of the Catholic Church. Its base was in the local neighborhood, where it was organized at the ward, precinct, and block level. Each ward or precinct (equivalent to the local parish) had its own boss (the parish priest), whose power rested in the neighborhoods. This locally elected boss had his block captains, who worked on his behalf on election day and throughout the year. These bosses were organized into a citywide organization like Tammany Hall and reported to the big boss, a Tweed or a Kelly. In the Church the citywide boss would have been the bishop.

Under Kelly, Tammany became a powerful army that could produce thousands of votes on election day. The key to victory at the polls was the patronage system, whereby the machine offered jobs in return for votes. Tammany was able to offer as many as forty thousand jobs to its supporters. On election day each of these jobs would produce several votes from the worker's family and friends.

Another key to Tammany's success was its alliance with businesses. Kelly allied Tammany with many successful businessmen. Chief among these was William R. Grace, an Irish-born immigrant who first settled in Peru. In the 1860s he moved to New York, where he opened his shipping company, W. R. Grace. Kelly chose Grace to be the Democratic nominee for mayor in 1880. Grace won the election, becoming the first Irish-born Catholic to hold that office. He served two terms, earning a reputation as an honest reform mayor. He appointed the first woman, Grace Dodge, to the city's board of education. He also reformed the city's corrupt street-cleaning department. A generous supporter of the Catholic Church, he died a multimillionaire.

Though Tammany's alliance with the business community improved its public image, it also forced the machine to adopt a conservative fiscal policy that limited spending. This meant a cutback in patronage jobs and services. This led to a working-class revolt in the 1880s, just as Kelly's time as boss was drawing to a close. In the forefront of this revolt were the Irish workers who supported the mayoral campaign of the reform candidate Henry George in 1886. But George challenged the hegemony of Tammany Hall. By this time Tammany was under the control of Kelly's successor, Boss Croker, one of the more flamboyant characters in

Tammany's history. Tammany's candidate won the mayoral election despite the large turnout of Irish support for George. The key to their victory was the support of the business community, together with Croker's ability to get out the vote despite the defection of many Irish workers who had traditionally supported Tammany.

Richard Croker had emigrated from Ireland with his parents in 1846 when he was three years old. He grew up in New York making his mark as a gang leader known for his skill as a street fighter. This attracted the attention of the local politicians, who recruited him into the Tammany machine. As an aide to Boss Kelly he rose to power in Tammany, eventually succeeding Kelly upon his death in 1886.

Croker immediately reversed course and severed Tammany's alliance with the business community, putting candidates in the mayor's office who would carry out his wishes. He built up an army of ninety thousand party workers whose task was to carry elections for Tammany candidates. George Washington Plunkitt, a Tammany ward boss, explained how these local district leaders worked:

> He plays politics every day and night in the year, and his headquarters bears the inscription, "Never closed."
>
> Everybody in the district knows him. Everybody knows where to find him, and nearly everybody goes to him for assistance of one sort or another, especially the poor of the tenements.
>
> A philanthropist? Not at all. He is playing politics all the time . . .
>
> He seeks direct contact with the people, does them good turns when he can, and relies on their not forgetting him on election day.
>
> If he holds his district and Tammany is in power, he is amply rewarded by a good office and the opportunities that go with it.[13]

Croker remained boss from 1886 until 1894. Under Croker, New York was a wide-open city with gambling, liquor, and prostitutes readily available. This was too much for reform-minded New Yorkers, who wrested control of the city from Tammany Hall for a brief period, 1894–97. But the reformers were too strict for the many New Yorkers who preferred the loosely controlled city associated with Tammany rule.

Especially irksome was the reformers' attempt to enforce a state law that would ban the sale of liquor on Sunday. As one writer commented, "The reformers had made the cardinal mistake: They got between the people and its beer."[14] With a campaign slogan of "To Hell with Reform," the Tammany candidate, Robert Van Wyck, won the mayoral election in 1897. Croker once again ruled the city until another reform movement ousted him for good in 1901.

Croker and his wife, Elizabeth Frazier, whom he married in 1873, had nine children, three of whom died at an early age. Ever since his youth Croker was known as a natty dresser. As boss he presented a striking figure with his fine suit of clothes, top hat, neatly clipped beard, piercing eyes, and square jaw. Known as the King of New York, he was admired by the common folk for his rise to power from the city's slums. When he sailed to Europe, as he frequently did, thousands of people lined the docks to send him off with rousing cheers. Croker became a rich man during the 1880s and '90s, accumulating a fortune of over eight million dollars. A lover of horses, he owned a farm where he raised Thoroughbreds; he also owned seven homes and traveled in a private Pullman car. He achieved such wealth by using his political clout to have the city award lucrative contracts to businesses in which he had invested. Turned out of power in 1901, he returned to his estate in England, where he spent his time raising racehorses. One of them won the English Derby in 1907 as well as the Irish Derby. Croker and his wife separated in 1897. Shortly after her death in 1914, he married Bula Benton Edmondson, a Cherokee Indian who was thirty years younger than him. They had met at the Democratic National Convention in 1900. He spent the last years of his life with his second wife at his mansion in Ireland, Glencairn, where he died in 1922, leaving an estate of several million dollars.[15]

Charles Murphy succeeded Croker as boss of Tammany. No two people could have been more different. His tenure lasted from 1902 to his untimely death in 1924. The son of Irish immigrants, he grew up on Manhattan's East Side in a neighborhood known as the Gas House District. He built a following in his neighborhood through his success as a baseball player and as owner of a saloon. By the time he was in his early thirties he was the owner of four prosperous saloons, one of which was the headquarters for the Anawanda Club, the district's Tammany organization. Under Murphy's direction the Anawanda Club was an efficient organization. The "secret of his success" as a district leader was, according to his biographer, Nancy Joan Weiss, "accessibility and Murphy made it a practice to station himself beneath the old gas lamp in front of the Anawanda Club for several hours each night and there conduct the business of the district leader. The Aldermen and Assemblymen were always within hailing distance, so that when a constituent had a favor to ask the matter could be settled then and there without any red tape." As boss of Tammany he offered this same accessibility to the scores of people who came to see him with their problems. As Fiorello H. La Guardia put it, "He was a great leader because he kept his hand on the pulse of the people."[16]

In addition to owning saloons Murphy was also in the trucking and construction business with his brother and a few friends. A shrewd businessman as well as a rising star in Tammany Hall, he was already a millionaire when he took over control of Tammany after the demise of Croker. Unlike Croker, "there was nothing crude or bombastic about him. He was clean-shaven," wrote Christopher M. Finan, "and his wardrobe consisted of immaculate business suits that he wore even on weekends." He had a reputation of "being puritanical in his personal habits." A man of few words, he was once asked why his ticket had lost the election. His reply was brief and to the point: "We didn't get enough votes!"[17]

Murphy took over a weakened Tammany Hall, cleansing it of its reputation for corruption and giving it an aura of respectability. At this time a new spirit of reform, known as progressivism, was gripping much of the nation. Advocating social justice, educational and legal reform, and the downsizing of government, progressive reform was most visible in the large cities, where reformers sought to alleviate the hardships brought on by industrial and urban growth. Murphy supported these initiatives by encouraging a good deal of social reform legislation. This turn to progressivism was primarily the work of a number of rising stars in Tammany whom Murphy backed. Chief among these was Al Smith, who with the boss's support would become governor of New York and eventually run for president of the United States. In the opinion of Christopher M. Finan, Murphy was "the shrewdest leader in Tammany's history."[18] Under his leadership Tammany reached the pinnacle of its success, becoming a powerful political machine whose influence extended beyond the city to the statehouse.

Another New York Irishman who gained notoriety as a local ward boss was "Big Tim" Sullivan. The son of immigrants, he was born and raised in poverty. He started working at age seven as a newsboy, left school at age eleven, and continued to work in the newspaper business for most of his teenage years. Eventually he bought a small saloon, which served as a gathering place for a local gang. This became the launching pad for his political career. He was an imposing figure at that time, about six feet tall and over two hundred pounds with a friendly demeanor that attracted others.

During the Croker era Sullivan was gaining power within Tammany as a district leader in the Bowery, located on the city's Lower East Side. He solidified his political base by giving away thousands of socks and shoes, providing free Christmas dinners, distributing coal, finding jobs for his constituents, and when necessary, bailing them out of jail. His political club sponsored an annual summer picnic for thousands of supporters. The all-day excursion began with a parade to the dock on the East River where steamboats ferried the people to a Long Island park. Once they arrived, they enjoyed lots of free food, beer, music, and dancing. The day ended with a journey back to the city highlighted by a "torchlight parade and fireworks." In the 1890s, the prime of his career, "the *Tammany Times* hailed Big Tim as 'the political ruler of down-town New York' and 'the most popular man on the East Side.'" His district was one of the best organized in the city with numerous neighborhood captains from different ethnic groups who would take care of their constituents and mobilize the voters on election day.[19]

Sullivan amassed considerable wealth by investing in the entertainment industry. The owner of a vaudeville theater, he also invested in storefront nickelodeons and penny arcades. With a partner he built a chain of forty vaudeville theaters across the country. Known as the King of the Bowery, he was also accused of being King of the Underworld because of his connection with gambling, as well as an alleged link with prostitution. Yet, as a state legislator he sponsored progressive labor legislation, such as limiting the hours of work for female factory workers, as well as the Sullivan Law, in 1911, that made it a felony to carry a concealed weapon. He also supported women's suffrage.

His life had a bizarre ending. After the death of his wife in September 1912, Sullivan suffered a nervous breakdown. As he was incapable of managing his affairs, his family and close friends took charge of his life, shuttling him "between sanitariums, trips to mineral baths in Germany, and private home care." On August 31, 1913, haggard, thin, and suffering from melancholy, he fled his brother's home in the Bronx, where he was living in seclusion. Intending to hop a freight train for Manhattan, he ended up dead on the tracks, run over by a train. His mangled body lay in the city morgue for two weeks unidentified. Finally, just before it was to be shipped off to Potter's Field for a pauper's burial, a policeman recognized the body as that of Big Tim.

His funeral was one of the largest in the city's history. Thousands filed past his coffin in the Timothy D. Sullivan Clubhouse where he was waked. His picture hung in the stores along the Bowery while as many as seventy-five thousand people lined the streets to view the funeral procession. The *New York Sun* reported, "There were statesmen and prize-fighters, judges, actors, men of affairs, police officials, women spendidly gowned and scrubwomen, panhandlers and philanthropists—never was there a more strangely heterogeneous gathering." Another newspaper acknowledged that "he had won his kingship through his friendship for the underdog." Historian Daniel Czitrom concluded his study of Sullivan with this assessment: "His power had rested upon an uncanny and shrewd melding of job patronage and legal services, charity and poor relief, urban carnival, protection of gambling and the saloon trade, and tolerance for a broad range of commercial entertainments . . . Above all, as a pure product of life among the city's poorest, Big Tim saw as no one else before him the political and cultural power latent in an urban underclass too easily dismissed as inherently criminal, depraved, and vicious."[20] This was the genius of the political machine. By championing the underdog, it gained considerable political clout.

Providing jobs for the underdogs became especially pronounced in the early twentieth century when, under Murphy's guidance, Tammany embarked on a spending spree. Money flowed out of the city treasury to pay for new parks, schools, hospitals, railways, and sewer lines. As a result, many new jobs were available for the machine to reward its supporters. One estimate suggests that more than half of all the new public-sector jobs in New York from 1900 to 1930 went to the Irish. In 1900, 37 percent of the city's employees were Irish. By 1930 it had increased to 52 percent. What this meant was that of all the Irish men and women who went to work in 1930, one out of four of them worked for the city government. These included jobs in the police and fire departments as well as city-owned subways, railways, and port facilities. Where once the refrain was "No Irish need apply," it now may as well have been "Only Irish need apply"! The spending spree of the machine also benefited the private sector, especially the construction industry, where the Irish had gained a strong presence. Contracts were awarded to companies friendly to Tammany. In turn, they awarded jobs to individuals recommended by the machine. This pattern of Irish hegemony in municipal employment was true in other cities controlled by the Irish such as Jersey City, Albany, and Boston.[21]

This increase in municipal employment benefited the second- and third-generation Irish. But it did not necessarily propel them into the middle class. As Stephen P. Erie wrote, they ended up in a "blue-collar cul de sac . . . solidly lower-middle rather than middle class."[22] Rather than rags-to-riches opportunities, the public sector provided the Irish with jobs that afforded respectability as well as security. Nonetheless, that was a significant achievement for an ethnic group whose ancestors were the poorest of the poor when they first set foot in New York.

In Boston also the Irish gained political ascendancy in the nineteenth century, finally muscling aside the Yankee Protestant elite who had treated them as second-class citizens for generations. Thomas O'Connor, who has written extensively on Boston's Irish, put it this way: "If there had existed in the nineteenth century a computer able to digest all the appropriate data, it would have reported one city in the entire world where an Irish Catholic, under any circumstance, should never, *ever*, set foot. That city was Boston, Massachusetts . . . Boston was a city that rejected the Irish from the very start."[23] Nevertheless, by the end of the nineteenth century the Irish were beginning to gain control of Boston politics. They would consolidate this control in the twentieth century, when for all but a few years for almost an entire century an Irishman was mayor of the city. No other city could match such Irish dominance. The day of the Puritan had passed. The Irish had taken over.

The first Irishman to achieve political prominence in Boston was Patrick Collins. Born near the town of Fermoy in county Cork, Ireland, in 1844, he emigrated to Boston in 1848 with his widowed mother. His father, a farmer, had died of pneumonia during the Great Famine. As a young man he worked as a recruiter for the South Boston Fenian Circle, an Irish American organization whose goal was to free Ireland from British control. Disillusioned with his work with the Fenians, he drifted into Boston politics quite by accident.

As a Fenian recruiter he had gained a reputation as a fine orator. At a caucus meeting of the South Boston Democrats, he was called upon to speak. Liking what they heard, his Democratic colleagues nominated him to run for the state House of Representatives. His victory at the polls in 1868, at the age of twenty-four, was the beginning of a long and distinguished political career. While in the state legislature he attended Harvard Law School, gaining his law degree in 1871. Collins is remembered best for his work in revitalizing the Democratic Party in Boston in the 1870s. The Republicans had gained considerable strength during the Civil War, leaving the Democrats disorganized and politically marginalized. Collins along with other young Irish Democrats revitalized the party by building an alliance between the old guard of the party, the Brahmin Democrats, and the young Irish newcomers. Collins was the key figure as chairman of the newly reorganized Democratic City Committee, thereby enabling the Irish to dominate the party in future years.[24]

Collins's popularity gained him a nomination for Congress in 1882. He easily won the election and remained in the House of Representatives until 1889. He later served as mayor of Boston from 1901 to 1905. By the time he ran for reelection as mayor in 1903, he was so popular that he carried every ward of the city.[25]

Patrick Maguire was an ally of Collins. Born in county Monaghan, Ireland, in 1838, he emigrated to Canada as a young boy. The family settled in Prince Edward Island, where young Patrick worked as a printer. When he was fourteen years old, he took off for Boston, walking most of the way, like many other Irish who had migrated from Canada to Boston. He eventually became a successful businessman, publishing a newspaper aimed at the Irish Catholic community and running a real estate business. Along with Collins he was a member of the Democratic City Committee, and though he never ran for political office, he soon became a force to be reckoned with in the Democratic Party. In 1876 he persuaded his colleagues to nominate a prominent Brahmin Democrat, Frederick O. Prince, for mayor. With Prince's victory on election day, Maguire had solidified his power within the party. With Collins heading off to Washington, D.C., to take his seat in Congress, Maguire emerged as the power behind the scenes, the acknowledged citywide boss. In the back room of Maguire's real estate office, the party made its key decisions. He succeeded by building a coalition between the Irish and the Yankee Democrats. His next move was to nominate an Irish Catholic to become mayor of Boston.[26]

Maguire's choice was Hugh O'Brien, an Irish-born immigrant. O'Brien was the ideal coalition candidate, highly respected in the Irish community and a successful businessman who could speak the language of the Brahmin Democrats. Though he lost the 1883 mayoral election, he made a successful comeback a year later. On January 5, 1885, he was

Charles Carroll of Carrollton, grandson of an Irish immigrant, American patriot, and signer of the Declaration of Independence. (Library of Congress)

Thomas Addis Emmet was a leading figure in the revolutionary Society of United Irishmen in the 1790s and later a distinguished lawyer in New York City. (Library of Congress)

John England, the Irish-born bishop of Charleston, South Carolina, who promoted a republican style of church government where clergy and laity worked together. (Diocese of Charleston)

The Famine in Ireland—Funeral at Skibbereen. One of a series of famous illustrations of 1847 by the Cork artist James Mahony, who was commissioned by the *Illustrated London News* to record the grim reality of the famine. This sketch depicts a funeral near Skibbereen in county Cork, a district that became notorious for the extent of its horror. (*Illustrated London News*)

THE EJECTMENT.

Ejectment of Irish Tenantry. Eviction of tenants from their homes became commonplace during the famine. In this sketch a hired crowbar brigade demolishes the cabin as the tenants plead for mercy from the landlord's agent. Soldiers were present to prevent any resistance. (*Illustrated London News*)

Emigrants Arrival at Cork—A Scene on the Quay. This sketch appeared in 1851; in that year alone almost 250,000 persons left Ireland. These emigrants faced a long, six-week journey across the Atlantic. (*Illustrated London News*)

Sunday morning Mass at the Civil War camp of the Fighting 69th of New York. Part of the Irish Brigade, they suffered heavy casualties in the battles at Antietam and Fredericksburg. (Library of Congress)

Two young Irish girls reading a letter from America. Such letters containing information about the United States inspired many Irish men and women to emigrate to America. (Library of Congress)

The Day We Celebrate, the Irish on St. Patrick's Day, *Harper's Weekly*, April 6, 1867. Thomas Nast generally portrayed the Irish as a cross between a professional boxer and an orangutan. (Reproduced from the original held by the Department of Special Collections of the University Libraries of Notre Dame)

The residents in Mullen's Alley in New York City pose for a snapshot in 1888. (Museum of the City of New York)

The American River Ganges, Harper's Weekly, September 30, 1871. Thomas Nast assailed the Roman Catholic Church in numerous cartoons. This cartoon depicts Catholic bishops as alligators attacking public school children and their teacher. In the background, Tammany Hall is portrayed as St. Peter's Basilica, with Irish and Papal flags. Nast continuously attacked such an alliance of church and state. (Library of Congress)

Archbishop John Hughes, an Irish immigrant who, as archbishop of New York, was a major spokesman for the Roman Catholic Church. (Library of Congress)

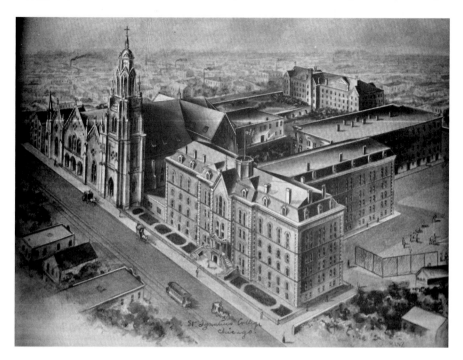

The Gothic Holy Family church and St. Ignatius College were the centerpiece of this huge parish complex of buildings and playing fields spread over acres of land on Chicago's Near West Side. (Midwest Jesuit Archives)

Young recruits, described as coming "from the leading and wealthy families of Ireland," aboard the *Pennland* as they sailed from Ireland to Philadelphia in February 1898. They entered the Sisters of St. Joseph of Carondelet in St. Louis, Missouri. (Sisters of St. Joseph Carondelet Archives)

Sister Mary Irene Fitzgibbon and her flock at the Foundling Asylum in New York City (ca. 1890), which she founded in 1869. (Museum of the City of New York)

Two old friends, Cardinal Gibbons and former president Theodore Roosevelt, share a warm welcome at the opening of the victory loan drive in Baltimore, September 1918. (U.S. Province Society of St. Sulpice Archive at Associated Archives at St. Mary's Seminary and University)

A Group of Vultures Waiting for the Storm to "Blow Over"—"Let Us Prey," Harper's Weekly, September 23, 1871. Thomas Nast was a political cartoonist whose attacks on the Tweed Ring helped to shape the public image of Tweed. This Nast cartoon appeared at a time when evidence of the corruption of the Tweed Ring was being published by the *New York Times.* The "storm" never blew over. (Library of Congress)

Sporting a top hat and a cigar, Boss Croker of Tammany Hall celebrates the victory of one of his racehorses with his jockey. (Brown Brothers)

John "Honey Fitz" Fitzgerald, mayor of Boston, and his eldest daughter, Rose, who was her father's favorite. She was often at his side at political functions and traveled with him on many of his official trips. (Boston Public Library)

Two legendary Chicago aldermen, Hinky Dink Kenna and Johnny Powers, with other Democratic politicians, circa 1910. (Chicago History Museum)

Mayor James M. Curley, in his signature fur coat and hat, speaking to his admirers during his 1921 mayoral campaign. (College of the Holy Cross Archives)

Women participating in a demonstration demanding self-determination for Ireland, 1920. (Library of Congress)

Neversweat mine crew, Butte, Montana, 1902. The Neversweat mine was known as an Irish mine. The miners strike a formidable pose, complete with their lunch pails, before they head down to the mine. (Montana Historical Society)

The legendary Mother Jones marching with striking workers in Trinidad, Colorado, 1913. Jones traveled throughout the country to support workers on strike. (Newberry Library)

Terence Powderly and Mother Jones, two labor leaders who were good friends. Mother Jones often stayed with Powderly when she was not on the road supporting striking coal miners. (Catholic University Archives)

Women delegates at the 1886 convention of the Knights of Labor. In the middle holding a twelve-day-old infant, the youngest of her twelve children, is Irish-born Elizabeth Rodgers who was head of the huge Chicago chapter of the Knights of Labor. (Library of Congress)

Al Smith with his wife, Katie, campaigning in Montana in 1928. Many farmers were suffering at this time and Smith sought their vote by promising to help them by raising agricultural prices. (Museum of the City of New York)

Cardinal Dougherty, the large person in the center-front, strides at the head of a group of civic leaders. This photo was most likely taken at his arrival in Philadelphia in 1918. Dougherty personified the big city Catholic prelate who lived and ruled like a Renaissance prince. (Library of Congress)

The labor leader Philip Murray speaking at a strike rally in Duquesne, Pennsylvania, 1949. "When he spoke," recalled one contemporary, "you hung on every word." (Philip Murray Papers, Historical Collections and Labor Archives, Pennsylvania State University)

The Boss, Mayor Richard J. Daley, exchanges sharp words with Alderman Jack I. Sperling at a Chicago City Council meeting in 1963. (Ralph Waters, photographer, Chicago History Museum)

President John F. Kennedy's motorcade in Cork, Ireland, in 1963 during a visit that he called "one of the most moving experiences" of his life. (Robert Knudsen, White House, The John F. Kennedy Presidential Library, Boston)

sworn in as the first Irish Catholic mayor of Boston. Many in Boston feared what this would mean for the city. A Harvard professor, Charles Eliot Norton, "wrote to his friend Frederick Law Olmsted informing him in ominous terms that 'the Irish dynasty has fairly settled itself upon the throne in Boston.'" But O'Brien fooled them. "To many native Bostonians," Thomas O'Connor wrote, "Hugh O'Brien was a pleasant surprise. Businesslike, sober, cautious, he displayed none of the disturbing characteristics Yankees usually associated with immigrants from Ireland." Even though he was Irish, the Yankees still liked him. His tenure as mayor was so successful that he was reelected four times before he went down to defeat in 1888.[27]

By the late 1880s a new surge of nativism appeared in the United States, especially in Boston, where a group of Boston Brahmins founded the Immigration Restriction League. Grounded in Anglo-Saxon racism, they sought to close the gates to all immigrants who were "most alien to the body of the American people."[28] Their target was the new immigrants from Eastern and Southern Europe, many of whom were Catholics. Also at this time the American Protective Association (APA) made its debut. An anti-Catholic organization founded in 1887, it had gained a strong following in Massachusetts by the early 1890s. Many Protestant ministers launched attacks against the Romanist threat. Anti-Catholic bigots, they feared most the increasing number of Catholic parochial schools being established at this time. The possibility that Catholics might demand public funding for their schools further angered them. Moreover, such a separate denominational school system meant that Catholic children were no longer under the influence of the public school, where they would supposedly learn to become respectful Bostonians. This would only further widen the breach between the Irish and the Brahmins. All of this suggested, as one minister put it, that "Rome was out to destroy the public schools."[29] Such prejudices against Catholics and immigrants coalesced in the late 1880s and early 1890s. They not only helped to defeat O'Brien in 1888, but also weakened the Democratic coalition of the Yankees and the Irish. Symptomatic of the division was the 1895 riot in East Boston. APA supporters, most of whom were Ulster Irish Protestants, marched through this Irish neighborhood on the Fourth of July taunting the Irish Catholic spectators. Fighting broke out, gunshots were fired, and one man lay dead with numerous others injured. "The incident earned national publicity, embarrassing the city by reviving its image as a community riven by ethnic hatred."[30]

The passing of Patrick Maguire in 1896 sounded the death knell of the alliance between Yankee and Irish Democrats. The election of Patrick Collins as mayor of Boston in 1901 was the last hurrah of this era of political harmony. A new period of Boston politics was about to begin. This time the Irish politicians, American-born rather than Irish-born, would emphasize the cultural differences that divided the Yankees and the Irish. Confrontation politics rather than coalition building would soon become the norm.

While Patrick Maguire was building a citywide alliance with the Yankee Democrats, other Irish politicians were building neighborhood political machines. Patrick J. Kennedy was the boss in East Boston; John F. Fitzgerald guided the political fortunes of the North End; in Charlestown, Joe Corbett was king; in Dorchester, Joe O'Connell ruled; "Smiling Jim" Donovan controlled the South End; P. J. Maguire, known as Pea Jacket, was in charge in Roxbury, until ousted by James Michael Curley, who would later become a legend in Boston.[31]

The most powerful of these local bosses was Martin Lomasney. He was born in Boston in 1859 to a young Irish couple, both refugees from the Great Famine, who had met and married in Boston. Before he was twelve years old, both his parents had died. He went to live with his grandmother, where he learned to speak Gaelic, a talent that would later serve him well with his Irish constituents. Having received a patronage job with the city, first as a laborer and later as a lamplighter, he took a liking to politics. Then in 1885 he made the key decision of his life. Together with his brother, Joseph, and a few friends, he founded a club in the West End of Boston. Known as the Hendricks Club, it became the base for his political activity, and within a few years he had established himself as the boss of Ward Eight, located in the city's West End.

For almost a half century Lomasney would hold court at the Hendricks Club. A man of routine, he would arrive there every weekday at nine in the morning and many days stayed until ten in the evening. Working day and night, he turned the Hendricks Club into what he described as "a machine for getting votes." He accomplished this, he said, "by working 365 days a year, caring for the people, being a big employment agency, being a generous benefactor, viewing with charitable and forgiving eyes lapses of human conduct." The key to his success was, as he put it, his ability to know "the whims, the fancies and the needs of the man in the street." In an interview published in the *Boston Globe*, he explained why he and other political bosses were so popular with the voters:

Is somebody out of a job? We do our best to place him and not necessarily on the public payroll. Does the family run in arrears with the landlord or the butcher? Then we lend a helping hand. Do the kids need shoes or clothing, or the mother a doctor? We do what we can, and since as the world is run, such things must be done, we keep old friends and make new ones.

Lomasney once said, "The great mass of people are interested in only three things—food, clothing, and shelter. A politician in a district such as mine sees to it that his people get these things. If he does, then he doesn't have to worry about their loyalty and support." Lomasney, known in Boston as the Mahatma, was reluctant to leave a paper trail. He was alleged to have coined the political maxim "Never write anything when you can say it; never say anything when you can nod your head."[32]

Through his ability to get out the vote in his district for the candidate of his choice, he became a powerful political presence in Boston for decades. His candidates won seats in the city council and the state legislature. He helped Democratic candidates become governors of Massachusetts; at the national level he controlled the party's congressional seat and was a delegate to several national Democratic conventions. A power broker, he was also an officeholder. Though he served briefly as alderman in the city, he truly excelled in the state legislature, where for some twenty years he distinguished himself as a supporter of progressive legislation on behalf of labor and education. Even his opponents acknowledged that he was the "most influential man in the legislature."[33] Though an opponent of prohibition, he himself was a teetotaler. A confirmed bachelor and a devout Catholic, he regularly attended church. When he died in 1933, Boston lost one of its most powerful political figures.

Another star in Boston politics was John F. Fitzgerald. He and Lomasney were political allies as well as bitter opponents. Like the Mahatma, Fitzgerald was a Boston-born Irishman whose parents, both of whom had fled famine-stricken Ireland, met and married in Boston. Fitzgerald was born in 1863 in the North End of Boston, where his family lived in an overcrowded tenement. His father soon prospered in the grocery and liquor business. This enabled him to move his large family to a bigger home in the North End. John, one of eleven children, was bright, handsome, gregarious, and ambitious. He attended Boston Latin School, a unique distinction for an immigrant's child. Then he was accepted to

Harvard Medical School, another indication of his ability, but his father's sudden death forced him to abandon his medical career. The political boss in the North End, Matthew Keany, got him a job with the city so Fitzgerald could help support the family.

His friendship with Keany kindled his interest in politics, beginning a whirlwind rise to political prominence. When Keany died in 1892, the young Fitzgerald, a natural leader of Napoléon-like stature, took control of the Sixth Ward political organization. After a brief time as a state senator, he ran for Congress in 1894. With the support of Lomasney, he triumphed on election day. He served three terms in Congress, where he became a strong opponent of restricted immigration, legislation championed by many Boston Brahmins. In 1900 he returned to Boston to pursue what had been his goal for some time—to be mayor of Boston. When Patrick Collins died in 1905, Fitzgerald was the first to announce his candidacy for mayor.

Caught off guard by Fitzgerald's announcement, the local Irish bosses opposed the politically ambitious Fitzgerald and nominated one of Lomasney's closest friends to run against Fitzgerald for the Democratic nomination. It looked as if the odds were stacked against Fitzgerald. David was taking on Goliath. But Fitzgerald waged an energetic campaign, outworking his older opponent, ironically promising that he, boss of the North End, would do away with bosses and political machines. He traveled the city "in the back seat of a large open-air touring car delivering more than ten speeches a day to enthusiastic crowds." On the eve of the primary he "organized the city's first motorcade, complete with honking horns and blazing red flares." He spoke in every ward of the city, ending his whirlwind tour at his political headquarters, the Jefferson Club, in the North End. One reporter wrote that it was the "most remarkable speaking tour ever made by a political candidate in Boston." Throughout his campaign Fitzgerald appealed directly to the voters rather than relying on party bosses. He crafted a media campaign that used the rhetoric of reform against his opponent, the candidate of the local bosses, whom Fitzgerald painted as corrupt. After winning the Democratic primary, Fitzgerald continued proclaiming his reform message in the mayoral election. An Irishman and a self-proclaimed reformer, Fitzgerald, in the opinion of historian James J. Connolly, "embodied the drive for civic respectability that appealed to so many Irish." This strategy was especially successful in the immigrant neighborhoods, propelling him to victory in the December election when he became the first Boston-born Irish Catholic to be elected mayor.[34]

His two-year tenure as mayor was notable for his cronyism in handing out city jobs to unqualified people as well as for bribery and corruption. Though Fitzgerald was never charged with any crimes, he lived a luxurious lifestyle complete with summers in Maine, trips to Southern resorts, and excursions to Europe with his eldest daughter, Rose. How he funded this lifestyle, given his modest legal income, raised the suspicion and indeed the "likely possibility that he was using his public office for private gain."[35] The cronyism and the graft were too much for Boston's reformers. They mounted a campaign to oust him from office, successfully defeating his attempt at reelection in 1907. But Fitzgerald would be back.

In the fall of 1909 he once again set out on the campaign trail. His opponent was a wealthy reformer who attacked the "evils of Fitzgeraldism." Fitzgerald made his opponent's wealth a campaign issue. Running as a "representative of the common man, a symbol to 'every father and mother that their boy needn't be a millionaire in order to be mayor of Boston,'" he ran a memorable campaign. He portrayed the Brahmin elite as hostile to the Irish. His stump speeches attracted large followings. Before the applause had ended he would ask "the crowd to join him in singing a rousing melody such as 'The Wearing of the Green,' 'When Johnny Comes Marching Home,' or 'Sweet Adeline.'" By incorporating music and song into his political rallies, he soon acquired the legendary title of "Honey Fitz, the man with the golden voice." By a slim margin Fitzgerald won the election. He called it "the greatest triumph of his political career."[36]

His second term, 1910–14, was much more successful and less controversial than his first. With his motto "A Bigger, Busier, Better Boston," he helped to revitalize the city and its harbor. He also built playgrounds, public baths, and schools. Another four-year term as mayor seemed almost certain. But a lack of discretion ruined his political career. A flirtatious relationship with a twenty-three-year-old cigarette girl known as Toodles became his Waterloo. Toodles, whose real name was Elizabeth Ryan, was a beautiful, vivacious woman who worked in a local restaurant where her job was to lure customers into an upstairs room where they could gamble at roulette. During a trial in which she was suing her former employer, Toodles stated that one of the men she lured into the gambling den was Fitzgerald. For hours he would flirt with her, she stated, hugging and kissing her as they danced. If this story ever got out, it would only be a matter of time before Fitzgerald's reputation would be ruined. As Doris Kearns Goodwin wrote, "Just one cartooned image of 'the Little Napoleon' kissing the voluptuous Toodles—with her enormous chest daringly revealed, her painted cheeks and her huge brown eyes—would be enough to transform this pillar of the community into a fool. Interestingly enough, there was no evidence that Fitzgerald had anything to worry about beyond his kisses."[37]

An upstart politician from Boston's Roxbury neighborhood, James Michael Curley, who wished to challenge Honey Fitz for the Democratic nomination, threatened to release news of Fitzgerald's indiscretion to the public if he would not drop out of the mayoral race. Facing public humiliation as well as intense pressure from his wife, Fitzgerald withdrew as a candidate in December 1913. Although he remained a political force for many more years, often running for office, he never won another election. Today he is perhaps best remembered as the father of Rose Fitzgerald Kennedy, mother of President John Fitzgerald Kennedy and the rock of the Kennedy clan. When Honey Fitz died in 1950, he was eulogized as "one of Boston's most beloved figures."[38]

By blackmailing Fitzgerald, James Michael Curley cleared the way for his election in 1914 as the mayor of Boston. Like many Irish politicians, he was born and raised in poverty. His parents were also immigrants who met and married in Boston. Curley's father worked himself to death when he was only thirty-four. Curley's mother kept food on the table and the family together by washing the floors of downtown offices. As a teenager Curley worked at a variety of jobs before becoming involved in ward politics. Besides being active in the local Catholic parish as well as the fraternal organization the Ancient Order of Hibernians, he attended night school so he could gain a high school education. These activities not only kept him busy day and night, but they also enabled him to build a circle of neighborhood supporters. In 1899 the young Curley was elected to the city council. Then, a year later, when he was only twenty-six, he was elected chairman of the Seventeenth Ward Democratic committee, becoming the the youngest political boss in the city. To strengthen his control of the local ward he founded an organization, the Tammany Club, named after New York City's infamous Tammany Hall. He served in the state legislature for one term, then ran for city alderman. Elected as alderman, he remained in city government until 1910, when he became a successful candidate for the U.S. Congress. In

Congress he distinguished himself as a fiery defender of unrestricted immigration.[39]

Like Fitzgerald before him, his dream had always been to be the mayor of Boston. He realized this in 1914. For the next thirty-five years James Michael Curley and the city of Boston were joined together in a political marriage unlike any other. Describing himself as the Mayor of the Poor, he became a hero whom the Irish worshipped as one of their own. "His triumph was their triumph," the *Boston Herald* wrote. His funeral in 1958 was the biggest in the city's history, with over one million people lining the streets "to watch the hearse carrying James Michael Curley through the streets of the city he had led," wrote his biographer Jack Beatty, "and to which he had given life and laughter, sorrow and scandal, for over fifty years."[40]

Though, as Beatty put it, he "tends to be thought of as a cross between a clown and a crook," he was "the most resourceful, eloquent, energetic, durable political personality of his time and place." He was mayor of Boston for four terms, in Congress for two terms, and governor for one term. He also spent two terms in jail, both times for fraud. During his first time in jail—he committed fraud by taking a civil service exam for an Irish immigrant—he ran for city alderman and won. In typical Curley fashion, he had turned a potentially disastrous episode into a political asset by proclaiming to all who would listen that "he had done it for a friend." Such loyalty endeared him to his Irish supporters who voted him into office. A devoted family man, he robbed the city treasury to build a mansion for his wife and children. This proved to be his downfall. As his biographer wrote, "The house swallowed the Curley administration. It led to graft; graft led to scandal; scandal led to defeat" when he ran for reelection in 1918. Though a regular churchgoer, he did not hesitate to blackmail his opponents and regularly used dirty tricks in his political campaigns.[41]

As the boss in the Seventeenth Ward he handed out jobs and favors to as many people as he could. As he put it, "We do our very best to help everyone." He tried to do "at least fifty favors a week." When he was mayor, people would line up in the corridor outside his office waiting to see him. He would call them in, twelve or fifteen at a time, ask them what they wanted, "and if he could give it to them, he gave it to them, and if he couldn't, he didn't. When he stood up, that was a sign for everybody to leave." His theory of government was simple: "to take care of the people."[42]

The anecdotes about Curley are legendary. One of the more enduring was recounted in his autobiography:

> My mother was obliged to work . . . as a scrubwoman toiling
> nights in offices downtown. I thought of her one night while
> leaving City Hall during my first term as Mayor. I told the
> scrubwomen cleaning the corridors to get up: "The only time a
> woman should go down on her knees is when she is praying to
> Almighty God," I said. Next morning I ordered long-handled
> mops and issued an order that scrubwomen were never again to
> get down on their knees in City Hall.[43]

He used this story countless times to win the hearts of his audience at political rallies. Decked out in a long fur coat topped by a derby hat, he re-
galed the crowds in a remarkable voice that was "smooth and rich and had
an extraordinary range. In a single sentence, he could shift from baritone
to tenor to countertenor." A reporter described his speech this way: "The
words roll off his tongue with a precision of diction, a clarity of expression, and an occasional vivid phrase which makes him a man well worth
hearing, even on casual subjects." He had worked hard to become such an
accomplished speaker, studying for eight years with a voice coach who
claimed that Curley was "his best pupil and the greatest American orator
since Daniel Webster." This was from the voice coach who later taught
public speaking to John F. Kennedy.[44]

James J. Connolly, who has written a perceptive study of Curley's
politics, described Curley as a representative of "ethnic progessivism" who
advocated "generous social welfare policies. He supported aggressive city
planning, built a hospital, playgrounds, bathhouses, and parks; and
sought greater streetcar service with lower fares."[45] Most of these endeav-
ors occurred in his second term as mayor (1922–26). He also endorsed
the restriction of child labor, pensions for mothers, and even women's
suffrage.

The key to his success was his ability to become a one-man political
machine. Unlike New York City, Boston had no citywide machine. The
local ward bosses such as Lomasney were the key power brokers. Curley
stripped them of their clout by making patronage—the foundation of
their power—"his exclusive domain, thereby cutting their political legs
out from under them." In addition, he successfully used the media and his
oratorical skills to create an image of himself as "the champion of

Boston's downtrodden," one who cared about the less fortunate. He appealed directly to the voters, continually reminding the Irish that Boston was an anti-immigrant, anti-Irish city. According to Curley, the Yankee elite had to be put in their place. The time of the Puritan had passed. It was now the time of the downtrodden Irish. This was not the Boston of Patrick Collins where Yankee and Irish worked together. It was a Boston that Curley had fashioned by "making cultural antagonism the defining feature of the city's public sphere." This depiction of Boston as a battleground between the Yankee Protestant elite and Irish Catholics became embedded in the minds of people in Boston and throughout much of New England for decades.[46]

Commenting on the lasting power of this stereotype, James J. Connolly wrote, "It is important to remember that this understanding was new and was largely the product of Curley's manipulation of Progressivism. It had not been the dominant conception even among ethnic Bostonians a dozen years earlier, when the eminently respectable and respectful Patrick Collins served as Mayor . . . Only when Curley turned Progressivism from an argument for Irish legitimacy into an indictment of Puritan Boston did the representation of Boston as a city defined by ethnic conflict fully take hold. The roots of modern Boston's ethnic polarization—and especially of blue-collar Irish Boston's clannish hostility—are not as deep as many believe; they rest mostly in the topsoil of the Progressive Era rather than in the deeper layers of the city's Anglo-Saxon past."[47] The flamboyant Curley has had more influence on Boston that he could ever have imagined.

Chicago was a third city where the Irish took control of the Democratic Party. Unlike Boston, Chicago was an ethnically diverse city. The Germans, not the Irish, were the largest ethnic group by the turn of the century, with sizable numbers of Polish and Italians. But the Irish ran the city. They first arrived with the building of the Illinois-Michigan Canal and never left. After the Great Famine they kept coming so that by 1900 Chicago had the third-largest Irish-born population in the country, even more than Boston. It was the Irish capital of the Midwest.

With a strong city council and a weak mayor, Chicago's government resembled Boston's rather than New York's. In 1900 at least twenty-three of sixty-eight of these council members were Irish. Since there was no citywide machine, political power was divided up among the local ward bosses. Dictators in their own wards, they became rivals in the city council, where the major political, and potentially lucrative, decisions would be made. Among the Irish, three ward bosses stood out: "Bath House" John Coughlin and Michael "Hinky Dink" Kenna in the First Ward, and Johnny Powers in the Nineteenth Ward. Their reign endured through the 1890s and early 1900s. They were colorful saloonkeeper-politicians whose names have become famous in Chicago's political history.

Bath House John was born in 1860, the son of Irish immigrants who had met and married in Chicago. Growing up in the city's First Ward, he spent his time at saloons and bathhouses. At the age of twenty-two he bought his first bathhouse. Soon he bought another one. Before long his patrons christened him with the nickname of Bath House John, a name that stuck with him for the rest of his life. In 1892, after building up a loyal following in the neighborhood, he was elected to the city council. He remained on the city council as the Democratic alderman from the First Ward until his death forty-six years later.

Michael Kenna was another Chicago-born Irishman, whose small stature gained him the distinctive nickname Hinky Dink. A successful saloonkeeper by age twenty-two, he teamed up with Coughlin after Bath House John was elected to the city council in 1892. Eventually he also served on the city council as an alderman from the First Ward. Together these two Irishmen ruled the First Ward for more than twenty years.

The First Ward was a diverse neighborhood in the heart of the city. It had department stores, mansions of the rich and famous, brothels, gambling houses, and numerous saloons. Its most notorious area was the Levee, near Clark and Taylor streets. This was the red-light district of gamblers, thieves, and prostitutes. The King of the Ward in the 1880s was the Irish-born Mike McDonald. A man of great wealth, acquired through his gambling houses and business enterprises, he controlled the election of mayors and congressmen through his political clout.

In the 1890s, Bath House John and Hinky Dink succeeded McDonald as the political power brokers in the First Ward. Christened the Lords of the Levee, they made sure that the lights never went out in the district. With the cooperation of the police they kept the brothels and gambling houses open. Through bribes from those who wanted to do business with the city, they acquired great wealth. Bath House had a second home in Colorado Springs as well as a stable of racehorses; Hinky Dink owned property in Arkansas in addition to a prosperous saloon in the First Ward. But the key to their power was their ability to deliver the votes of their district on election day for their chosen candidates. They would do this by any means possible, for in those days Chicago politics did not follow the

Marquis of Queensbury rules. Being strong allies of Mayor Carter Harrison II, who governed the city from 1897 to 1905, and again from 1911 to 1915, they would deliver the vote for Harrison and in return acquired control over the vice, gambling, and insurance interests in their district. The alliance enabled them to remain in power for a number of years.[48]

Bath House John was the more flamboyant of the two. His sartorial elegance was renowned. At one of the First Ward balls that he sponsored, he showed up in a green tail coat, a mauve vest, and lavender pants with a glowing cravat and pale pink gloves, shining yellow shoes, and on top of his head a silk hat "that sparkled like the plate-glass windows of Marshall Field's department store." He was the star of the dance that night. He would show up in the city council in equally splendid attire. Kenna was more modest and worked behind the scenes. He was the organizer, the troubleshooter, and the brains of the operation. The *Chicago Tribune* described him as "the absolute overlord of Chicago vice." He was also reputedly the "wisest of all Chicago ward politicians." The reformers continually tried to get rid of Kenna and Coughlin, but could never succeed.[49]

Johnny Powers, another Irish chieftain, ruled the Nineteenth Ward, on the city's South Side, as its elected alderman. This was the home of Irish and Italian immigrants. Powers was one of the most powerful politicians in Chicago. As chairman of the Finance Committee of the city council, he was personally responsible for giving away the city's money to whomever he chose. One reporter described him as "coolheaded, cunning and wholly unscrupulous."[50] Like Coughlin and Kenna, whose politics he often opposed while on the city council, he was popular in his district, where he was known as the Mourner, since he always appeared at wakes and funerals. On Christmas Day he would distribute as many as six tons of turkey and four or more tons of ducks and geese to the families in his district. He visited the sick and dying, provided jobs for those who were in need, and took care of his constituents. Jane Addams, the well-known settlement worker whose Hull House was in Powers's district, waged a concerted campaign to get rid of Powers, whom she described as a "corrupt alderman." But she failed. She acknowledged that he always got elected because "he is a good friend and neighbor." For her it was that simple. Powers, she wrote, "understands what the people want, and ministers just as truly to a great human need as the musician or the artist does." Powers and his fellow ward bosses, she went on to say, "stand by and for and with the people." That was why they were so popular.[51]

The Mourner, Hinky Dink, and Bath House represented one style of

Irish politician at the turn of the century—the saloonkeeper and neigh-borhood boss. New York had Big Tim Sullivan, and Martin Lomasney ruled in Boston's Ward Eight. But as the American-born Irish moved up the social ladder and out of the old immigrant neighborhoods, a new type of politician was replacing the old-style boss. In Chicago, Edward Dunne represented this new generation of politicians.

Dunne's parents were both Irish immigrants who settled in Peoria. After high school Edward studied at Trinity College in Dublin, Ireland. After his return to Illinois he studied law, eventually becoming a judge in Chicago. Known as the "people's judge" because of his support for the underdog, he was also a devout Catholic as well as a vigorous promoter of Irish nationalism. In 1905 he gained the Democratic nomination for mayor as an advocate of municipal reform. The centerpiece of his cam-paign was municipal ownership of the city's transit system. Dunne was never able to implement this radical proposal in Chicago, as municipal ownership challenged the prevailing arrangement of private ownership of the transit system. The majority of the public and the city's power brokers were too firmly committed to the system of private ownership to embrace Dunne's proposal. The source of Dunne's liberalism was his Irish Catholicism. In the opinion of historian John D. Buenker, being Irish gave him "an empathy with the disadvantaged and the oppressed. Equally important was his belief in Catholic social liberalism, a world view founded on a corporatist conception of society that stressed the interde-pendence of social classes, [and] the responsibility of the more fortunate for the less."[52] Such a social gospel reflected the urban progressivism that Irish politicians such as Al Smith in New York and James M. Curley in Boston were advocating.

Supported by such notables as Jane Addams and Clarence Darrow, as well as the powerful ward bosses, Dunne won the mayoralty, but his tenure was brief, only two years, 1905–7. Nonetheless, despite failing to gain municipal ownership of the transit system, he forced the companies to accept regulation as well as rate reductions. He also championed the rights of teachers and parents to have a role in shaping educational policy. His administration raised the salaries of teachers; enforced public health and building codes; and forced corporations to pay higher real estate taxes. In 1912 he was elected governor of Illinois, the first Irish Catholic to gain that honor. Once again his administration was noted for its pro-gressive record in the areas of labor and welfare. Defeated for reelection in 1916, he devoted himself to his family and the cause of Ireland's sovereignty. In 1919 he led an Irish American delegation on an unsuccessful mission to the Versailles Conference, where they lobbied for Irish independence.[53]

Another representative of the new breed of politician in Chicago was Roger C. Sullivan. Born in rural Illinois in 1860, he got involved in Chicago politics at an early age. In the early 1890s he formed an alliance with another Irishman, John Hopkins, who became the first Irish Catholic mayor of Chicago in 1893. This partnership would last a lifetime. Sullivan came from the West Side of Chicago, where the middle-class Irish lived, while Hopkins's roots were in Hyde Park on the South Side of Chicago. Unlike Dunne, they were not reformers. Contemporaries of Bath House and Hinky Dink, they represented the businessman-politician rather than the saloonkeeper-politician. But, they were just as corrupt as the Lords of the Levee, just not as unsavory. One of their biggest coups was persuading their cronies in the city council to pass laws granting franchises to electric and gas companies that they owned. They planned to sell them later at a sizable profit.[54] After his two-year term as mayor, Hopkins stepped out of the limelight, preferring to work in the shadow of Sullivan. As businessman-politicians, their goal was not to control the city's vice and gambling enterprises, but to take over politically related businesses such as construction, utilities, and transportation.[55] Sullivan was a citywide power broker, but he could never unite the rival Democratic factions into a single machine. Chicago was too much of a political jungle for such unity. Sullivan also focused his energies on state and national politics. From 1892 until his death in 1920 Sullivan was a delegate to the Democratic National Convention, controlling the votes of the Illinois delegation for many of these years. He ran for the U.S. Senate in 1914 but lost. He moved from the West Side to a more fashionable address on Lake Shore Drive and belonged to the best clubs in Chicago. When he died, the bishop of Chicago presided at his funeral in Holy Name Cathedral. A shrewd businessman as well as an enterprising politician, he left an estate of over 1.5 million dollars.

The Sullivan faction of the Democratic Party fought frequently with the Coughlin-Kenna bloc. To gain control of the party Sullivan had to get rid of Mayor Carter Harrison II. Harrison was a popular reform mayor who had served for five terms. As long as he had the support of Coughlin, Kenna, and other ward bosses, Harrison was unbeatable. He lost their support when he closed the brothels in the city's red-light district. This was too much for the Lords of the Levee, who controlled the business, which reportedly had an annual revenue of sixty million dollars. They abandoned Harrison and joined the Sullivan Democrats, who were now able to wrest control of the party from Harrison. The Irish, corrupt as they were, had finally gained control of the Democratic Party in 1915. Sullivan would remain the kingpin of the party until his death five years later. But his coup d'état in 1915 was a hollow victory. The Democrats lost the 1915 mayoral election to a rising star, William "Big Bill" Thompson, who would become one of the most colorful mayors in Chicago's history. The Democrats would have to wait until the 1930s, after the reign of Thompson, before they could regain political control of the city.

These sketches of three cities where the Irish achieved political prominence provide an understanding of the Irish political style and how they were able to succeed in the political arena. The Irish left their imprint on other cities as well. Philadelphia was an anomaly. An Irishman, James McManes, emerged as the acknowledged king of Philadelphia politics in the post–Civil War era, but he was an Ulster Presbyterian who was boss of the Republican Party, not the Democratic Party. Irish Catholics still gravitated to the Democratic Party, but the Republican machine kept them out of leadership positions in the city. In Worcester the Irish dominated the Democratic Party. The election of one of their own as mayor in 1900 marked the arrival of the Irish, who had been struggling for years to overcome Yankee prejudices. Providence, Rhode Island, had its first Irish Catholic mayor in 1895. Then in 1906 another Democrat, Patrick J. McCarthy from county Sligo, Ireland, became mayor, the first foreign-born Catholic to hold that office. In St. Paul, Minnesota, the Irish-dominated Democratic machine controlled city politics. In San Francisco the Irish achieved political prominence in the early years of that city's history. Frank McCoppin became the first Irish Catholic mayor of the city in 1867, long before William Grace was elected mayor of New York. The most renowned Irish politician was James D. Phelan. Son of an Irish immigrant who struck it rich in San Francisco, Phelan was not only one of the wealthiest men in the city, but also one of its major boosters. He served as mayor from 1897 to 1901. A Progressive Democrat, he promoted the public ownership of city utilities as well as new schools and parks. As one of California's leading Democrats, he was elected to the U.S. Senate in 1914.

The Irish took to politics with gusto. In the nineteenth century no other ethnic group could compare with them when it came to building urban political machines. Moreover, no other ethnic group could match their electoral participation. As Stephen Erie pointed out, "Irish naturalization, registration, and turnout rates regularly exceeded those of other groups, even the early arriving Germans."[56] For the Irish, politics was a road to success in the nineteenth century. Nor did their skill in deal making and power brokering disappear. It would continue throughout the twentieth century, culminating in the election of one of their own to the nation's highest office in 1960.

CHAPTER 7

Strike

On Monday, July 16, 1877, the workers on the Baltimore and Ohio Railroad heard that their wages were going to be reduced by 10 percent. This was too much. Along with the rest of the country they had suffered through hard times for three years as an economic depression crippled the nation. During this time they were forced to take wage cuts of 10 percent or more a year so that the railroad could squeeze out more profits. The railroad was the major industry in the country at this time, employing thousands of workers. Its strategy during the downturn was to slash wages to offset declining profits. But the workers, who worked from twelve to fifteen hours a day, would now get as little as $1.50 for a day's work. Who could support a family on such wages? So at Camden Junction, outside Baltimore, a number of workers walked off the job. In Martinsburg, West Virginia, workers also went on strike. In the next few days hundreds of others joined the protest all along the B and O railroad network, which stretched west to St. Louis. The strike, eventually involving thousands of workers, crippled the nation's railroad system. Though it lasted less than three weeks, over a hundred people were killed, scores more were injured, and as much as ten million dollars' worth of property was destroyed.[1]

Pittsburgh was the scene of one of the bloodiest battles. To keep the strike under control six hundred National Guard troops from Philadelphia were dispatched to Pittsburgh. As they marched to the railroad yards, they made an impressive sight with their blue-and-gray uniforms, their plumed hats, and brightly polished rifles. A large crowd of men, women, and children had gathered to support the striking workers and their leaders.

The crowds heckled the soldiers as they sought to clear the tracks. Then the soldiers were ordered to advance with fixed bayonets. Several people were stabbed. Seeing blood, the crowd arose in anger. Stones flew, striking a number of soldiers. The soldiers fired into the crowd, and in minutes twenty-six people were killed and many more badly wounded. Newspapers later described the massacre as the "slaughter of the innocents." That night a mob of some twenty thousand people turned its wrath on the Pennsylvania Railroad Company. Burning and looting went on all night and throughout the next day. By the time the rioting was over, twenty more strikers were killed, as well as several soldiers. The railroad yards were littered with as many as thirteen hundred burned-out freight cars, engines, and passenger cars. Virtually all the buildings of the railroad company were smoking ruins.[2]

The strike of 1877 awakened the nation to the discontent of the working class. As the *New York Times* said, "Whatever else the disturbances have done, at least they have opened the eyes of the American people to the order of things which has grown up among them so gradually as to be unobserved . . . Beneath the vicious elements which produced the riots, the country traces evidence of hardship, of suffering, of destitution to an extent for which it was unprepared." The strike also energized the labor movement. Labor now knew its strength, but "nothing could be accomplished by the working people without a system of perfect national organization," as one labor newspaper put it. The labor leader Samuel Gompers later remarked that "the railroad strike of 1877 was the tocsin that sounded a ringing message of hope to us all."[3]

In subsequent years the nation witnessed an unprecedented level of labor violence with as many as 36,757 strikes between 1881 and 1905, involving over six million workers. Miners, carpenters, longshoremen, steelworkers, and scores of other working people joined together in unions with the goal of changing conditions in the workplace. As one union banner proclaimed in a parade in 1880, "Each for himself is the bosses' plea, Union for all will make you free."[4] In the forefront of this labor movement were the Irish.

Most people acknowledge the influence the Irish have had on politics and the Catholic Church. But few, I suspect, realize the impact the Irish had on the American labor movement. Yet, to write its history without including the Irish would be to tell only part of the story. By the 1850s and '60s Irish workers had already gained leadership positions in two major labor organizations in New York City, the Longshoremen's and Laborers

United Benevolent Society and the Tailor's Trade Association. In Fall River, Massachusetts, they took over the textile workers' union, and in 1868, the Irish-born John Siney founded the Workingmen's Benevolent Association in Pennsylvania, an organization that mobilized over thirty thousand mine workers within a year. From the 1870s to 1890s, when the modern labor movement was taking shape, the Irish prominence was so dominant that "by the 1880s the majority of American labor unions would be headed by Catholics of Irish descent." During the first decade of the twentieth century, when the American Federation of Labor had become the dominant labor organization, the Irish occupied the presidencies of more than 50 of the 110 unions in the AFL. A biographical dictionary of American labor leaders offers another indication of the widespread presence of the Irish. More than one quarter of the 503 leaders profiled from the late 1830s to the 1970s were Irish, with a similar percentage being Roman Catholic. No other ethnic group or religious denomination came close to challenging such dominance.[5]

Several reasons help to explain why the Irish were so prominent in the labor movement. The Irish were predominantly working-class—ditchdiggers, coal miners, hod carriers, longshoremen, domestic servants, and teamsters—whose presence was critical to the success of an emerging industrial nation. Stuck in low-paying jobs and working from sunup to sundown, they stood to benefit most from organized labor's efforts to gain some measure of justice in a capitalist system that was exploiting working-class wage earners. Irish immigrants had experienced oppression and poverty in the old country and hoped for a better life in America. Yet, economic depression in the 1870s, low wages, and, worse, unemployment drew them to a social movement that promised justice for the working class in the form of better wages and more humane working conditions.

Another key reason for the Irish's prominence in the labor movement was timing. The Irish arrived just when the modern labor movement was taking shape and were in position to gain leadership roles. As in politics, that they spoke English gave them an advantage over other immigrants seeking to join the leadership ranks of labor. Later, when new immigrants arrived from Eastern and Southern Europe, the Irish would serve as brokers for these newcomers who spoke little or no English by helping them find work. Also, more than a few Irish labor leaders were gifted orators, a skill deeply rooted in Irish tradition.

Irish nationalism and the urge for social justice in America reinforced each other. In Ireland a crusade for land reform was under way. In the

1870s and '80s, "the land of Ireland for the people of Ireland" was the battle cry of this crusade. Large numbers of Irish workers in the United States not only supported this cause, but they linked it with labor's crusade for social reform. As the journalist and social reformer Patrick Ford put it, "The cause of the poor in Donegal is the cause of the factory slave in Fall River."[6] This nationalist impulse would inject a spirit of radicalism into the nation's labor movement.

Finally, the Catholic clergy's support of the labor movement was important. At first the clergy were suspicious of, indeed downright hostile to, labor organizations, fearing that they were secret societies, antagonistic to religion. But by the late 1880s this attitude began to change as Church leaders, the pope included, endorsed the right of workers to organize to seek justice in the workplace. The Church's endorsement made the appeal of the labor union especially powerful to Irish Catholics who were closely attached to their Church.

The first major labor union in the post–Civil War era was the Knights of Labor, founded in 1869. Its goal was to "to abolish wage slavery and emancipate the wage earner." To achieve this it gathered all types of workers regardless of race, religion, nationality, or sex into an organization whose guiding principle was solidarity. Those who joined also believed in the Knights' dream of a reformed society, "a working man's democracy" where there would be no conflict between workers and employers.[7]

Founded in Philadelphia by Uriah Stephens as a secret society, the Knights of Labor grew slowly at first, limited to the Pennsylvania, Mid-Atlantic region. After the national strike of 1877, membership soared as the Knights spread to the nation's major cities. By the summer of 1885 it had thousands of supporters across the country. They had "accomplished something no one else before had been able to do in American history," wrote historian Melvyn Dubofsky, "they built a genuine labor federation from the ground up." Then in 1885 they won a labor victory over Jay Gould's Southwestern rail system—one of the largest rail systems in the country. One of Gould's rail lines, the Wabash, had begun to lay off shopmen who belonged to the Knights of Labor in an effort to break the union. When the Wabash refused to halt the layoffs, the Knights still working on the Wabash went on strike. This strike spread throughout Gould's entire Southwestern system. With his entire railroad system under attack, Gould, a Wall Street tycoon, came to terms with the Knights of Labor's leadership, agreeing to end all discrimination against Knights of Labor members working on his rail lines. The *St. Louis Chronicle* proclaimed, "No such victory has ever before been secured in this or any other country."[8] News of this victory flashed across the country, and within a year the membership of the Knights skyrocketed to over seven hundred thousand. This was unprecedented.

Their success, however, was short-lived. They lost a second strike to Gould's railroad in the spring of 1886 when he refused their demand for higher pay. Then, on May 1, 1886, thousands of Knights went on a nationwide strike for an eight-hour day that was unsuccessful. Two days later in Chicago, police stormed an area near the McCormick Harvester plant to break up a fight between striking unionists and strikebreakers. During the melee, the police shot and killed four men, wounding several others. The next evening workers rallied at Haymarket Square to protest police brutality. Anarchists had fanned the flames of anger by circulating leaflets throughout the city urging workers to even the score for the deaths of their comrades. In spite of inflammatory speeches by anarchist leaders, the rally was peaceful. But just as the meeting was breaking up, a detachment of two hundred policemen arrived with orders to disperse the remaining crowd. Someone threw a bomb into the ranks of the police, killing one of them instantly. They opened fire on the workers, who answered with shots of their own. At the end seven police and four workers were dead and close to one hundred injured. Blaming the anarchists for the deaths and the injuries, the police combed the city rounding up anarchist leaders, eight of whom they charged with murder. In an atmosphere inflamed by fear and revenge, they were convicted, in spite of little evidence of their guilt. Four were executed, one committed suicide in jail, and the other three were later pardoned by Governor John Peter Altgeld.

The head of the Knights, Terence V. Powderly, condemned the Haymarket bombers as anarchists. He also failed to support the strike on behalf of the eight-hour day. This turned many workers against the union. Such internal dissension weakened the Knights, and within a few years they went into a decline from which they never recovered.

At the height of their popularity in the mid-1880s at least one half of the Knights were Irish, most of the officers in the organization were also Irish, and the man who led them during their triumphant period, Terence V. Powderly, was the son of Irish immigrants.

Powderly was born in Pennsylvania coal country in 1849, the eleventh of twelve children born to Terence and Madge Powderly. His parents, who had emigrated from county Meath, Ireland, in 1827, had settled in the small mining community of Carbondale after a brief time in Ogdensburg, New York. At a young age Powderly began his working career as a machinist. But before long he was out of work as the economy deteriorated. By 1872 he had become active in the machinists' union in Scranton. A year later he was elected president of the local. His union activities got him blacklisted just as the nation was entering a prolonged period of economic depression. Unable to find work, for two years he wandered poor and depressed about the region. He described this period as "my tramp life."[9] This experience made him even more aware of the hardships of the working class.

Abandoning his career as a machinist, Powderly became a labor organizer in Scranton, where in 1877 the Greenback-Labor Party, capitalizing on labor unrest, had won control of the city council. By this time Powderly was well-known in labor circles across the country, having attended national conventions of the machinists' union as well as being a district officer of the Knights of Labor. A strong supporter of Irish nationalism, he had also become active in Irish fraternal organizations. With a strong following in the Irish community and good labor credentials, he became the Greenback-Labor Party's mayoral candidate in Scranton in 1878.[10] He won the election with more than 55 percent of the vote and remained mayor for six years, winning reelection in 1880 and 1882. In this brief time Powderly had transformed himself from a blacklisted, unemployed "tramp" to mayor. His rapid rise to prominence continued when in 1879 he was elected as the grand master workman of the Knights of Labor, replacing the founder, Uriah Stephens. He remained head of the organization until 1893, when a power struggle within the organization forced him to resign. After a brief period as a lawyer, he went to work for the federal government as the commissioner general of immigration. He still kept in touch with the concerns of the labor movement, most especially through his friendship with the legendary Mother Jones, who gained fame as a union organizer for the mine workers. She often stayed at his house when she was not on the road supporting the coal miners. In 1999, seventy-five years after his death, he was inducted into the Department of Labor hall of fame.

As head of the Knights, Powderly was the voice of labor throughout the country. One historian portrayed him as "the first American working-class hero of national stature." Described as a "superlative orator," he was "one of the most charismatic men of his day." In Kansas City, one listener wrote, "For two hours we sat in serene felicity. It was one of those soul-elevating, Pentecostal efforts that men are only privileged to hear once or twice in a lifetime." Another historian claimed, "He was the first labor leader in American history to become a media superstar . . . To his contemporaries Powderly was the Knights of Labor, and the Knights of Labor were a symbol of the central dilemma of a new industrial age: 'the labor question.' " As one Indiana worker put it, he was " 'our Moses,' the man chosen . . . to lead us through this 'Valley of the Shadow' of cursed rock-ridden monopoly and wage slavery."[11]

Powderly, a teetotaler throughout his life, was a tireless advocate of temperance. This was not uncommon among the Irish working class. The Church strongly advocated this by encouraging people to take the pledge at parish missions and organizing local temperance societies. Powderly belonged to one such temperance organization, and in his speeches he frequently endorsed temperance. The Knights even had a temperance oath called the Powderly Pledge.[12] A particular target for Powderly and other leaders in the Knights was the saloon. In one of his talks, he said:

> Workingmen, shun strong drink as you would a scorpion. It debases, it weakens, it ruins you . . . The saloonkeeper may be your personal friend, even your relative, but he is your worst foe if you patronize him . . . I shall never stand on a platform while I hold office in a labor organization without warning my hearers against strong drink, without asking them to shun the saloon, and so far as my influence will go no man who sells liquor shall ever darken the door of a local assembly of this Order.[13]

This commitment to temperance and opposition to the saloon on the part of Powderly as well as other leaders in the Knights was an integral part of the organization's effort to promote individual and social reform by endorsing values that cut across boundaries of class, religion, and ethnicity.

Powderly was also a strong advocate of women in the labor movement, believing in equal rights for both sexes. When he first became grand master, women were not admitted into the Knights. But within two years he persuaded his colleagues that women should be admitted. As a result, in 1881 the first women Knights were organized in Philadelphia as an all-female local of shoemakers. Within the next few years as many as sixty-five thousand women joined the Knights, organizing their own local assemblies or joining the men's assemblies.[14] Two Irish-born women who rose to prominent positions in the Knights were Leonora Barry and Elizabeth Rodgers.

Barry was the Knights' leading female organizer. A widow with three children, she worked in a knitting mill in Amsterdam, New York, earning only eleven cents a day. With the hope of remedying her miserable situation, she joined the Knights in 1883, and within three years she was named the general investigator of women's work. Her charge was "to investigate the abuses which women were subjected to by unscrupulous employers as well as to agitate the principles which our Order teaches, of equal pay for equal work and the abolition of child labor." She traveled the country lecturing and organizing new assemblies. A gifted speaker, she delivered more than five hundred lectures on behalf of the Knights. In addition to speaking on labor issues, she also promoted temperance and women's suffrage. In 1890 the widow Barry remarried, left the Knights, and moved to St. Louis, where she continued to work on behalf of women's suffrage and temperance. A dramatic and entertaining speaker who never used a prepared text, she won a wide following on the lecture circuit, speaking under the name of Mrs. Barry-Lake or sometimes Mother Lake.[15]

Elizabeth Rodgers was not as eloquent as Barry, but she was equally tough. She married George Rodgers, an ironworker and union activist. They had twelve children, nine of whom lived to adulthood. After moving to Chicago in 1876 she became involved in the labor movement, organizing workingwomen into a citywide union. Like Powderly she was an Irish nationalist, serving as president of a Land League chapter. It did not take long for her to join the Knights, and reportedly she was the first Chicago woman to do so. Because her work on behalf of the organization was so admired, in 1886 she took over as the head of the Knights in Chicago, overseeing a membership of fifty thousand workers. She was the first woman to hold such a position. An aggressive unionist, Rodgers said she had "a great deal of experience in strikes."[16] Despite Powderly's disapproval she endorsed the nationwide strike in 1886 on behalf of an eight-hour working day. She was also a supporter of the anarchists who were arrested for the bomb explosion in Haymarket Square in May 1886, much to Powderly's chagrin. The Chicago branch of the Knights began to decline after they lost a strike at the stockyards later that same year. About three years later Rodgers left the Knights. Though her career as a labor organizer was over, she directed her energies to the Catholic Order of Foresters, a fraternal organization and insurance society, establishing a women's branch and eventually serving as the head of this organization that paid death and insurance benefits to its female members. In 1908 her public career came to an end after thirty years.[17]

The commitment of so many Irish men and women to the labor movement posed a serious problem for the Catholic clergy, who were hostile to secret organizations, fearing that they might be anti-Catholic or, worse, antireligion. This was especially true of the Knights since it was not only a secret organization, but its initiation ritual had a quasi-religious character that used Christian phraseology in invoking individual moral responsibility and human brotherhood. Such features made it anathema to most Catholic clergy. Some priests denied the sacraments to people who belonged to the Knights; others went so far as to deny them burial. Such strong opposition slowed the growth of the Knights among Catholics, leading one worker to declare, "The greatest curse to our order seems to me to be the priests." Given the influence of the priest among the people, all it took was a word of condemnation from the pulpit and the local chapter of the Knights would be sure to collapse.[18] Powderly sought to defuse such opposition by having religious references and the secret oath removed from the order's initiation ritual in 1881. Nonetheless, secrecy remained a feature of the union, and so clerical opposition stood firm.

In 1884, at the request of the archbishop of Quebec, the Vatican issued a ruling that forbade Catholics to belong to the Knights of Labor. Most American clergy interpreted this as applying only to Canada, but Quebec's archbishop wanted Rome to make this condemnation universal. At this juncture, Cardinal Gibbons of Baltimore, persuaded by Powderly that nothing in the Knights' constitution was hostile to the Church, intervened at the Vatican in 1887 on behalf of the Knights. He defended the rights of workers to organize and urged that the Knights of Labor not be condemned. Gibbons's statement marked a major turning point in the Church's position on labor and social reform. The Vatican finally rendered a decision a year and a half later, lifting the ban on the Knights. It was too late to save the Knights, who were already in a downward spiral. What did matter was that Gibbons's intervention officially put the Catholic Church on the side of labor. This was a dramatic turnabout. A few years later, in 1891, Pope Leo XIII issued the encyclical *Rerum Novarum*, which reinforced the Church's official support for the labor movement. While condemning socialism in no uncertain terms, the pope also spoke out against the excesses of capitalism and individualism. He upheld the right to private property, the right of workers to organize, and the need of the state to protect the rights of people.

The Church's support for labor was also manifest in the emergence of the labor-priest tradition. While most priests were caught up with the daily challenges of parish life, a number of Irish priests did become active in the labor movement. Among them was Peter C. Yorke of San Francisco. He rallied support for the dockworkers who went on strike in 1901. He continued to champion the cause of the workers in later strikes and founded a labor newspaper, the *Leader*. At his death he was eulogized as the "Father of the organized labor movement in San Francisco." John J. Curran of Wilkes-Barre, Pennsylvania, was known as the miners' friend and worked closely with John Mitchell, head of the United Mine Workers of America. During the coal strike of 1902 practically all the priests in the Pennsylvania mining region were solidly behind the strike. A number of them had worked in the mines themselves and personally understood the grievances of the workers. Thomas H. Malone of Denver was another priest with a social conscience. Through his newspaper, the *Colorado Catholic*, he promoted his views. "He believed that the complete unionization of the working class was necessary . . . 'to protect the laboring man from the greed and heartless aggressiveness of capital.'"[19]

One reason the clergy had been so suspicious of the Knights in its early years was the fear that it was somehow linked to the Molly Maguires, a secret Irish workingmen's society notorious for its violent tactics. The Molly Maguires terrorized the coal mining region of Schuylkill County in eastern Pennsylvania in the 1860s and '70s.

Their name came from rural Ireland, where in the nineteenth century secret societies with names such as the Molly Maguires, Ribbonmen, and Whiteboys used violent tactics to attack the landlord system. Irish miners, resentful of the unfair labor practices of the mine owners, transplanted this tradition of violent protest to Pennsylvania's coal mining country. The Molly Maguires' first wave of violence, which included six assassinations, took place in the 1860s, during and after the Civil War. This was a time of labor organizing among the miners as well as resistance to the military draft, both of which the mine owners considered treasonous. The violence subsided with the emergence of a powerful union, the Workingmen's Benevolent Association, that championed the cause of the miners. But the long strike in 1875 that lasted from January to June doomed the union. With its collapse, the Molly Maguires surfaced once again as a number of Irish workers turned to violence as the only remedy to gain justice in the mines. Six assassinations took place in the summer of 1875. The arrests of more than fifty men followed. Accused of a string of at least sixteen assassinations that took place in the 1860s and '70s, they were brought to trial based on evidence, much of it fabricated, provided by an undercover Pinkerton detective.

The chief prosecutor was the main enemy of the union, Franklin B. Gowen, president of the Philadelphia and Reading Railroad, which effectively controlled the mining economy in the region. No Irish Catholics were allowed to sit on the jury. The trials, which historian Kevin Kenny concluded "bordered on a travesty of justice," took place over two years. At the end, twenty Molly Maguires were sent to prison and twenty were executed, ten of them hanged on a single day—June 21, 1877, a day known as Black Thursday to the people of the region.[20] Like some other outlaw organizations, the Molly Maguires gave rise to a legend that was embellished and romanticized in later decades and enshrined in a 1970 Hollywood film.

Like the wandering canal diggers, Irish miners traveled to wherever there were jobs. Many left Pennsylvania and headed to Leadville, Virginia City, or Coeur d'Alene, western mining towns where the dream of striking it rich provided powerful motivation. A few Irishmen did strike it rich. The Irish-born John Mackay lived this dream, becoming a millionaire overnight when he and his partners struck gold in Virginia City's famous Comstock Lode in March of 1873. Together they amassed incredible wealth.

In the West's mining towns the Irish were so active in the growth of local unions that they eventually became identified with the labor movement throughout the West. A more radical phase of the American labor movement also emerged here.

The most Irish town in America was Butte, Montana. A mining outpost in the 1860s and '70s, it attracted several hundred Irish miners. Among them was the Irish-born Marcus Daly, who arrived in 1876. Within a few years he purchased the Anaconda Silver Mine. When he converted the mine from silver to copper, he launched the Anaconda Copper Mining Company, eventually amassing a legendary fortune for himself and his family. Born into a peasant family in Ireland, the life of this "stocky, ruddy, blue-eyed Irishman who chewed tobacco" resembled the celebrated Horatio Alger rags-to-riches story.[21]

During the 1880s and '90s Irish miners flocked to Butte, attracted by the good pay, steady work, and the worker-friendly policies of their countryman Marcus Daly. By the turn of the century Butte was no longer a frontier town but a thriving city. The county's population was over forty-seven thousand. A copper capital at that time, its three banks had deposits in excess of three million dollars. "Its wealthier classes lived in elegant homes and worked in handsome business residences; its miners and mill-men received over $500,000 monthly in wages and over 100 smoke-stacks poured out their residue night and day." One of four residents in Butte was Irish Catholic. They worshipped at five parishes, with St. Patrick's alone claiming a membership of ten thousand. No Protestant church had more than eight hundred members. David Emmons, author of a history of the Butte Irish, stated, "It would be difficult to overstate the importance of the churches to the Irish community. Indeed, for some they were the Irish community. They baptized the babies, educated the children, . . . married the young adults, comforted the sick, buried the dead. In the process they provided a continuity, a sense of group solidarity that no other organization, fraternal, political, or labor, could match."[22] In politics the Irish were also the dominant force. As loyal to the Democratic Party as they were to the Church, they ran the city. Between 1893 and 1919 Butte had eight Irish mayors. So pervasive was their influence that in 1905 the Irish held twelve of the sixteen aldermanic posts on the city council and most of the important jobs in the city as well. This pattern persisted through the end of World War I.

Butte was a union town with thirty-six different unions at the turn of the century "representing everyone from barbers and musicians to cigar makers, bricklayers, cooks and waiters, and brewers." But it was the Butte Miners Union (BMU) that gave the city its reputation as the "Gibraltar of Unionism" in the western mining region. The Irish ran the BMU, the largest union in the West with six thousand members by 1900. They determined its policies and the rank and file followed along with little unrest or dissension. What was unique about the BMU was its conservatism. Founded in 1878, it thrived until 1914, when a rival union emerged to replace it. For these thirty-six years the union "participated in no . . . work stoppages, job actions, or worker protests." This was unheard of in the western mining region, where strikes, frequently violent, were commonplace. The principal reason for the union's conservatism was the Irish control of the workforce. By cooperating with Marcus Daly and other officials in the Anaconda Mining Company, "Irish workers became active partners in a collaborative effort to maintain" Butte's Irish enclave. They were not transient, itinerant workers, but men who had settled down, owned a home, had a family, and enjoyed the steady work that the Anaconda Mining Company provided. Though working-class, they were not radicals who wanted to challenge the capitalist structure that kept the mines open and the copper flowing.[23]

The Western Federation of Miners (WFM) was the most important radical miners' union that emerged in these years. The federation grew out of the BMU, which many believed was under the complete control of Marcus Daly. Disillusioned with the conservatism of the BMU, union activists organized the first local of the WFM in Butte in 1893. Its goal was to unite all the miners' unions in the West. Most of the first officers of the federation were Irish, and its president from 1896 to 1902 was Edward Boyce. Born in county Donegal in Ireland, Boyce emigrated to the United States at age twenty. He made his way West, where he worked in the mines in Colorado and Nevada. Involved in several strikes, he spent time in jail for his role in the violent strike at Coeur d'Alene in 1892. Radicalized by this experience, he traveled to Butte, where, together with a host of delegates from other unions throughout the West, he helped to form the WFM. Butte was its first home and the main source of financial support. In 1896 he became the president of the federation, giving it the aggressive leadership it needed. Under his direction it grew to more than two hundred locals within the next five years, becoming the most powerful labor union in the West. Then, in an ironic twist of good fortune, the rebel miner married the daughter of a millionaire Idaho mine owner, an alliance that forced him to leave the federation.[24] Now he gave his money, not his time, to the labor movement.

During Boyce's presidency the federation took a decisive turn to the left. Dissatisfied with the increasing power of mine owners, who had the armed support of the government to put down striking workers, the federation moved left toward socialism and radical unionism. No longer concerned only about wages and jobs, the federation advocated revolutionary change by endorsing socialism as the best alternative to the political status quo.[25] The radicalism of the federation eventually served as a catalyst for the organization of the Industrial Workers of the World (IWW), clearly the most radical labor union in the nation in the early twentieth century. Like the federation, the IWW, in its manifesto, endorsed class struggle between "the working class and the employing class, . . . a struggle that must go on until the workers of the world organize as a class, take possession of the earth and the machinery of production, and abolish the wage system."[26] Present at the organizing meeting of the IWW in 1905 was the

Irish-born Mary Jones, better known as Mother Jones. As well as anyone, she personified the radical spirit within the Irish working class.

She was born Mary Harris in Cork, Ireland, in 1837. The Great Hunger of the 1840s drove her father and one of her brothers to North America. The rest of the family later joined them in Toronto, where their father, described as an illiterate Irish laborer, worked on the railroad. After her schooling she became a teacher and later a seamstress. In Memphis she met and married George Jones, an iron molder, with whom she had four children. Tragedy struck Memphis in 1867 when yellow fever attacked the city. Her husband and all her children caught the fever and died. The young widow moved to Chicago to make a living as a seamstress, but tragedy struck once again as the great Chicago fire of 1871 wiped out her seamstress shop. Thirty-four years old, she now began a new chapter in her life as a labor activist.

In the late nineteenth century Chicago was a hotbed of labor radicalism. This is where Mary Jones, a struggling seamstress, was transformed into Mother Jones, the radical labor organizer. A member of the Knights of Labor, she participated in a number of strikes across the country. The doctrine of socialism was emerging at this time, and Jones embraced it as the cure for the nation's economic ills. She became a supporter of Eugene Debs, the icon of the Socialist Party, who was the party's candidate for president five times. She also supported the IWW in its efforts to change the nation's capitalist system. But she gained her fame as a union organizer and platform speaker.

In the late 1890s she adopted the moniker Mother Jones. For the next thirty years and more she would always be known as Mother Jones. This is how she signed her correspondence and how other labor leaders addressed her. The workers also called her Mother, and she referred to them as her boys. "The image she cultivated," wrote historian Elliott Gorn, "did not represent motherhood victimized and docile, however, but motherhood aroused. In speeches and articles, she elaborated her image as a woman who faced down old-age and gun-toting thugs for the family of labor . . . A fiercely proletarian political radical, Mother Jones imposed her presence on the national consciousness."[27]

Mother Jones worked as an organizer for the United Mine Workers. A small woman with striking blue eyes and white hair, Jones dressed like a Victorian housewife in a black dress, "with its fussy touches, and her bonnet of black lace, with its violets and lavender ribbon." Beneath this demure presence, however, was a self-described hell-raiser known for her fiery speeches and colorful language. Once when she found some workers meeting inside a church, she ordered them outside, where she told them, "Your organization is not a praying institution. It's a fighting institution . . . Pray for the dead, but fight like hell for the living." Described by historian Gorn as "the Johnny Appleseed of American activists," this aging widow traveled through the foothills of Pennsylvania, the mining towns of Colorado and West Virginia, to support striking miners. In 1912 at the age of seventy-five, she was in Butte, Montana, speaking to the copper miners when she heard the news of a coal miners' strike in West Virginia. She canceled her speaking dates, "tied up all my possessions in a black shawl—I like traveling light," as she put it in her autobiography, "and went immediately to West Virginia."[28] There she rallied the striking miners in her typical fierce style. One labor activist described what she was like on the podium:

> She might have been any coal miner's wife ablaze with righteous fury when her brood was in danger. Her voice shrilled as she shook her fist at the coal operators, the mine guards, the union officials . . . She prayed and cursed and pleaded, raising her clenched and trembling hands, asking heaven to bear witness . . . The miners loved it and laughed, cheered, hooted, and even cried as she spoke to them.

Another miner wrote, "The miners loved, worshipped, and adored her. And well they might, because there was no night too dark, no danger too great for her to face, if in her judgment 'her boys' needed her." She was arrested and put in jail, where she boldly proclaimed, "I can raise just as much hell in jail as anywhere."[29] After more than a year, one of the longest and bloodiest strikes in American labor history came to an end. After three months in jail, Jones was released, free to carry her crusade to Colorado, where she rallied support for the miners during a violent strike against John D. Rockefeller's mining company. By 1913, at age seventy-six, she had become one of the most famous women in America. She continued her crusade into her tenth decade. She died in 1930 at age ninety-three, the end of an amazing life that helped to change modern America.

As an organizer for the UMW, Mother Jones had worked closely with John Mitchell, who had become president of the UMW in 1898. During his tenure the UMW was one of the most progressive unions in the country.

Like Mitchell, many of its officers were Irish, and this appeared to be one reason why Mother Jones felt comfortable with the union. But, unlike Jones, who represented the more radical wing of the UMW, most of the union's leaders were conservative, preferring to negotiate rather than strike. As part of the AFL, they were trade unionists who focused on key issues of wages and the right to collective bargaining. As John Mitchell put it, "I am a strict trade-unionist. I believe in progress slowly—by evolution rather than revolution. I believe a better day is in store for the American workingman, but it has to come through no radical change in the organization of human society. It must come one step at a time, and through a slow upward movement, by his own efforts."[30] Under Mitchell's leadership the UMW prospered, reaching a membership of three hundred thousand by the early twentieth century.

Irishmen were also presidents of many other unions affiliated with the American Federation of Labor. One of the more well-known was Peter J. McGuire. Born in New York City to immigrant parents, he grew up in the tenements of the city's Lower East Side. A labor organizer with strong socialist beliefs, he traveled widely throughout the East and Midwest. Then in 1881 the key event in his life occurred in Chicago, where he helped to establish a national organization of carpenters. By the time the meeting was over he had been elected general secretary of the union, known as the United Brotherhood of Carpenters and Joiners of America. In the next twenty years McGuire would emerge as one of the great labor leaders in the nation. When the American Federation of Labor was organized in 1886, McGuire, along with Samuel Gompers, was one of the key founders of this organization. He was elected secretary of the AFL.[31] McGuire was also the prime mover to have a national Labor Day holiday, which Congress finally proclaimed in 1894 as the first Monday in September. Suffering from ill health brought on by his alcoholism, a new breed of unionists challenged his leadership in the carpenters' union. Finally, in 1902 he resigned from office and spent the last four years of his life in poverty, neglected and forgotten by his colleagues in the labor movement. Born in poverty, he died in poverty at age fifty-three, a sad ending to a remarkable life.

The dark side of the Irish presence in the labor movement was their prejudice against minority groups such as the Chinese and African Americans. The antagonism toward African Americans was most visible during the New York draft riots in 1863. In subsequent years, as the Irish gained leadership positions in the labor movement, they kept African American workers out of many unions. Their anti-Asian prejudice was most evident in San Francisco, where the Irish immigrant Denis Kearney led the charge for the exclusion of Chinese immigrants. The Irish and Chinese had been competing for jobs since the days of the Gold Rush. Such competition sowed the seeds of intense antagonism between the two groups. This reached a fever pitch in the 1870s and '80s when a campaign to curtail Chinese immigration took hold under the charismatic leadership of Kearney. A fiery speaker, he helped to form the Workingmen's Party, serving as its president for a time. His slogan, repeated at the end of every talk, was "And whatever happens, the Chinese must go."[32] For a brief time the party gained wide support from the laboring class, endorsing some harsh anti-Chinese measures such as denying them the right to vote. Kearney's star fell as rapidly as it soared. Nonetheless, his anti-Chinese campaign, supported by the Irish working class, was a catalyst in the passage of the Exclusion Act by Congress in 1882, prohibiting the immigration of Chinese laborers to the United States. Other Irish politicians and labor leaders in California lobbied to exclude Asians, including James D. Phelan, mayor of San Francisco and U.S. senator. They used the same harsh rhetoric against the Chinese that nativists had used against the Irish not long before.

The Irish moved up the occupational ladder at the expense of other minority groups who were also struggling to gain a foothold in the American economic system. Being white was a key advantage over African Americans and Chinese, and speaking English and being well-adjusted in their new home gave the Irish a decided edge over the new immigrants from Southern and Eastern Europe. Add to this their prominent presence in the labor movement and the Irish had a formula for success.

No one prototype personified the Irish labor leader. Most were men, but there were numerous women. Most were raised Catholic, and, influenced by their Church's vigorous opposition to socialism, they endorsed the more conservative model of the AFL in deciding what was best for the American worker. The sizable presence of the Irish among the leaders as well as the rank and file of the AFL enabled this union to adhere to its conservative approach in meeting the challenges confronting labor in an age of big business. A liberal strain of a Catholic social gospel was also present in the Irish community, so much so that by the turn of the century a number of Catholics were demanding not just charity, but social justice as the key to solving the nation's economic problems. This was most visible among labor priests such as Edward McGlynn of New York,

Thomas Malone of Denver, and Peter Yorke of San Francisco, who championed the right of workers to organize and seek better wages and working conditions. Such a concern reinforced labor's efforts to achieve justice for the worker. Alongside the conservative tendencies of most Irish workers and labor leaders was a deep vein of radicalism, rooted in the history of resistance to English oppression. From Mother Jones to the Molly Maguires, some of the most radical figures in American labor were Irish. From left to right, radical to conservative, the Irish were everywhere, leaving a distinctive imprint on the labor movement.

CHAPTER 8

Nation Among Nations

Easter Monday was a public holiday in Dublin. On a beautiful sunny day, thousands of Dubliners left the city to spend the holiday in the country, many going to the Fairyhouse horse races. At around midday a contingent of about 150 men and boys, some in military uniform, others in civilian clothes, carrying an assortment of rifles, pistols, and shotguns, marched down Sackville Street, Dublin's main avenue. People strolling the street watched in curious wonder. Then, as the marchers approached the General Post Office, Patrick Pearse, the poet leader of the group, shouted, "Charge!" Without firing a shot, they took over the building, which they used as their headquarters for the next six days. Other rebels, numbering about fifteen hundred, occupied St. Stephen's Green and several other key locations throughout Dublin. April 24 marked the beginning of the 1916 Easter Rising.

Shortly after seizing the General Post Office, Patrick Pearse stood in front of the building and read a proclamation:

> Irishmen and Irishwomen: In the name of God and the dead generations from which she receives her old tradition of nationhood, Ireland, through us, summons her children to her flag and strikes for freedom.
>
> Having organized and trained her manhood through her secret revolutionary organization, the Irish Republican Brotherhood, . . . having resolutely waited for the right moment to reveal herself, she now seizes that moment, and *supported by her*

exiled children in America [italics mine] . . . she strikes in full confidence of victory.

. . . We declare the right of the people of Ireland to the ownership of Ireland, and to the unfettered control of Irish destinies, to be sovereign and indefeasible.

We hereby proclaim the Irish Republic as a Sovereign Independent State and we pledge our lives and the lives of our comrades-in-arms to the cause of its freedom, of its welfare, and its exaltation among the nations.

Then they hoisted the tricolor flag of the Republic over the building, where it remained for the next six days.

The fighting was centered in Dublin, where for six days a force of about sixteen hundred fighters, now known as the Irish Republican Army, took over several buildings in the city. When British troops assaulted the rebels, they battled each other as fire ravaged the city, destroying over one hundred buildings. Finally, on Saturday, April 29, the rebels surrendered. As many as five hundred people had died and more than twenty-five hundred were wounded.

The rebellion was doomed to fail given the might of the British army, which far outnumbered the Irish band of rebels. Nonetheless, the rebels, later christened patriots, were prepared to die. As one of their leaders, Sean MacDiarmada, wrote from his jail cell the night before his execution, "We die that the Irish nation may live. Our blood will rebaptise and reinvigorate the land."[1] MacDiarmada's prophecy was fulfilled as the Easter Rising set in motion a series of events that would lead to Irish independence in 1922.

The Easter Rising would not have taken place without the support of Ireland's "exiled children in America," as Patrick Pearse put it. For decades they had been enthusiastic supporters of Ireland's struggle to gain its independence as a sovereign nation.

Irish nationalism intensified in the years during and after the Great Famine. Daniel O'Connell was the chief spokesman for constitutional nationalism during the 1840s. His goal for the Repeal movement was to abolish the Act of Union, thereby gaining independence for Ireland but within the United Kingdom. Frustrated with the aging O'Connell, a group of Irish writers, activists, and journalists broke with him and formed their own movement, known as Young Ireland. Like O'Connell their goal was freedom for the Irish people, but they wanted total independence rather than some form of home rule within the United Kingdom. Moreover, the Young Irelanders, led by Thomas Davis and Charles Gavan Duffy, were willing to endorse an armed revolution, which O'Connell would not accept. This disagreement about the best way to gain Ireland's freedom drove the Young Irelanders out of the Repeal movement. They promoted their version of nationalism through their poetry and prose, recalling for their readers the glories of Ireland's history. One symbol of their romantic expression of Irish nationalism was the tricolor flag, with green representing the Catholic Irish, orange representing the Protestant Irish, and white symbolizing the unity of the two. This flag, which would eventually become the flag of the Republic of Ireland, expressed their hope for an Ireland where all Irish men and women, Catholics as well as Protestants, would be united into one nation. They also founded a newspaper, the *Nation*, read by as many as 250,000 people, in which they published much of their ideology.

Their long-awaited uprising took place on July 29, 1848, in Ballingarry, county Tipperary. Leading the rebellion was William Smith O'Brien, a Protestant aristocrat and a member of Parliament whose ancestral home was Dromoland Castle in county Clare. This refined, polite gentleman was a reluctant revolutionary who had been thrust into a leadership position after more militant Young Irelanders had been arrested. The Irish police swiftly routed his small brigade. The Young Irelanders' rebellion was a noble gesture, but it ended in humiliating defeat. The uprising lacked popular support. After three years of famine the Irish people were too physically exhausted and mentally wounded to become revolutionaries. Smith, along with several of his coconspirators, was arrested, tried, and exiled to the penal colony of Tasmania.

The Young Ireland movement's romantic version of Irish nationalism would inspire later generations. In addition, many of these revolutionaries ended up as exiles in the United States, where they would continue their crusade to free Ireland of British rule. This link between Ireland's nationalists and Irish America was the indispensable ingredient in the development of Irish American nationalism throughout the nineteenth and twentieth centuries.

One of the more prominent Young Irelanders who emigrated to the United States was John O'Mahony, who in 1858 founded the Fenians in New York City, a sister organization to the Irish Republican Brotherhood (IRB), founded in Ireland at the same time by another rebel, James

Stephens. Eventually all who belonged to these revolutionary societies would be known as Fenians, a name that recalled the deeds of ancient Irish warriors. The aim of the Fenians was to gain Ireland's independence through an armed rebellion.

As the logical successors to the Young Ireland movement, the Fenians promoted the cause of revolutionary nationalism, while at the same time another wing of Irish nationalism, personified by Daniel O'Connell, wanted an independent Ireland, but sought to achieve this by constitutional means. These two expressions of Irish nationalism, one revolutionary and the other constitutional, were transplanted to the United States, where they competed for the support of the Irish American community.

In the United States the Fenians flourished in the 1860s, numbering as many as fifty thousand, who took an oath that committed them "to labor with earnest zeal for the liberation of Ireland from the yoke of England."[2] But many more Irish men and women supported the Fenian cause. At just one Fenian rally in New York, as many as one hundred thousand attended. One event that was especially effective in promoting the Fenian organization was the funeral of Terence McManus. This Young Irelander, sentenced to prison in Tasmania, escaped to the United States, landing as a fugitive in San Francisco in 1851. After a hero's welcome in San Francisco, McManus led an unremarkable life until his death in January 1861.

At first the death of McManus did not attract much attention, and he was buried without any fanfare. But the San Francisco Fenians thought that they could promote their cause by honoring this Irish rebel in a more public manner. They came up with the audacious idea of having him reburied in Ireland in Glasnevin Cemetery, home of some of Ireland's most famous people.[3] In August 1861, the body of McManus was exhumed and placed in a new casket. Then for two days the San Francisco Irish honored McManus with a public wake followed by a Mass in the cathedral church presided over by the archbishop. As many as twenty thousand people lined the streets as a procession of more than sixteen hundred people escorted the body from the church to the pier where a steamship was waiting to begin the long journey to Ireland by way of Panama and New York City.

The body arrived in New York twenty-four days later, receiving a hero's welcome complete with a solemn high requiem Mass in the cathedral. When the Mass was over, Archbishop Hughes mounted the pulpit to deliver a nationalistic address that linked McManus's love for Ireland with the right of lawful resistance to the state. A month later another grand procession took place with the Fenian founder, John O'Mahony, leading the way through the streets of New York to the pier where the casket was placed aboard a ship bound for Ireland, where the body of McManus once again received a hero's welcome. Thousands of people lined the tracks from Cork to Dublin as the funeral train passed through the Irish countryside. Archbishop Cullen of Dublin was not as welcoming as his American counterparts, refusing the use of any churches for another funeral service. This did not deter the Fenian loyalists. They organized a weeklong wake in Mechanics' Institute, followed by a mammoth procession, "the largest affair of its kind that Dublin had seen since the funeral of Daniel O'Connell fourteen years earlier, and the grandest they would see until the funeral of Parnell over thirty years later." After a day's journey through the streets of Dublin, the body of Terence McManus finally found a permanent resting place in Glasnevin Cemetery, accompanied by yet more nationalist speeches. "The grandfather of Irish wakes," the reburial of McManus lasted eleven months. Carefully staged in each city to gain as much publicity as possible for the Fenians, it was a huge success.[4]

In many respects this event was the high point of Fenianism in the United States. Membership increased across the country, mainly in the urban areas where the Irish were heavily concentrated. The Fenians were also successful in recruiting many Irishmen who were fighting in the Civil War. Organized in Irish brigades, these soldiers had gained a new sense of Irish identity that strengthened their commitment to the nationalist cause. Fenianism also appealed to large numbers of the Irish working class. In 1863 the Fenians held a national convention in Chicago. Two years later they met in Cincinnati and again in Philadelphia, where a representative from the Canadian branch of the Fenians joined them. By this time they had become what historian Kerby Miller called "the most popular and powerful ethnic organization in Irish American history."[5] But their rapid rise would end in an equally speedy demise, so that by 1870 the American branch of the Fenians had collapsed. A major reason for their downfall was a failed assault on Canada.

As preposterous as it may seem, some Fenian leaders thought that if they could overthrow British rule in Canada, they could use this as a bargaining chip to persuade the British to give up their rule over Ireland. Such a victory might even persuade the United States to take up arms against England, thereby opening the door to a rebellion in Ireland while England was distracted by war with the Americans. O'Mahony and

Stephens both opposed such a confrontation. But their prestige, especially that of O'Mahony, was at a low point by this time. First in 1866 and again in 1870, a contingent of Fenians, mostly recruits from the Civil War, led by former Civil War officers, invaded Canada, only to be defeated both times by Canadian and British troops. This military fiasco spelled doom for the Fenians and demoralized Irish American nationalists. But the hatred of England was too strong for Irish American nationalism to remain dormant for long.

Though Anglophobia was a key reason for the popularity of Irish American nationalism, there were other reasons as well. One was the poverty and oppression the immigrants experienced upon their arrival in the United States. This was especially true of those who had fled the Great Famine. It would be hard to imagine a more desperate group of immigrants. Hungry, broke, and exhausted from their long journey across the ocean, they arrived with little more than the clothes on their backs. In addition, they encountered a great deal of discrimination once they set foot in the United States. As one immigrant put it, "This is an English colony and its people inherit from their ancestors the true Saxon contempt for everything Irish."[6] In addition, a sense of exile haunted them. Famine and poverty had driven them from their homeland. Exiles in a foreign land, they experienced loneliness as well as alienation. Who was to blame for all this misery? No one but the English. The Act of Union had promised prosperity, but all the Irish got was famine, poverty, and exile. The Irish nationalist John Mitchel spoke for many when he claimed, "The English created the famine." A popular Irish American ballad put it more powerfully by recalling the famine tragedy that decimated the town of Skibbereen:

> O Father dear . . . the day will come when vengeance loud will call
> And we will rise with Erin's boys to rally one and all.
> I'll be the man to lead the van beneath our flag of green,
> And loud and high will raise the cry, "Revenge for
> Skibbereen."[7]

The link between the famine graves in Skibbereen and the battle for Ireland's freedom would inspire a generation of Irish immigrants to support the nationalist cause.

Another reason why Irish Americans became so nationalistic was self-respect. If Ireland gained its independence, the Irish hoped to gain more respect from their American neighbors—something they were in dire need of given the prejudice they encountered. This desire for respect was most visible among the lace-curtain Irish, who had gained some measure of success. Michael Davitt, an Irish-born nationalist, articulated this feeling in one of his speeches: "You want to be honored among the elements that constitute this nation . . . You want to be regarded with the respect due you; that you may thus be looked on, aid us in Ireland to remove the stain of degradation from your birth . . . and you will get the respect you deserve."[8]

When the immigrants arrived in the United States, they settled in Irish neighborhoods where they shared a common experience with their fellow countrymen and countrywomen that transcended any previous loyalties they had to village, county, or region. The Irish worked together and worshipped together. Nationalism further strengthened their common identity as an Irish people. They were not just individual laborers or servants, but Irish men and women proud to belong to a cause larger than themselves—the struggle to gain Ireland's freedom. This is the heritage that they would pass on to their children.

These urban Irish enclaves promoted a nationalism that was more defined by hatred of England than love of Ireland. As historian Brian Jenkins wrote, in these neighborhoods they "were reminded that the English had oppressed them, that the English were responsible for Ireland's chronic poverty, that the English were responsible for the calamity of the Famine, that the English were responsible both for their exile and their rejection by native-born Americans." Many of the Catholic clergy who followed the immigrants to America were born and raised in the same nationalistic environment as their parishioners. The seminaries where they studied in Ireland fostered nationalism.[9] They carried this national loyalty with them, encouraging their parishioners to support the cause. In parochial schools children learned as much about the history of Ireland as they did about the United States. Readers used in these schools celebrated the glories of Irish history, most especially the loyalty of the Irish to their faith during the dark days of the penal times. The Irish American press also fueled the nationalist movement. Local newspapers supported Irish pride by recalling the glories of Ireland's past as well as providing extensive coverage of Irish affairs. This strengthened the sense of Irish identity among the newcomers. Irish organizations such as the Ancient Order of Hibernians were also hothouses of nationalist fervor, sponsoring social gatherings where nationalist propaganda was readily promoted. Mr. Dooley, Finley Peter Dunne's quintessential Irish bartender, captured the link between the Irish fondness for Sunday picnics and nationalism when he remarked, "If Ireland could be freed by a picnic, she'd be an Empire now." All of these neighborhood institutions—church, school, newspaper, and clubs—taught the Irish to love Ireland, hate England, and support the cause of Irish independence.

The failed invasion of Canada was only a momentary check to this nationalist fervor. A new organization, known as the Clan na Gael (Family of the Irish), emerged as heir to the revolutionary wing of Irish American nationalism. Founded in New York in 1867, it grew to a membership of close to ten thousand by the late 1870s, gaining most of its support from the working class. Linked with the Irish Republican Brotherhood in Ireland, it would become by the end of the 1870s, according to Thomas N. Brown, "the single most powerful Irish revolutionary society in the United States."[10] Its most illustrious member was John Devoy, whom his biographer labeled "America's greatest rebel."[11]

Devoy was born in county Kildare in 1842. While his father worked as a farm laborer, his mother took care of their eight children. In 1848, when famine was ravaging the countryside, John's father, out of work and facing starvation, moved his family to Dublin, where he would have a better chance of providing for his family. As a teenager in Dublin, Devoy was attracted to nationalist politics. Realizing that if a revolution was to take place, it would involve guns and warfare, skills which he did not possess, the eighteen-year-old decided to join the French Foreign Legion to learn how to be a soldier. After a brief sojourn in French North Africa, he returned to Dublin eager to take up arms against the British government in Ireland. He joined the IRB, quickly gaining the confidence of its leader, James Stephens, who appointed him as an organizer in the British army stationed in Ireland, 60 percent of whom were of Irish ancestry. His task was to infiltrate the army and recruit members for the IRB. But the British government, learning of the revolutionary schemes of the IRB, arrested several of its members. By 1865 the young Devoy was a wanted man. He was finally captured in an Irish pub in February 1866 and thrown in Kilmainham jail. He spent the next five years in jail, released with the understanding that he could live anywhere except the United Kingdom of Great Britain and Ireland. So, along with four other Fenian rebels who had also served time in jail, Devoy set sail for the United States. When he landed in New York in January 1871, the revolutionary wing of Irish American nationalism finally got the leader it needed.

Joining the Clan shortly after his arrival in New York, Devoy quickly made his mark. One of his most remarkable achievements was orchestrating the successful rescue of six Fenians who had been sentenced to life in prison in Freemantle, Western Australia. Moved by letters from these prisoners, Devoy decided to send an American ship to rescue them. As unlikely as it may have seemed, the rescue attempt succeeded. The Clan raised the money to purchase a ship, called the *Catalpa*, which set sail from the harbor of New Bedford, Massachusetts, in April 1875, reaching Western Australia eleven months later. Two of Devoy's Fenian allies sailed to Australia on another ship to coordinate the rescue in Freemantle. Remarkably, the rescue took place more or less as planned. When news of this daring escapade finally reached Ireland, the streets of Dublin lit up with torchlight parades hailing this revolutionary victory over the English. In August the *Catalpa* sailed into New York Harbor, where the Fenian prisoners received a triumphal welcome. In cities across Irish America salutes were fired to celebrate the *Catalpa*'s return. Devoy's name would forever be linked to the journey of the *Catalpa* and the most daring rescue in Irish American history.

Events in Ireland during the 1870s revived nationalistic fervor on both sides of the Atlantic. The founding of the Home Rule movement in 1870 inaugurated a prolonged campaign to gain a measure of independence for Ireland. The Home Rule movement represented the constitutional, nonviolent version of Irish nationalism at this time. Unlike O'Connell's Repeal movement, which sought to abolish the 1800 Act of Union, the goal of Home Rule was the establishment of an Irish parliament that would legislate for Ireland's domestic affairs, but would remain subordinate to the English parliament. For the die-hard revolutionaries any compromise that still recognized English rule over Ireland was unacceptable. Nonetheless, the majority of the Irish population supported this constitutional compromise as a more pragmatic way to achieve a measure of political freedom for their homeland. The Home Rule campaign took off in the late 1870s when its leadership passed to a new and promising young member of Parliament, Charles Stewart Parnell. A Protestant landlord in county Wicklow, Parnell appeared to be destined to live the life of a country gentleman, spending his time at parties and dances as well as hunting and shooting. But he decided to enter politics, and in 1875, at the age of twenty-nine, he was elected to Parliament. Before long he would be hailed, like Daniel O'Connell before him, as "the uncrowned king of Ireland."[12]

While the Home Rule movement was gaining momentum in Parliament, Ireland was in the midst of another potential famine. With a poor harvest in 1877 and again in 1878 and 1879, the west of Ireland was once again on the brink of starvation. Falling prices for grain and beef further hurt small farmers. Since people could not pay their rents, evictions soon followed, more than doubling in number between 1877 and 1879. Emigration to the United States was not a solution since America was suffering a severe depression. With evictions rising and unemployment increasing, discontent became widespread. For political activists the solution was to find some type of land reform that would return the land of Ireland to the people of Ireland by doing away with the hated landlord system. In a speech in New York, John Devoy put it emphatically:

> The landlord system is the greatest curse inflicted by England on Ireland, and Ireland will never be prosperous or happy until it is rooted out. The land of Ireland belongs to the people of Ireland and to them alone, and we must not be afraid to say so . . . I believe in Irish independence, but I don't think it would be worthwhile to free Ireland if that foreign landlord system were left standing.[13]

The answer was the organization of the Land League, whose ultimate goal was the abolition of the landlord system. The founder of the Land League was Michael Davitt, a Fenian rebel who had spent time in jail for gunrunning. Upon his release he traveled to the United States, where he and John Devoy brainstormed about how best to gain Ireland's freedom. They came up with the idea of joining the two strands of Irish nationalism, the revolutionary and the constitutional, into one grand coalition known as the New Departure. Land reform would be a crucial phase in launching this new mass movement.

Upon his return to Ireland, Davitt traveled to county Mayo, a region where Fenian influence was strong and agrarian unrest was boiling over. There, at a meeting in Castlebar in August 1879, he organized the National Land League of Mayo. Later that fall, Charles Parnell took over the leadership role as the Mayo Land League expanded into a national organization. Within a year more than a thousand branches of the Land League came into existence, numbering more than two hundred thousand members. By persuading Parnell to join their crusade for land reform, Devoy and Davitt were able to build a coalition between Fenian nationalists and constitutionalists. Large numbers of parish priests supported the league, speaking at rallies aimed at gaining popular support for the cause of land reform. For the next three years Ireland came as close as it ever had to a national uprising as a war against the landlord system erupted throughout much of the country.

As the land war exploded, nationalist fever gripped Irish America. Feeding this fever was the "cry of distress" from Ireland as the danger of starvation was becoming more real. The Catholic clergy became involved in a nationwide campaign to provide relief, with dioceses across the country sponsoring special collections. In addition, public rallies were held in cities such as St. Louis and Richmond to raise funds for the starving people in the west of Ireland. The best estimate is that such church-sponsored fund-raisers sent about five million dollars to Ireland by 1881.[14] While this relief effort was taking place, Charles Parnell arrived in the United States to promote the cause of the Land League as well as raise funds for famine relief.

Parnell's first speech was in New York's Madison Square Garden, where he spoke to over four thousand people, whom Devoy described as "the very best Irish people in New York City."[15] After New York he traveled some sixteen thousand miles across the United States and Canada, visiting over sixty cities in less than three months. He raised as much as three hundred thousand dollars from the adoring crowds that welcomed him along the way. Without question this triumphal tour enhanced his stature as Ireland's most celebrated politician. His message to his audiences highlighted the need for relief for the starving Irish, the evils of the landlord system that led to such famine, and, of course, the dream of Ireland's freedom. As he put it in a speech in Cincinnati:

> I feel confident that we shall kill the Irish landlord system, and when we have given Ireland to the people of Ireland we shall have laid the foundation on which to build up our Irish nation . . . None of us, whether we be in America or in Ireland, or wherever we may be, will be satisfied until we have destroyed the last link which keeps Ireland bound to England.[16]

Though this speech would haunt him in later years because it linked him with revolutionaries such as Devoy, it clearly indicated how closely allied constitutional and revolutionary nationalism had become.

Parnell left New York in a howling snowstorm on March 11, 1880, to return to Ireland, where he would take over leadership of the Home Rule Party. His visit helped to strengthen the nationalist spirit of Irish Americans, proving to him that they were, in his words, "even more Irish than the Irish themselves in the true spirit of patriotism."[17] One of his last acts was to meet with Irish American leaders to discuss the formation of an American branch of the Land League. That took place two months later in New York with the formation of the Irish National Land League of America. The delegates at the convention elected Michael Davitt, who had just arrived in the country, as their first secretary. Davitt had come to the United States to help organize Land League clubs and raise funds for the cause. He traveled across the country for several months drumming up support for the Land League, speaking in lecture halls and at huge picnics organized by the Clan na Gael, whose members were officers in many of the Land League clubs. One highlight of his travels was meeting a young woman, Mary Yore, in Oakland, California, who would become his bride in 1886. Davitt's tour was so successful that within a few months hundreds of clubs were in operation. At its peak the American Land League had as many as fifteen hundred branches located in nearly every state and territory and raised five hundred thousand dollars to support Ireland's Land League.

Parnell's sister Fanny was instrumental in organizing an American Ladies Land League in 1880 that also raised money for Ireland's land war. A year later, her sister, Anna, founded a similar organization in Ireland. Given its militant and masculine character, the Fenian organization excluded women, but the Land League encouraged them to join its campaign. Some clergy criticized this, protesting, in the words of one Irish prelate, that the organization was asking "the daughters of our Catholic people . . . to jeopardize the modesty of their sex and the dignity of their womanhood." In the United States the bishop of Cleveland threatened to excommunicate any women who joined the league. Undaunted, Cleveland's women patriots continued their work with the league. In other cities, such as Worcester, Massachusetts, and New York, the clergy were much more receptive to women's participation in the Ladies Land League. New York had so many branches "that they were organized ward by ward in Irish neighborhoods."[18] The league provided these women with an opportunity for political involvement that would pave the way for later activity in the nationalist movement, as well as the labor movement and the suffrage campaign.

Support for the American Land League came mainly from the working class, those who, in historian Eric Foner's judgment, comprised "the grass roots of Irish-American radicalism." One *New York Times* reporter wrote,

"The money that has kept the Land League together has come mostly from the day laborers and the servant maids of America."[19] This was most true of those who sent their money to the *Irish World*, a newspaper edited by the Irish-born Patrick Ford. His newspaper, one of the most widely read papers in the country, enthusiastically endorsed the Land League. In fact, Ford had established his own land league organization, using his newspaper as a collection agency. Most of the contributions collected at the local branches and sent to Ford were for less than one dollar. Often branches were organized at places of work—at railroads and steel factories. A sizable amount of funds came from the mining towns of Pennsylvania, such as Scranton and Carbondale. Another center of support was western mining cities such as Butte and Leadville. Terence Powderly personified this link between the working class and nationalism. He was not only a powerful labor leader, but also an official in the Land League as well as an officer in the Clan na Gael. He spoke frequently on the land question, never failing to connect the American labor movement with the Irish land movement. In his words, they were "almost identical."[20] Support for the Land League also came from the Irish middle class, most especially in the urban centers of the Northeast where they were most concentrated. They were inclined to send their contributions to the American Land League, founded in New York shortly after Parnell's visit to the United States. This division within the Irish American community over raising funds for the land war underscored the fatal tendency of Irish American nationalists to fight among themselves. A key figure in this controversy was Patrick Ford.

Born in Galway in 1837, he emigrated to Boston with his parents in 1845, never to return to the land of his birth. As a young boy he found a job with William Lloyd Garrison's abolitionist newspaper, the *Liberator*. He later worked for another Boston newspaper before he volunteered for the Union army. After surviving the bloody battle at Fredericksburg, he returned to civilian life with an honorable discharge. In 1870 he moved to Brooklyn with his wife, where he founded the *Irish World*, remaining as its editor until his death in 1913. At its height, when Ford was regarded as the most prominent Irish American journalist in the country, the *Irish World* had a weekly circulation of one hundred thousand. Throughout the 1870s and '80s it was the newspaper of choice for labor leaders and Irish nationalists. According to Ford, it was read by "every reform advocate in the land." It was equally popular in Ireland. William O'Brien, an Irish nationalist, recalled, "There was scarcely a cabin in the West to which some

relative in America did not dispatch a weekly copy of the *Irish World* . . .
It was as if some vast Irish-American invasion was sweeping the country
with new and irresistable principles of Liberty and Democracy."[21] Without the funds collected by the newspaper, the Land League would never
have lasted as long as it did. William Gladstone, Great Britain's prime
minister at the time, allegedly admitted, "But for the work the *Irish World*
is doing and the money it is sending across the ocean, there would be no
agitation in Ireland."[22]

The economic depression of the 1870s had a profound effect on Ford,
turning him into a radical reformer. Blaming America's miseries on the
economic system, he condemned capitalism and supported unions, as well
as the eight-hour day and the right to strike. For him land monopoly was
the "prime evil" both in America and Ireland. The "land robbers," he
wrote, were the "foremost social enemy" in both countries.[23] This commitment to social reform through land reform pushed Ford to the forefront of
the Land League movement. Rather than support the American Land
League, over which he had no control, he founded his own Land League,
which grew to as many as twenty-five hundred branches throughout the
country, raising as much as $350,000 by 1882. One attraction of Ford's
organization was that he published each donor's name in his newspaper as
well as the amount donated. The contributions, averaging less than one
dollar, came from "poor and unpretentious workingmen," according to
Ford. The money sent to Ireland was primarily used to fund relief efforts
and to pay the legal costs of those who were challenging their evictions.[24]

John Devoy, who was equally doctrinaire, never got along with Ford,
believing that Ford's advocacy of land reform diverted attention from Devoy's lifework, the violent overthrow of British rule. Nor did Ford's radical ideas and his dogmatic attitude sit well with the more moderate Irish
who supported economic reform in Ireland, but not in the United States.

One person who did support Ford's call for land reform was Henry
George. Born in Philadelphia in 1839, he was raised in a devout Episcopalian family. As a teenager he moved to San Francisco to seek his fortune,
but within a few years he was flat broke. Married and with children, he
was reduced to begging for food to feed his family. Good fortune came his
way by the late 1860s when he finally found a job as a journalist. In 1871
he published a pamphlet that "outlined the basic idea to which he devoted
the rest of his life: that society's 'fundamental mistake is in treating land
as private property.'" He spent the next eight years developing these ideas,
finally publishing them in a book, *Progress and Poverty*. In time it "became

the most widely read economic treatise ever written" in the United States, selling as many as two million copies by 1900. Like Ford and Davitt, George singled out the land monopoly as the cause of the "central problems of the age—the unequal distribution of wealth, the growing squalor of the cities, and the declining status of labor."[25] His solution was to have a single tax on the unearned profits derived from the land. This would end land monopoly, while the monies collected from this tax would eliminate the need for other taxes and would ensure social progress.

As utopian as it was, George's single-tax idea captivated the popular imagination, gaining for him an international reputation as a political economist. Ford endorsed the work of George, publishing some of his essays in the *Irish World*. Popular among the Land League followers, George traveled through the Northeast speaking in various cities, drumming up support for the league. Ford even sent him to Ireland as a correspondent for the *Irish World*, to report back on the land war. Another ally of George was Michael Davitt. Not only did he read his book, but he shared his views on land monopoly.[26] They became close friends as well as coconspirators in the battle against the land monopoly. This only enhanced the reputation of George among Irish Americans. Another enthusiastic supporter of George and his single-tax solution was the New York priest Edward McGlynn. He, too, took to the lecture circuit on behalf of the Land League, promoting the nationalist agenda of land reform with rhetoric that was decidedly evangelical. The alliance between McGlynn and George joined together the Catholic social-gospel priest and the Protestant evangelical reformer in a common crusade for social justice.

This alliance became most public for a brief time in 1886, when Henry George ran for mayor of New York. The Democratic Party, traditionally the party of the working-class Irish, had nominated Congressman Abram Hewitt as their candidate for mayor. The city's labor unions, unhappy with Tammany Hall and the Democratic Party, who they believed had lost touch with the working class, nominated Henry George as their choice to run against Hewitt. Patrick Ford backed George, his fellow Irish nationalist, viewing his candidacy as an opportunity to gain a measure of social reform. Father Edward McGlynn supported George, while Terence Powderly spent an entire week campaigning for him. George lost, coming in second to Hewitt, with Theodore Roosevelt, the Republican choice, finishing third. This was the last hurrah for the radical alliance of Irish nationalism, labor, and social reform. Powderly and the Knights of Labor were about to experience a rapid demise. Patrick Ford soon abandoned his

radical reform ideas, severed relations with George, and became more conservative, supporting Home Rule and opposing the Clan na Gael. George
continued to promote his single-tax idea, but it never caught on, while
McGlynn's work on behalf of George was dealt a fatal blow when his refusal to abandon his political activities led to his excommunication.

Because of this alliance of Irish nationalism with social reform during the brief period when labor unrest was tearing apart the United States
and a land war in Ireland was erupting, the Land League movement, as
Eric Foner wrote, "introduced thousands of Irish Americans to modern
reform and labor ideologies and helped to transform specifically Irish
grievances and traditions into a broader critique of American society in
the Gilded Age."[27] By joining Irish nationalism with American social reform, the Land League encouraged a radical working-class consciousness
among Irish Americans that took root in the 1880s in the Knights of Labor and then later among the western mining communities. By emphasizing the need for social justice it helped to nurture a Catholic social gospel
that was beginning to emerge at this time. A better understanding of this
chapter in Irish American history should dispel the myth that the conservatism of the respectable lace-curtain middle class defined Irish America.
This was but one characteristic of the community. Another equally significant feature emerged from the working-class Irish who were committed
to a radicalism that did not hesitate to critique the American economic
system. This radical spirit, also present among the Irish in the labor movement, remained within the Irish American community as long as it maintained its working-class identity.

During the land war Ireland's tradition of agrarian violence reemerged.
Brutality spread across the rural areas, ranging from intimidating letters to
landlords to assassinations. Assaults increased, cattle were maimed or killed,
and property was attacked. One of the more notable tactics was the shunning of anyone who took over the land of an evicted tenant. You must treat
him "as if he were a leper of old," as Parnell put it, and "show him your de-
testation of the crime he has committed."[28] Shortly after Parnell urged this
nonviolent tactic, it was applied to an estate in Mayo where Charles Boycott
was the agent. The local Land League, under the leadership of the parish
priest, initiated a campaign of shunning against anyone who cooperated
with Boycott. It was so effective that Boycott had to import workers from
the north, who, protected by soldiers, harvested the estate's crops. As a result, a new word entered the English language, *boycott*, and the American labor movement acquired a new weapon in its arsenal.

The increasing violence persuaded the British government to suspend habeas corpus and imprison some of the leaders of the Land League, including Parnell, who was incarcerated in Kilmainham jail. Shortly afterward, the Land League was declared an unlawful organization. William Gladstone, the British prime minister, had persuaded the English parliament to pass land reform legislation in 1881 in the hope of defusing the discontent of the Irish tenant class. Though the law passed, the violence only increased while Parnell was in jail. To end the violence Gladstone sought to persuade Parnell to support Parliament's land reform legislation. After six months in jail without the benefit of trial, Parnell finally came to an arrangement with Gladstone in April 1882 that became known as the Kilmainham Treaty. It gave to the tenant class fair rents and freedom from arbitrary eviction, already spelled out in the 1881 law, as well as a guarantee of relief to the small tenants who were in arrears in their rent. This brought an end to the Land League campaign.

The Kilmainham Treaty began a long legislative process that would eventually give the land of Ireland back to the people of Ireland. It was finalized in 1903 with the Wyndham Act, whereby the government financed the transfer of land ownership from landlord to tenant. By 1920, outside of Ulster, which was mostly Protestant, Irish Catholics finally owned the land they lived on. Without the efforts of the Land League, strengthened financially and politically by Irish America, it is doubtful that this massive land transfer would ever have taken place, even though it took more than twenty years to achieve.

Parnell was at the height of his popularity in the mid-1880s as the Home Rule movement, largely financed by Irish America, gained headway in Parliament. But as rapid as his rise to fame had been, his downfall was even more spectacular. It was revealed in late 1889 that for ten years he had had a liaison with Katherine O'Shea, the wife of Captain William O'Shea, a former member of the Home Rule Party. Between 1882 and 1884 Parnell and Katherine had three children. Once the affair became public and the "nauseous details" were revealed at one of Ireland's most sensational divorce trials in November 1890, Parnell's career was over.[29] His colleagues in the Home Rule Party, as well as the Catholic hierarchy, turned against him. While on the campaign trail seeking to regain his power in Parliament, he became fatally ill. He died in October 1891 in the arms of Katherine, whom he had married only weeks before. At the age of forty-five, Parnell was dead.

The intensity of Irish American nationalism declined considerably af-

ter the collapse of the Land League and the death of Parnell. The New Departure alliance between revolutionary and constitutional nationalists was a
failure in the eyes of radical revolutionaries, though it had aided Parnell in
gaining popular support for the Home Rule movement. In the United
States, what enthusiasm there was for Irish nationalism was now concentrated on raising funds to support the campaign for Home Rule, struggling
to maintain its momentum after Parnell's demise. The revolutionary wing
of Irish American nationalism, the Clan na Gael, was in disarray by 1890.
In Chicago, a hothouse of radical nationalism, the murder of one of the
leaders of the Clan, allegedly by a rival Clan member, marked the low
point of the organization, which to the unknowing public seemed no more
than a gang of murderers. Discredited and riddled with factionalism, the
Clan had lost whatever influence it once had among the Irish.

In Ireland the death of Parnell left the Home Rule Party without a
leader and in disarray. In 1900 John Redmond, a member of Parliament,
reunited the party under his leadership. Like Parnell and Davitt before
him, he traveled to the United States to raise funds. At his urging Irish
American activists founded the United Irish League of America to raise
money and gain support for the Home Rule movement in Ireland.
Launched in Chicago in 1901 at a gathering attended by some fifteen
thousand people, it spread across the country with centers in most major
cities. Redmond and other Irish politicians frequently traveled to the
United States to garner support for Home Rule and raise the funds
needed to sustain their political campaign in Ireland. After several failed
attempts, a Home Rule bill was finally passed in Parliament in 1914. By
this time Irish America had sent hundreds of thousands of dollars to Ireland to support the cause.

As the campaign to pass the bill gathered momentum, it rekindled
bitter sectarian feelings in Ulster, where Protestants wanted no part of a
united Ireland in which they would be a minority. For them Home Rule
meant Rome Rule. As a result, the final bill left this issue and the possible
partition of Ireland unresolved. On August 4, six weeks before the bill
was signed into law, the United Kingdom declared war on Germany. This
forced the bill to be shelved until the war was over. After thirty years of
struggle Home Rule was finally achieved. But the triumph meant little for
the revolutionary nationalists since it was not Home Rule for all of Ireland, whereas the unionists in Ulster would not participate in an Irish
state unless it was governed by British Protestants. Home Rule became a
moot issue two years later when on April 24, Easter Monday morning,

more than fifteen hundred hard-core republicans launched the long-awaited revolution in Dublin. John Devoy's dream had finally been realized, or so it seemed.

During the 1890s Devoy committed himself to the revival of the Clan na Gael, which had split into separate factions. Finally, in 1900 the feuding nationalists were reunited after years of bitter infighting. Chosen as secretary of the revitalized Clan, Devoy would be its driving force as it conspired with its revolutionary brotherhood in Ireland, the IRB, to initiate the long-awaited rebellion. Supporters of the Clan, now numbering in the thousands, had no use for John Redmond, the United Irish League of America, and their goal of Home Rule. Many of Ireland's hardened revolutionaries who would lead the Easter Rising in 1916 had traveled to New York to meet with Devoy to plan strategy for the rebellion. In 1903 he began publication of a weekly newspaper, the *Gaelic American*, that became the mouthpiece for Clan propaganda. Over the next decade the Clan sent money and arms to Ireland—even conspiring with the Germans, who by 1914 were at war with Britain, to send arms to Ireland.

Working alongside Devoy during these years was an unlikely ally, Daniel Cohalan, a Tammany Democrat and a judge on the New York Supreme Court. A jurist who did not hesitate to break the law when Ireland's future was at stake, he became a major player as the planned rebellion gathered momentum.

Given the secretive nature of the Clan and the limited circulation of the *Gaelic American*, Devoy and his allies decided that they needed to get their message out to the Irish American public. They called a meeting in New York in March, scarcely six weeks before the Easter Rising, of some twenty-five hundred Irish American leaders. At the convention they founded the Friends of Irish Freedom, which would serve as the leading Irish American revolutionary organization for the next ten years. One of its main tasks was to raise money to support the Irish revolution. Indicative of its success, shortly after the convention ended, Devoy wired ten thousand dollars to his IRB contact in Ireland.

As early as the spring of 1915 the IRB had been planning a rebellion while England was at war with Germany. "England's danger is Ireland's opportunity" was their saying. Critical to the success of the rebellion was a shipment of arms from Germany. Together with Roger Casement, an Irish nationalist, John Devoy had arranged this shipment with the assistance of German diplomats in New York. But the British discovered the plot. A Royal Navy gunship intercepted the *Aud*, a German ship disguised as a Norwegian trawler, which was carrying twenty thousand rifles. Ordered to proceed to Queenstown harbor, the ship's captain scuttled the ship as it reached the harbor. The shipment of guns sank to the bottom of the sea. Casement, who was returning to Ireland in a German submarine, was arrested soon after he got to shore. The conspiracy was falling apart. When word got back to Dublin about the arrest of Casement and the scuttling of the arms shipment, the military council of the IRB was in a state of confusion. Nonetheless, they decided to go ahead with the rebellion scheduled for Easter Sunday, but put it off until the following day.

The Easter Rising lasted less than a week. The vast majority of Irish looked upon the small band of revolutionaries as fools. As one local newspaper put it, "The Dublin revolution has ended, as everybody not a sheer lunatic must have known it would, in unutterable disaster, defeat and ruin."[30] As the rebels were led off to prison, people booed and heckled them. Then a few weeks later the British did something that would change the course of Ireland's history. They turned a military victory into a political debacle by executing the leaders of the rebellion. Over several days in May, fourteen republicans were shot to death in a small yard in Kilmainham jail. The executions turned the tide of public opinion against the British, ushering in a decisive chapter in Ireland's century-long struggle to gain freedom from British rule.

The Clan na Gael had an important influence on the Easter rebellion by providing money, support, and inspiration to the IRB, who launched the uprising. Patrick Pearse, a key figure in the rebellion, acknowledged this when he read his proclamation announcing the formation of the Irish Republic. Several of the leaders of the rebellion, including Pearse, had met with John Devoy in New York. Thomas J. Clarke lived and worked in New York for several years, becoming a confidante of Devoy. James Connolly, a labor activist both in America and in Ireland, was another Irish exile who lived in the United States for several years before he returned to Ireland to lead the revolution. Along with Pearse, they were all executed by a British firing squad.

Reaction to the uprising in Irish America was similar to that in Ireland—shock and sadness at such a foolhardy attempt to overthrow the world's most powerful government. Then, once the executions became known, the tide of public opinion shifted. The Clan organized meetings in Boston and in Philadelphia, condemning the executions and rallying support for Ireland. Father Peter Yorke presided over a rally in San Francisco that sent a letter to President Woodrow Wilson denouncing the executions.

A huge rally took place in Carnegie Hall two days after the execution of James Connolly. Five thousand people filled the hall, listening to speeches, while thousands more stood outside. John Devoy was there and heard Congressman W. Bourke Cochran proclaim, "The vilest murders ever committed in Irish history are fresh before our eyes. The noblest Irishmen that have ever lived are dead, dead by the bullet of British soldiery, shot like dogs for asserting the immortal truths of patriotism." "On both sides of the Atlantic," wrote Terry Golway, "men and women who regarded the rebels as fools and the rebellion as a fool's errand . . . now saw the rising as the sacrifice of martyrs." The executions had transformed Pearse and his colleagues "from rioters to patriots."[31] As public opinion shifted to support the revolutionary nationalists, support for John Redmond and the Home Rule Party disappeared. In the Irish general election of 1918, Sinn Fein, the nationalists' political party, attracted a huge following, garnering 70 percent of the vote. When the new Parliament convened in Westminster, the newly elected Sinn Fein members of Parliament refused to take their seats. They established their own parliament in Dublin, declared Ireland independent, and elected Eamon de Valera, one of the survivors of the Easter Rising, president of the new republic. This bold step ushered in a war with Great Britain that lasted until July 1921, when the British army and the Irish Republican Army signed a truce.

When the United States declared war against Germany in April 1917, Irish nationalism took a backseat to American nationalism as patriotic fervor swept the country. When the war ended in November 1918, Irish Americans wasted no time in taking up the cause of Irish nationalism. This time it was not Home Rule or the Land League that became their rallying cry, but self-determination: the quest to become a nation among nations. This was the proposal of President Woodrow Wilson for the national groups of Europe such as Poland and Austria, and Irish Americans wanted the same recognition for Ireland. In December 1918, Devoy's group, the Friends of Irish Freedom, proclaimed an "Irish Self Determination Week" of large public meetings. As many as twenty-five thousand people gathered in Madison Square Garden in New York to show their support for Ireland's quest for independence. One of the featured speakers was the cardinal archbishop of Boston, William O'Connell. Devoy was ecstatic that such a high-ranking prelate would support the movement for Ireland's independence. Amid the cheers of some twenty-five thousand people, O'Connell noted, "This war, we are told again and again . . . was for justice for all, for the inviolable rights of small nations, for the inalienable right, inherent in every nation, of self-determination. The purpose of this meeting tonight is very specific. The war can be justified only by the universal application of those principles. Let that application begin with Ireland." A few months later another rally took place in Philadelphia, where Cardinal Gibbons of Baltimore, in a speech partially crafted by Devoy, endorsed self-determination for Ireland. Gibbons urged the delegates at the peace conference in Paris where the victors would determine the spoils of the war to "apply to Ireland the great principle of national self-determination."[32]

The huge rallies had little influence with President Wilson, who had always been suspicious of ethnic groups such as the Irish Americans because of their presumably divided loyalties between the United States and their original homeland. As a result, the peace conference adjourned without taking up the question of self-determination for Ireland. Disillusioned with Wilson, Irish American political activists were among those who lobbied Congress not to ratify the Treaty of Versailles, which included the concept of a League of Nations, Wilson's dream for a new world order.

In June 1919, while President Wilson was trying to persuade Congress to ratify the Treaty of Versailles, Eamon de Valera decided to travel to the United States, where he hoped to gain public support for Ireland's struggle for independence. This decision shocked some of his allies, who believed that as president of the new Republic of Ireland he should stay home while Ireland was at war. De Valera, who was born in New York and raised in Ireland, spent eighteen months traveling across America. Warmly greeted wherever he went, he not only publicized the Irish cause, but also raised millions of dollars. His reception in Worcester was typical of how the Irish welcomed him. The mayor greeted him, a war hero "led a parade in his honor, and thousands lined the streets to cheer him despite a howling blizzard."[33] The local branch of the Friends of Irish Freedom launched a drive to raise funds and claimed to have raised over $130,000. But not all was happy behind the scenes, as a prolonged feud broke out between Devoy and Cohalan on one side and de Valera and some of the dissident members of the Clan on the other.

At issue were not only the personalities of such strong and determined individuals, but also the question of who would speak for Irish American nationalism. De Valera, as president of the Irish Republic, claimed to be the spokesman for the Irish at home and abroad. Devoy and Cohalan considered themselves best qualified to promote Ireland's cause in America. Bitter conflict erupted among these Irish rebels, and once again factionalism weakened the cause of Irish nationalism. Devoy continually attacked de Valera in the *Gaelic American.* De Valera, in referring to Cohalan, claimed, "Big as the Country is, it is not big enough to hold the Judge and myself."[34] When he realized that he could not control Devoy and the Friends of Irish Freedom, de Valera established his own organization, the American Association for the Recognition of the Irish Republic. De Valera's organization soon eclipsed Devoy's as it enrolled more than eight hundred thousand members by the summer of 1921 when the war with Great Britain came to an end. By that time de Valera was back in Ireland.

In October 1921, de Valera sent a delegation to London to negotiate a treaty with Great Britain. In December both sides signed the Anglo-Irish Treaty. Though the vast majority of the population supported it, dissatisfaction was widespread in the Irish parliament, where it was ratified by the narrowest of margins in January 1922. Though the treaty gave Ireland autonomy, it was not the total independence that many republicans wanted. The Irish Free State, established by the treaty, became a self-governing dominion within the British Empire. As part of the Commonwealth, it enjoyed the same constitutional status as Canada, while remaining subordinate to the British Crown. Another major source of contention was the requirement that members of the Irish parliament had to take an oath of allegiance to the king of England. This was too much for many nationalists to accept. In June, civil war broke out as the IRA split apart, dividing families and pitting brother against brother in a conflict that claimed more lives than the earlier war with England. The pro-treaty army, led by Michael Collins (who was killed during the conflict), prevailed when the antitreaty forces, led by Eamon de Valera and under the banner of the Irish Republican Army, stopped fighting in May 1923. The brutal conflict, with numerous executions and killings, left a legacy of bitterness that would last for years. As Irish historian J. J. Lee said, "The terrible beauty had become more terrible than beautiful."[35]

The Anglo-Irish Treaty partitioned Ireland into two separate political entities: the six counties of Northern Ireland and the Irish Free State, which became the Republic of Ireland in 1948. The partition would rankle Irish nationalists for the rest of the twentieth century.

Once the Irish signed the Anglo-Irish Treaty, enthusiasm for the nationalist movement in Irish America dissipated. This marked the end of the nationalist movement in the United States. When Irishmen began to kill Irishmen during the civil war, Irish Americans became utterly disillusioned. Devoy was particularly bitter. He put it this way:

> The present split has developed into a savage civil war which is devastating Ireland, ruining her economic life, breaking the morale of the people, and filling the world with the idea that the old English theory is correct, that when England's firm hand was removed, the Irish would start to cut each other's throat. Can we blame the world for accepting that theory when thousands of Irishmen are busily engaged in proving its apparent truth?[36]

There was no doubt in his mind who was to blame. It was de Valera, who, in opposing the Anglo-Irish Treaty, had plunged the country into war. As far as Devoy was concerned, de Valera was "a monster who must be punished for his crimes."[37] When he spoke those words, Devoy was eighty years old. The old warrior was tired, deaf, and going blind. His dream of an Irish republic had not been realized after a lifetime of struggle. What he accepted was what Michael Collins, one of the signers of the Anglo-Irish Treaty, described as "the fullest measure of freedom obtainable—the solid substance of independence." Collins believed it would "lead inevitably and in a short period to the complete fulfillment of our national aspirations."[38]

PART THREE

Becoming American,
1920–1960

CHAPTER 9

Up from the City Streets

A defining moment for Irish Americans in the 1920s was the presidential campaign of 1928, when Al Smith, the Democratic Party's nominee, suffered a humiliating loss to the Republican candidate, Herbert Hoover. Al Smith had achieved a level of popularity across the country that was unprecedented for an Irish Catholic politician. His selection as the party's unanimous choice indicated how far Irish Catholics had come since the famine decades, but his defeat, in a campaign noted for its attacks on Smith's religion, reminded them that they were still outsiders in Protestant America. Al Smith's rise to power began, as his campaign song put it, on the "sidewalks of New York."

Alfred E. Smith was born and raised on the Lower East Side of New York City. Proudly Irish, he began his autobiography by recalling, "My mother's father and mother, Thomas and Maria Mulvehill, were born in Westmeath, Ireland."[1] Though he did not say much more about his Irish ancestry in this autobiography, his contemporaries as well as historians have always remembered him as the quintessential Irish politician, the first Irish Catholic chosen to be the Democratic candidate for president of the United States. Growing up in a predominantly Irish neighborhood and parish, his Irish ancestry formed his self-identity. His involvement in the local Catholic parish, where Irish priests and Christian Brothers shaped the lives of the young children, teaching them the glories of Ireland's saints and scholars, was a memory he always cherished. As a young boy, Smith and his friends would watch the St. Patrick's Day parade as it marched through their neighborhood, up the Bowery to Twenty-third Street. When it came time to marry, he chose a young Catholic colleen from the Bronx. He loved the camaraderie of the Irish saloon, where he would hold court with a cigar in hand and his trademark brown derby atop his head. On many a St. Patrick's Day Smith was the featured speaker at the gala dinner sponsored by the Friendly Sons of St. Patrick, where the elite Irish proudly celebrated their heritage. It is hard to imagine any politician more Irish than Al Smith.

Smith had to grow up fast because his father, a teamster of German and Italian descent, had worked himself to death when Al was only twelve years old. The family was so poor that his father's friends had to pay for the funeral. His mother did not know how she would survive, but young Al told her, "I'm here, I'll take care of you." He quit school right before his graduation and became the breadwinner for his mother and younger sister. Growing up in the city's Fourth Ward, the heart of Irish New York, Smith could not help but be impressed by the popularity of the Tammany politicians, who ruled like Irish kings. He fondly remembered Big Tom Foley, a saloonkeeper and Tammany politician, who was Smith's political godfather. He recalled that his acquaintance with Foley "dates back to when I was a small boy. He was the proprietor of a café on the corner of James Slip and South Street, one block from the house in which I was born. My earliest recollection of him is of an enormous big man with a jet-black mustache, known to all the children in the neighborhood for his extreme generosity . . . The friendship formed, practically in childhood, between Tom Foley and myself lasted up to the minute of his death."[2]

Foley chose Smith to be a candidate for the state assembly in 1903 when he was only twenty-nine years old. He won the election and would continue to serve in the assembly until 1915. Smith was also a favorite of Tammany boss Charles Murphy, who selected him as the party's nominee for governor in 1918. He won that election, but failed in his attempt to be reelected in 1920. Smith thought about retiring from public life, but urged on by an up-and-coming Democrat, Franklin D. Roosevelt, Smith accepted the party's nomination for governor in the 1922 election. He won and would be reelected in 1924 and 1926.

Smith first gained widespread attention as a result of the tragic Triangle Shirtwaist factory fire on March 25, 1911, in New York City, which claimed the lives of 146 workers, 125 of whom were young immigrant women. The factory, a sweatshop on the top three floors of a ten-story building, had too few fire exits, some of which were locked; narrow stairways; and fire escapes that collapsed under the weight of too many women, plunging them to their deaths. Trapped by the spreading flames, sixty-two women jumped to their death, some of them with their arms wrapped around each other. The public outcry was so great that the state assembly established a Factory Investigating Commission, chaired by Smith's Democratic colleague Robert Wagner, with Smith as vice chairman. The commission worked for over a year, visiting factories where women worked ten to twelve hours a day, where fire escapes ended in midair. As Frances Perkins, a member of the commission and later secretary of labor, recalled, "We made sure" that Smith and Wagner saw "little children . . . five, six and seven year olds, snipping beans and shelling peas," and "machinery that would scalp a girl or cut off a man's arms."[3]

Visiting these sweatshops transformed Smith into a reformer who would henceforth fight for legislation to protect workers, especially women and children. As a result of his legislative skills, he persuaded the legislature to pass some of the most progressive labor laws in the country. These included child labor laws, legislation limiting the hours women could work, as well as a widows' pension law that sought to provide a pension to women who were left destitute after the death of their husband. As governor he continued his advocacy of progressive social legislation by signing laws that gave women teachers equal pay with men, increased public funding for education, aligned the state government with private enterprise to promote slum clearance and low-cost housing, and reorganized state government. He proved that an Irish politician could be a good governor. But ironically, what Smith is best remembered for is not his victories as a progressive politician, but his defeat in the 1928 presidential election.

The 1920s witnessed the revival of the Ku Klux Klan. By this time the Klan had over one million members, had helped to elect governors in Georgia, Alabama, California, and Oregon, and dominated local politics in many communities. It gained such popularity because many white Protestants believed that their values and traditions were under attack. The Klan singled out Catholics, Jews, immigrants, and blacks as the ones tearing apart the social fabric of the nation. Catholicism, Klansmen believed, was incompatible with American democracy because it was "fundamentally and irredeemably . . . alien, un-American, and usually anti-American." As one Klan leader put it, "Our government is on the banks of the Potomac, and not on the Tiber in Rome."[4] Flush with political power, the Klan prevented the national Democratic convention in 1924 from passing an anti-Klan resolution. This debate over the Klan bitterly divided the convention, claiming as one of its victims Al Smith, who was seeking the party's nomination for president. Smith's religion, his opposition to Prohibition, and his Irish ancestry were everything the Klan opposed.

An underlying issue at the 1924 convention was Smith's stance on Prohibition. In 1919 Congress had passed the Volstead Act, outlawing the brewing and selling of beverages containing more than one half of 1 percent alcohol. The goal was the moral reform of the nation by regulating the private lives of people. Though a dismal failure, Prohibition divided the nation into wets and drys until its repeal in 1933.

By 1919 most Catholics were not sympathetic to Prohibition. Temperance had gained wide support among Catholics in the post–Civil War era, most especially through the Catholic Total Abstinence Union of America, founded in 1872 to promote temperance. By 1903 the group reached the zenith of its popularity with a membership of more than ninety thousand, the vast majority of whom were Irish. But by this time Prohibition, the outlawing of alcoholic beverages, had replaced temperance as the chosen strategy to reform the nation's morals. However, among the Irish, where the saloon was such a popular institution, the idea of outlawing beer and whiskey was not only outrageous, but an infringement on their personal freedom. Cardinal Gibbons, who was not a teetotaler, was quoted in the *New York Times* in 1917 as saying that the passage of Prohibition would be a "national catastrophe, little short of a crime against the spiritual and physical well-being of the American people."[5] Most bishops shared Gibbons's misgivings about the wisdom of Prohibition. By this time they had lined up with Al Smith, one of the most prominent wets in America, who would publicly flaunt his opposition to Prohibition by serving liquor in the governor's mansion in Albany.

After his defeat in 1924, Smith reemerged four years later ready once again to seek his party's presidential nomination. Smith, a four-term governor of New York, was one of the most powerful and popular Democratic politicians at the time. He easily won the party's nomination for president on the first ballot. To balance the openly wet New York governor, the Democrats chose a dry Methodist, Arkansas senator Joseph T. Robinson. Smith pledged to those gathered at the convention to make repeal of the Volstead Act one of his top priorities. But another issue would haunt Smith throughout the campaign—his religion. Was a Protestant country ready to elect a Catholic president?

Smith had not wanted to confront the religious question publicly, fearing that this would only fuel the debate. But he was forced to when in April 1927 an article appeared in the *Atlantic Monthly* that questioned the legitimacy of a Catholic president. Written by Charles C. Marshall, a New York lawyer and prominent Episcopalian, this open letter to Smith questioned whether Smith as president could remain loyal to both his church and the nation. Quoting a number of papal encyclicals, Marshall argued that in a conflict between Roman Catholic teaching and American constitutional law, Smith would, as a loyal Catholic, have to accept the authority of the Church over the state. Reading like a dull legal brief, Marshall's essay posed the fundamental question to Smith:

> Citizens who waver in your support would ask, whether as a Roman Catholic, you accept as authoritative the teaching of the Roman Catholic Church, that in case of contradiction, making it impossible for the jurisdiction of that Church and the jurisdiction of the State to agree, the jurisdiction of the Church shall prevail; whether as statesman, you accept the teaching of the Supreme Court of the United States that, in matters of religious practices which in the opinion of the State, are inconsistent with its peace and safety, the jurisdiction of the State shall prevail; and, if you accept both teachings, how you will reconcile them.[6]

After reading the article, Smith was supposed to have said, "What the hell is an encyclical?" He had never read one and did not even know how to spell the word, let alone pronounce it. He told his Jewish aide Judge Joseph M. Proskauer to write a response. "Well," said Proskauer, "that would make it perfect. A Protestant lawyer challenges a Catholic candidate on his religion, and the challenge is answered by a Jewish judge." Smith relented, and with the help of Proskauer and Father Francis P. Duffy, a New York priest, respected theologian, and famous army chaplain who had served in World War I, Smith put together a response entitled "Catholic and Patriot: Governor Smith Replies." Smith's response was received favorably by the press, putting to rest Marshall's accusation that Smith could not be both a faithful Roman Catholic and a loyal American.

Smith wrote that Marshall implied that "there is conflict between religious loyalty to the Catholic faith and patriotic loyalty to the United States." Smith said, "I have taken an oath of office in this State nineteen times. Each time I swore to defend and maintain the Constitution of the United States. All of this represents a period of public service in elective office almost continuously since 1903. I have never known any conflict between my official duties and my religious beliefs. No such conflict could exist."[7]

In responding to Marshall's point that Catholics believed in a union of Church and state in which the Church dominates the state, Smith replied that such a teaching was the ideal articulated in Catholic theology. But no purely Catholic states existed where this ideal would apply. Moreover, this traditional teaching, quoting the archbishop of St. Paul, "may well be relegated to the limbo of defunct controversies." In other words, such a teaching was no longer applicable in the twentieth century. Marshall's other main contention was that Catholics must always side with the Church in case of a conflict with the state. Smith responded by reminding Marshall, "Your church just as mine" endorses "the injunction of our common savior to render unto Caesar the things that are Caesar's and unto God the things that are God's." For Catholics then, "conscience is the supreme law which under no circumstances can we ever lawfully disobey." He ended his reply with his own lengthy "creed as an American Catholic," in which he reaffirmed his commitment to his faith and his country, ending with "a fervent prayer that never again in this land will any public servant be challenged because of the faith in which he has tried to walk humbly with his God."[8]

The religious issue would not go away, however, hounding Smith throughout the campaign. Numerous pamphlets attacking Smith and his religion littered the landscape, reminiscent of the Know-Nothing era. Over one hundred anti-Catholic newspapers were also spreading their propaganda to millions of readers. Ministers assailed Smith from their pulpits. One Protestant divine asked an audience of Lutherans, "Shall we have a man in the White House who acknowledges allegiance to the Autocrat on the Tiber, who hates democracy, public schools, Protestant parsonages, individual right, and everything that is essential to independence?"[9] Anti-Catholic lecturers traveled the country denouncing Smith and his Church. Fueling this religious bigotry was an organized campaign orchestrated by dry leaders who realized that Smith's candidacy presented a formidable challenge to Prohibition. They called him "Alcohol Al" and "the cocktail President," portraying him as a drunkard who would show up at rallies intoxicated. A poem written by a factory worker captured some of these feelings:

A vote for Al is a vote for rum
A vote to empower America's scum.
A vote for intolerance and bigotry,
In a land of tolerance and of the free.[10]

Frances Perkins, an aide of Smith's, recalled, "We who campaigned for Smith in 1928, and also the candidate himself, were not prepared to deal with the degree of prejudice we encountered . . . and were surprised and shocked by the way in which our opponents appealed to the basest passions and lowest motives of the people."[11]

Smith confronted the religious issue head-on at a campaign stop in Oklahoma. The Ku Klux Klan had welcomed the campaign train by burning crosses along the way to Oklahoma City. Rumors of pending violence had been circulating, but the roar of more than seventy thousand well-wishers at the train station quieted the fears among Smith's aides. In his talk Smith addressed the issue of anti-Catholicism, stating that such hatred was "so out of line with the spirit of America." He closed his talk by saying, "I do not want any Catholic to vote for me . . . because I am a Catholic . . . But on the other hand I have the right to say that any citizen of this country [who] votes against me because of my religion, he is not a real, pure, genuine American."[12]

Smith continued his travels through the Midwest, stopping in Nebraska, Kansas, Missouri, Colorado, Montana, and Minnesota. At every stop enthusiastic crowds welcomed him. He was not a large man, only about five feet seven inches, built more like his mother than his father. But he transcended his stature by performing for the crowds, cigar in hand, waving his brown derby, and leading them in song as together they sang "Sidewalks of New York." A great speechmaker, he could talk for two hours or more without any notes. Audiences loved him. In St. Louis, where over two hundred thousand people greeted him, one of Smith's aides recalled:

The behavior of the crowds was a surprise. I recognized their liking him, but they cried. Tears rolled down the cheeks of many people. I saw people rush out, so that the Secret Service men who were supposed to be guiding him couldn't cope with the crowds. Men and women would rush up and try to touch the automobile. I remember saying to somebody . . . My God, they're trying to touch the hem of his garment.[13]

At a train stop in a small rural town in Minnesota, a young Catholic girl, dressed in her Girl Scout uniform, recalled how she and her family went to the train station to greet Al Smith. She remembered him as so very New York, not quite refined, and "so alien to the Minnesota landscape," but she did not dare tell her father.[14] Her instincts were prophetic since a vast majority of voters thought the same. Smith was too wet, too Irish, too urban, and, of course, too Catholic for their taste. In the election, he went down in a resounding defeat. When the final votes were counted, Herbert Hoover had won 444 electoral votes to Smith's 87. It was a tragic defeat for Smith as well as the Irish. As historian Michael Lerner observed, Smith was the victim of "an organized campaign of bigotry orchestrated by the dry crusade."[15] By joining Smith's opposition to Prohibition with his religion, the dry leaders created a deadly combination that killed any chance he had of winning in 1928.

On election day, whatever optimism Smith and his advisers had faded once the votes started to come in. In the South, a Democratic stronghold since the Civil War, Smith lost Virginia, North Carolina, Kentucky, Tennessee, Florida, Oklahoma, and Texas. He lost every state in the West and all the industrial midwestern states. He even lost New York. As Walter Lippmann wrote, this was "more than he could stand." He lost in his home state for much the same reasons as in the rest of the nation—his Catholicism and his stance against Prohibition. In addition, a large number of independents voted for Hoover rather than Smith. Such a loss was a blow to his pride. Not only was he tired and spent after such a grueling campaign, but on election night he looked bewildered. One of his aides recalled, "Al looked hurt that night and said to me, 'I never could believe it. I never could believe it. You saw them crowds in St. Louis, didn't you?' He remembered that I was there. I said, 'Yes.' He said, 'It was just the same everywhere . . . After the way they felt how could you believe they wouldn't vote that way?' "[16]

Once the outcome was decided, Smith returned to his apartment at the Biltmore, where he joined his family. Amid tears of consolation they celebrated his daughter's birthday, sharing cake with friends and family. Shortly after midnight he sent Herbert Hoover "a telegram congratulating him on his victory."[17]

Ever since then, historians have attempted to explain the outcome of the 1928 election. Some said that the decisive issue was the voters' attitude toward Prohibition. Others claimed that the voters' nativity, either American-born or foreign-born, was the critical factor. Still others claimed that the economic prosperity of the 1920s assured the Republicans of victory. But the most comprehensive study, done in 1979, concluded that "the religious issue was by far the most important influence on voting." Smith's contemporary Republican senator George W. Norris acknowledged, as did many others in 1928, that "the greatest element involved in the landslide was religion." Moreover, Norris added, "the religious issue" has sowed "the seeds of hatred, prejudice, and jealousy, and they will grow and bear fruit long after the present generation has passed away."[18]

The campaign of 1928 clearly revealed the deep division between Catholics and Protestants as religion remained as a major fault line running through American society. Recalling her reaction as a young girl to Smith's defeat, Abigail McCarthy remarked, Smith's loss "was my loss as well as his." She was sad, "afraid that if I went up Main Street people would taunt me and jeer at me." A Catholic high school student in Chicago confessed that Smith's defeat "left us with the feeling that 'we couldn't be president; that we were just dealt out.' "[19] The election showed how far the Irish could go, but also how far they still had to go. Embittered by such a crushing blow, McCarthy and countless other Catholics turned to the Church for comfort and solace, building it into a powerful citadel, unrivaled by any other religious denomination.

Al Smith represented the new generation emerging in the early twentieth century who would redefine what it meant to be Irish in America. Proudly Catholic, they strongly protested the bigotry they encountered because of their religion, always asserting that they were as American as the descendants of the Puritans. Smith's rise personified the Irish success story that was taking place as increasing numbers of American-born Irish moved into the middle class. His climb up the social ladder began in a tenement on the Lower East Side and ended in an apartment on Fifth Avenue where his neighbors were the Vanderbilts and the Rockefellers, not the Foleys and the Murphys.

A key element in this emerging self-identity was respectability, a distinctive feature of the emerging Irish Catholic middle class, whose lace curtains and steam heat signaled their arrival. Realizing, as Al Smith put it, that "we are watched a little more than anybody else," Irish Catholics wanted to shed the Paddy image to gain respect from their neighbors.[20]

Reinforcing this shift in ethnic identity was the decline in Irish immigration. In the 1920s, amidst a rising tide of anti-immigrant sentiment, Congress passed new immigration laws that severely limited the number of immigrants allowed into the United States. As a result only 220,591

Irish emigrated to the United States in the 1920s, most of them arriving in the early years of the decade, whereas in the first decade of the century more than 339,000 Irish had emigrated. In the late 1920s, after the passage of new laws, the Irish could not even fill their annual quota of 28,567. Then in the 1930s Irish emigration dropped dramatically, with only 801 arriving in 1931, and in no year until after World War II did it ever reach 1,000. The 1930s, not the 1920s, was the watershed in post-famine migration from Ireland. When the American economy began to recover after World War II, emigration to the United States picked up, but it only averaged a few thousand a year as the bulk of Irish emigrants now chose England as their favorite destination. One critical reason for this was the safety net provided by the British welfare state. As immigration declined, the number of foreign-born Irish in the United States also declined, to less than one million by 1930. This further weakened the link with Ireland as it became a lived memory for fewer Irish in America.[21]

Not only did the Depression of the 1930s influence immigration, but it also weakened the bonds between Irish America and Ireland. Widespread unemployment and long bread lines were hardly appealing to anyone contemplating emigration. The United States was no longer considered the "land of golden opportunity." In fact, a significant number of Irish decided to return to their native land, arriving broke and disillusioned. As a Donegal newspaper put it, "The wild geese are returning, but their footsteps are slow and their faces are haggard. They are here because they can no longer get bread or work in the land of their adoption." Also weakening the link with Ireland was the decline in remittances sent home by immigrants. By 1940 the level had declined to about a half million dollars a year, or one-third less than the pre-Depression levels. This, too, weakened the bond between family in Ireland and those in America. No more money arrived to help repair a leaky roof; First Communion dresses were no longer shipped to young nieces; fewer people were able to send the usual Christmas remittance, creating additional hardship. One Irish newspaper predicted, "There will be a serious loss in the west, where the American letter is awaited with expectancy and hope on the eve of the Christmas season."[22]

Those Irish who did emigrate in the post-1920 period resembled the typical nineteenth-century emigrant—single, unskilled laborers, not highly educated, and as many women as men. They were the silent victims of an inheritance system that still favored the oldest son and daughter, disinheriting the other siblings. Leaving a country that was economically stagnant, they traveled to the United States hopeful of a better life. Like those before them, they settled in the big cities, with New York being the favorite destination.

Leaving home and breaking away from all that one had known was never easy, whether it was in 1880 or 1940. A young Irish emigrant described her feelings and the events leading up to her departure in 1947, which included a vestige of the traditional American wake:

> Everybody came with me as far as the cove, you know, and went out on the small ship [the ferry to the ocean liner] with me. I didn't get really lonely till I got on the big ship. And then I realized that there's no turning back. There were callers for two days and nights [before she left], when everybody was coming by, and parties and everything. It's sad, you know, it's sad. To think of breakin' up with all your chums. I then, well I just got to New York, when I got a telegram saying my father was dead. So I was very lonely, but there was nothing I could do—I was so far away. It's hard breaking away, but when you're young and you have to decide your future you just can't turn back.[23]

Contributing to the transformation from an Irish American identity to an American Irish identity was a marked decline in nationalism. The signing of the Anglo-Irish Treaty in 1922 had silenced Irish American nationalism until it flared up again in the 1960s and '70s. Along with this weakening in nationalist fervor was a sharp drop in the number of those joining Irish fraternal organizations, most notably the Ancient Order of Hibernians. Their flagship publication, the *National Hibernian*, suffered such a serious decline in circulation that by 1935 it had only thirty-five thousand readers, just over one third of its pre-Depression membership. During the Depression, many state chapters of the Hibernians lost as much as 75 percent of their members, with the result that nationwide the Hibernians had declined to an estimated twenty thousand members on the eve of World War II. The two flagship newspapers of Irish America, the *Gaelic American* and the *Irish World*, also lost many readers. Their Anglophobia, evident during the nationalist struggle, proved to be less appealing to a people becoming more American.[24]

One other indication of the transformation of the Irish was the rise of the Knights of Columbus. Founded in 1882 by Michael McGivney, a young parish priest in New Haven, Connecticut, as a fraternal insurance society, it became popular throughout the Northeast. Before long the Knights of Columbus were present in every state of the union, boasting a membership of over two hundred thousand by 1909. Though it was not an exclusively Irish organization, its founding members and its key officers throughout the nineteenth and much of the twentieth century were of Irish descent. As a fraternal society with an array of social and educational programs as well as an attractive insurance benefit, it had a special appeal to the emerging Irish middle class.

What was particularly notable was the Knights' emphasis on American patriotism. To prove their loyalty to the nation the Knights took as their patron the Catholic explorer Christopher Columbus, proclaiming both their Catholic faith and their American patriotism. As their oath put it, "The proudest boast of all time is ours to make, I am an American Catholic citizen."[25] Though it was first and foremost an insurance organization that would eventually have millions of dollars of assets, through its rituals and ethos it fostered a spirit of Catholic Americanism that was unique. Unlike the Hibernians, who were an exclusively Irish organization, rooted in a love for all things Irish and a disdain for everything English, the Knights were ethnically inclusive and visibly patriotic. This Catholic Americanism proved to be widely popular, so much so that by the 1920s the Knights numbered over 782,400 members. The Hibernians were no match for the Knights and their Catholic Americanism.

Another indication of the waning of Irish nationalism and the rise of American patriotism among the Irish was the popularity of the American Legion and the Veterans of Foreign Wars. In the post–World War II period, many Irish veterans who had served in the war joined these fraternal organizations rather than the Hibernians.

The U.S. entry into World War II had sparked a wave of patriotism across the country. War-bond rallies, air-raid drills, and scrap drives instilled a sense of national purpose in local communities. Soldiers of different ethnic backgrounds fought side by side on the battlefields of Europe in a crucible of war that melted away their ethnic differences. Strengthening this emphasis on interethnic unity was the prevailing belief in the melting-pot metaphor to explain the cultural assimilation by which many diverse peoples blended into one people. Being American trumped being Irish. Adding to this reshaping of ethnic identity was a decline in Anglophobia as Britain became America's ally in war. As the war continued, Ireland's neutrality as well as Prime Minister de Valera's strong opposition to allowing any British soldiers or ships on Irish soil fostered resentment toward Ireland by those who identified with America in the global struggle.

After the war, the Ancient Order of Hibernians underwent a transformation that reflected this reshaping of Irish ethnic identity. Facing competition from the Knights as well as other patriotic fraternal organizations, the new leadership in the Hibernians sought to promote a more tolerant American ethos, calling for a new sense of fellowship among Catholic ethnic groups. As one spokesman put it, "Hibernians should take the lead in civic celebrations that develop the true American way of life, celebrations such as Columbus Day, Saint Patrick's Day, and all church holy days." For this Hibernian, St. Patrick's Day had become an American holiday, no longer reserved for the Irish alone. Uncle Sam had trumped St. Patrick. He went on to speak out for equality and tolerance, declaring, "We must be broad . . . loving not merely our own members but all God's children, irrespective of their race, unmindful of their color, regardless of their creed."[26] Such a posture would make the American Irish more respectable and accepted.

In 1947 the Hibernians founded a new newspaper, the *Hibernian Digest*, which also sought to redefine Irish ethnic identity. In it the national secretary reminded readers, "The Ancient Order of Hibernians is an American organization, dedicated to the support and protection of American institutions and the American way of life." Such civic patriotism was oceans removed from the intense nationalism that had animated the Hibernians during Ireland's struggle for independence.[27] Paul Blanshard, a famous anti-Catholic publicist in the 1950s not known for his kindness toward the Irish, even acknowledged that the Irish American people "are on the whole, eagerly and sincerely patriotic. Probably they are more deeply and emotionally attached to America than any other national group in American society, and their remarkable record as volunteers in American wars would bear this out."[28]

Even as they became ardent patriots, the American Irish never lost their Irish heritage. It continued to be an important element in their self-identity, but as historian Matthew O'Brien wrote, "The basis of that identity shifted away from the land of origin and became more firmly rooted in American patriotism." For Americans of Irish descent, Ireland had become but a point of ethnic reference in a multicultural America.[29]

Fueling this reshaping of ethnic identity was the economic mobility experienced by the Irish in the post–World War I era. In the 1920s the Irish were still a blue-collar community, with as many as six out of every ten workers being manual laborers. The rest were in low white-collar oc-cupations or skilled trades. Few families had a breadwinner with a high white-collar profession.[30] This occupational profile remained fairly con-stant through the mid-1940s. But among the American-born Irish a no-ticeable pattern of economic mobility was apparent, confirming the trend that, for the most part, each successive generation did better economically, with fewer manual workers and more middle-class, white-collar workers than their predecessors. In Newburyport, Massachusetts, for example, 66 percent of the all Irish workers were blue-collar working-class and 34 percent were middle-class. But, when the third generation was consid-ered separately, the figures were almost reversed, with 60 percent in the middle class and 40 percent described as working-class. This pattern of occupational mobility was prevalent throughout the nation.[31]

In those cities where the Irish political machine was in control, the Irish gained economic advancement. In New York City, for example, more than half of all the workers in the city-owned subways, street railways, waterworks, and port facilities were Irish (52 percent). Large numbers of Irish were also employed in the city's fire and police departments. These municipal jobs were secure, respectable occupations, but offered little op-portunity for advancement out of the lower middle class. Except for the construction industry, which had traditionally been an Irish stronghold, the Irish chose the public sector rather than the riskier private sector, where opportunities for advancement were greater. This reflected the con-servative nature of the Irish, who sought security first rather than risk the uncertainty of possible economic gain.[32]

The 1930s were hard times in America as the economy went into a tailspin. The Irish suffered, as did all Americans. A woman living on Manhattan's West Side recalled, "Things were rough at that time. The poverty of the Depression was different from the poverty I knew growing up, because here I could see there were few jobs for anybody . . . There were thousands out of work." Her Irish neighbor echoed her observation, recalling that "it was very, very hard" during the Depression as jobs disap-peared. Families lost their homes, small businesses went bankrupt, and what government relief there was provided little help.[33]

Another feature of the post–World War I era was the exodus of the American-born Irish from the immigrant enclaves to new neighborhoods being developed beyond the old city limits. Some of these changes of ad-dress were by necessity, as growing families needed more living space. For others, just the promise of indoor plumbing was enough of a motivation to move. Though not every change of address meant a step up the economic ladder, most often it did signal a move to a more respectable neighborhood. In New York the expansion of the subway to northern Manhattan sparked a housing boom in the nineteenth-century suburbs of Washington Heights and Inwood, located north of 155th Street. Jewish and Irish families left their tenements in Lower Manhattan to settle in these new neighborhoods. By 1940 the Irish numbered 23,900, or almost 12 percent of the neighborhood's population, with the Jewish population comprising about 73,100, or 36 percent of the total.[34] The Bronx was another area that underwent a housing boom in the 1920s, pushing the population of the area to 1,265,258 by 1930—almost double what it was in 1920. Once again it was the Irish and the Jews who led the migration out of Manhattan to new homes and apartments in the Bronx. Most of the Irish who settled there worked for the city, enjoying better incomes than those in the suburbs of northern Manhattan. Their new address had anointed them with the chrism of respectability.

In Chicago, the streetcar pushed the city limits into the prairie bordering the city's South Side. As new neighborhoods developed in the 1920s, Irish families moved out of their old enclaves in the Back of the Yards and Canaryville to Auburn Park, located around Seventy-ninth Street and Ashland Avenue. By 1930 the population of the area had soared to 57,381, nearly triple what it was ten years earlier. The attraction of new homes in a countrylike setting persuaded many inner-city dwellers to pack up and move. One resident recalled that his family "had lived in a four-room apartment on 58th and Peoria and it was too small for two children and parents." Another mentioned that the opportunity to have indoor plumbing was reason enough to move. The Irish who settled in what would become known as St. Sabina's parish were blue-collar working-class. As one person said of them, "They didn't have a lot. It [the parish] was made up of . . . small people—streetcarmen, policemen, firemen, city workers, who in those days didn't get much in the way of pay—people with big families."[35] Yet, they considered themselves middle class who had moved up a notch in respectability, signaled by the lace curtains hanging in the windows of their new bungalows.

The same pattern of urban expansion and residential mobility took place in San Francisco. In the late nineteenth century, scores of Irish left their downtown neighborhoods, adjacent to the docks, for the Mission District in the southeastern part of the city near the old Mission San Francisco de Asis. The earthquake and fire of 1906 forced more people to abandon the burned-out downtown and move to the Mission District. By this time the area had become a working-class neighborhood of mostly Irish and German immigrants and their descendants. More and more Irish settled in the neighborhood in subsequent years, attracted by the Catholic flavor of the area, nurtured by St. Peter's parish and its charismatic priest, Father Peter Yorke. Until World War II "many Mission residents were consciously Irish, often consciously working class, and very conscious of being residents of 'the Mish.'" As in Auburn Park and the Bronx, many worked in civil service jobs or were police or firemen.[36]

These Irish neighborhoods of the pre–World War II era shared certain features, the most prominent being their tightly knit, insular character. Though other ethnic groups lived in each area, the Irish had their own network of pubs and parishes that enabled them to live in their own world. Their homes, families, and friends further defined this world. As one New Yorker in Washington Heights put it, "Your whole life was your neighborhood, your home, your parish, your block." A Chicago Irishman put it this way: Catholics "were raised in a kind of an enclave, maybe you should call it a ghetto, but we didn't feel persecuted in it. We thought we were on top of the world. But I think we did close ourselves in."[37] They might as well have been living in an Irish village. Such clannishness persuaded them to marry within their own ethnic group. In those days a "mixed marriage" did not mean a religiously mixed marriage, which was rare, but an ethnically mixed marriage, which, though less rare, was generally discouraged.

Another feature was the prominence of the Catholic parish. Each parish was generally a large complex that occupied as much as an entire city block. With its cross rising high above the rooflines of the neighborhood, the church bells ringing throughout the week, and the processions winding their way through the city streets on special holy days, the church gave the neighborhood a special, sacred character. So tied to the neighborhood was the parish that people identified themselves as living in St. Sabina's or Incarnation rather than Auburn Park or Inwood. In San Francisco's Mission District they even adopted the name Peterites to identify who they were and where they lived. When real estate agents, many of whom were Irish, wanted to advertise homes for sale, they would identify them by the name of the parish, such as "a St. Sabina bungalow." In many ways the parish was the glue that held the community together during this interwar era. Residents rarely left the neighborhood. Everything they needed could be found along the neighborhood's main thoroughfare, whether it was Seventy-ninth Street on Chicago's South Side or Mission Street or Twenty-fourth Street in San Francisco's Mission District. For children growing up in New York's Washington Heights, Times Square might as well have been in London, since they rarely ventured far from home.

One other feature people remembered was how order was kept in the community. They all claimed to know each other, enabling them to keep a watchful eye on the children. Smoking was taboo for young people, and anyone seen smoking by a neighbor was duly reported to his or her parents. It was a "word of mouth" culture where mothers were an especially effective network of communication, spreading the news, good or bad, through the neighborhood in hours. The police were often neighborhood residents who knew the children by name and would not hesitate to report any misdeeds to their parents. Certainly crime existed in these enclaves, along with teenage gangs, domestic abuse, and alcoholism, but on the streets parents and police kept a watchful eye out for any delinquency in the hope of preserving order in the neighborhood.[38]

Foreign-born Irish who had arrived prior to the Depression as well as the newcomers who came after World War II helped to give these neighborhoods a visible and audible ethnic flavor. On Chicago's South Side, in St. Sabina's parish, people claimed "that you could stand on 79th Street and hear the brogue of every county in Ireland."[39] Most Irish communities sponsored ceilis (dances) that featured Irish dance and music. In New York the future labor leader Mike Quill first gained notoriety as a popular master of ceremonies at many Irish ceilis. The popular Irish dance hall City Center was packed with hundreds of Irish every Saturday night, dancing to both American dance tunes and Irish jigs and reels. Such dances, held in dozens of dance halls scattered throughout New York, reflected the changing nature of Irish identity as the dancing Irish adapted to the prevailing American commercial culture while maintaining a loyalty to Ireland's traditional culture. The New York Irish not only supported such cultural events but also were avid fans of hurling and Gaelic football, athletic contests that attracted large crowds at Gaelic Park, located in the Bronx. The love for such sports was so widespread that in 1947 the New York Irish sporting community persuaded their counterparts in Ireland to hold the All-Ireland Gaelic Football championship in New York, where it took place at the Polo Grounds, attracting a crowd of thirty-five thousand fans. This was the only time the All-Ireland Final was played outside Ireland. This was not only a gesture of friendship on the part of Ireland toward the Irish American community, but also a calculated attempt to encourage the development of Gaelic sports in the New York area.

The post–World War II era ushered in a new age in American history. For the American Irish working class—as for many other Americans—everything changed. The GI Bill, enacted in 1944, enabled many veterans to attend college, thus gaining an education that opened doors to new and better job opportunities. The population exploded, new suburbs appeared, and there emerged "a prosperity and materialism that scarcely anyone had expected and few knew how to handle."[40] Wages and salaries doubled during the war years, ushering in an age of prosperity unprecedented in American history. The rising tide lifted large numbers of the Irish into the middle class. By 1960 they had become one of the best-educated and most prosperous ethnic groups in the nation, with as many as 66 percent in white-collar occupations and 49 percent having a college education. Not surprisingly the American-born Irish had done much better than the more recent Irish-born immigrants, who were still a blue-collar community.[41]

Just as the post–World War II era ushered in an unprecedented age of affluence, it also marked the beginning of a transformation throughout urban America that forever changed the Irish neighborhoods of the pre-war period. This was a time of urban renewal, when freeways demolished city neighborhoods, city planners tore down old buildings and replaced them with new high-rises, and a building boom took place in the nation's suburbs. On top of this was a massive African American migration from the South to the Northern cities where the Irish, along with other European ethnic groups, had established their ethnic enclaves. In time, African Americans, along with newly arrived Latino immigrants from Latin America, would move into these Irish enclaves. This demographic pressure occurred throughout the urban North just at a "point of triumph" for the Irish, who, as John McGreevy put it, "having weathered the depression, built the school, and finished the church, now confronted the possibility that, given patterns of racial transition in American cities, the painstaking work of generations might be rendered obsolete in a handful of years."[42] Their loyalty to neighborhood and church intensified their resistance to change, thus making the transition all the more difficult.

In San Francisco it was not the migration of African Americans, but the arrival of new immigrants from Central and South America that changed the city's Mission District. Low rents and the working-class nature of the Mission attracted a steady flow of new Latino immigrants. Construction of a new freeway in the eastern part of the Mission forced many of the old-time Irish to move. Reflecting the changing nature of the neighborhood, St. Peter's church began to offer services in Spanish, much to the distress of the old-time parishioners. By 1960, 30 percent of the Mission District was Latino. This demographic shift would continue until eventually the Mission District became a predominantly Latino neighborhood.

Where did the Irish go? Those who enjoyed the fruits of the postwar prosperity moved to more affluent and newer neighborhoods in the Sunset and Richmond districts of the city. Others moved beyond the city to the new suburbs developing in the Bay Area. Those who could not afford to move adapted to the cultural diversity of the Mission.

In New York, a similar transformation took place in the Irish neighborhoods of Washington Heights. People said that the Heights began where Harlem ended, but by the 1950s the migration of African Americans had pushed the boundaries of Harlem north into the Heights. Alongside blacks, Puerto Ricans moved into the neighborhood. Both groups came for the same reason that the Irish first settled in the area— better housing, low rents, and convenient transportation. Crime rose as gangs from different racial and ethnic groups battled for control of the Heights. Fear took over the streets, persuading many Irish residents to leave. Some moved just a few blocks north to Inwood, where the Irish were still a sizable presence. Others, enjoying the prosperity of the times, could afford to move to New Jersey or north to New York's Rockland County. Throughout the 1960s, newcomers replaced the Irish in the Heights and eventually Inwood as well.[43]

By the 1940s Chicago was already a black metropolis. This was most evident in the city's South Side, where throughout the 1950s African Americans continued to settle in racially segregated neighborhoods bordering Irish Catholic enclaves. As the city's black belt began to expand south and west into the Irish enclaves, the majority of the Irish lived in fear that African Americans would move into their neighborhoods. Some Irish neighborhoods, supported by their priests, resisted the possibility, exhibiting the racism that the Irish had displayed ever since the days of the New York draft riots in 1863. Racial epithets were hurled, stones were thrown, and riots broke out as the Irish did everything they could "to keep Negroes out."[44] By 1950 the black belt was approaching the neighborhood of Auburn Park and the Irish parish of St. Sabina. The fear of change traumatized the neighborhood. The pastor of the parish, Monsignor John McMahon, urged the people to be tolerant and disavow the racism on display in other Catholic neighborhoods. He refused to believe "that the presence of blacks meant the death knell for a neighborhood."[45] Unlike many clergy, he believed in the integration of the races rather than segregation. This was the model he hoped to establish in St. Sabina's. But the fear of neighborhood change was just too great. White flight took place in the 1960s as St. Sabina's, once an Irish Catholic citadel, became a prominent black Catholic parish. The Irish who left moved to the city's southern and western suburbs.

During the 1920–60 era the Irish had advanced economically, gaining parity with much of the nation's population. They had built their Church into a powerful institution, feared if not admired by their Protestant neighbors. Respectability, so ardently desired since the postfamine era, was no longer a goal since the Irish had now achieved it. They had become more American than Irish, loyal patriots who claimed an Irish ancestry but an American identity. The breakup of the old neighborhoods hastened the change as the Irish moved out to new suburban neighborhoods where being American trumped being Irish. But as Al Smith's defeat had demonstrated, their Catholicism was still a liability. Politically, Irish Catholics might rule such cities as Chicago and Boston, but socially, they were still not wanted at the elite country clubs. The one institution that had held the Irish community together throughout this period was the Church.

CHAPTER 10

Irish Catholicism's Golden Age

I n July 1918 the city of Philadelphia witnessed a spectacle never before seen: the triumphal entry of the new Catholic archbishop, Dennis Dougherty. Traveling by train from Buffalo, where he had been bishop for three years, Dougherty arrived at the train station greeted with the sound of church bells ringing throughout the city. Along with an entourage of priests who had accompanied him on the journey, Dougherty stepped off the train into an open limousine waiting to take him on a motorcade through the city. Accompanying the motorcade were fifty brass bands, seventy-five automobiles, and a police escort of roaring motorcycles. As Dougherty's parade made its way to the Catholic cathedral, thousands of people lined the streets, cheering the arrival of the new archbishop. The Irish prelate loved the attention, smiling and waving to the crowds from the open limousine. People even broke through the police barriers so they could touch him and kiss his ring as he reached out to greet the exuberant faithful. That evening the governor-elect, the state attorney general, the mayor, and the city's leading citizens welcomed Dougherty at a splendid reception.[1] It was a day that he would long remember.

The son of Irish immigrants, Dougherty would reign in Philadelphia like a Renaissance prince for the next thirty-three years. He lived in a sixteen-room mansion purchased during the Depression, when many Catholics could hardly afford to pay their rent or mortgage. In addition, he had a winter home in Florida and would take lengthy, three-month trips to Europe, always with a stopover in Rome to strengthen his ties to the pope and the power brokers in the Vatican. He had studied in Rome at the North American College, where bishops sent the best of their seminarians. Dougherty reportedly said that next to his baptism and ordination, his education in Rome was the most important event in his life. Living in Rome in the shadow of St. Peter's Basilica and the Vatican powerhouse, he acquired a spirit of *Romanita* that shaped his entire life. His loyalty to the pope was unrivaled, and he was so well connected that within three years after his arrival in Philadelphia he was named a cardinal, an honor reserved for a select few Americans at that time. He loved the pomp and circumstance of religious ceremonies, so reminiscent of the spectacles in St. Peter's. In addition, he modeled the seminary in Philadelphia on his Roman experience, insisting that its faculty be Roman-educated just as he was. As a Catholic, he was clearly more Roman than American. In Philadelphia he was pope, ruling with an iron fist and instilling fear among his clergy, whom he transformed into a marinelike battalion, demanding complete obedience and tolerating little dissent. When he celebrated Mass, the clergy showed up with shoes shined, hair combed, cassock and surplice clean, with the obligatory biretta properly worn atop the head, and if you had the honor—some would say the burden—of assisting the cardinal at Mass, you had better not make any mistakes for fear of being publicly reprimanded. The cardinal did not suffer fools graciously.

Dougherty had come a long way from the hardscrabble Pennsylvania coal-mining region where he was born and raised. Not only was he a prince of the Church, but he was also a real estate genius. He bought up acres of land throughout the diocese, anticipating the expansion of Philadelphia's suburbs. At the time of his death, the diocese had assets in the range of several hundred million dollars. As an administrator he was typical of many bishops of his era, who, as historian Edward Kantowicz wrote, "brought order, centralization, and business like management to their dioceses." In a city ruled by WASPs, he still wielded considerable political power, quietly but effectively. In 1934 he issued an edict forbidding Catholics to go to the movies, under pain of sin. The people did as they were told, effectively shutting down the movie industry in the city. A brick-and-mortar bishop, who referred to himself as "God's bricklayer" because he was so often photographed laying a cornerstone, he built an unprecedented number of schools and parishes. Education was such a top priority of Dougherty's that he ordered that all parochial schools could not charge any tuition.[2]

Dougherty was not unique. Other Catholic prelates, most of whom were also Irish, wielded similar power and enjoyed comparable benefits.

One of the more notorious was William O'Connell of Boston. The son of famine immigrants, he traveled far from his humble origins, becoming known early on in his priesthood as Monsignor Pomposity. As a bishop and later cardinal, he enjoyed a lavish lifestyle with Florida vacations and European holidays. Like Dougherty he was educated in Rome, so absorbing the city's *Romanita* that his newly built residence resembled an Italian villa. His travels were so numerous that he acquired the nickname Gangplank Bill, as photos of him boarding a ship appeared so often in the press.[3]

By the 1920s Catholics in the United States numbered about twenty million. On any Sunday the gospel was preached in as many as twenty-five languages. In many respects it was still an immigrant church, with as many as 60 percent of Catholics being first- or second-generation immigrants. The largest groups were the Irish, Germans, Italians, and Polish. But the Irish controlled the seats of power, with more than half the bishops in the country being of Irish descent, and if, as in Chicago, the boss was not Irish, the men whom he chose to run the Church were likely to be. Not all the bishops lived like Dougherty and O'Connell, but they did enjoy unprecedented authority and the respect that the office of bishop commanded. In addition, more than one third of the clergy was of Irish descent. In fact, seminaries in Ireland were still sending priests to the United States; more than twelve hundred arrived from 1900 to 1949. Their presence was strongest in California and the Southeast, especially in Florida, where even today Irish-born clergy are still numerous.[4]

Though the Irish were not a majority of the people in the pew, in the popular mind *Catholic* meant "Irish." One reason for this was the way the movie industry portrayed Catholicism. As America's leading mass medium in the 1930s and '40s, its portrayal of Catholics shaped the popular understanding of Catholicism. When Hollywood produced a film about Catholics, it often chose an Irish priest as the hero. There were Italian, Polish, and German Catholics, but the Irish were Hollywood's Catholics. For many Americans who were not Catholic, this was the only image of Catholicism they would ever know.

In the 1930s and '40s Hollywood produced a number of classic films in which the Irish priest was featured. In 1938 Spencer Tracy won an Academy Award portraying Father Flanagan in the movie *Boys Town*. Flanagan, the founder of the Boys Town orphanage, epitomized the saintly, down-to-earth Irish priest who lived by the gospel that "there is no such thing as a bad boy." In that same year, the film *Angels with Dirty*

Faces featured two Irishmen raised in the Church, James Cagney as Rocky, the tough dead-end kid, and Pat O'Brien as Father Connolly, the childhood friend of Rocky's and the heroic priest who saves Rocky's soul as he is led off to the electric chair. In 1944, Hollywood produced a blockbuster film, *Going My Way*, that won seven Oscars. It starred Barry Fitzgerald as the aged Irish pastor and Bing Crosby as the young Irish priest, Father Chuck O'Malley, who showed up at his new assignment in a baseball cap and sport clothes, a golf bag over his shoulder. Here was a virile, athletic, good-looking, worldly young man who could charm audiences with his beautiful voice and transform a bunch of rough kids into angelic choirboys. A Hollywood hero, he became the best-known priest in the United States. He reappeared a year later with Ingrid Bergman starring as Sister Mary Benedict in another award-winning film, *The Bells of St. Mary's*. Both of these films not only glorified the Irish priest, but also underscored the central role of the parish in the Irish community. Al Smith reportedly said, after watching *Going My Way*, "It reminded me of the days when I was a boy at St. James."[5] For him and many other Catholics it confirmed their memories. In 1954 another film, *On the Waterfront*, celebrated the Irish priest. This time he was not a romantic crooner, but a tough labor priest who sought to reform the New York waterfront. Father Pete Barry, played by Karl Malden, even traded punches with the longshoreman Terry Malloy, played by Marlon Brando. Such romantic portrayals of the Irish Catholic priest only served to enhance his reputation among the faithful. In their eyes he was still the *Sagart aroon* (the Dear Priest) who could do no wrong. Hollywood could not agree more.

Such a romanticized portrayal of the priest appealed to many young men, who began to enroll in the seminary. By the 1950s large dioceses such as Chicago, Boston, and Philadelphia were ordaining as many as fifty to sixty priests a year, many of them, a third or more, from Irish Catholic families.

One reason for Hollywood's fascination with movies celebrating the Catholic culture was that they were profitable. Since Catholics constituted a huge market, films extolling the heroism of Catholic priests were potential blockbusters. This proved to be true as award-winning movies such as *Going My Way* were on lists of the top-grossing movies for a number of years. These films also promoted values that most Americans found appealing—loyalty, hard work, kindness, strong communities. The men portrayed were often tough but caring, regular churchgoers who worked hard to support their family. But, these were not the only reasons for the large numbers of Catholic movies at this time.

Hollywood had a reputation for producing films that many people considered indecent. To combat this, several states established censorship boards, but they were not very successful. Another attempt to control what was coming out of Hollywood was the Motion Picture Production Code, drawn up in 1930 by Martin Quigley, a Chicago Irish Catholic who was the publisher of the *Motion Picture Herald*, a weekly publication, and Daniel Lord, a Jesuit priest. In Quigley's opinion the public demanded "that pictures be made clean and wholesome to the last detail." If not, they would no longer support the film industry. To save the industry, he believed that a decency code was needed. Written by Lord, the new code was designed to keep movies free of indecent and objectionable material by detailing the relation of moral principles to the production of motion pictures. But it was a failure since much of the movie industry ignored the code. Something more effective was needed. With the aid of a new ally, Joe Breen, another Chicago Irish Catholic, and the support of the bishop of Los Angeles, the Irish-born John Cantwell, Quigley persuaded leading members of the hierarchy to take on the movie industry. To put some teeth into their support of the code, the bishops established a Legion of Decency, a nationwide campaign in which Catholics would pledge only to attend decent movies. The success of the campaign was startling enough to persuade Hollywood to take the code more seriously and produce films that were moral and inoffensive to Catholics.[6]

Joe Breen, whose office was in Los Angeles and whose salary was paid by the film industry, became the moral watchdog of Hollywood. With Breen and the Legion of Decency looking over their shoulders, Hollywood's movie studios portrayed Catholics favorably. If the movie industry wanted to make money and avoid censorship from millions of moviegoers, it needed the support of Catholics. There was no better way to achieve this than by producing films extolling the culture of Catholicism.

One of Hollywood's heroic priests, Father Pete Barry, was a labor priest who sought to gain justice for the thousands of longshoremen on the docks of New York. In real life Barry was the Jesuit priest John Corridan. Like a large number of other clergy of Irish descent, Corridan became known for his work in a ministry that had a distinctive liberal quality. Part of this orientation was rooted in the struggle for justice that was so much a part of the Irish heritage. Social justice was also an issue among the blue-collar, Irish working class, who were often victims of a fickle

economy. Another impulse behind their liberal reform ideas was the social encyclicals issued by the popes in the late nineteenth and early twentieth centuries. Included in this group of activists would be Bernard J.
Sheil, a Chicago priest and later auxiliary bishop whose claim to fame
was his role in establishing the Catholic Youth Organization, "a veritable
social-work empire" in Chicago that soon spread across the country.[7]
Charles Owen Rice was a Pittsburgh priest who championed the organized-
labor movement. The founder of the Extension Society, which sought to
aid the Church in poor rural areas, was Francis Clement Kelley. During
his tenure as head of the organization, 1905–40, over twelve million
dollars was distributed to these rural mission churches. Edwin V. O'Hara
was also involved in ministering to Catholics along the rural frontier,
eventually organizing a National Catholic Rural Life Conference. Other
Irish priests who could be included in the clerical hall of fame would
be James A. Walsh, a cofounder of the Maryknoll Society, a Catholic
foreign-missionary society; John A. O'Brien, prolific author and
preacher who dedicated his life to winning converts; Fulton J. Sheen,
another renowned preacher and televangelist; and the theologian John
Courtney Murray, whose picture graced the cover of *Time* magazine in
1960.

Certainly near the top of this list of notable Irish priests would be
John A. Ryan. The oldest of eleven children, Ryan was born in 1869 to
Irish immigrant parents who lived in the small farming community of
Vermillion, Minnesota. Ryan grew up in a rural Irish enclave where pop-
ulism and reform were frequent topics of conversation. The Ryan family
kept in touch with Ireland through their subscription to Patrick Ford's
Irish World. "Week by week," he wrote, "it maintained and reinforced" his
"interest in the cause of Ireland . . . One could not read the *Irish World*
week after week without acquiring an interest and a love of economic justice, as well as political justice."[8] Throughout his life Ryan maintained a
keen interest in the Irish struggle for independence, visiting Ireland four
different times as well as writing essays defending the Irish struggle for
freedom.

After his ordination to the priesthood in 1898, Ryan went to
Catholic University for further studies. His doctoral dissertation, "A Living Wage," was published in 1906, propelling him onto the stage as a rising star for social reform. The book argued "that wages should be
sufficiently high to enable the laborer to live in a manner consistent with
the dignity of a human being." As an advocate of the minimum wage, he

began to write numerous articles for Catholic publications as well as promoting social reform in his lectures across the country. He mingled freely with reform groups not associated with the Church, becoming a recognized advocate of minimum-wage legislation, even helping to write the new minimum-wage legislation in Minnesota.[9]

Ryan's significance lay in his ability to blend Catholic social thought with the American current of reform emerging during the Progressive Era. By formulating a system of social ethics that was both Catholic and American, he provided the foundation for a social gospel that would gain increasing support during the post–World War I era when the stock market crash and the Depression intensified the need for economic justice. From his position as head of the Social Action Department of the bishops' National Catholic Welfare Council, based in the nation's capital, he kept the torch of social Catholicism burning through his essays, lectures, and personal involvement. Ryan's assistant in the Social Action Department was another Irish priest, Raymond A. McGowan. Though less well-known, he was responsible for making the department an effective agency for promoting social reform at the local level.

Ryan's advocacy of a social gospel did not sit well with many Catholics who were more comfortable with a gospel of individual self-help. His close identification with President Franklin Delano Roosevelt and his New Deal reforms spurred his detractors to label him derisively the Right Reverend New Dealer. Roosevelt honored Ryan's support for him by having him deliver the benediction at his 1937 inauguration, where Ryan articulated his appreciation for the president by asking God to "bless abundantly our Chief Magistrate. Inspire his leadership. Grant him . . . the light and the strength to carry through the great work he has so well begun, and to pursue untiringly his magnificent vision of social peace and social justice."[10]

A contemporary of Ryan's who rose to national prominence in the 1930s as a radio preacher was another Irishman, Charles Coughlin. At first pleasant talks on religious subjects, his Sunday radio sermons became exclusively political. A ruddy-faced Irishman, with black hair neatly combed and rimless glasses, he had a strong baritone voice that boomed over the airwaves. With the Depression as a backdrop, he preached a message of "want in the midst of plenty." This appealed to his listeners, many of whom were unemployed Irish men and women. His Sunday *Golden Hour* had the largest radio audience in the country with as many as thirty million listeners. Thousands of letters, most with contributions to support his work, flooded his office in Royal Oak, Michigan. The volume was so large that he employed more than one hundred secretaries to handle his mail. High school football games even stopped so that players and fans could listen to his Sunday-afternoon sermon. People remember walking down the street and "hearing out of every window the voice of Father Coughlin blaring from the radio. You could walk for blocks, they recalled, and never miss a word."[11]

At first he was a supporter of Roosevelt and the New Deal as the answer to the nation's economic problems, but by the 1936 election he had become an outspoken opponent of Roosevelt. Fiercely anticommunist, he also began to attack Jews, blaming them for the nation's troubles. By the late 1930s his anti-Semitic attacks found a receptive audience among many young unemployed Irish living on the margins of society. Tapping into their discontent, he supported them as they formed neighborhood clubs to act as self-defense units to defend America against the threat of communism and other anti-Christian forces. Known as the Christian Front, these clubs were popular among the Irish in Boston and New York. Gangs of Irish youths attacked Jews in the Bronx and northern Manhattan as well as in South Boston and Roxbury. They vandalized synagogues and boycotted Jewish merchants, breaking store windows and painting anti-Semitic graffiti.[12]

By the late 1930s and early '40s Coughlin's weekly paper, *Social Justice*, had become blatantly anti-Semitic, condemning Jews as Bolsheviks and greedy capitalists. It even featured favorable profiles of Hitler, whose picture appeared on the journal's cover more than once. This was too much for the federal government, which shut down the paper in 1942 and informed Coughlin's archbishop, Edward Mooney, that the radio priest would be indicted under the Espionage Act if he was not silenced. Mooney ordered Coughlin to end his broadcasts. The radio priest retired from public life, but he continued as pastor of Little Flower church in suburban Detroit until his retirement in 1966.

As the nation struggled to cope with the economic distress unleashed by the Depression, Catholics found solace in the one institution that followed them wherever they went—the parish. This was the institution that nurtured the Catholic sectarian compound by fostering the culture of Catholicism, strengthening the barriers that separated Catholics from the rest of society.

Most of the Irish parishes founded in these years were located in the streetcar suburbs emerging in the post–World War I period. As with their nineteenth-century predecessors, the centerpiece of the parish was a large, richly decorated church. Many parishes had an elementary school attended by hundreds of children. Some parishes even had large community centers, where basketball tournaments, boxing bouts, and Sunday-evening dances entertained the youth of the parish. This focus on activities for the young people of the parish received a great deal more emphasis after World War I than in previous years. A main reason was to protect the young people from the perceived dangers lurking in dance halls and movie theaters popular at this time. By offering alternative entertainment and activities, the priests hoped to keep the youth within the orbit of the parish and its influence.

To promote their Irish heritage, parishes also sponsored Irish nights, featuring Irish music and dance. In Chicago, St. Sabina's parishioners organized the South Side Irish parade on St. Patrick's Day in 1953. From a neighborhood parade loosely organized with families and friends pushing baby carriages or riding bikes, it blossomed into a full-fledged parade the following year with twenty-three bands, forty floats, and thousands of spectators. In 1955 the parade marshal was the popular television personality Ed Sullivan, whose parents were born in county Cork, Ireland. He claimed that "it was the happiest day of his life."[13]

But by this time Irish identity was waning as being American became more important than being Irish. The parish had become an agent of Americanization rather than a promoter of ethnic identity. The American flag, not the flag of Ireland, was prominently displayed in the sanctuary of the church. Schools discontinued classes in Irish history, stressing American history along with the Pledge of Allegiance. But first and foremost, parishioners were reminded that their Catholicism was all-important.

Without question the key institution in the parish was the elementary school, consuming at least one half of a parish's entire budget, eventually as much as 75 percent. Some parishes even sponsored high schools, but, for most, running a grammar school was enough of a challenge. In most Irish neighborhoods the Catholic parish had a monopoly on education as few parents sent their children to the public school. Tuition was minimal, one dollar a month in most places. In Philadelphia it was free. By cornering the market on elementary education, the school solidified the sense of belonging that people had toward the parish.

The sisters who taught in the schools were held in high esteem by the people. In the nineteenth century, women religious were involved in a variety of ministries, but by the early twentieth century they were becoming more and more concentrated in teaching in parochial schools. The reason for this was clear—the bishops had made a concerted effort to establish a school in every parish. Though they could never reach this ideal, the number of schools steadily increased. This created a critical need for teachers, and the bishops turned to the religious orders of women to meet this demand. The sisters provided a cheap labor pool since they worked for meager wages. By the late 1950s as many as two thirds of all the sisters in the country were teaching in parish schools, doing what one of their young students described as the "wageless work of paradise." Their lives were totally focused on teaching. As one sister recalled, in the 1940s and '50s "we talked school all the time . . . it was a *life* dedicated to schools and children."[14]

Many of the sisters who taught in these schools were not only young, but ill prepared. In addition, they had to teach classes of fifty to sixty students. To do this effectively they had to have control of the classroom. They gained this by instilling discipline, and indeed fear, into their students. Their word was law, and the discipline they fostered has become legendary. Students had to line up for everything—going to the bathroom, to church, or to recess. Stepping out of line or talking in line was not acceptable. All students wore the same school uniform, and no one dared to show up out of uniform. "The nuns had almost complete control over you," recalled one Chicago Catholic. "If they wanted to whack you or punch you, they could just do it. The parents would go along with it, and if you complained, you'd be in trouble with your parents. A lot of the parents gave up their authority to the school and to the religion." As the Catholic saying had it, "If you caught it in school, you'd get it at home!"[15]

But the sisters offered more than just discipline. In St. Sabina's parish, the Sinsinawa Dominicans were fondly remembered as good teachers. As one parishioner put it, "They ran a fine school. You got a very good basic education."[16] Another Irishwoman recalled her parochial education in "the tender hands of the Sisters of Mercy." They specialized "in simple repetitive exercises through which everyone seemed to be learning how to read and write. On the whole these nuns were kindly, modestly educated women, who willingly tackled classes of fifty to sixty students. They were experts at handwriting and grammar and deportment as well as small domestic tasks like sewing, which they enjoyed themselves. Their expectations for us (as far as this world was concerned) were modest too. There was no talk of professional careers beyond teaching or nursing. They didn't press us to enter the convent—that was a matter of grace, a rare thing. Most of us were expected to become good wives and mothers of large families; there was perhaps more emphasis on the latter vocation. How this was to transpire remained a mystery."[17]

As all-important as the school and the parish's social and recreational activities were, in the eyes of the clergy at least they could never match the importance of the religious events that took place in the parish. The centerpiece of a parish's religious life was still the Sunday Mass. The Irish had set the standard for all Catholics to follow, regardless of their ethnic background. The most important requirement was attendance at Mass on Sunday. Skipping Sunday Mass was a serious sin to be avoided at all costs. For this reason parishes had to schedule numerous Masses on Sunday to accommodate the large number of people in the parish. Chicago's St. Sabina's, for example, scheduled eleven Sunday Masses to accommodate the more than thirty-four hundred families in the parish.

For Catholics, Sunday was the high point of the week. It began at midnight with fasting before Mass and Communion. "Whatever you were up to the night before," recalled one woman, "whatever tasty snack was in your hand, you partied with one eye on the clock. At midnight the dance went on, but neither food nor drink would pass those Catholic lips. There was a certain pleasurable pang in all this self-denial that no doubt went beyond the religious impulse. It set us apart as people who lived up to high standards; it gave us a sense of rigor, of fine aristocratic purity and reserve."[18]

Next to the Mass were the numerous Marian devotions that had become quite popular in the twentieth century. Devotion to Mary had always been part of Catholic piety, but in the first half of the twentieth century it became even more popular, with the spring ritual of the May crowning of Marian statues being a special event for the young girls of the parish, especially the one chosen to crown the statue. Novenas, nine days of prayer, became the most popular Marian devotion at this time, filling churches on weekday evenings with standing-room-only crowds. Praying the rosary—the centerpiece of which was the Hail Mary—was another favorite ritual, performed both publicly and privately. Devotion to the Eucharist—the presence of Jesus Christ in the sacred host—became more widespread in the post-1920 period. Such devotion included not only frequent Communion, but also adoration of the Eucharist in the church night and day for forty hours. This would begin and end with a grand celebration of priests and laity, usually young children, marching in procession in and around the church. In addition, just about every parish had organizations for adult men and women. The Holy Name Society was the flagship organization for the men. Irish parishes again set the norm with Communion Sundays where members of the society would receive Communion as a group, followed by a breakfast often featuring a special speaker, generally a distinguished athlete or politician. For women, the altar and rosary society attracted those who wanted more involvement in the life of the parish.

These religious devotions and organizations strengthened the Catholic ethos that had developed during the immigrant era. Authority still remained a keystone in Catholic culture—the authority of the priest and the bishop was seldom publicly challenged, though it could certainly be ignored privately. In this period the cult of the pope gained popularity. This was especially true during the pontificate of Pius XII (1939–58), who became widely known through newsreels and television. He became an iconic figure whose portrait often decorated the homes of the devout. Catholics still loved religious rituals, with the Mass and the novena being the most popular. The miraculous also remained a trademark of Catholic devotionalism, with certain saints having a special appeal, such as Therese of Lisieux, the French Carmelite nun whom the Church declared a saint in 1925.

What took on new sense of urgency during this period was the Church's battle against sin. Catholics outdid most religions when it came to waging war against sinful behavior, with the Irish leading the way. The Irish God could be loving and generous or terrifying and judgmental. In this period He remained as He had been in the nineteenth century—terrifying and judgmental. Sunday sermons often reflected this by focusing on sin in one way or another. "The push was that sin is everywhere," recalled one Catholic, with Satan lurking just "around the corner."[19] Parish missions were especially terrifying. Recalling missions in her parish, a woman wrote,

> The missionaries who presided over our annual retreats at our parish church and in high school were in league with Torquemada. They roared from the pulpit, summoning up visions of hellfire and eternal suffering reserved for those guilty of "impurity" (that is, those with sexual impulses). By a curious twist of logic, women (the weaker vessels?) had a responsibility to set the proper example and keep the men at bay. Virginity was our greatest treasure, "a bright jewel," so precious to God that we

should be ready to die rather than to yield it up (without permission from the Church).[20]

For Catholics, temperance was no longer a hot topic. The Prohibition
crusade had replaced temperance as the cure for society's evils, but Irish
Catholics were not sympathetic to the outlawing of alcohol. The chief evil
to be resisted now was birth control.

Initially identified with radical feminists, in particular Margaret
Sanger, daughter of an Irish-born stonemason, birth control became the
centerpiece of a significant reform movement by the 1920s. At first, virtually all religious denominations opposed the use of any contraceptives, but
by the mid-1930s the more liberal, mainline denominations approved
birth control. Even though conservative Jews and Protestants together
with Catholics remained opposed to the use of contraceptives, the
Catholic Church was singled out as the chief enemy of what many regarded as a liberal and enlightened understanding of marriage. The main
reason for this view was that Margaret Sanger and other birth control advocates, capitalizing on the anti-Catholic atmosphere of the 1920s, convinced the American public not only that the Catholic Church's position
on birth control was old-fashioned, but also that it was trying to force its
morality on the American public.

In the 1930s and '40s the Church had mounted an aggressive campaign against artificial birth control, with a papal encyclical issued in 1930
providing the rationale. The parish mission, still popular at this time, had
a "near obsession with birth control" according to historian Leslie Tentler.
Preachers painted gruesome consequences for those who shamelessly used
contraceptives. Sunday sermons on the evils of birth control were less
gruesome and florid, but no less condemnatory. One priest recalled that
the lines for confession would stretch around the block, "and it would all
be birth control."[21] Such strong opposition to birth control increased
Catholics' sense of standing apart from mainstream American culture.
This meant, as Tentler suggested, "that the issue of birth control came to
loom almost unnaturally large in the mind of the Catholic community.
Opposition to birth control was a veritable badge of tribal membership
for growing numbers of Catholics, and a touchstone of loyalty to the
Church."[22]

Such a preoccupation with sin meant that confessing one's sins
became quite regular, monthly if not weekly. This fit well with the practice of frequent Communion, which had become more common in this

period. Catholics remembered well the long lines in church during Saturday confessions when they waited patiently, and often nervously, to enter the darkened tomb of the confessional, where they would kneel, asking the priest to absolve them of their sins.

Another crusade against sin was the clergy's attempt to clean up the movies, ridding them of "indecency and immorality." They achieved this through the Legion of Decency, a movie-rating system that became immensely popular throughout the 1930s and '40s, as every year Catholics took the Legion of Decency pledge in which they condemned "all indecent and immoral motion pictures," promising to stay away from movies not approved by the Legion office as well as the theaters that showed them. Large parades of young people, wearing their Legion buttons, marched in support of the Legion's goal to clean up the movie industry. On occasion certain bishops would mount a crusade against a particular movie thought to be immoral. Surely one of the most famous incidents was New York's Cardinal Spellman's personal crusade against the 1956 film *Baby Doll*. Written by Tennessee Williams, the movie featured a nineteen-year-old virgin and two older cotton-gin owners who competed for her love. Its steamy sexual content was too much for many people, including Spellman. He had previously issued pastoral letters condemning certain movies, but in this instance he personally mounted the pulpit in St. Patrick's Cathedral to denounce a movie that *Time* magazine condemned as "the dirtiest American-made motion picture" ever produced. Of course, Spellman never saw the movie, leading one pundit to remark later that "Justice Potter Stewart asserted that he knew pornography when he saw it; Spellman knew it even when he did not see it."[23] Predictably, Spellman's condemnation boosted ticket sales.

In many ways Francis Cardinal Spellman personified the Irish in the 1950s. Though only one generation removed from the bogs of Ireland, his parents had become respectable, upper-middle-class Irish. Though their son, who would one day become the most powerful Catholic in America, preferred to be called an American rather than an Irishman, he was proud of his Irish heritage. Describing himself as "an American with Irish blood in his veins," he never failed to express his "veneration and appreciation of all that Ireland" had given him. But it was the United States, "this land of the free, this home of liberty, this country of opportunity, my country, your country," that he extolled.[24] He became a Cold War warrior, a passionate anticommunist who traveled across the globe visiting American soldiers who were defending the nation's freedom. No one supported him more in this effort than the Irish American community. Like many an Irish politician he was a power broker, a one-man Tammany Hall whose influence reached into the White House, Congress, and City Hall. Theologically he was conservative, a traditionalist for whom sexual morality was the bedrock of the faith. He was very Irish in this regard, becoming the Church's public moralist, who never hesitated to censure what he considered to be indecent movies and plays. As the writer John Cooney put it, Spellman's "moral concerns were almost always of a sexual nature—rarely did he condemn such sins as lying, cheating, or hypocrisy."[25]

Like Dougherty and O'Connell, Spellman studied in Rome and later worked in the Vatican for several years. During this time he made friends with several powerful clerics, among them Eugenio Pacelli, who would become pope in 1939. Spellman's close friendship with Pacelli, along with the large sums of money that he sent to the Vatican, enabled him to become the most powerful prelate in America. An American pope, his influence in Rome was so great that he could control who would be appointed to the hierarchy in much of the United States.

When Spellman died in December 1967, President Lyndon B. Johnson attended his funeral in St. Patrick's Cathedral, along with numerous other dignitaries who filled the church. Flags in the city flew at half-mast, and the stock exchange halted trading for a minute of silence in honor of this American Catholic Irishman. No Catholic bishop would ever again be so powerful.

During the 1940s and '50s Cardinal Spellman was the public face of American Catholicism. Though small in stature, he loomed large on the American landscape—confident, militant, even pugnacious—symbolizing the triumph of the immigrant Church. But Catholics were still regarded with suspicion. Paul Blanshard, a well-known anti-Catholic bigot, wrote a bestseller in 1949, *American Freedom and Catholic Power*, in which he portrayed Catholicism as a power to be feared and held in check. The book went through ten printings in less than a year, selling more than one hundred thousand copies. The respected Protestant journal *Christian Century* published a series of articles in the 1940s entitled "Can Catholicism Win America?" Many people actually believed that Catholics were planning to overthrow American democracy. In addition, Catholic opposition to birth control raised the fear that Catholics were attempting to force their own moral code on the rest of society. Such accusations not only offended Catholics, but they also reminded them of their outsider status. This would change somewhat by the late 1950s, but it never entirely disappeared.

The outsider status of Catholics strengthened the cultural enclave fostered by the parish. As one commentator wrote, "The church at the parish level . . . was a thriving, self-confident institution at the peak of its influence. It was not searching for a new identity. It was simply not very interested in change."[26] But all around it the world was changing with bewildering speed, challenging not only the culture of Catholicism but also the continued existence of the Irish neighborhood parish. Adding to these changes was the emergence of a new breed of educated Catholics who were in search of a Catholicism more in tune with American culture. They wanted a new Catholicism to replace the religion of the immigrant era fashioned by the Irish clergy. Within a few short years such a transformation would take place, bringing an end to a chapter in American Catholic history in which the Irish ruled.

CHAPTER II

City Hall and the Union Hall

Al Smith's run for the presidency in 1928 confirmed the rise of the Irish in American politics. For the next thirty years they would continue to advance, dominating the Democratic Party and eventually avenging Smith's defeat by putting one of their own in the White House. Loyal Democrats, they helped Franklin Delano Roosevelt win the presidential election in 1932. His victory opened the door for the Irish at the federal level, where many partnered with Roosevelt in his efforts to fashion a New Deal for a nation stuck in the midst of an economic depression. At the local level the Irish still had a well-oiled political machine, but it was in need of an overhaul as the growth of the federal government, with its publicly funded programs, challenged the patronage system of the Tammany-style machine. To keep up with the changing times a new breed of Irish politician would retool the machine in cities such as Chicago and Pittsburgh to keep the party in control. It is ironic—or perhaps symbolic—that the epitome of this new breed of Irish politician, John F. Kennedy, would arise out of Boston, a city dominated for nearly forty years, from before World War I until after World War II, by James M. Curley, an iconic figure who personified everything that was bad, as well as good, in the old-style big-city Irish politician.

Curley's success rested, in the words of William V. Shannon, in "his ability to define, dramatize, and play upon the discrimination, resentments, and frustrations suffered by the Irish community" at the hands of Boston's Brahmins.[1] He practiced the art of personality politics by adopting a confrontational style that pitted Irish Catholic Democrats against Yankee Protestant Republicans. As he put it in a letter to a member of the

Harvard Board of Overseers, "The Massachusetts of the Puritans is as dead as Caesar, but there is no need to mourn the fact. Their successors— the Irish—had letters and learning, culture and civilization when the ancestors of the Puritans were savages running half naked through the forests of Britain. It took the Irish to make Massachusetts a fit place to live in." This was vintage Curley, and it played well in Boston for a number of years. But the city's Irish community was changing. The new, more assimilated Irish were becoming tired of the "steady diet of ethnic rivalry, class animosity, and religious antipathy with which they had grown up." They were looking for a change, for someone different from Curley who could inject new life into a weary New England city whose sleazy center, Scollay Square, stood as a continual reminder of economic depression and civic fatigue.[2]

In 1945 Curley ran for mayor once again. Though under indictment for mail fraud, the seventy-year-old Curley easily won the election. Then, in July 1947, having exhausted all his appeals, he was sentenced to jail for six to eighteen months. Boston had to suffer the embarrassment of its mayor serving time in jail. As the *Boston Herald* put it, "It would be perhaps a little regretful that a city of 770,816 should be run from a jail." Pardoned by President Truman after only five months in jail, Curley returned to Boston greeted by thousands of well-wishers and a brass band that played "Hail to the Chief."[3] But this was Curley's last hurrah. Full of himself and brimming with a self-inflicted sense of invincibility, he announced that he would run for reelection in 1949. His opponent was John Hynes, the city clerk, whom the governor had appointed to act as mayor while Curley was in jail.

What prompted Hynes to run against his old boss was a cutting remark Curley made after his first day in office. Speaking to a group of reporters, he remarked, "I have accomplished more in one day than has been done in the five months of my absence."[4] This wisecrack infuriated Hynes, who then and there decided to oppose Curley in the upcoming mayoral election. Curley thought he was invincible, but he misjudged the Boston Irish community, which had changed remarkably in the past thirty years. Hynes won the election, bringing an end to the reign of the Irish "tribal chieftain" who ruled in Boston for almost forty years.

Hynes, son of Irish immigrant parents, brought a new style of politics to the city. A quiet man, he attended Mass every day, looked and dressed like a banker, and repudiated the confrontational style of Curley. His accommodating manner enabled him to build a coalition between the Yankee Protestant Republicans who dominated Boston's banking community and the Irish Catholic Democrats. This partnership enabled him to begin to revitalize the city during the 1950s, thus paving the way for the remarkable urban renewal that took place during the following decade.

Another personality emerged in the 1940s who also contributed to the changing climate in Boston. This was the new Irish Catholic archbishop, Richard J. Cushing. Unlike his predecessor, Cardinal O'Connell, who like Curley thrived on portraying the Irish as victims of Yankee Protestant prejudice, Cushing adopted a more irenic approach, reaching out to Boston's Protestant and Jewish communities. In contrast to the pompous O'Connell, Cushing had a down-to-earth, disarming style that appealed to people. He related to all segments of the community—the poor, the imprisoned, the elderly, as well as the rich and powerful—breaking down the barriers dividing Yankee Protestants and Irish Catholics.

The 1940s also witnessed the arrival of a new face in Boston politics, John F. Kennedy. Kennedy ran for Congress in 1946, taking the seat vacated by Curley, who had decided to run for mayor once again. Reportedly, Kennedy's father, Joseph P. Kennedy, a multimillionaire, promised to pay off Curley's sizable debts and in return "all Curley had to do was run for mayor—and resign his congressional seat if he won." This would enable the young Kennedy to run for Congress in a district so heavily Democratic that "people said the Lord himself could not have won on the Republican ticket."[5]

Kennedy's arrival on the political scene did not excite many people at first. Thomas P. "Tip" O'Neill, a member of the Massachusetts legislature in 1946 when he met Kennedy for the first time, commented, "I couldn't believe this skinny, pasty-looking kid was a candidate for *anything*." He remarked that Kennedy "was twenty-eight, but looked younger, and he still hadn't fully recovered from his war injuries. He also looked as if he had come down with malaria. Certainly he was nothing like the hearty and extroverted types who dominated public life in Boston."[6]

With the financial support of his father and after numerous cocktail parties and teas where his sisters and mother showed up along with young Jack, Kennedy won the Democratic Party's nomination, which guaranteed him a seat in Congress. When Kennedy arrived in Washington, he joined another Boston Irish politician, John McCormack, who had been

in Congress since 1928. McCormack, who had risen to a powerful position in the House of Representatives, eventually would become Speaker
of the House in 1962, the first Roman Catholic to hold that position.
When Kennedy decided to run for the U.S. Senate in 1952, Tip O'Neill
left his powerful position as Speaker of the House in the Massachusetts
legislature to campaign for the congressional seat vacated by Kennedy.
O'Neill won the election, joining his Boston neighbor John McCormack
in the House of Representatives, where one day he, too, would gain the
coveted position of Speaker of the House. These three Boston Irishmen
would leave an indelible mark on the nation's politics.

The political landscape in Chicago was very different from Boston's.
Though the Irish had their share of powerful politicians such as Hinky
Dink Kenna and Johnny Powers, by the early twentieth century the
Democratic Party in the Windy City was so divided into rival factions
that no one person controlled city politics as Curley did in Boston. Then,
in the late 1920s, an individual emerged who would become the most
powerful boss that Chicago had seen since the days of its founding. He
ruled not only Chicago, but the state of Illinois as well. But he was not
Irish. He was Anton Cermak, a Czech immigrant who came to the United
States as an infant with his parents in 1874. His family settled in the mining town of Braidwood, Illinois, where young Tony worked in the mines.
At sixteen he hopped a boxcar headed for Chicago, settling in a Czech
neighborhood that eventually became his political base. Over time he rose
to power in the Democratic Party by building a multiethnic political machine that united Bohemian, Irish, Jewish, German, and Polish factions
into an effective organization. By 1928 he had become the leader of the
Cook County Democrats. Three years later he ran for mayor. His opponent was the Republican William Hale Thompson.

Big Bill, as he was known, had been a three-term mayor, controlling
City Hall from 1915 to 1923 and from 1927 to 1931. But Chicagoans
had tired of Thompson's flamboyant theatrics, his links with organized
crime, and his corrupt city government. It was time for a change. Capitalizing on the public's dissatisfaction with Thompson, Cermak emerged
victorious in a watershed election that ushered in the Democratic reign
over city government that has lasted, at this writing, more than seventy
years.

In fashioning a "House for all Peoples," Cermak appointed numerous
Irishmen to important positions in the party. Chief among them was
Patrick Nash, the American-born son of an Irish immigrant laborer. By

the time of Cermak's victory in 1931, Nash, who had inherited a sewer-contracting business from his father, had become one of Chicago's wealthiest citizens as well as Cermak's right-hand man in running the Democratic machine. At the age of sixty-eight, an elder statesman in the party who was financially secure and lacking political ambition, he was the perfect person to work in the shadow of the Bohemian Boss. Then, on a fateful day in February 1933, when Cermak was in Florida recuperating from dysentery contracted in a luxury hotel in Chicago, he went to visit the newly elected president, Franklin D. Roosevelt, hoping to gain favor with the man whom he had campaigned for in the decisive 1932 election. Cermak's fragile health had placed him in Florida, while chance had brought him together with Roosevelt, who was passing through Miami on his way home from a yachting trip. Cermak attended a reception given for Roosevelt, who addressed the crowd from his automobile. After his remarks the president beckoned Cermak over to his car, where they talked briefly. Suddenly, shots rang out. A deranged gunman, Giuseppe Zangara, was evidently targeting Roosevelt, but struck Cermak and four others. In less than three weeks Cermak was dead.

With the death of the Bohemian Boss, the way was now open for the Irish to gain control of the political organization that Cermak had built. Pat Nash, now in control of the machine, convinced the city council to appoint Edward J. Kelly as the new mayor of Chicago. Thus began the reign of the Kelly-Nash machine, which would rule Chicago until Nash's death in 1943. "Chicago's Irish," wrote the political analyst Paul M. Green, "after almost a hundred years of effort, were in command of city affairs. The Mayor was Irish, the Cook County board president would be Irish in 1934, and the head of the Democratic party was Irish. Late a half century by Tammany Hall standards, they had succeeded at last."[7]

Kelly, born in 1876, grew up on the city's South Side, the son of an Irish-born Chicago cop. Like Al Smith he left school at an early age to help support his family. One of his first jobs was with the Chicago Sanitary District, where he remained for twenty-six years, reaching the pinnacle of his career when he became the district's chief engineer in 1920. A few years later he became head of the South Park Board. As head of the board, he filled in the city's lakefront and transformed Grant Park from a "tin can dumping ground" into a spacious park. During his tenure such Chicago landmarks as the Shedd Aquarium, the Adler Planetarium, and Buckingham Fountain were constructed. He also supervised the construction of Soldier Field and the renovation of the Museum of Science and

Industry. His ten-year reign as park president was so spectacular that he became known at the Father of the Lakefront. Though he was active in Democratic politics and had awarded many contracts worth millions of dollars to Pat Nash's sewer-construction company, he had never held an elective office. His friendship with Nash was the key that opened the door to the mayor's office.

Tall and robust, he dressed like a LaSalle Street banker in suit and tie, a model of the new breed of Irish politician. Several times he was voted one of the nation's best-dressed mayors. Gregarious and charming, he kissed babies, attended wakes, cut ribbons, and seldom passed up a chance to give a speech. One admirer said, "He looked like a Mayor."[8] He also lived like a king, with a summer home in Wisconsin and a winter home in Palm Springs, along with his plush residence on Chicago's lakefront. He could afford such luxuries because of all the kickbacks he received both as chief engineer and later as mayor. Since the days of the saloonkeeper politicians, Chicago had acquired the reputation as one of the more politically corrupt cities in the nation. As mayor, Kelly did little to change that reputation.

At first Kelly was reluctant to take Nash's offer to become mayor, telling Nash, "I don't want the damned job." But he finally relented, saying he would take the job but only on his own terms. As he put it, "All right, Pat, I'll take it. But I want you to understand this: That I am the Mayor and nobody else. I will be the boss of city hall. I will never be a figurehead." He lived up to his promise by becoming one of the most ironfisted bosses in Chicago's history. One Democratic colleague said of Kelly, "He could even give a lesson in bossism to Hitler and Stalin."[9]

Kelly became mayor in the midst of the Depression, which had crippled the city. Schoolteachers, policemen, firemen, and other city employees had not been paid for months. Shantytowns sprouted up in the city as close to seven hundred thousand workers, almost half the workforce, were unemployed. But Kelly rose to the challenge and saved the city from collapsing into chaos. He trimmed the city's budget, paid the schoolteachers, established good relations with the state legislature to obtain tax legislation favorable to the city, and lobbied the federal government for financial aid. Within two years, when he was running for his first election as mayor, he was hailed as one of the best mayors in the country. Commenting on his victory at the polls, the *New York Times* concluded, "Why did the people of Chicago give him an unparalleled vote of confidence? Because he turned one of the worst-governed cities into one of the best governed . . . He is a good model of mayors and even offices of loftier title to follow."[10]

A major reason for Kelly's success in saving the city from financial collapse was his close alliance with President Roosevelt, who placed great confidence in the Chicago mayor, frequently seeking his advice. Their relationship enabled Kelly to obtain significant financial aid for the city. He gained control of the New Deal's Works Progress Administration projects in Chicago, which employed close to two hundred thousand people. These jobs translated into patronage and power, thereby strengthening the Kelly-Nash machine. Chicago also got a significant face-lift as federal funds helped to build roads and subways, parks, schools, and public housing. When Roosevelt decided to run for reelection in 1940, Chicago was the chosen site for the Democratic convention. Kelly, ever loyal to Roosevelt, put his political machine to work, helping to engineer FDR's nomination to an unprecedented third term as president.

Kelly built on his achievements by attracting the city's large black population to the Democratic Party. Traditionally Chicago's black voters supported Republican candidates, but Kelly changed that by reaching out to the black community. He appointed blacks to major positions in the city government, such as assistant city prosecutor, deputy coroner, civil service commissioner, and chairman of the Chicago Housing Authority. By providing many jobs to black Chicagoans, made possible by the federal largesse of the New Deal, Kelly strengthened the appeal of the Democratic machine among blacks. Despite the protests of whites, he took a courageous stand in favor of integration of high schools on the city's South Side. He also favored the integration of the city's public housing, another unpopular position in the white community, especially among the Irish. But such bold decisions gained him a large following among the city's black population. Known affectionately among blacks as Big Red, he won their allegiance by appearing at many South Side functions, appointing the boxing champion Joe Louis as mayor for ten minutes in a highly publicized ceremony, and showing up at the annual black-college football game at Soldier Field. Kelly's ability to win over the black vote to the Democratic Party would become even more significant in the 1950s and '60s when white flight from the city made the votes of a growing black population essential to the continued success of the Democratic machine.

When Pat Nash died in 1943, the machine began to split apart. Kelly took over Nash's position as party chairman, but not for long. Criticism of Kelly's autocratic rule increased, forcing him to relinquish his party chairmanship. Kelly had once said, "Either you run the machine or the machine runs you."[11] The time had now come for the machine, with a new party chairman, Jacob Avery, to run Kelly out of office.

As the time for Kelly's reelection approached, Avery conducted public opinion polls that revealed Kelly's popularity to be at an all-time low. When respondents were asked whether they would vote for Kelly, they replied, as Avery put it, "Are you kidding? We'd sooner vote for a Chinaman." The voters were no longer willing to accept his tolerance of organized crime, a corrupt police department, poor garbage collection, high taxes, and poor city services. In past times the machine had survived such discontent, but this time, in the opinion of Avery, "one new issue . . . crystallized public opinion against Kelly: the open housing controversy. The Mayor's repeated pledges to guarantee the availability of housing citywide to blacks galvanized the public" against him.[12] The South Side Irish, along with their German and Polish neighbors, would not support Kelly's open housing policy. Such public opposition, coupled with discontent among the party regulars, persuaded Kelly not to seek reelection in 1947.

Comparing the political landscape in Chicago with that in Boston, two striking conclusions emerge. Chicago had none of the religious and class antagonism between the Catholic Irish and the Protestant Yankees that Curley, and his clerical contemporary Cardinal O'Connell, cultivated. On the other hand, in Chicago, where large numbers of African Americans had settled pre-1960, racial antagonism became a defining feature of city politics, with the Irish leading the opposition against integrated neighborhoods and schools. Racial conflict would scar Boston as well, but it did not affect city politics until the 1960s and '70s.

The Chicago machine slated another Irish Catholic, Martin H. Kennelly, to run for mayor in 1947. Born and raised in Bridgeport, a South Side neighborhood where four of the city's mayors grew up, he represented the new style of Irish politician—a successful businessman who was a respected civic leader. After the scandals of the Kelly era, Kennelly gave the Democratic organization just what it needed—respectability. The perfect choice to replace Kelly, he won the mayoral election in 1947, keeping the Democrats in control of city politics for the next eight years as he won reelection in 1951. As mayor he modernized the city's administration; he also promoted civil service reform by filling city jobs according to a merit system rather than political patronage. But as the *Chicago Tribune* noted, this hardly went over well with the "ward bosses, who [gave] up patronage about as cheerfully as they sacrifice an arm or an eye." He also encouraged development of the city's downtown and promoted urban renewal. But he was mostly an inept mayor who could not cope with scandals in the police department and alienated the black community by allowing the Chicago Housing Authority to become a "bulwark of segregation."[13] When he sought reelection in 1955, the organization abandoned him by running the new party chairman against him in the party's primary, none other than Richard J. Daley.

Daley had climbed the political ladder, rising from office assistant, state representative, and ward committeeman to Cook County clerk. In 1953, he was elected chairman of the Cook County Democratic Party. Two years later he defeated Kennelly in the party primary and went on to victory in the mayoral election. Daley built one of the most powerful political machines in the nation in the 1960s and ruled Chicago until 1976.

David Lawrence, mayor of Pittsburgh and later governor of Pennsylvania, was another Irish political boss who rose to power in the years following World War I. The grandson of Irish immigrants, he was raised in a blue-collar Irish Catholic family that lived in a heavily Irish neighborhood in the city's Point District. He inherited his love for politics from his father and his commitment to Catholicism from his mother. In 1920, as the new chairman of the Democratic Party in Allegheny County, he began building a political machine that would change the political landscape of Pittsburgh and the state of Pennsylvania for the rest of the twentieth century. Like Kelly in Chicago, Lawrence rose to power during the New Deal, benefiting from the federal largesse that funneled as many as 150,000 jobs to Pennsylvania, a patronage pool that Lawrence used to reward party loyalists. In 1945 he ran for mayor of Pittsburgh and won. During his term as mayor, 1945–58, he partnered with Richard K. Mellon and other civic leaders in guiding the city through an urban-renewal project, labeled the Pittsburgh Renaissance, that gave new life to a decaying city. He also promoted fair-housing and fair-employment legislation in the city council. In 1958 he won election as governor of Pennsylvania, retiring from politics at the end of his four-year term. Like Kelly and later Daley, Lawrence was a political boss who learned, as Father Owen Rice, Pittsburgh's labor priest and one of his supporters, wrote, "to adapt an old style political machine into modern usage. Democrats had to be elected to positions of power, but once in, they had to serve the community. The faithful had to be fed, but they could not be allowed to gorge themselves and in office they had to perform with acceptable efficiency. It was quite a challenge and he brought it off."[14]

Two Irish bosses whose style of politics was quite different from that of David Lawrence were Thomas Pendergast of Kansas City and Frank Hague of Jersey City. Born into an Irish immigrant family, Pendergast rose to power in Kansas City during the 1920s and '30s. His political machine controlled the city, reaching its zenith in the 1930s when he was one of the first city bosses to support Roosevelt in his bid for the presidency. His control of the vote in Kansas City helped Roosevelt win the critical 1932 election. It paved the way for a federal payback in huge work-relief programs that not only provided thousands of jobs but also transformed the skyline of Kansas City. A close relationship with James Farley, who was Roosevelt's chief adviser, was also a major reason why the Pendergast machine benefited from the New Deal largesse. Pendergast's fall was as swift as his rise to power. Convicted of federal income-tax evasion in 1939, he was sentenced to fifteen months in jail and five years' probation. His machine collapsed, and after serving time in jail, Pendergast retired from public life. Historians have praised Pendergast for running a well-organized jobs program and relief agency. But they have also acknowledged that his tenure as boss turned Kansas City into one of the most corrupt cities in the nation.

Frank Hague ruled Jersey City with an iron fist during his reign as mayor from 1917 until his retirement in 1947 at the age of seventy-two. The son of Irish immigrants, Hague's early years followed the pattern of other Irish bosses. Raised in a Catholic working-class family in an Irish neighborhood, he took a liking to politics early in his life, benefiting from the mentoring of experienced politicians. As he rose to prominence in the Democratic Party, he gained a reputation as someone who could deliver the votes on election day. Once he became mayor, he began to build a political machine that would control not only Jersey City, but the state of New Jersey as well. By supporting Roosevelt in the 1932 election, he gained favor with Roosevelt and his key aides, James Farley and Harry Hopkins. All the funds from the New Deal that came to New Jersey were funneled through Hague. By 1939, Jersey City had received nearly fifty million dollars from the Works Progress Administration, turning Hague's machine into a huge social relief agency that provided thousands of jobs to his supporters. Once he retired, the Hague machine lost its power. But, like the other Irish bosses of this era, he has become legendary.

Across the river from Jersey City was New York's Tammany Hall. The oldest political organization in the city, it began to decline after the death of Charles Murphy, who had guided Tammany during its glory days in the early twentieth century. With the demise of Tammany the fortunes of the Irish who had built one of the most powerful machines in the country declined. Having supported their own Al Smith in his bid for the presidency in 1928, Tammany backed him again in 1932 when he once again sought the Democratic presidential nomination. This time, however, Smith lost out to Roosevelt. His defeat not only soured Smith's relationship with Roosevelt, but it also foreshadowed the end of Tammany's influence since it had backed the wrong man. To add to its troubles the Democratic mayor of New York—another colorful Irishman, Jimmy Walker—was forced to resign because of corruption in the city government. The final blow came in 1933 with the election of Fiorello La Guardia, the Republican reform candidate who would serve as mayor of New York until he retired in 1945. For all practical purposes Tammany Hall was finished, and so was the Irish era in New York City politics.

The Bronx boss Edward J. Flynn, another American-born Irishman, whose parents had emigrated from Ireland, survived the fall of Tammany since he had been a close ally of Roosevelt's throughout his entire political career. A lawyer, devout Catholic, and the political boss of the Bronx Democratic machine for more than thirty years, his close friendship with Roosevelt propelled him onto the national political stage. Then in 1940 when James Farley resigned as chairman of the Democratic National Committee, Flynn replaced him.

A contemporary of Flynn's who was also a loyal New Dealer was Dan O'Connell of Albany, New York. Unlike Flynn, who came from a middle-class family, O'Connell was the more typical poor Irish boy who pulled himself up by his own bootstraps to become a powerful political boss. He first emerged as a political force in 1921 and remained the boss of Albany until his death in 1977—a reign unparalleled in the twentieth century. He turned Albany into a Democratic town, whose Irish working-class world has been celebrated in the writings of one of its own sons, the Pulitzer Prize–winning novelist William Kennedy.

All of these Irish politicians profited from the relief programs launched during the New Deal. The notable exception was Curley, whom Roosevelt viewed as a corrupt boss who would waste any federal funds that came to him. The Works Progress Administration alone provided millions of jobs across the nation, mostly in hard-pressed urban areas. A major beneficiary of this jobs program was the Irish, whom the machine rewarded for their loyalty on election day.

Patronage politics worked the same way in the 1930s as it did in the

1880s. The machine was based in the neighborhood, where the local precinct captain worked under the ward boss, who was responsible for all the precincts in his district. All the ward bosses reported to the citywide boss or his subordinates. On election day the precinct captains and the ward bosses had to produce votes for the party's candidates. If they were successful, they gained some patronage positions, with the ward boss receiving better positions than a precinct captain. These included such jobs as street inspector or building inspector or better-paying, white-collar jobs in the city government. If they did not deliver, they would not be rewarded. It was simple—if you deliver the votes, you will reap the rewards.

In the years following World War II the big-city political machine collapsed as the political climate changed. One major change was the introduction of civil service reform, which depleted the machine's pool of jobs that it could give to faithful supporters. Unions also began to push for more collective bargaining, threatening the machine's control over many public-sector jobs. Affirmative action programs in the 1960s further weakened the patronage system. The major exception was Chicago, where the new mayor, Richard J. Daley, overhauled the old-style political machine.

During the Roosevelt era the Irish not only built some formidable political machines, but for the first time a new generation of Irishmen began to move into important positions at the national level. James Farley first helped Roosevelt get elected as governor of New York, and later, as chair of the Democratic National Committee, he played a major role in helping FDR get elected president. Roosevelt rewarded his loyalty by appointing him postmaster general. By 1940 Farley had his eye on the party's nomination for president, but Roosevelt's unprecedented decision to run for a third term ruined his hopes as well as his long relationship with FDR. A few years later he retired from politics. Thomas G. Corcoran, whom Roosevelt nicknamed Tommy the Cork, was a brilliant, young New Dealer who became the prototype of the modern lobbyist. He also acted as a talent scout for Roosevelt, recruiting other young, capable people to work in the administration. Corcoran's biographer, David McKean, described him as a deal maker as well as an influence peddler and wrote, "He never held a position of great stature, but nevertheless he played a major part in some of the most significant events in the nation's political history during the twentieth century."[15] He left the administration in 1940 and returned to the practice of law in the nation's capital, where he became a successful lobbyist and adviser to many Democratic politicians.

In the House of Representatives, two Irish politicians from Massachusetts, John W. McCormack and Joseph Casey, were champions of New Deal legislation. Roosevelt appointed Frank Murphy, governor of Michigan, to be attorney general. In that capacity Murphy successfully prosecuted boss Tom Pendergast of Kansas City as well as the Republican boss of Atlantic City. Then in 1940 Roosevelt appointed him to the Supreme Court when Pierce Butler, the only Catholic on the Court, died. Twenty-five percent of Roosevelt's other judicial appointments went to Catholics, undoubtedly as a reward for the loyal support Catholics gave to the Democratic president on election day. Another Irishman who gained the favor of Roosevelt was Joseph P. Kennedy, father of the future president. Described as the man with "nine children and nine million dollars," he became the first Irish Catholic to be appointed ambassador to the Court of St. James.[16] As England moved closer to war with Germany, Kennedy's isolationist views ultimately strained his relationship with Roosevelt, until finally Kennedy resigned his post. He spent the rest of his life and much of his money advancing the careers of his sons.

One Irish politician who, for a brief period, gained a large national following because of his campaign to rid the government of alleged communist spies was Joseph McCarthy, the Republican senator from Wisconsin. In the early 1950s the nation was in the midst of the Cold War, a climate that generated a pathological fear of communism. McCarthy tapped into this fear by alleging that hundreds of communists had infiltrated the federal government. Even though such accusations were greatly exaggerated, they gained McCarthy the publicity he was seeking. From 1950 to 1954 he waged a relentless campaign, based on innuendo and false accusation, to rid the government of suspected communists. Some of his most ardent supporters were Irish Catholics who had always viewed communism as a threat to their Church. Now McCarthy convinced many of them that it was also a threat to the nation. On one occasion McCarthy appeared in New York at the annual Communion breakfast of the Holy Name Society of the New York Police Department. The heavily Irish crowd gave him a rousing reception, loudly cheering his diatribe against the Pentagon, the army, and college professors with their "screwy ideas." Cardinal Spellman had invited McCarthy to the breakfast and spoke in praise of the senator. His support was widely seen as an endorsement of McCarthy's crusade; as one biographer wrote, Spellman "consecrated McCarthyism" that day.[17]

For the most part such an endorsement went over well in the Irish

Catholic community, especially among the more conservative Irish who had earlier supported the radio priest Charles Coughlin and his anti-Semitic tirades. As William Shannon wrote, their "cultural isolation and the residual resentment against past discrimination convinced many Irish that they had a special mission to save America for religion in the struggle against communism."[18] But the Irish tradition of political liberalism and concern for social justice produced opposition to McCarthy as well, with Bishop Bernard J. Sheil of Chicago and the Catholic journals *America* and *Commonweal* in the forefront. The senator's downfall took place in the fall of 1954, when the Senate, in condemning his reckless behavior, censured him. Discredited and abandoned, McCarthy lost his following. In less than three years he was dead, a tragic victim of alcoholism.

By the 1960s the Irish domination of the Democratic Party and the urban political machines first fashioned in the mid-nineteenth century had waned. Individual Irish politicians would gain prominence at the national level, but the heyday of boss politics was over. A new era was beginning that would witness a tectonic shift as the new American Irish, comfortable in their middle-class homes, began to drift into the Republican Party, an affiliation they had resisted ever since they first arrived as exiles from Ireland.

Another area where the Irish made their mark in the post–World War I era was in the labor movement. One of the first manifestations of this influence took place in September 1919, when across the country as many as three hundred thousand steelworkers walked off their jobs in an attempt to unionize the steel industry. Steelworkers were unhappy with working twelve-hour days, six days a week, for low wages. To remedy their discontent they organized, but the industry refused to allow the workers to form a union. For the workers the only solution was to walk off the job. One of the key leaders of the strike was William Z. Foster, a Philadelphia Irishman.

Foster was raised in a poor Irish neighborhood in Philadelphia and, like many others, went to work at an early age to help support his family. But the comparison ends there. In 1900, at the age of nineteen, he joined the Socialist Party, and a few years later the Industrial Workers of the World. After a few years with this radical union, he abandoned the IWW, eventually moving to Chicago, where he became an organizer for the Chicago Federation of Labor. Recognized as an able organizer, he captured the attention of the AFL leadership, who assigned him to lead the steel strike. Samuel Gompers, head of the AFL, described Foster as "a man of ability, a man of good presence, gentle in expression."[19] Foster traveled the country, trying to organize the steelworkers. But his efforts were in vain. The long and bitter strike ended in January 1920, a dismal failure for the workers and a crippling blow to organized labor. The steel industry was just too powerful for the AFL and Foster. A few years later, Foster joined the American Communist Party, where he would hold a leadership position for more than thirty years. After failing to unionize the steelworkers, the AFL declined in membership from its high of five million on the eve of the strike to less than three and a half million in 1929. The crash of 1929 and the subsequent economic depression further weakened the AFL as more members left the federation. But quite unexpectedly organized labor underwent a remarkable recovery, with its membership soaring to almost nine million by 1939.

The Depression had forced union leaders to increase their recruitment of workers, arguing that joining the union would improve their lives. In addition, the National Industrial Recovery Act, passed in 1933, sanctioned the right of workers to bargain collectively. As a result, the United Mine Workers, under the leadership of John L. Lewis, experienced a dramatic increase as organizers traveled to the nation's coal-mining towns from New Mexico to Pennsylvania. The AFL unions in the construction trades, traditionally very Irish, recruited so many new members that they could not keep up with the applications from workers.[20] In 1933 and 1934 the AFL gained almost a million new members. Then in 1935 occurred one of the most significant developments in labor history as a number of labor leaders in the AFL, led by John L. Lewis, broke away from the AFL and formed the Congress of Industrial Organizations (CIO). Its goal was to organize the mass-production industries such as steel and automobiles, a policy that the AFL leadership refused to endorse. Under the energetic leadership of Lewis, the CIO achieved two major victories in 1937. First, its affiliate the United Auto Workers, after a prolonged sit-down strike at the General Motors plant in Flint, Michigan, signed a union contract with General Motors. Three weeks later, U.S. Steel "surrendered without a struggle" when it recognized the Steel Workers Organizing Committee (SWOC) as the bargaining agent for its employees. "From a modest plan to encourage organizations of neglected workers, the CIO had emerged in less than two years as a mass movement of over 4 million members"—as many members as its rival, the AFL. Philip Murray, an Irish immigrant who was a charter member of the CIO and chairman of SWOC, proudly asserted, "We are the dominant labor force in this nation."[21]

When the CIO first formed its charter committee in 1935, four of the eleven members of the committee were Irish. Such prominence of the Irish in the leadership of the CIO reflected a pattern set in the nineteenth century when the Irish had gained a dominant position in the American labor movement. A study done of more than thirty-five hundred labor leaders in the New Deal years concluded that the group described as Old Stock American was the only group that had a higher percentage of labor leaders than the Irish. Close to 40 percent of these leaders were Roman Catholic, with 60 percent being Democrats, the party of choice for most labor leaders during the 1930s and '40s.[22]

Along with Philip Murray, the other Irishmen who met with John L. Lewis to create the CIO were John Brophy, Tom Kennedy, and Thomas McMahon. Brophy, born in England to an Irish Catholic coal-mining family, emigrated to the United States at the age of nine, settling with his family in the coal-mining region of Pennsylvania. Working in the mines as a young man, he joined the United Mine Workers, eventually rising to the position of district president. Disagreeing with Lewis over union strategies, he challenged the latter's rule by running for president of the UMW in 1926, but he lost. After a reconciliation with Lewis, Brophy rose to prominence in the CIO, becoming a national director. Thomas McMahon was born in Ireland and emigrated to the United States in 1887 at the age of seventeen. A member of the Knights of Labor, he eventually joined the United Textile Workers, where, over sixteen years, he rose from business agent to national organizer and finally to president of the union in 1921, serving until 1937. The other Irishman present at the creation of the CIO was the American-born Thomas Kennedy. Kennedy was a Pennsylvania coal miner and, like Brophy, became a district president of the UMW. He eventually became the secretary-treasurer of the UMW and later its vice president. Kennedy, together with Lewis and Murray, was a key partner in what Lewis's biographer described as an "unshakable triumvirate that dominated the United Mine Workers."[23] When Lewis retired in 1960 as president of the UMW, Kennedy succeeded him. But it was Philip Murray who would rise to the pinnacle of union prominence, emerging as a giant in the labor movement during the 1930s and '40s.

Murray was born in Scotland in 1886 to an Irish couple who had emigrated from Ireland just a few years before. His father, a coal miner and devout Catholic, left an indelible impression on his son, who left school at an early age to work in the mines with his father. Murray learned his first lessons in labor organizing from his father, who was a union activist. Murray would remain a union man for the rest of his life as well as a committed Irish Catholic. In 1902, Philip and his father journeyed to the United States hoping to build a better life for their family of thirteen. They settled in Madison, Pennsylvania, a mining town where Philip's uncle had already established himself. Philip and his father worked together in the mines, earning enough to bring the whole family over within a year.

Shortly after his family was reunited in Pennsylvania, "Murray got into a fight that had a lasting impact on him." He recalled, "One night as I came out of the pit, I complained at the weighman's office that I was being short-weighted and thereby losing money every day. Words led to a knockdown, dragout fight, and the next morning I was fired." Six hundred workers walked out in support of Murray and voted to strike. The strike was unsuccessful, and then, "the day after the strike," Murray said, "my father and his eight children, including myself, were thrown from their homes out into the street." Blackballed, Murray was forced to leave town. From that moment, "Murray decided to devote his life to the union movement."[24]

Still working in the coal pits, he was elected president of a UMW local in 1905. Though a young man, he was making an impression on union leaders in the region. Historian Ronald Schatz described him as "an attractive young man, who had an unusual talent for retaining facts and figures, was sincerely devoted to the miners' betterment, was not afraid to fight, and yet could get his way usually by speaking softly." As one miner put it, "He was very likable, and he's probably on his way up in the mine workers' affairs."[25] His prediction came true. Within a few years Murray was appointed to the international executive board of the UMW, soon after he became a district president. One man behind Murray's rise was John L. Lewis, who became president of the UMW in 1920. Soon after his election Lewis appointed Murray vice president. Only thirty-three years old, Murray became the second-ranking officer of the nation's largest labor union.[26]

Murray was Lewis's right-hand man for the next twenty years, a loyal supporter in bad times as well as good. Lewis gave the orders and Murray carried them out. They were two entirely different personalities, labor's odd couple. "Lewis was imperious," wrote Melvyn Dubofsky, "Murray was more egalitarian. Lewis lived in a regal style . . . Murray lived modestly . . .

Lewis never attended church . . . Murray was a devout Catholic. Lewis was a teetotaler; Murray enjoyed a few beers with the boys in the neighborhood tavern. Lewis did not associate with the ordinary workers, preferring the company of businessmen . . . and the socially eminent . . . while Murray never did enjoy sitting and talking with the so-called great. He always felt much better going back to the homely people, and getting the feel of what was going on in the mines, with the guys back home."[27]

As vice president of the UMW, Murray took on numerous responsibilities. He testified before Congress, worked with the federal government to improve the situation of workers, negotiated contracts with mine operators, and calmed the anger of dissident union members. After the creation of the CIO, Lewis appointed Murray chairman of SWOC, which later became the United Steelworkers of America. When Lewis resigned as president of the CIO in 1940, he anointed Murray as his successor. Their friendship cooled considerably after this, eventually degenerating into open hostility. The major reason was Murray's support of Roosevelt, whom Lewis had repudiated by supporting Wendell Willkie, the Republican candidate for president in the 1940 election. In addition, Murray supported Roosevelt's pro-war policy, which Lewis opposed. For Lewis, Murray's support for Roosevelt amounted to a personal betrayal. The two men remained at odds until the death of Murray in 1952.[28]

As head of SWOC, Murray built the steelworkers union into one of the most powerful unions of the day. An accomplished administrator, he was also a great orator. "When he spoke," recalled one contemporary, "you hung on every word." One of his favorite themes was the responsibility of the union to its members. His most famous line, in describing what the union meant for each worker, was "a picture on the wall, a carpet on the floor, and music in the home." The journalist Murray Kempton said that Murray's special quality was "to touch the love and not the fear of men." This warmth and benevolence inspired "a fierce loyalty among the rank and file unionists he led. 'He became like a god to the members of this union,' one activist remembered. 'You couldn't say anything about him. Say anything about Philip Murray and you'd probably be killed.'" One labor historian wrote, "Few labor leaders in American history enjoyed the public esteem awarded to CIO president Philip Murray, who combined an appealing humility with outspoken humanitarian values."[29]

Murray rose to prominence at a time when the federal government became increasingly involved with organized labor. Favoring such federal intervention in labor disputes, Murray found a friend in Franklin D. Roosevelt, with whom he formed a strong alliance. This began in 1932 when Murray and a UMW delegation traveled to Albany to meet the Democratic presidential candidate. Murray remembered the occasion vividly. "Those few Miners' leaders, he recalled, . . . presented to the Governor of New York the condition of the Miners. You know the Miners in 1932 were eating garbage, yes garbage, and getting $1.50 a day for a ten-hour day . . . I lived with them, I worked with them. All my family were miners and I felt that something ought to be done for them. But one day, they found a friend. He was sitting on the end of a divan in his library at the Executive Mansion in Albany, New York. He knew the miners and their problems, and he said he would help them. Another day he was found sitting at a desk in the White House, and he said, 'I will help you by giving you the means of helping yourself.' The miner helped himself, Murray concluded, and he shouted the name of Roosevelt as loudly as he shouted the words United Mine Workers."[30] Murray organized the CIO's Political Action Committee, which worked on behalf of Roosevelt and other Democratic Party candidates. This alliance between Murray and the White House enabled the USWA and the CIO to become powerful organizations during the 1940s.

When war broke out in 1941, Murray unveiled his plan for industrial councils that would guide the U.S. economy during the war. He based this idea on his experiences in the coal industry and with the National Recovery Administration during the New Deal era as well as Pope Pius XI's encyclical *Quadragesimo Anno*, which addressed the issue of social justice. As an involved Catholic, Murray was in touch with such Catholic activists as Monsignor John A. Ryan and Father Charles Owen Rice, a close friend and labor priest in Pittsburgh. For Murray "the teachings of the church provided moral authority for the belief in interest group cooperation." The idea behind these councils was that each industry would have its own council made up of an equal number of union and management people and chaired by a federal official. According to Ronald Schatz, their responsibility was to run the industry "determining expansion needs, allocating orders, scheduling production, determining priorities, and establishing labor policies." Given the status and power of labor in such an arrangement, business leaders rejected the plan, nor did Roosevelt and his administration warm to the idea. Such lack of support prompted Murray to acknowledge that "labor's chief difficulty in America today, as in days gone by, lies in the unwillingness, the obvious unwillingness of government and business to accept labor in good faith."[31]

Another area where Murray's religion had a strong influence was his opposition to communism. As fierce opponents of the rise of communism in Europe, Catholics were especially suspicious of any communist influence in the United States. Communist influence was quite strong in the labor movement at this time, most especially within the CIO, where John L. Lewis had welcomed communists because of their energetic and capable organizing ability. Since the Communist Party in the United States took its orders from Moscow, support for them within the CIO depended on what position the Soviet Union took during and after the Second World War. When the Soviet Union allied with Nazi Germany in the Nazi-Soviet Pact (1939–41), labor leaders spoke out against the alliance between Lewis and the communists. Once the Soviets became our allies during the war, however, criticism was muted. Nor was Murray anxious to proceed decisively against the communist influence as almost one third of the CIO membership belonged to communist-led unions. In the postwar years in the Cold War atmosphere, President Truman adopted a strong anti-Soviet policy. At the national CIO convention in 1948 and again in 1949, Murray spearheaded a purge of communist-led unions from the CIO. Murray's confidant Father Charles Owen Rice, who was well-known for his strong anticommunist beliefs, had been warning Murray since at least 1942 of the threat of communism in the CIO. With Rice encouraging him and the anticommunist climate reaching scary intensity, Murray led an onslaught against the communists, railing against those whom he labeled "sulking cowards . . . apostles of hate" who were corrupting the CIO with their propaganda.[32] It was a fierce fight, but he succeeded in largely eliminating the communist influence from the CIO.

At this time the Jim Crow mentality of separate but equal was pervasive, and the lynching of African Americans still took place. Advocating equal rights for black workers in such an environment was uncommon, yet that is just what Murray did. Though the AFL had long discriminated against black workers, the UMW had a good reputation regarding issues of race. The association of the UMW with the founding of the CIO added prestige to the new organization as far as black workers were concerned. As head of SWOC and later the CIO, Murray spoke out on behalf of racial equality, helping to "make the CIO an important voice in support of fair employment practice and a wider civil rights agenda." Although racial discrimination persisted within the union, "in 1950, and for a number of years thereafter, there was a moment of racial equilibrium within the union that convinced the leadership that its policies were . . . advancing the cause of civil rights." A key reason for this was Murray's reputation among black workers "as a man of honor who cared deeply about the goal of racial equality." When he died suddenly in November 1952, there was no better tribute to him than the admiration expressed by an African American gospel group in Alabama, the CIO Singers:

> The Congress Industrial Organization assembled
> The whole world began to tremble.
> Men, women and children cried,
> When they heard the sad news Mr. Murray had died.
> He was the CIO's loss, but he's Heaven's gain.
> In the day of Resurrection we'll see him again.
> Good God Almighty our best friend is gone.
> I want you boys to help me, just sing this song.[33]

Philip Murray not only achieved a level of prominence unique within the Irish American community, but he also symbolized, as Al Smith did, the Irish success story. From city streets and coal-mining towns the Irish were moving up.

In terms of national prominence the only Irish labor leader who could match the stature of Philip Murray was the Bronx-born plumber George Meany. Meany was the grandson of Irish immigrants who fled the Great Famine. Though he was raised in a family two generations removed from Ireland, he still recalled how Ireland was often a topic of conversation in his family—"a household," he said, "where Ireland and its troubles and history were subjects of daily discussion." In speaking about the Irish contribution to the labor movement, he explained why he thought they were so significant. It was not just their "inherited flair for language and love of the spoken word—but I would like to think, he said, that they were equally spurred by the deep centuries-old indignation which injustice stirred in them . . . The yearning for freedom—the insistence on human dignity—are forever enshrined as part of the Irish character. Similarly, they are the well-spring of the American trade union movement."[34]

Meany inherited his union activism from his father, who was president of a plumbers' union in the Bronx, New York. From plumber to business agent in the local plumbers' union to head of the New York State

Federation of Labor in 1934 at forty years of age, Meany had become, as historian Robert Zieger wrote, the "consummate union functionary—shrewd, articulate, honest, and always respectful of the labor movement's protocols and rituals of deference and influence. 'A plumber with brains,' judged one observer. 'No,' corrected another, 'all plumbers have brains. The difference is that Meany *uses* his.' "[35]

As head of the New York labor movement, he flourished as a political power broker supporting President Roosevelt and other Democratic politicians in New York State. He was a New Dealer who worked the state legislature to pass laws benefiting the workers. By 1939 Meany had achieved considerable influence in the state.

As with Murray, Meany's Catholicism led him to become a fervent anticommunist, viewing the Soviet Union as a foremost enemy. In the postwar period he became a Cold War warrior supporting President Truman's anti-Soviet foreign policy. One speech in particular anointed Meany as the heir apparent to the presidency of the AFL. It took place at the AFL convention in 1947 when he clashed with John L. Lewis. Lewis, who refused to endorse the government regulation that union officers sign affidavits that they were not communists, lashed out at the delegates, as one observer put it, "with a tongue like a butcher's knife" that "could chop a man to little pieces." Challenging their courage, he described the leadership of the AFL as "fat and stately asses." Meany rose to rebut Lewis, giving a stunning performance. Meeting Lewis head-on, he lashed out with his own attack that challenged Lewis's patriotism by accusing him of allowing communist "comrades" to work as organizers and officials in the CIO. Meany declared, "I am prepared to sign a non-Communist affidavit. I am prepared to go a step further and sign an affidavit that I was never a comrade to the comrades," as he broadly implied "Lewis had been." As one observer recalled, "Meany . . . knocked the stuffing out of Lewis." When William Green, president of the AFL, died in 1952, it was a foregone conclusion that Meany would succeed him as president. At the age of fifty-eight he had joined the ranks of the nation's top labor leaders. He achieved this not by leading strikes or standing on picket lines, but by his skill as an administrator, lobbyist, and bureaucrat.[36]

One of Meany's first priorities as president was to reunite the labor movement by merging the CIO and the AFL. Working with Walter Reuther, who had succeeded Murray as head of the CIO, he achieved his goal in December 1955. Since the AFL was now twice as big as the CIO,

Meany became the president of the newly minted labor organization. He later stated, "The merger of the AFL and CIO—reuniting the house of labor—was the accomplishment I take the most pride in."[37] As president of the AFL-CIO, he would dominate the labor movement until his retirement in 1979.

By the end of the 1950s labor seemed poised to reap the achievements of the previous era. But the 1960s ushered in a period of social and economic changes that would challenge the labor movement as it had never before been challenged.

PART FOUR

Irish and American, 1960–2000

CHAPTER 12

The Triumph of the Irish

The presidential election of 1960, in the words of the NBC news commentator Chet Huntley, was a "cliff-hanger." John F. Kennedy and his wife, Jacqueline, voted that morning, November 8, in Boston, the town where he had been born and where his immigrant ancestors had settled more than a century earlier. Then he and Jacqueline, who was eight months pregnant, boarded the family plane, the *Caroline*, and flew to the Kennedy compound located at Hyannis Port on Cape Cod to await the returns of the election. The entire clan was there—father, mother, brothers, and sisters, along with many of his campaign staff, who were manning the telephones to keep abreast of the election returns. In the early evening, a sense of euphoria swept across the compound as the early returns were full of good news. Ken O'Donnell, one of Kennedy's aides, recalled that "the three Kennedy sisters were jumping with glee, assuming that Jack had already been elected." But as returns came in later that evening from the Midwest and the West, the mood became somber. Kennedy was losing in Ohio, Wisconsin, Kentucky, Tennessee, and in the farm belt west of the Mississippi, and not doing as well as he had expected in Michigan and Illinois. John Chancellor, the NBC reporter in Chicago, had even predicted "a Nixon sweep." The election was not going as they had hoped.[1]

What was especially puzzling, and so reminiscent of the Smith campaign of 1928, was what happened in Ohio as well as other states that ultimately went for Nixon. In Ohio, huge crowds greeted Kennedy at every stop on the campaign trail. Theodore White, who wrote the classic account of the 1960 election, *The Making of the President 1960*, described these crowds as "spectacular," not so much in terms of numbers but because of their "frenzied quality," so reminiscent of the crowds that greeted Al Smith. Ohio seemed like a "certain Kennedy victory," as White put it. Even Kennedy himself thought he would carry Ohio. But Nixon won Ohio with 53 percent of the vote. According to White, that was "the greatest upset of the election."[2] As the night wore on with the election still undecided, thoughts of Al Smith's defeat in 1928 must have crossed the minds of the Kennedy clan as gloom set in at the family compound. Was the nation still not yet ready to elect an Irish Catholic president?

Kennedy went to bed around four in the morning, still uncertain if he would be the next president. Shortly afterward the Michigan vote was finally official, giving Kennedy the prize coveted so long by his family and the American Irish community. It was a razor-thin victory, but a victory nonetheless. The Irish Catholic community finally had one of their own in the White House. More important, by his victory the American people had finally repudiated an ancient taboo against a Catholic in the White House.

As in 1928, religion was a major issue in Kennedy's bid for the presidency. It surfaced in the Wisconsin primary in April 1960 when Kennedy defeated his Democratic opponent, Hubert Humphrey. Though he won in a close election, the vote split along the lines of religion, with Kennedy losing the predominantly Protestant districts and winning decisively in Catholic areas. Such a clear Catholic-Protestant split convinced Kennedy that he could no longer avoid publicly discussing his religion. Though his aides tried to discourage him, he had made up his mind. "Let's face it," he said. "It's the most important and the biggest issue in this campaign." He had to address it head-on in the next primary in West Virginia, whose population was 95 percent Protestant. In a speech in Morgantown, he struck a theme that he would repeat throughout West Virginia. "Nobody asked me if I was a Catholic when I joined the United States navy," he said to a stunned crowd. His aide Ken O'Donnell recalled that Kennedy went on "with a fire and dash that I had seldom seen in him, asking if forty million Americans lost their right to run for the Presidency on the day when they were baptized as Catholics. 'That wasn't the country my brother died for in Europe,' he said, 'and nobody asked my brother if he was a Catholic or Protestant before he climbed into an American bomber plane to fly his last mission.'" By stressing the theme of religious tolerance rather than intolerance, he won over a majority of the Protestant voters, defeating Humphrey, who then withdrew from the primary campaign.[3]

Nonetheless, the religion issue did not die. Throughout the presidential campaign hundreds of anti-Catholic tracts were distributed to millions of homes, along with radio broadcasts and television advertisements attacking Kennedy's religion. The issue came to a head in September with the founding of the National Conference of Citizens for Religious Freedom, an organization of prominent Protestant clergymen. After a daylong meeting, they issued a public statement, read by the well-known clergyman Norman Vincent Peale, that claimed Kennedy's religion made him unacceptable for the presidency. The prestige of Peale gave a measure of respectability to the prejudices of millions of Americans fearful of what a Catholic presidency might mean for the country. The bigotry evident in 1928 when another Catholic ran for the presidency was still prevalent across the land.

Kennedy knew that once again there was "only one way to separate the bigots from the honestly fearful," as Theodore White wrote, "and that was to face the issue of religion frankly and in the open, stripping it of the darkness, incense, and strange rituals that so many Protestants feared."[4] Kennedy did this in Houston, Texas, on September 12, 1960, when he addressed a meeting of the Greater Houston Ministerial Association. The ministers had invited him to discuss his religion and defend the right of a Catholic to be president. Kennedy's brother Robert; Lyndon B. Johnson, Kennedy's vice-presidential running mate and a senator from Texas; and House Speaker Sam Rayburn, also from Texas, did not want Kennedy to accept the invitation. They feared that "it might be a trap to embarrass Kennedy." As Rayburn put it, "They're mostly Republicans and they're out to get you."[5] Kennedy's instincts persuaded him to accept the invitation.

In a speech that has become one of his most famous, he defended the right of a Catholic to be president. Theodore Sorensen, who wrote the speech, described it as "the best speech of his campaign and one of the most important in his life." "Only Kennedy's Inaugural Address could be said to surpass it in power and eloquence," wrote Sorensen. Addressing three hundred Protestant ministers and a crowd of three hundred spectators, Kennedy said:

> Because I am a Catholic and no Catholic has ever been elected President, the real issues in this campaign have been obscured . . . So it is apparently necessary for me to state once again—not what kind of church I believe in for that should be important only to me, but what kind of America I believe in.

I believe in an America where the separation of church and state is absolute—where no Catholic prelate would tell the President (should he be a Catholic) how to act and no Protestant minister would tell his parishioners for whom to vote . . .

I believe in an America that is officially neither Catholic, Protestant nor Jewish—where no public official either requests or accepts instructions on public policy from the Pope, the National Council of Churches or any other ecclesiastical source . . . and where religious liberty is so indivisible that an act against one church is treated as an act against all.

I believe in a President whose views on religion are his own private affair, neither imposed by him upon the nation or imposed by the nation upon him as a condition to holding that office.

This is the kind of America I believe in—and this is the kind of America I fought for in the South Pacific and the kind my brother died for in Europe.[6]

After the speech Kennedy answered a barrage of questions, "none of them wholly friendly," noted Sorensen. Though the speech did not end the controversy, it was widely applauded in Texas and beyond. Sam Rayburn, who had been lukewarm about Kennedy, became an enthusiastic admirer after hearing the speech. "As we say in my part of Texas, he ate 'em blood raw." He then went on to say, "This young feller will be a great president."[7]

When the voters cast their ballots on election day, Kennedy's religion hurt him more than it helped him. Though he received a majority of the Catholic vote, he clearly lost votes because of his religion. One analyst summed it up best by stating, "Kennedy won in spite of rather than because of the fact that he was a Catholic."[8]

Kennedy's victory not only broke through the age-old American bigotry against Catholics, but it also overcame the prejudice against the Irish. Kennedy was 100 percent Irish. All of his great-grandparents were born in Ireland and were part of the great exodus that took place during the famine. His father's grandfather, Patrick Kennedy, left Dunganstown in county Wexford in the 1840s and landed in Boston, where in 1849 he married Bridget Murphy, another immigrant. Within a few years, the Irish laborer was dead of cholera, leaving Bridget a widow with four small children. To this day the Kennedys remember her as the heroine who kept the family together in spite of all the odds stacked against a young widow struggling to make it in a strange and, at times, hostile new world. Kennedy's mother's family traced their roots back to county Limerick and the village of Bluff, where Thomas Fitzgerald, her grandfather, was born. After trying to survive the famine, he gave up the family's land and joined the exodus to America. Landing in Boston in the 1850s, this Irish peddler met Rose Anna Cox, an Irish immigrant from county Cavan, whom he married in 1857. The Kennedy and Fitzgerald families created the Kennedy dynasty when Rose Fitzgerald, the granddaughter of Thomas and Rose Anna and daughter of the legendary Boston mayor John "Honey Fitz" Fitzgerald, married Joseph P. Kennedy, the grandson of Patrick and Bridget and son of the Boston politician Patrick "P.J." Kennedy. This was President Kennedy's Irish heritage, a legacy he cherished throughout his life. This became most apparent in 1963 when, as president, he visited Ireland.

Kennedy had visited Ireland a few times prior to becoming president. Recalling these earlier visits to his relatives in county Wexford, he told the American ambassador to Ireland, Matthew McCloskey, that he was "anxious to visit Ireland" again. His aides were cool to the idea because, as his chief aide Ken O'Donnell said, "it wouldn't do you much good politically. You've got all the Irish votes in this country that you'll ever get. If you go to Ireland, people will say it's just a pleasure trip." Kennedy replied, "That's exactly what I want, a pleasure trip to Ireland." So his staff added an Ireland stopover to his tour of Europe, a tour that included Kennedy's memorable speech in Berlin where he praised the West Berliners' resistance to communism by proudly claiming, *"Ich bin ein Berliner"* (I am a Berliner).[9]

For four days in June, President Kennedy did everything in Ireland but kiss the Blarney stone. In Dublin he delivered an eloquent address to the Irish parliament. In this speech, featuring "flashes of easy wit, graceful literary quotations, moving praise of Ireland's courageous history, its contributions to culture and to America," he first used a well-known quotation from the Irishman George Bernard Shaw: "Other people see things, and say why. But I dream things that never were, and say, why not?" At Wexford he laid a wreath at the monument to Commodore John Barry, the Irish-born father of the American navy; he attended a memorial for the executed leaders of the 1916 Easter Rebellion; he visited his relatives in Dunganstown and the docks at New Ross where his great-grandfather boarded the ship for America. In the ceremony at New Ross, he told the townspeople, "When my great-grandfather left here to become a cooper in East Boston, he carried nothing with him except two things, a strong religious faith and a strong desire for liberty. I am glad to say that all of his great-grandchildren have valued that inheritance." David Powers, who worked closely with the president throughout his political career and had arranged the Ireland trip, recalled that during this trip Kennedy was "getting so Irish, the next thing you know, he'll be speaking with a brogue." Powers, along with Ken O'Donnell and Larry O'Brien, were three of Kennedy's closest associates in the White House. All Irishmen skilled in the art of politics, they worked with Kennedy in his senatorial campaign and throughout the presidential campaign. The White House press corps dubbed them the Irish Mafia.[10]

In Limerick, before Kennedy left Ireland, he told the crowd that Ireland "is not the land of my birth, but it is the land for which I hold the greatest affection, and I will certainly come back in the springtime." Of course, he never returned. But this trip to Ireland was, in his own words, "one of the most moving experiences" of his life.[11]

Kennedy was an Irish Catholic Brahmin. A Harvard man who wore London-tailored suits, he was quite unlike most Irish Americans. Yet, he was 100 percent Irish, not just in his family roots, but in his personality as well. Loyalty was a key virtue for Kennedy, most especially loyalty to his family. His father and mother fostered this trait among all their children, turning their family into an American icon that has fascinated people for decades. As was true with so many other Irish, politics became the road to power for Kennedy. Raised in a political family, he loved the rough-and-tumble world of politics. His charismatic personality that exuded sophisticated cool enabled him to stand out. He possessed a beguiling wit sprinkled with self-mockery that appealed to his audiences. A lover of the English language, he was one in a long line of gifted Irish orators. His talks featured literary quotations, humor, and a sense of idealism that seldom failed to move those who listened to him. His inaugural address still remains one of the most inspiring presidential speeches. An Irish romantic, he had a deep sense of melancholy that would overcome his periods of joy.

Another key element in his personality was his Catholicism. He was born into the faith and was devoted to his Church. But his Catholicism was quite different from the pietism, the prudery, and the defensiveness that had characterized so much of the Irish Catholic community in America. Though he seldom missed Sunday Mass, he was a secular Catholic, more comfortable in the world than in the Church. He struggled with his religion as he sought to seek some reconciliation between the traditions, both intellectual and moral, of Catholicism and the challenges of modernity. A womanizer who cheated on his wife, he was hardly a candidate for sainthood. Nonetheless, he was born a Catholic and died a Catholic, and as president he proved that there was no conflict between Catholicism and American democracy.

Kennedy's presidency was a triumph for Irish Americans, signaling their final arrival and acceptance in a land where, for so long, their name and their religion were held against them. As William Shannon wrote, Kennedy's election "wiped away the bitterness and disappointment of Al Smith's defeat in 1928; it removed any lingering sense of social inferiority and insecurity."[12] His death at the hands of an assassin transformed the young Irish Brahmin into a legend of what might have been. Anyone who was alive on that fateful day in November 1963 remembers where he or she was on hearing the news of the president's death. The news not only shocked Americans, but touched people across the globe. Grief settled over Ireland at the loss of the man Pete Hamill described as "the young and shining prince of the Irish diaspora." In Belfast, people ran into the streets wailing, crying, *"Oh, sweet Jesus, they shot Jack!"* and *"They killed President Kennedy!"* In Irish America, "Jack Kennedy was forever and always someone special," Hamill wrote. "His election in 1960 had redeemed everything: the bigotry that went all the way back to the Great Famine; the slurs and the sneers; *Help Wanted No Irish Need Apply*; the insulting acceptance of the stereotype of the drunken and impotent stage Irishman; the doors closed in law firms, and men's clubs, and brokerage houses because of religion and origin. After 1960, they knew that their children truly could be anything in their chosen country, including president of the United States." Irish Catholics had come a long way since 1928, when Al Smith bemoaned, "The time hasn't come when a man can say his beads in the White House."[13]

Kennedy's election marked the culmination of the immigrant era for the Irish that began during the Great Famine when Kennedy's great-grandparents and thousands more set out on a journey of hope to America. It ended at the White House more than a century later, where this fabled son of Erin held court. His election suggested that Irish Catholics had become accepted as fully American. As the *Irish Independent* wrote, the election of an Irish American president symbolized "the closing of a chapter in our history . . . After three generations a young man of fully

Irish stocks [*sic*] has reached the last point of integration into American life—the chief executive of the nation."[14]

Commenting on the significance of Kennedy the politician, Daniel Patrick Moynihan wrote, "The era of the Irish politician culminated in Kennedy . . . He served in a final moment of ascendancy. On the day he died, the President of the United States, the Speaker of the House of Representatives, the Majority Leader of the United States Senate, the Chairman of the National Committee, were all Irish, all Catholic, all Democrats. It will not come again."[15]

One of the most visible developments in this time of triumph was the economic mobility of Irish Americans. Though the first signs of this appeared by the 1920s as the children of immigrants began to go to college, it became clearly evident in the 1950s as the rising tide of prosperity lifted most Americans into the middle class. By 1960 the Irish had become one of the most prosperous and best-educated ethnic groups in the nation. In the following decades the trend continued as the American Irish were not only excelling in educational achievement and income, but also began to gain prestige jobs that had been closed to them.[16] The success of the Irish in Boston was a clear example of this achievement.

In a city where they had faced years of discrimination, most especially in the world of business and banking, they joined the business elite. In the 1970s the Irish were already making inroads in Boston's banking and business communities, but they had clearly arrived by the 1990s, when two of the city's major banks, US Trust and Fleet Bank, had an Irishman at the helm; Peter Lynch, a Boston College graduate, became a financial guru who put the Fidelity investment firm on the map with his management of the Magellan Fund from 1977 to 1990; Patrick Purcell was the president and publisher of the *Boston Herald*. The Irish-born Thomas Flatley, who'd arrived in this country with just a few dollars in his pocket, became not only one of the richest men in Boston but in the entire world through his real estate developments. The Irish were also key players in the advertising business.

A major reason why these Boston Irishmen, as well as other Irish men and women, have made it in the world of business and finance is because of education, most especially in the Catholic school system, which has educated young men and women from first grade to graduate school. As a Boston Irish banker put it, "The only way to get out of Dorchester was to get an education."[17] For many Boston Irish that meant going to one of the city's Catholic high schools and then enrolling at Boston College, a school whose alumni dominate the city and its business. What took place in Boston has occurred in New York, Chicago, and San Francisco, where large numbers of the Irish also settled.

The economic triumph of the Irish becomes evident each fall when *Forbes* magazine publishes its annual list of the richest Americans. In 1996 one hundred people on the *Forbes* list of the four hundred wealthiest Americans were Irish. In 2006, when assets of at least one billion dollars were needed to make the *Forbes* list, about 10 percent of the four hundred wealthiest billionaires had Irish names. Many more, of course, are mere millionaires, whose names decorate the buildings of many Catholic colleges.[18]

The other side of the Irish story is of those who were never able to make it. Boston was especially notable in this regard. Despite the prominent presence of the Irish in the city's business and banking communities, another segment of the Irish community lived in an entirely different world. In Dorchester or South Boston they were some of the city's poorest residents. The media labeled the Irish enclave of South Boston the "white underclass capital of America." Michael Patrick MacDonald wrote about growing up in South Boston, where the vast majority of Irish were on welfare. He described it as a neighborhood of "junkies, the depressed and lonely mothers of people who'd died, the wounded, the drug dealers, and a known murderer."[19] In Southie, as it was known in Boston, Whitey Bulger and his gang of drug pushers and murderers became a legend. For years he fooled everyone, even the FBI. Hollywood captured this Irish underworld in the award-winning movie *The Departed*, starring Jack Nicholson as Boston's Irish mob boss. In New York, the Irish mob, known as the Westies, were major players in the city's underworld of crime. Based in Hell's Kitchen, an Irish district for decades, they controlled organized crime on the West Side for more than twenty years, from the mid-1960s to the 1980s. In other New York neighborhoods Irish residents had to resort to food stamps and unemployment insurance. These places were the underside of Irish America, where all the social problems associated with poverty kept many people stuck there forever.

For those Irish who rode the economic escalator up to middle-class respectability, a move to the suburbs generally followed. But more was involved than just an increase in income. A decisive influence was the migration of blacks and Hispanics into the old Irish neighborhoods. In Chicago, New York, Boston, and San Francisco large numbers of minority newcomers transformed the ethnic complexion of these cities. Chicago experienced the most dramatic change. In 1950 blacks and Hispanics represented 14 percent of the city's population. By 1980 they had increased to 55 percent. In this period the city's black belt was steadily moving south and west into the old Irish neighborhoods. A priest in St. Sabina's parish recalled the atmosphere when blacks first arrived in the neighborhood: "It was a classic Irish ghetto which saw itself under threat. When I got there in 1963, the black movement was right at the border. There was one black family that lived in the parish at that time. So it was like a 'The barbarians are at our border! The Huns are at the wall!' kind of experience." Within five years a parish of almost three thousand Irish Catholic families had become a congregation of less than four hundred families. Despite the efforts of the pastor, who endorsed an integrated parish; the uphill struggle of a community organization led by reformer Saul Alinsky that sought to prevent white flight; and the hard work of parish organizations that reached out to the newcomers, the majority of the Irish abandoned the parish and the neighborhood for the suburbs.[20]

What finally tipped the scales of racial balance in the neighborhood was the fatal shooting of a young parishioner in the summer of 1965. Crime had been on the increase in recent months, spreading fear throughout the parish. Then tragedy struck on a sunny August afternoon as a group of teenage boys headed over to the parish center after their baseball game and met some of the girls from the parish. When three black teenagers appeared, insults were exchanged, and two of the black youths drew guns and fired at the group. One girl was wounded, while seventeen-year-old Frank Kelly was shot in the chest and died minutes later as the parish priest was administering the last rites. "It was that incident, probably more than anything else, that convinced hundreds of people to leave," recalled a priest in the parish.[21] As the middle-class Irish left, middle-class blacks moved in, many of them joining the old Irish parish. By 1980 St. Sabina's, once an Irish citadel, had become one of the premier black parishes in the city.

The population shift in St. Sabina's parish was replicated throughout the city's entire South Side. It was hardly a smooth transition. Many Irish resented the intrusion of blacks into their neighborhood. They resisted as much as they could, hurling insults at the newcomers, throwing rocks through their windows, and shunning those who attended Catholic services. Then, in the summer of 1966, one year after the fatal shooting in St. Sabina's, Martin Luther King led a series of civil rights marches through heavily Catholic neighborhoods of the Southwest Side, demanding open housing in Chicago. Joining him and other civil rights activists were a number of priests, nuns, and Catholic laypeople. Angry crowds, eventually numbering in the thousands, greeted the marchers each time they took to the streets, hurling bricks and bottles and screaming, "Two, four, six, eight, we don't want to integrate," and, "Kill those niggers." Andrew Young recalled, "Bottles were flying and cherry bombs were going off. We felt like we were walking through a war zone." King remarked that he had "never seen—even in Mississippi and Alabama—mobs as hostile and hate-filled as I've seen in Chicago."[22] The campaign for open housing hardly changed the minds of the residents in these neighborhoods. Then, in 1968 King was assassinated. The pent-up anger among blacks burst forth across the country as rioting set many cities on fire. In Chicago rioting swept through the city's West Side, leaving blocks of buildings destroyed by fire and looting. The South Side neighborhood of Englewood, not far from the Irish enclaves west of Ashland Avenue, the line of demarcation at that time, was another area torched by rioters. Along Sixty-third Street, the pungent odor of smoke from burning stores filled the air and chaos was everywhere as fear gripped the city. The National Guard, and even federal troops, had to be called in to restore order. These riots hastened white flight, and it never stopped as the line of demarcation separating black and white neighborhoods moved steadily west and south.

The Irish were too numerous and too complex a group to be identified with only one side of the controversy. Many were conservative bigots, hurling epithets at King and his supporters; many were numbered among the liberal activists marching shoulder to shoulder with King. The same type of division present in Chicago was true in Philadelphia and other cities where the migration of blacks into old immigrant neighborhoods led to racial confrontations. Despite such differences, a study done in the 1980s by the sociologist Andrew M. Greeley concluded that a majority of the Irish "have been more sympathetic to integration" than other Catholic ethnics as well as all Protestants during the 1970s.[23]

Once the Irish arrived in the suburbs, they mingled with people from different ethnic backgrounds. Uprooted from the Irish parish, they began to think of themselves as being lawyers, teachers, doctors, and business men and women rather than as being Irish. Moving to the new suburbs of the 1960s and '70s clearly hastened their Americanization. It also marked the end of the era of the big-city Catholic parish, the glue that had held the old Irish neighborhood together. The unique culture created in these enclaves was gone, as extinct as the dodo.

Further accelerating the Americanization of the Irish was a decline in Irish immigration. A major reason for this was an economic upsurge in Ireland. An expanding economy had produced more jobs and more opportunities, so long denied in a country where agriculture, not industry, reigned supreme. Ireland's entry into the European Economic Community in 1972 provided a significant boost to the economy as well. As a result, fewer people left Ireland. Only about thirty-five hundred emigrated annually to the United States during the 1960s, and even fewer came in the 1970s, about fifteen hundred a year. In fact, by the early 1970s more people were immigrating to Ireland than leaving. The new U.S. immigration law of 1965 also contributed to this decline. The law did away with the national-origins quota system that had been in place since the 1920s, replacing it with legislation in which family unification took precedence, along with a maximum quota of twenty thousand for each country. Since so few new Irish had arrived in the 1950s and '60s, scarcely any Irish had relatives in the United States who could sponsor them.

In the early 1980s Ireland's economy went into a tailspin. Between 1979 and 1985 unemployment rose from 7.8 percent to 18.2 percent. With no jobs, as many as one third of the population, or one million people, were living in poverty. Ireland had a young, well-educated population with no work and a future of poverty staring it in the face. Emigration surged again: as many as 360,000 Irish left home during the 1980s. They were single men and women under the age of thirty, the majority of whom headed to England, where as many as one million Irish-born people lived.[24] Many also came to the United States. As one young clerk in Boston put it, "Back home there is absolutely no work to be had. Here there is plenty of work and the money is decent. All we want is work."[25] Those who immigrated to the United States with proper documentation averaged about one thousand a year in the early 1980s, but after successful lobbying efforts by Irish American congressmen, the number of visas granted to Ireland increased so that by the end of the decade close to thirty thousand Irish had arrived. Many more, however, came with a six-month tourist visa and overstayed it, hanging on for months or years. Without proper documentation, these new Irish immigrants survived as undocumented aliens in an underground world, seldom entering the mainstream of American society. How large their number was is difficult to determine, with estimates ranging from 40,000 to as high as 150,000.

These undocumented, or illegal, immigrants settled in traditional Irish neighborhoods in cities such as New York, Boston, and Chicago, where there were existing Irish communities. Not surprisingly, New York attracted the largest number of the new Irish. Relying on ethnic networks in these communities, they found jobs in construction, in restaurants, or as domestics. Their arrival often revitalized the old neighborhoods as the young newcomers patronized Irish businesses, joined Gaelic athletic teams, and supported a resurgence in Irish festivals.

Yet the new Irish were very different from the older immigrants who had arrived in the 1950s and before. Children of a modern Ireland, they could not identify with the old culture of rural Ireland in which Church and family were so central. Television, with its pop culture and rock music, had opened up a new world to them. In America, they viewed themselves as transients, migrant workers who would eventually return home to Ireland. A priest in New York described the difference between the two waves of immigrants in the following manner: "People don't mix easily outside of their own social group. The older Irish tend to be more family oriented, better established and more upwardly mobile. The younger, single people are into a totally different lifestyle. Bars are their cultural center and they tend to close in on themselves."[26] Many of the older immigrants believed that the new Irish were arrogant, too self-centered, and ungrateful for the work the old-timers had done to preserve Irish cultural traditions in America. Because of such attitudes, the two waves of immigrants never jelled, resulting in a fragmented Irish community.

In the 1990s Ireland underwent a remarkable transformation. What sparked this was a booming economy led by the computer and pharmaceutical industries, including many American companies. The old, rural, agriculturally based Ireland was disappearing. A new nation emerged as over half a million new jobs were created. The Irish economy expanded like the "tiger" economies of Southeast Asia, earning the label the Celtic Tiger. In addition, the European Union poured millions of dollars into Ireland to build up its roads and infrastructure. Ireland had become the envy of Europe, economically outperforming its partners in the European Union. Who would want to leave Ireland now? Not only did emigration dry up, but more and more people were immigrating to Ireland. These included the younger Irish who had temporarily settled in the United States as well as thousands of Eastern Europeans and Africans, mainly from Poland, Lithuania, and Nigeria. In 2006 about 10 percent of Ireland's population was foreign-born. A sign of the times occurred in June 2007 when Ireland elected its first black mayor, Rotimi Adebari, a Nigerian who had arrived in Ireland seven years earlier, seeking asylum. Backed by both political parties, he was elected mayor of Portlaoise, a small city in county Laois, southwest of Dublin.

The return to Ireland continued throughout the early years of the new century. The Irish were being driven out of America not just by the attraction of Ireland's booming economy, but also by the American government's attitude toward all illegal immigrants and an economy in which people found it more difficult to make ends meet. Longtime illegal residents found it difficult to drive or work without a valid Social Security number. Others, who were naturalized citizens, found the price of health care and education too high, and life exhausting. As the *New York Times* described one couple's plight, "Ireland's style of prosperity promises a better life for their children. After the birth of their first baby, they rebelled against the toll of seven-day workweeks to pay rising costs in a sluggish American economy." They left New York and returned to Ireland, where they started their own business. They were not alone. One woman commented, "Everybody's leaving and nobody's coming over anymore," as she listed the friends who had moved back to Ireland.[27] Such an exodus marked a historic milestone in the history of Irish immigration to the United States, as more Irish returned to Ireland than emigrated to America. Without a doubt, such a change will strengthen the American identity of the Irish American community, where the Irish brogue can scarcely be heard anymore.

Another major development in the post-Kennedy era was the reformation—some called it a revolution—in the Catholic Church in the closing decades of the twentieth century. One of the distinguishing marks of the Irish had been their loyalty to the Catholic Church. Throughout the nineteenth and twentieth centuries the Irish clergy had promoted a distinctive brand of Catholicism that shaped the lives of their parishioners. In the 1960s this religious world began to come apart. A major reason for this was the emergence of a new breed of Catholic—a college-educated, more independent-minded individual who began to question many of the rules of the Church. Another key influence was the Second Vatican Council, which ushered in a new era in the Church as it sought to bring Catholicism up-to-date.

Among the Irish, Catholicism had become a religion of dos and don'ts. There were rules for everything, and if you wanted to be a Catholic, you kept to the rules. You had to eat fish on Friday. You could not marry a Protestant unless you got special permission, and then the ceremony took place in the dark confines of the parish rectory rather than the church. You had to attend Mass every Sunday, and if you didn't, you would go right to hell when you died. Catholics were not allowed to be divorced. You had to be buried in a Catholic cemetery if you wanted to be buried as a Catholic.

In the 1960s a new breed of Catholic began to assert the rights of individuals, challenging the authority of the Church and its right to make rules governing an individual's behavior. Then the council began to change such long-lasting traditions as the Latin Mass, replacing it with Mass in the vernacular. The Church changed its sectarian, defensive posture toward modern society, and Protestants suddenly became allies rather than enemies. As this ecumenical alliance gained momentum, the militant attitude of Catholics slowly disappeared. Sectarianism did not play well in such an environment. Religious freedom and the right to choose one's religion was another change proclaimed by the council. All of these changes swept through the Catholic community in a few years, pleasing many and disillusioning others.

Within a decade the behavior of Catholics underwent dramatic and permanent change. Attendance at Sunday Mass went from 70 percent in 1963 to 50 percent in 1974, as fewer people believed that missing Mass was a ticket to hell. By 2005 the number had declined to 37 percent. The practice of regular confession declined; today more than half of the Catholic population seldom or never goes to confession. Parish missions, notorious for their fire-and-brimstone sermons, became extinct; many of the laity no longer regarded premarital sex as always wrong; Catholics married Protestants with increasing frequency. Cremation became accepted, and meatless Fridays were a thing of the past. What really undermined the teaching authority of the Church was the papacy's adamant prohibition of any form of artificial birth control, spelled out in the encyclical *Humanae Vitae*, issued by Pope Paul VI. Despite the papal encyclical, the vast majority of laypeople, along with many of the clergy, upheld the legitimacy of birth control. This more than anything else eroded the authority of the Church and its right to make rules governing the behavior of people. The old-style religion, in particular the sexual moral code that had shaped the behavior of Irish Catholics for generations, had collapsed.

As the old-time religion disintegrated, the priest fell from his pedestal, where he had ruled for decades with unquestioned authority. The revelations of widespread sexual abuse on the part of the clergy, many of whom were Irish, further damaged their reputation. News about such crimes became public in the mid-1980s and further revelations occurred in the 1990s. Then in January 2002, the *Boston Globe* began an exposé of Boston Catholic priests who had preyed on young boys and the Church authorities who had covered up the scandal. Many news stories appeared in the *Globe* for several weeks. Such shocking revelations about the behavior of priests, not just in Boston but in many other Catholic communities across the country, became a major media event. Over the next few months "more than twelve thousand sex-abuse-by-priests stories had been carried by the major TV networks, cable outlets, wire services, and magazines and the nation's fifty top newspapers."[28] Catholics were outraged. No longer did the Irish speak fondly of the *Sagart aroon*.

As the religious world of Catholics changed, the institutional Church began to shrink. The number of priests and women religious declined. Seminaries across the country closed their doors as the number of new recruits dwindled. In Boston, a citadel of Irish Catholicism that had regularly ordained as many as fifty priests a year in the 1950s, ordinations had declined to fewer than ten a year by the 1980s and '90s. No longer could bishops turn to Ireland to replenish the supply of clergy since the Church in Ireland was collapsing as well. Rather, they turned to Africa and Asia for new recruits. The days when Irish clergy ruled the Church were over. As Catholics left the old urban neighborhoods, many of the churches and the parish schools they left behind closed their doors. In the suburbs, new churches were built, but fewer parish schools, as many parents turned to the public schools for their children's education. Within a decade, 1964 to 1974, the number of children attending parochial schools declined from 44 to 29 percent.

The closing of churches and schools in the old neighborhoods, as much as anything else, signaled a transition for the immigrant Church. As the Irish moved to the suburbs, Church and religion no longer dominated their lives as in times past. They remained Catholic, but a new breed of Catholic who could love the pope while ignoring what he had to say.

The loyalty of the Irish to the Democratic Party was as legendary as their loyalty to their Church. There was no better symbol of this marriage in the 1960s and '70s than Richard J. Daley, mayor of Chicago. When John F. Kennedy made his last trip to Chicago shortly before election day in 1960, Daley welcomed him with a torchlight parade that attracted a crowd of over one million people, lining the streets of Chicago as the mayor and the young candidate led a cavalcade of bands, floats, and roaring motorcycles. Starting in the heart of downtown Chicago, the parade ended at the Chicago Stadium, several blocks south, where a capacity crowd of twenty-eight thousand welcomed the mayor and his presidential hopeful.[29] A few days later, on election day, Illinois and the Daley machine cast their votes for Kennedy, helping him to a razor-thin victory. Ever since then, observers have questioned the legitimacy of the Illinois victory, accusing Daley and the Democrats of stealing the election.

Chicago has always had a reputation for voting fraud at election time. "Vote early and vote often" was the motto of the machine for years. A joke often told around Chicago as well as in Washington had Mayor Daley, President Kennedy, and Nikita Khrushchev in a sinking lifeboat with only one life preserver. Kennedy said that as leader of the free world he should have the life preserver; Khrushchev replied that as leader of the most powerful nation in the world, he should have it; Daley, a true Chicago politician, suggested that they take a vote to see who would get the life preserver. Daley won, 8 to 2.[30]

Daley and the machine could never escape the charge that they had stolen the election for the Democrats and their Irish Catholic idol. Powerful as he was, Daley survived this accusation as well as many others during his reign as mayor from 1955 to 1976.

Richard J. Daley (1902–76) was born and raised in Bridgeport, a working-class neighborhood on Chicago's South Side. Several ethnic groups lived in Bridgeport, each claiming their own turf. Daley grew up in Hamburg, an Irish enclave anchored by three institutions synonymous with the Irish—the Church of the Nativity, the Democratic headquarters of the Eleventh Ward, and Shaller's Pump, the local saloon. Remarkably, Daley never left Bridgeport. He was buried from the same church where he was baptized. Daley was the only child of Michael and Lillian Daley. His father, whom he always remembered with great fondness, was a sheet-metal worker and a union man. His mother, Lillian, was the dominant personality in the family. A suffragist, she often took her son along to marches in support of women's right to vote. She was also active in the local parish, where she acquired the reputation of being a formidable force. One parishioner remarked that when the Daley family walked by on the way to church, a neighbor "pronounced with dark Irish humor, 'Here they come now, the Father, the Son, and the Holy Ghost.' "[31] Close to her throughout his life, Daley never lived more than a block away from his mother.

Like most Irish boys in Bridgeport, Daley attended Nativity parochial school, and after graduation he went to De La Salle Institute, a three-year Catholic high school known as the Poor Boys College. After graduating from De La Salle at age seventeen, he went to work in the city's stock-yards, located close by Bridgeport. A few years later Daley enrolled at De-Paul University, where he began taking classes four nights a week while continuing to work. After eleven years, he finally got his law degree. Shortly afterward, he married Eleanor Guilfoyle. Their first of seven children, Patricia, was born about a year later on St. Patrick's Day, 1937.

Like Al Smith, Daley had a patron, "Big Joe" McDonough, a former football player who was the boss of the Eleventh Ward. McDonough took a liking to the young De La Salle graduate, appointing him precinct captain. This was Daley's baptism into Democratic machine politics. From his base in the Eleventh Ward and with Big Joe's endorsement, Daley slowly began his ascent in the Democratic Party. When McDonough was elected county treasurer in 1930, he took Daley with him. While Big Joe was carousing in the local saloons, Daley was on the job, learning the intricacies of balancing the city budget. Then, in 1936, one of the state legislators from Bridgeport died, opening up a slot for the ambitious Daley. He announced his candidacy, called upon all his supporters in Bridgeport, and with the endorsement of the Democratic organization won election to the state House of Representatives. He served in Springfield for eight years, where he gained a reputation as an honest, hardworking legislator. He was a rising star in the Kelly-Nash machine. One commentator described him as "probably the best exhibit of the hard-working, decent, honest organization politician that the Kelly machine can produce."[32]

After Springfield, he returned to Chicago and his home base in the Eleventh Ward, where he had become a powerful presence. Gathering together the ward's precinct captains, he got himself elected ward committeeman, a position that guaranteed him a seat on the Cook County Democratic Central Committee. As boss of the Eleventh Ward, he joined the ranks of the machine's inner circle. Thirsting for power rather than money, Daley coveted the big prize, leadership of the Democratic Party. He won this in 1953 when the party power brokers elected him chairman of the Cook County Democratic Party. Two years later, having gained the party's nomination, he won the mayoral election.

When Daley became mayor, only 10 percent of the city's population was Irish. Polish and black voters far outnumbered them, but the Irish ran the city, holding one third of the seats in the city council. By 1970, even with the Irish population dwindling, they still held the following positions in the city and county government: mayor, president of the Cook County Board of Commissioners, county assessor, county clerk, state's attorney, clerk of the circuit court, president of the Chicago park district, superintendent of police, fire commissioner, president of the board of education, as well as numerous other offices. According to one estimate, all of these offices, together with the citywide machine, controlled as many as forty thousand patronage jobs, which on election day produced as many as four hundred thousand votes. Each job generated about ten votes: the worker's vote, those of his family and friends, and the votes that the worker's campaign efforts produced.[33]

As mayor, Daley rewarded his own kind. The Irishman in him highly valued loyalty—loyalty to family, friends, and neighbors. Despite much criticism, he took care of his sons. When it was revealed that two of his sons, both lawyers, benefited from lucrative appointments, an enraged Daley told his colleagues, "If I can't help my sons, then" these critics "can kiss my ass." He went on to say, in a line that became famous, "If a man can't put his arms around his sons, then what kind of a world are we living in?" As many as one hundred of his relatives held government jobs. He groomed his oldest son, Richard M., who would eventually become mayor of Chicago, for a career in politics. The elder Daley displayed his sentimental Irish nature when he broke down in the middle of a speech congratulating his son for his election to the state constitutional convention in 1969. "I hope and pray to God," said the father, holding back tears, "when he's on the floor of the convention, he'll always remember the people from whence he comes and that he'll always fight for the people." Then his voice broke and tears welled up in his eyes.[34]

Most of the mayor's friends were Irish as were most of his appointments. His press secretary once said that Daley's "idea of affirmative action was nine Irishmen and a Swede." He was also loyal to his neighbors in Bridgeport. Though the population of the Eleventh Ward was perhaps only 4 percent Irish, they ruled the ward. Daley funneled as many as two thousand patronage jobs to his neighbors in the Eleventh Ward, three or four times the number given to other wards.[35]

Daley was proud of his blue-collar background. He described himself as the "son of a Chicago working man . . . reared in a working man's community . . . played on the sand lots in the great stockyards . . . worked in the stockyards and dreamed."[36] He never moved from the small bungalow home in Bridgeport where he raised his family. He was unpretentious, unlike his predecessors, who had homes on the city's Gold Coast as well as in Florida or California. A loyal and devout Catholic, he attended Mass every week, rubbing shoulders with the common folk in Nativity parish. He sent his children to the parochial school and the local Catholic colleges, where Chicago's Irish gained the education that put them on the economic escalator.

When Daley took over as mayor in 1955, Chicago was in decline, a gritty city known more for its stockyards and its run-down housing than for its skyscrapers. As black migrants from the South continued to crowd into the city's South Side, whites moved out to the suburbs. Businesses were taking their money out of the city, investing it in the new suburbs ringing Chicago. For twenty years, city government had been a mess, with corruption widespread. Daley gave the city new life. As boss of the party and mayor of the city, he gained complete control over city government by taking control of the city council. Following his motto "Good government is good politics," he modernized the city government so that Chicago became known as "the city that works." He built alliances with big businesses, persuading them to invest in the city, thus enabling Chicago to become one of the nation's great cities. New skyscrapers of epic proportions turned Chicago into a living museum of modern architecture. He used his clout to build O'Hare International Airport, Sears Tower, and the Dan Ryan Expressway. McCormick Place, one of the world's largest exhibition halls, was built during his tenure, as was the downtown Civic Center, anchored by an eye-catching fifty-foot-high steel sculpture designed by Picasso. He also encouraged the development of the Magnificent Mile on North Michigan Avenue, one of the nation's premier shopping districts.

Daley was a masterful politician who wielded tremendous power. For twenty-one years he was the Boss of Chicago who ruled like an Irish chieftain. No political appointment was made without his approval. His influence reached beyond the city to the state and national level, where his word would determine who would be governor, state legislator, U.S. senator, or congressman. Anyone seeking the Democratic presidential nomination had to pass through Chicago and obtain the mayor's blessing. Otherwise it was a hopeless endeavor. Nonetheless, as powerful as he was, Daley could not control the social forces that were challenging the nation during the 1960s. Chief among these was race.

Race had been a source of tension in Chicago since the First World War. Racial conflict erupted on and off for thirty years as blacks and whites fought over ownership of the city's changing neighborhoods. In the 1960s the city became the Northern battleground in the civil rights movement. At this time Chicago had one of the most segregated and dilapidated public housing programs in the nation, while its public schools were deteriorating. When Martin Luther King brought his civil rights campaign to Chicago in 1966, he hoped to overturn a pattern of segregation in the city's housing and school system. But King's campaign failed. Daley was too powerful an opponent. By refusing to acknowledge the need to integrate the city's schools and public housing, the mayor maintained the color line in Chicago, gaining it the dubious distinction of being one of the most racially segregated cities in the nation. Like many other mayors at this time, he could not resolve the issue of racial conflict. He presided over the building of one of the nation's wealthiest cities, but its public housing projects were some of the poorest neighborhoods in the country. He made Chicago a city that works, but not for all of its people.

With Daley's death one of the last of the mighty Irish machines was gone. The only other one left was the Democratic machine built by Dan O'Connell in Albany, but that, too, went into decline after O'Connell's death in 1977.

After Daley's death in 1976, Chicago politics entered a period of readjustment. For thirteen years no one figure emerged who ruled over the city as Daley had. In 1983 Chicago elected its first black mayor, the Democratic congressman Harold Washington. His sudden death from a heart attack in November 1987 opened the door for Daley's son Richard M. Daley, who was elected mayor in 1989, the city's fifth mayor since 1976. For two more decades, another Irish Catholic from Bridgeport has presided over the city. His political success rested in his ability to build a citywide coalition of white ethnics, blacks, and Latinos. He accomplished this not by relying on his father's old-style machine, based in the ward and precinct, but by building a new machine that focused on loyalty to a person—Richard M. Daley—and not an organization.[37] By 2003 he was so popular that he won nearly 80 percent of the votes cast in the mayoral election. Like his father, Richard M. Daley also courted the city's business community. Unlike his father, he managed the city as a political chief executive officer rather than a boss politician. But he has continued the legacy of his father by strengthening Chicago's reputation as the nation's unrivaled Second City. When he completes his sixth term as mayor in 2011, he and his father will have occupied the mayor's office for forty-three of the last fifty-six years.

As the old urban machines passed away, many of the politically inclined Irish moved to the national arena, where they made their mark in Congress. John F. Kennedy's brother Robert was a senator from New

York as well as the leading Democratic candidate for the 1968 presidential nomination until his assassination in Los Angeles. Another Democratic candidate running for the White House in 1968 was Senator Eugene McCarthy from Minnesota. Both Kennedy and McCarthy were the liberal, antiwar candidates during that primary season. Robert's brother Edward has been a distinguished member of the Senate since 1962. Daniel Patrick Moynihan, who grew up in the Irish neighborhood of Hell's Kitchen in New York City, was a noted academic at Harvard University who served in cabinet or subcabinet positions under Presidents Kennedy, Johnson, Nixon, and Ford. He represented the state of New York in the Senate from 1977 to 2001. Patrick Leahy of Vermont has served in the Senate since 1975. Christopher Dodd of Connecticut is another Irish Democrat who has had a long and distinguished record in the Senate. He was a member of the House of Representatives for six years prior to his election to the Senate in 1981. The people of Connecticut have reelected him four times since then.

Without a doubt the most memorable Irish member of the House of Representatives was Thomas P. "Tip" O'Neill, the Democratic congressman from Massachusetts from 1953 to 1987. As Speaker of the House from 1977 to 1987 he played an important role in persuading Presidents Carter and Reagan to intervene with the British to bring peace to Northern Ireland. In the House of Representatives, Peter King, the Republican representative from the Third District of New York, was also involved in seeking to resolve the conflict in Northern Ireland. Thomas Foley was another prominent Irishman who served in the House of Representatives. During his thirty years in Congress, 1965–95, he emerged as an influential leader in the Democratic caucus. In 1989 he became Speaker of the House, holding that office until 1995.

One significant development among the Irish in the post-Kennedy era was a noticeable shift to the Republican Party. For some, such a conversion was tantamount to losing the faith. In 1938 John Danaher from Connecticut was the first Irish Catholic ever elected as a Republican to the U.S. Senate. A story was told about an old Irish Catholic woman who, hearing the news that Danaher's father had switched his allegiance to the Republicans, said to her friend, "It can't be true. I saw him at Mass just last Sunday."[38] Well, it was true. The first realignment took place in the 1950s when large numbers of Catholics voted for Dwight Eisenhower, the Republican president. They returned to the Democratic Party when Kennedy ran in 1960, with as many as 78 percent of Catholics voting for

JFK. But, in the mid-1960s a number of Irish Catholics voted for Barry Goldwater, the conservative Republican who lost in a landslide presidential election to Lyndon B. Johnson. This was most noticeable in New York City, where Irish Catholics led the shift to political conservatism. The most eminent of this group was William Buckley, who, through his journal, *National Review*, would become a leading spokesman for conservative thought. Even though as many as 78 percent of the Irish voted for Johnson, a trend of conservative Irish Catholics moving to the Republican Party was under way.[39]

In the 1968 presidential election 64 percent of the Irish Catholic vote went to the Democratic candidate, Hubert Humphrey. Then in the 1970s as more Irish settled in the suburbs and moved up the ladder economically, they adopted a more conservative political stance. This political shift to the right was gaining momentum across the country during the decade of the seventies. By 1980 many Irish had become loyal Reaganites in an election in which the majority of Catholics voted for the Republican. This was a seismic shift from the New Deal era and the 1960 Kennedy election. This trend continued during Reagan's presidency, 1981–89, when the country moved to the right, becoming more socially and morally conservative. Reagan led this shift by promoting prayer in public schools and opposing abortion. Many Americans also supported Reagan's tough anti-Soviet policy. When he ran for reelection in 1984, the majority of Irish in New York and several other states voted for Reagan. Reagan directly appealed for the Irish vote when in June 1984 he traveled to the town of Ballyporeen in county Tipperary, Ireland, where his great-grandfather had been born. In rediscovering his Irish roots Reagan was playing the Irish card. His aides were delighted with the possible influence the visit could have with Irish American voters. His trip was carried live on American television, and these scenes would later be used in campaign commercials. That fall he won reelection in a landslide.

The Irish turn to the Republican Party continued through the early 1990s when in the 1994 congressional election, the majority of Irish Americans voted Republican. Since then, some of the Catholic Irish have moved back into the Democratic Party. In the 2000 presidential election, the Catholic vote was just about evenly divided between Al Gore, 49 percent, and George Bush, 47 percent. This political realignment over the past forty years was clearly illustrated in the 2004 Congress, where Irish Catholic Republicans in the House of Representatives outnumbered Irish Democrats twenty-one to nineteen. In the Senate, however, Irish Catholic

Democrats far outnumber Irish Republicans, by an estimated ten to one. Such differences between the House and the Senate suggest that perhaps the shift to the Republican Party has not been as decisive as it appears at first glance. As one study of the Irish vote concluded, from 1952 to 1992, with the exception of the 1960 election, when Catholic support for the Democratic candidate was unusually high, "their tendency to favor Democratic candidates in all other elections [relative to the corresponding preference of Protestant voters] shows no distinctive net trend [either toward or away from the Democratic Party]."[40]

A key reason for the political realignment of many Irish Catholics has been the emergence in recent years of a cultural divide in the United States. Culture wars over such hot-button issues as abortion and same-sex marriage have sharpened the boundaries between the two political parties, with political partisanship dividing the country into ideological camps. Many Irish Catholics, who view opposition to abortion as the litmus test of their faith, have moved into the Republican Party, while the Democratic Party has attracted those Catholics who respect a woman's right to privacy and choice on issues such as abortion. Such a division was apparent in a 2005 survey in which 42 percent of Catholics identified themselves as Democrats and 39 percent as Republicans. This was a far cry from the days of Al Smith when finding a Catholic Republican was as rare as spotting Halley's comet.

Despite the shift of some Irish to the Republican Party, Irish labor leaders remained committed to the Democratic Party. After he became president of the AFL-CIO in 1955, George Meany entered the high point of his career and influence. In the print media and on television, he was the public face of labor, who defended the rights of workers and the liberalism of the New Deal. During his tenure the AFL-CIO became a formidable political force aligned with the Democratic Party, helping President Lyndon B. Johnson gain passage of his Great Society programs. Meany became a close friend of the president, and Johnson, on more than one occasion, made a late-night call to Meany to come to the White House, where "Johnson would talk into the night, detailing his plans and venting his frustrations."[41] In the halls of Congress Meany was a key lobbyist on behalf of civil rights, emphasizing the need to abolish job discrimination. Throughout the sixties the AFL-CIO waged political campaigns across the country, supporting Democratic pro-labor candidates. The presidential campaign of 1968 proved to be a decisive moment for the labor movement. Despite their Herculean efforts on behalf of

Hubert Humphrey, the Democratic candidate, union workers saw their efforts go down to defeat at the hands of Richard M. Nixon and the Republican Party. This defeat not only marked the weakening of New Deal liberalism, but also ushered in a period of decline for organized labor.

Manifesting the complexity of what it meant to be an Irish Catholic, Meany, a devout Catholic, embraced the social liberalism of the Catholic social gospel and the New Deal, strengthening this vision within the labor movement. He was also a Cold War warrior who was unrivaled in his opposition to communism. This became most apparent in the 1960s when he enthusiastically supported the Vietnam War. As public opposition to the war intensified, Meany's support for the war grew stronger. In a speech in 1966 he told an audience that he "would rather fight the Communists in South Vietnam than fight them here in the Chesapeake Bay." Conservative in his personal values, he had little tolerance for the young activists of the 1960s who were challenging the establishment on issues of race, gender, and war. Describing them as "kooks," he said, "There is more venereal disease among them . . . There are more of them smoking pot and . . . they have long beards and look dirty and smell."[42]

When Meany became president of the AFL-CIO in 1955, unions had reached their peak of influence with as many as 35 percent of workers carrying a union card. At the time of his retirement in 1979, union membership had declined to 19 percent. Ironically, George Meany, perhaps the most powerful and prominent union leader in the twentieth century, also presided over labor's decline, a weakening that would continue for the rest of the century.

Lane Kirkland succeeded Meany as president in 1979. When he retired from office in 1995, two Irish Americans—John Sweeney, president of the Services Employees International Union, and Thomas R. Donahue, secretary-treasurer of the AFL-CIO—squared off in an election to see who would be the next president. Sweeney, a son of Irish immigrants who proudly celebrates his Irish working-class background, won the election and has remained head of the union into the twenty-first century.

Sweeney's commitment to the labor movement began when, as a student at Iona College, he took classes at Xavier Labor School, where the labor priest Philip A. Carey, S.J., taught him the principles of Catholic social teaching. Commenting on this experience, Sweeney said, "I came to understand that working people have God-given rights; and that there is a moral connection among the church, the rights of workers and economic justice."[43] For Sweeney, as well as for Philip Murray and George Meany, Catholic social teaching had a major influence on his work on behalf of the labor movement. This son of Irish immigrants presides over a federation of seventy-five national unions and forty thousand local unions. Though not as strong as in times past, the Irish presence in the American labor movement is still significant.

A major development in the post-1960 period was the rise of nationalism in the Irish American community. This was linked to the civil rights uprising in Northern Ireland in the 1960s that sought to abolish discrimination against Catholics in housing, jobs, and education. Eventually this campaign spilled over into a prolonged armed struggle aimed at the reunification of Ireland. This battle, involving revolutionary nationalists who wanted a united Ireland, militant Ulster unionists who opposed this idea, and British troops attempting to keep the peace between them, lasted for more than thirty years, claiming more than thirty-three hundred lives and injuring at least thirty-eight thousand people. One event that aroused American support for the nationalist cause happened on Sunday, January 30, 1972, in the city of Derry in Northern Ireland, when British troops fired into a crowd of civil rights marchers, killing thirteen unarmed civilians. The local coroner described what happened that day, labeled Bloody Sunday, as "murder . . . sheer unadulterated murder."[44] Many Irish Americans took sides, some supporting the revolutionaries, who believed that only through guns and bombs could Ireland be reunited, and others supporting a constitutional, nonviolent solution to the conflict in Northern Ireland.

The most widely supported militant organization was the Irish Northern Aid Committee (NORAID). The driving force behind NORAID was Michael Flannery, a veteran of the Irish Civil War who had emigrated to New York. Flannery, who had never lost his hunger for militant nationalism, lived a relatively peaceful life as an insurance man until the troubles erupted in Northern Ireland in the late 1960s. Encouraged by leaders in the Provisional IRA, who were leading the armed struggle against the British presence in Northern Ireland, Flannery announced the formation of NORAID at a news conference in New York in April 1970. The stated purpose of NORAID was to raise money for humanitarian relief in Northern Ireland. By the early 1970s NORAID reportedly had as many as seven to ten thousand members scattered across the country in about eighty chapters.[45] NORAID was popular among Irish Americans because it appealed to the traditional Irish American nationalism that viewed the conflict in Ulster as a classic struggle between Irish nationalists and British invaders.

Chapters in New York, Chicago, Philadelphia, Boston, and San Francisco contributed the most funds, sending as much as several thousand dollars a month to the NORAID headquarters in New York. Much of this money was collected in Irish bars. In addition, NORAID sponsored raffles, concerts, and festivals to raise money for the cause. Irish-dominated branches of teamsters', carpenters', and longshoremen's unions were another source of funds. Over about twenty years, 1971–90, NORAID sent as much as three million dollars, if not more, to Ireland.[46] Authorities in the United States and Ireland have always asserted that much of the money raised was used to buy weapons for the IRA. NORAID has continually denied this accusation.

In addition to raising money for the cause in Ulster, the more militant Irish Americans also sent weapons and ammunition. Much of these were stolen from military bases in the United States. If not stolen, they were purchased from gun shops. These weapons were smuggled into Ireland in cargo ships, hidden in crates listed as containing machine parts or packed among furniture. Sympathetic Irish longshoremen in East Coast ports cooperated with these gunrunners. IRA supporters even transported weapons aboard the cruise liner *Queen Elizabeth II*.[47]

NORAID reached its peak of notoriety in the early 1980s. The hunger strikes of IRA prisoners in Northern Ireland in 1981, in which ten men died, protesting the refusal of the authorities to recognize them as political prisoners, intensified support of Irish Americans for the militant nationalists. The death of Bobby Sands in May 1981, the first hunger striker to die, became an international media event. The subsequent deaths of each hunger striker intensified criticism of the British government, most especially Margaret Thatcher, the prime minister. A group of Irish American politicians who had been working together to bring about a peaceful solution to the conflict in Ulster sent her a telegram condemning her intransigence and urging her to end the "posture of inflexibility that must lead inevitably to more senseless violence and more needless deaths."[48] Then in 1982 the steering committee of New York's St. Patrick's Day parade, made up of members of the Ancient Order of Hibernians who supported the militants' cause, elected Bobby Sands as the honorary grand marshal of the parade. The following year, the Hibernians selected Michael Flannery of NORAID as grand marshal. Crowds along the parade route, waving IRA flags, cheered their republican hero.

Needless to say, this display of nationalist fervor generated tremendous publicity for the IRA. But, it also rallied opposition among the more moderate wing of Irish American nationalists against the IRA and its American supporters.

One of the first groups organized to counteract the appeal of NOR-AID was the Ireland Fund, a group led by wealthy, well-connected Irish-born and American-born Irishmen. Tony O'Reilly, a rugby star in Ireland and an extraordinarily successful businessman in the United States, was the driving force behind the establishment of this organization in 1976. Its goal was to raise money for peaceful initiatives in Northern Ireland in the hope of achieving reconciliation among the opposing factions. It was quite successful, raising fifty million dollars by 1992 to fund its projects. It could do little, however, to stop the fighting in Ulster. Political support was needed in Congress and at the White House to influence the British government to seek a political solution to the Ulster conflict.

Irish American politicians had traditionally been reluctant to speak out against the militant nationalist tradition since so many of their constituents supported it. Tip O'Neill typified this position. Raised in an Irish working-class neighborhood in North Cambridge, Massachusetts, he recalled:

> We had a tremendous hatred for the English. In addition to our fierce Irish pride, there was our American heritage as well. Kids in other neighborhoods were playing cops and robbers, or cowboys and Indians, but with us it was patriots and redcoats. Each year on Easter Sunday, men in our neighborhood would go from door to door, collecting for the IRA. On the front window of almost every house you would see a sticker: "I gave to the Army."[49]

One person who was instrumental in changing the reluctance of Irish American politicians to speak out against the militant nationalists was John Hume. Raised in a poor Catholic family in Derry, Northern Ireland, Hume was a schoolteacher turned civil rights activist. Nurtured by the writings of Martin Luther King Jr., he became an advocate of nonviolence as the best way to abolish discrimination against Catholics in housing, jobs, and education. To achieve this goal Hume entered politics and was elected to the Northern Ireland parliament in 1969. A year later, along with five other members of Parliament, he founded the Social Democratic Labor Party (SDLP). As head of the SDLP, Hume played a key role in the march toward peace in Northern Ireland. The significance of his role was recognized in December 1998 when, along with David Trimble, leader of the Unionist Party, he was awarded the Nobel Prize for Peace.

Hume had made several trips to the United States trying to gain support for the SDLP's constitutional approach to peace in Northern Ireland. He finally persuaded Senator Edward M. Kennedy to endorse his ideas. Hume and Kennedy then approached O'Neill, Senator Daniel Patrick Moynihan, and New York governor Hugh Carey, convincing them to join their efforts to promote a nonviolent solution to the Ulster conflict. These four Irish Americans, dubbed the Four Horsemen, worked to gain further support for their position in Congress. On St. Patrick's Day 1981, together with Senator Christopher Dodd and Congressman Thomas Foley, they announced the organization of the Friends of Ireland. Composed of some of the most influential members of Congress, the Friends of Ireland sought to promote constitutional nationalism and condemn Irish American support for militant nationalism. They played a key role in persuading Margaret Thatcher, prime minister of Great Britain, and Garret FitzGerald, taoiseach of the Republic of Ireland, to sign the Anglo-Irish Agreement in 1985, which established an intergovernmental conference in which British and Irish officials would discuss matters related to the government of Northern Ireland. For the first time the Republic of Ireland had a formal role in the affairs of Northern Ireland.

By the late 1980s Irish nationalists were persuaded that an armed struggle was unlikely to achieve victory, given the continued presence of so many British troops in Ulster. Gerry Adams, head of the Sinn Fein, the political wing of the IRA, spearheaded the transition from a purely military approach to a more political campaign aimed at gaining more popular support. John Hume was instrumental in convincing Adams to endorse a political solution to the conflict. He and Adams had met on several occasions with Hume urging Adams to convince the IRA to declare a cease-fire in its military campaign. Hume was bitterly criticized for sitting down with Adams, whom most regarded as an IRA terrorist. But Hume said that "if talking with one man could save even one life, he had to try."[50] These talks led to a new peace undertaking by Ireland and Britain. Enter once again the Irish Americans.

Edward Kennedy, Christopher Dodd, and Jean Kennedy Smith,

JFK's sister and the new ambassador to Ireland, along with others persuaded President Bill Clinton to grant a visa to Gerry Adams, the terrorist turned politician. Despite vehement opposition from the British government as well as disagreement among his advisers, Clinton authorized the visa with the hope that he could convince Adams "to get on the peace train and leave violence behind," as Albert Reynolds, the Irish taoiseach, put it in a phone conversation with Clinton.[51] Adams made a brief, two-day visit in January 1994 to New York, where the Irish American community welcomed him as an Irish Nelson Mandela. The publicity generated by his visit helped Adams gain the support of many Irish Americans in his journey toward peace. But the one person he needed to convince of the sincerity of his commitment to a political solution to the Ulster conflict was President Clinton. He demonstrated that commitment when on August 31, 1994, the IRA announced a complete end to their campaign of violence. A group of influential Irish Americans, led by former congressman Bruce Morrison, had a key role in convincing Adams and the IRA leadership to come to this decision. Fifteen months later, in November 1995, Clinton traveled to Northern Ireland and later to Dublin and the Republic of Ireland. Though he had some Irish roots on his mother's side of the family, he did not play the Irish card in seeking to gain votes. Rather he came to Ireland not in a search for his roots but as an advocate of peace and reconciliation. He described this visit as "two of the best days of my Presidency."[52]

One of the most memorable moments in his brief visit was when a young schoolgirl offered a welcome to the American president. She read her letter to a crowd of fifteen hundred people at a factory in Belfast:

> My first Daddy died in the troubles. It was the saddest day of
> my life. I still think of him. Now it is nice and peaceful. I like
> having peace and quiet instead of having people shooting and
> killing. My Christmas wish is that peace and love will last in
> Ireland for ever.[53]

In his speech at the factory Clinton told the crowd that they "must not allow the ship of peace to sink on the rocks of old habits and hard grudges. You must stand firm against terror. You must say to those who would still use violence for political objectives, 'You are the past. Your day is over. Violence has no place at the table of democracy and no role in the future of this land.' "[54] Then he and his wife helicoptered to Derry, where

John Hume introduced him to an adoring crowd of twenty-five thousand and he reiterated his call for peace and promised the support of the United States in the peace process. The next day he traveled to Dublin, where as many as eighty thousand people welcomed him on College Green. In Dublin he was "feeling full of my Irishness," as he put it. He even met some of his distant relatives who were related to his maternal grandfather, whose family had come from Fermanagh. Maureen Dowd wrote in the *New York Times*, "In Ireland, the prodigal son of the Cassidy clan was celebrated as a statesman, a saint, an angel of peace, a ruddy handsome devil 'with a bottomless bucket of charm,' the most powerful man on earth, and 'King Billy.' "[55] Clinton's triumphal visit persuaded the politicians in Northern Ireland that the people wanted peace, not war.

The next major step toward achieving this was the 1998 Good Friday Agreement, an accord negotiated by Senator George Mitchell, Clinton's envoy, who chaired the conferences that led to this landmark decision. Nine years later in May 2007 its main provision took effect when the leaders of the two political parties, Martin McGuinness of Sinn Fein and the Reverend Ian Paisley of the Democratic Unionists, were sworn in as first minister and deputy minister, respectively, of the Northern Ireland executive government. This was the final act in the thirty-year struggle for peace.

Peace would never have come to Northern Ireland without the participation of the Irish American community—its politicians and business leaders most especially. Throughout the 1980s and '90s politicians put pressure on the British government to negotiate with the Irish government. Through their lobbying efforts the U.S. government also contributed millions of dollars to the International Fund for Ireland, which was established after the Anglo-Irish Agreement in 1985. These funds supported economic development in Northern Ireland. Venture capital companies were also set up to promote business and provide jobs. During the Clinton administration support for the International Fund continued, but more emphasis was put on encouraging private investment in Northern Ireland. Irish American politicians also brought the Irish republican leaders, Gerry Adams in particular, into the mainstream of these discussions, pushing them along when they stalled. But few will doubt the critical role that President Bill Clinton played in helping the divided community in Northern Ireland to sit down together with the common goal of bringing an end to violence and inequality. It was one of his most notable foreign policy achievements.

In the late nineteenth century Irish Americans supported the Irish as they struggled to gain independence. It is doubtful that the uprising in 1916 and the subsequent establishment of the Irish Free State could have taken place without the support of the Irish American community. Much the same can be said about the achievement of the Good Friday accord a century later. Though they are generations removed from the Emerald Isle, Irish Americans have never lost touch with the land of their ancestors. The Irish have always been known as a people with a high regard for loyalty. Support for their homeland has been the highest form of such loyalty and has bound together the histories of Ireland and Irish America ever since the Irish first set foot on American soil.

CHAPTER 13

It's Chic to Be Irish

One of the most remarkable achievements of the Irish in America is that they have stayed Irish. In becoming American they have acquired a national or political identity, but they also chose to remain Irish. The Pulitzer Prize–winning author William Kennedy put it this way:

> I believe that I can't be anything other than Irish-American. I know there's a division here, and a good many Irish-Americans believe they are merely American. They've lost touch with anything that smacks of Irishness as we used to know it. That's all right.
>
> But I think if they set out to discover themselves, to wonder about why they are what they are, then they'll run into a psychological inheritance that's even more than psychological, that may also be genetic, or biopsychogenetic, who the hell knows what you call it? But there's something in us that survives and that's the result of being Irish, whether from North or South, whether Catholic or Protestant, some element of life, of consciousness, that is different from being Hispanic, or Oriental, or WASP. These traits endure.[1]

The ethnic awareness that Kennedy is describing is more than just a subconscious feeling of being Irish. It is a deliberate choice that people make and is not unique to the Irish.

In 1965 Congress passed new immigration legislation, the Immigration and Nationality Act. This legislation, signed into law by President Lyndon Johnson at the Statue of Liberty, ushered in a new chapter in the nation's history of immigration by eliminating racial and ethnic discrimination from its immigration policy. The new law opened the nation's gates to all the countries of the world, and millions of people from Asia and Latin America arrived in the United States. The presence of so many people from diverse cultures fueled the sense of ethnic consciousness among all Americans. Ethnicity mattered now more than ever. At the same time scholars cast aside the melting-pot ideology, which stated that the nation's different ethnic groups would blend into one homogeneous people. As Daniel Patrick Moynihan put it so succinctly, "The point about the melting pot . . . is that it did not happen."[2] The idea of cultural pluralism, which stressed the persistence of ethnicity rather than the inevitability of assimilation, became normative. Taking a cue from the black power movement, white ethnics began to emphasize their heritage. Suddenly it was fashionable to be Irish, Polish, or Italian. For the first time the U.S. Census began to ask people to identify themselves by their ethnic origin. A new ethnic awareness was abroad in the land in the late 1960s and early '70s.

What fueled this has been described as the *Roots* phenomenon. Alex Haley's book *Roots: The Saga of an American Family*, published in 1976, was a Pulitzer Prize–winning account of Haley's family history. Tracing his roots back to Africa, he wrote a gripping saga of one American family. Though criticized as more a work of Haley's imagination rather than historical scholarship, it sold millions of copies and was the basis for a prize-winning television miniseries. Both the book and the television production sparked a surge in genealogical research as people traced their own family roots. In 1976 Irving Howe published *World of Our Fathers*, a study of the immigrant Jewish experience on New York's Lower East Side. Though Howe's book never gained the acclaim of Haley's, it was a landmark study that confirmed the increased interest in the nation's ethnic history. Another indication of this was Mario Puzo's 1969 bestseller, *The Godfather*, a fictional account of the primacy of family loyalty among Italians, which was adapted into Francis Ford Coppola's hugely successful film. In 1980, Harvard University Press published the *Harvard Encyclopedia of American Ethnic Groups*. Edited by the historian Stephan Thernstrom, it included the work of 120 scholars, who wrote essays on 106 ethnic groups as well as 29 thematic essays. This landmark publication was another testament to the resurgence of interest in ethnicity.

As individual Americans began to research their ethnic heritage, the nation underwent a quest for its identity. The bicentennial in 1976 celebrated the birth of the nation. Ten years later the centennial commemoration of the Statue of Liberty took place. Both of these events celebrated the nation's cultural pluralism. But more than any other event in recent history, the opening of the Ellis Island Museum in 1990 redefined the national identity. From 1892 when it opened to its closure in 1954, Ellis Island was the reception center that welcomed more than twelve million immigrants to America. After its closing, the entire complex of buildings deteriorated. A successful fund-raising campaign enabled the National Park Service to restore the main building as a museum of the nation's immigration history. It became so popular that as many as ten to fifteen thousand people a day journey by ferryboat to Ellis Island to learn about their nation's history as well as their own immigrant heritage. The museum celebrates the immigrant success story of the "tired . . . poor . . . huddled masses" whose descendants rose to become middle-class Americans. The historian Matthew Frye Jacobson has argued that the new emphasis on ethnic identity replaced an older notion of American identity that focused on the Anglo-Saxon heritage of the Pilgrims, but both identities leave little space for people of color. As he put it, "Ellis Island whiteness" replaced "Plymouth Rock whiteness."[3] Minorities today such as African Americans or Latinos still face prejudices remarkably like the ones that confronted the Irish or the Italians a century and more ago. The current debate over immigration, revealing a palpable suspicion and resentment of Hispanics, eerily echoes the anti-Irish rhetoric of the Know-Nothing era.

Yet the example of the Irish, many of whom arrived in America destitute, can only offer hope for today's immigrants. The Irish in America are a prototypical immigrant success story. During the 1980s and '90s when the ethnic revival was gaining momentum, there was a resurgence of interest in things Irish. Seamus Heaney, Irish poet and Nobel laureate, commented, "It is the manifestation of sheer, bloody genius. Ireland is chic."[4] It was fashionable to be Irish. The evidence for this was widespread. In 1985 a new glossy magazine, *Irish America*, appeared. In 1993 the University of Notre Dame and New York University both established endowed centers for Irish studies. By 1996 twenty-six universities were offering Irish studies courses, double the number in 1981. The 1990s was the high point of this renaissance. In 1995, Riverdance, an Irish dance show, made its debut in Dublin. One year later it opened at Radio City Music Hall in New York City to a sold-out audience. Since then more than eighteen

million people in Europe and North America have enjoyed the music and
dance of this spectacular production. In 1996, *Angela's Ashes* appeared, a
Pulitzer Prize–winning memoir of growing up poor in Ireland. Written by
Frank McCourt, a high school English teacher in New York, it has been
translated into nineteen languages, sold over four million copies world-
wide, and inspired a feature film in 1999. In 1998 Alice McDermott won
the National Book Award for her novel *Charming Billy*, which depicted
Irish family life in post–World War II New York. Reinforcing this awakening was a similar cultural renaissance in Ireland, highlighted by the
work of poets such as Seamus Heaney, writers such as Seamus Deane and
Roddy Doyle, and film directors Neil Jordan (*The Crying Game*) and Jim
Sheridan (*In the Name of the Father*), whose award-winning films introduced the realities of modern Ireland to an admiring audience in the
United States.

The Chieftains, the award-winning Irish musical group, have brought
traditional Irish music to the world's attention. Their success sparked a revival of Irish folk music in America. Irish dance also became popular, inspiring the establishment of numerous academies of dance for young
children. Irish *feis*, or festivals, lasting for a few days or more, have become
common. Seeking to promote Irish heritage, they feature traditional Irish
music, dance, food, and all sorts of imported items. At these festivals travel
agencies promote Irish tourism—an industry that has exploded in recent
years. Between 1988 and 1998 the number of Americans traveling to Ireland almost doubled, from 2.8 million to 5.5 million. In 1996, seventy
thousand of these tourists spent more than thirty million dollars tracing
their family history.

Another way to explain the Irish renaissance is to recognize that in
moving out of Irish neighborhoods into the American suburbs, the Irish
have experienced a loss of identity. To fill this void, they have sought to
recapture their ethnic heritage at the same time that other ethnic Americans were also connecting with their roots and redefining what it meant to
be American in a nation of immigrants. As the sociologist Mary Waters
wrote, "Being ethnic makes them feel unique and special and not just
vanilla . . . They are not like everyone else. At the same time, being ethnic
gives them a sense of belonging to a collectivity. It is the best of all
worlds: they can claim to be unique and special while simultaneously
finding the community and conformity with others that they also crave."[5]

In the 1990 U.S. census, forty-four million people, about 18 percent
of the nation, identified themselves as Irish. Such a number is much more

than what would be expected given the size of Irish immigration, about five million, along with natural population increase. It reflects that down through the decades the Irish intermarried with other ethnic groups, most often of the same religion. This increased the number of individuals with Irish ancestry. In the census, individuals with such dual (or multiple) ethnic heritages could choose one or the other as their own. And as sociologist Michael Hout said, "Given a choice, people pick Irish." They choose Irish because of the positive traits associated with that group—gregariousness, wit, charm—and because this choice enables them to identify vicariously with the underdog and claim as their own the Irish success story.[6]

What is remarkable is that after three hundred years of history and many generations removed from Ireland, millions of Americans still choose an Irish ancestry as an essential ingredient of their identity. They have preserved an ethnic heritage that has had a profound influence on the history of the United States. That is the real Irish success story.

Acknowledgments

Writing is a solitary experience. A writer is a lot like a monk who works alone, cut off from the rest of the world. I know at times I felt like that. I was so focused on the task before me that everything else took a backseat to my work. But I could not have written this history without the support of so many colleagues. First and foremost, I must acknowledge my appreciation to the staff of the University of Notre Dame library. Not only does the library have a rich collection of books, but it has a wonderful staff. Individuals at the reference desk, and the interlibrary loan and circulation departments, were always pleasant and cooperative. No request was too difficult for them. The Cushwa Center for the Study of American Catholicism and its director, Tim Matovina, supported this project from the beginning. During my retirement the center has become my academic home. It provided funding for the collection of illustrations and enabled me to hire a student assistant, Amelia Schmidt, to gather these illustrations. Her assistance was invaluable. I called on Paula Brach, the center's administrative assistant, for help many times, and she always responded graciously. Kathleen Cummings, historian, colleague, and dear friend, who also works at the Cushwa Center, was always ready to offer support whenever I needed it. The conversations we shared about our work as historians continually energized me over the many months that I was working on this project. Notre Dame's Keough-Naughton Institute for Irish Studies and its director, Christopher Fox, funded a research trip to Ireland. Chris's enthusiasm for my work on this book has never wavered and is much appreciated.

Philip Gleason, emeritus professor of history at Notre Dame, and

Kevin Kenny, professor of history at Boston College and an acknowledged authority on Irish American history, read the entire manuscript. Their comments were invaluable and enabled me to proceed with confidence knowing that they would be reviewing everything I wrote. Patrick Griffin of the University of Virginia reviewed my chapter on the Irish in the eighteenth century and persuaded me to revise and improve my rendering of this period in Irish American history. James Donnelly of the University of Wisconsin read the chapter on the famine and emigration. Moreover, he generously shared with me his collection of illustrations on the Irish famine. Dan Graff of Notre Dame and Bruce Nelson of Dartmouth College read what I had to say about the Irish and the labor movement. Enda Leaney, a Fellow at the Keough-Naughton Institute for Irish Studies, offered a valuable critique of the chapter on nationalism. Peter Quinn also read parts of the manuscript and has provided encouragement along the way. Ellen Skerrett has been an invaluable friend and resource person who not only read what I wrote on Irish Catholicism but shared her vast knowledge of Chicago history with me and aided me in locating photos for the book.

Walter Nugent and Suellen Hoy also were supportive and helped out whenever I needed their assistance, and I could always rely on John McGreevy, chair of the department of history at Notre Dame. Paul Wieber generously offered his time and expertise in arranging the illustrations in a digital format ready for publication. Another colleague, Marion Casey of New York University, provided assistance along the way. Conversations with Andrew Greeley and Michael Hout were not only enjoyable, but most helpful in understanding the more recent history of the Irish in America. Frank Cunningham and Tom Grady of Ave Maria Press offered good advice about the business of publishing when I needed it. I would be remiss if I failed to note the contribution of Kerby Miller, whose writings have revitalized interest in the history of Irish America. For years I have been an admirer of his work, as is evident from my reliance on his many publications.

I am indebted to Peter Ginna, my editor at Bloomsbury Press. He was not only eager to publish this book, but read every line I wrote with a keen eye and a razor-sharp mind. His editorial comments and suggestions greatly improved the manuscript. Katie Henderson, assistant editor at Bloomsbury Press, also provided helpful comments on the manuscript and efficiently handled many of the administrative details of its publication.

I have dedicated this book to my wife, who has read everything I ever wrote whether she wanted to or not. She has been a wonderful companion for more than thirty-five years and has blessed my life in more ways than she will ever realize.

Notes

CHAPTER 1: HERE COME THE IRISH

1. Padraig Lenihan, *1690: Battle of the Boyne* (Gloucestershire: Tempus, 2003), p. 156.
2. Patrick Griffin, *The People with No Name: Ireland's Ulster Scots, America's Scots Irish, and the Creation of a British Atlantic World, 1689–1764* (Princeton: Princeton University Press, 2001), p. 23; and Kerby A. Miller, *Emigrants and Exiles* (New York: Oxford University Press, 1985), p. 158.
3. Griffin, *People with No Name*, p. 80.
4. Ibid., p. 67.
5. Kerby A. Miller, Arnold Schrier, Bruce D. Boling, and David N. Doyle, *Irish Immigrants in the Land of Canaan: Letters and Memoirs from Colonial and Revolutionary America, 1675–1815* (New York: Oxford University Press, 2003), pp. 23, 83.
6. Griffin, *People with No Name*, p. 94; and Miller et al., *Immigrants in the Land of Canaan*, p. 24.
7. Miller et al., *Immigrants in the Land of Canaan*, p. 32.
8. Ibid., p. 420.
9. Ibid., p. 42.
10. Miller, *Emigrants and Exiles*, p. 154; and Griffin, *People with No Name*, p. 96.
11. Miller, *Emigrants and Exiles*, pp. 142–43.
12. David Hackett Fisher, *Albion's Seed* (New York: Oxford University Press, 1989), p. 620.
13. Russell Menard, "Economy and Society in Early Colonial Maryland" (Ph.D. diss., University of Iowa, 1975), p. 448.
14. Beatriz Betancourt Hardy, "Papists in a Protestant Age: The Catholic Gentry and Community in Colonial Maryland, 1689–1776" (Ph.D. diss., University of Maryland, 1993), p. 122.
15. Ronald Hoffman, *Princes of Ireland, Planters of Maryland: A Carroll Saga, 1500–1782* (Chapel Hill: University of North Carolina Press, 2000), p. 267.
16. Ibid., p. 97.
17. Ibid., p. 142.

18. Sally D. Mason, "Charles Carroll of Carrollton and His Family, 1688–1832," in Ann C. Van Devanter, ed., *Anywhere So Long as There Be Freedom: Charles Carroll of Carrollton, His Family and His Maryland* (Batimore: Baltimore Museum of Art, 1975), p. 19.

19. Ibid., p. 21.

20. Ibid., p. 26; and Scott McDermott, *Charles Carroll of Carrollton: Faithful Revolutionary* (New York: Scepter Publishing Co., 2002), p. 51.

21. Hoffman, *Princes of Ireland*, p. 205.

22. Ibid., p. 283.

23. Ibid., p. 297.

24. Ronald Hoffman, "Charles Carroll of Carrollton," *American National Biography*, www.anb.org.

25. Hoffman, *Princes of Ireland*, p. xiii.

26. Ronald Hoffman, "A Worthy Heir: The Role of Religion in the Development of Charles Carroll of Carrollton, 1748–1764," Cushwa Center for the Study of American Catholicism, Working Paper Series, Fall 1982, pp. 2, 42–44, 60.

27. See Hardy, "Papists in a Protestant Age," and Jay P. Dolan, *The American Catholic Experience: A History from Colonial Times to the Present* (Garden City, NY: Doubleday, 1985), for information on Maryland Catholicism.

28. Miller, *Emigrants and Exiles*, p. 147.

29. Miller et al., *Immigrants in the Land of Canaan*, p. 254.

30. Bernard Bailyn, *Voyages to the West* (New York: Random House, 1986), p. 173; and Thomas M. Truxes, *Irish-American Trade, 1660–1783* (New York: Cambridge University Press, 1988), p. 127.

31. Bailyn, *Voyages to the West*, p. 173.

32. Miller et al., *Immigrants in the Land of Canaan*, pp. 254–57.

33. Ibid., pp. 91–92.

34. Fintan O'Toole, *White Savage: William Johnson and the Invention of America* (New York: Farrar, Straus and Giroux, 2005), p. 38.

35. Ibid., pp. 23, 26.

36. Ibid., pp. 44, 285.

37. Ibid., pp. 280, 283, 288.

38. Francis Jennings, "Sir William Johnson," *American National Biography*, www.anb.org.

39. Kevin Kenny, *The American Irish: A History* (New York: Longman, 2000), p. 24.

40. Griffin, *People with No Name*, p. 108.

41. Ibid., pp. 114, 124.

42. Miller, *Emigrants and Exiles*, p. 165.

43. Truxes, *Irish-American Trade*, p. 117.

44. Miller et al., *Immigrants in the Land of Canaan*, p. 585.

45. Ibid., p. 287.

46. Maurice J. Bric, "Ireland, Irishmen, and the Broadening of the Late Eighteenth Century Philadelphia Polity" (Ph.D. diss., Johns Hopkins University, 1991), pp. 438–39.

47. Truxes, *Irish-American Trade*, pp. 78, 108–9.

48. Bric, "Ireland, Irishmen, and the Broadening," pp. 410–11.

49. Truxes, *Irish-American Trade*, p. 113.

50. Joyce D. Goodfriend, "'Upon a Bunch of Straw': The Irish in Colonial New York City," in Ronald H. Bayor and Timothy J. Meagher, eds., *The New York Irish* (Baltimore: Johns Hopkins University Press, 1996), p. 36.

51. Miller et al., *Immigrants in the Land of Canaan*, p. 418.

CHAPTER 2: A TIME OF TRANSITION

1. Edward C. Carter II, "The Political Activities of Mathew Carey, Nationalist, 1760–1814" (Ph.D. diss., Bryn Mawr College, 1962), p. 36.

2. Mathew Carey, *Autobiography* (Research Classics, 1942), p. 10.

3. David A. Wilson, *United Irishmen, United States* (Ithaca: Cornell University Press, 1998), p. 2.

4. Michael Durey, *Transatlantic Radicals and the Early American Republic* (Lawrence: University Press of Kansas, 1997), p. 10.

5. Wilson, *United Irishmen, United States*, p. 8.

6. Ibid., p. 45.

7. Ibid., p. 152.

8. Carey, *Autobiography*, p. 2.

9. Wilson, *United Irishmen, United States*, p. 44.

10. Michael S. Carter, "Under the Benign Sun of Toleration: Mathew Carey, the Douai Bible, and Catholic Print Culture, 1789–1791," *Journal of the Early Republic* 27 (Fall 2007): p. 443.

11. Carey, *Autobiography*, p. 25.

12. Carey Diary, December 1, 1824, November 2 and 15, 1825, Rare Book Room, University of Pennsylvania.

13. *Niles National Register* (Baltimore), 5th ser., no. 4, 7 (September 21, 1839); and David Kaser, "The Retirement Income of Mathew Carey," *Pennsylvania Magazine of History and Biography* 80, no. 4 (October 1956): pp. 410–15.

14. Durey, *Transatlantic Radicals*, p. 97.

15. Ronald H. Bayor and Timothy J. Meagher, eds., *The New York Irish* (Baltimore: Johns Hopkins University Press, 1996), p. 635; and George Potter, *To the Golden Door* (Boston: Little, Brown, 1960), p. 216.

16. Cormac O Grada, "Poverty, Population and Agriculture, 1801–45," in W. E. Vaughan, ed., *A New History of Ireland*, vol. 5, *Ireland Under the Union, 1801–1870* (Oxford: Clarendon Press, 1989), p. 110.

17. Ibid.

18. Kevin Whelan, unpublished manuscript, p. 113. My thanks to him for sharing this with me.

19. David Fitzpatrick, "Emigration, 1801–1921," in Michael Glazier, ed., *The Encyclopedia of the Irish in America* (Notre Dame, IN: University of Notre Dame Press, 1999), p. 259; and Kerby A. Miller, *Emigrants and Exiles* (New York: Oxford University Press, 1985), p. 199.

20. David Fitzpatrick, *Irish Emigration, 1801–1921*, no. 1, *Studies in Irish Economic and Social History* (Dublin: Dundalgan Press, 1984), p. 7.

21. David T. Gleeson, *The Irish in the South, 1815–1877* (Chapel Hill: University of North Carolina Press, 2001), pp. 2, 26.

22. Graham Hodges, "Desirable Companions and Lovers: Irish and African Americans in the Sixth Ward, 1830–1870," in Bayor and Meagher, *New York Irish*, p. 110.

23. Tyler Anbinder, *Five Points* (New York: Free Press, 2001), pp. 1, 4.

24. Ibid., p. 121.

25. Potter, *To the Golden Door*, pp. 163–64.

26. Ibid., p. 183; and Jay P. Dolan, *The Immigrant Church: New York's Irish and German Catholics, 1815–1865* (Baltimore: Johns Hopkins University Press, 1975), pp. 52–53.

27. Paul A. Gilje, "The Development of an Irish American Community in New York City Before the Great Migration," in Bayor and Meagher, *New York Irish*, pp. 72–73.

28. Maldwyn A. Jones, "Scotch Irish," in Stephan Thernstrom, ed., *Harvard Encyclopedia of American Ethnic Groups* (Cambridge: Harvard University Press, 1980), p. 906.

29. Peter Way, *Common Labour: Workers and the Digging of the North American Canals, 1780–1860* (Cambridge: Cambridge University Press, 1993), p. 90, and also pp. 94, 97, 279–78; and Peter Way, "Evil Humors and Ardent Spirits: The Rough Culture of Canal Construction Laborers," *Journal of American History* 79, no. 4 (March 1993): p. 1405.

30. Way, *Common Labour*, p. 94.

31. Ibid., p. 138.

32. Ibid., p. 194.

33. Ibid., pp. 200–201.

34. Ibid., pp. 145–47.

35. Earl F. Niehaus, *The Irish in New Orleans, 1800–1860* (Baton Rouge: Louisiana State University Press, 1965), pp. 31, 46.

36. Way, *Common Labour*, p. 160.

37. Ibid., pp. 270–71.

38. Wilson, *United Irishmen, United States*, pp. 1, 2, 5.

39. Ibid., p. 76.

40. Anbinder, *Five Points*, pp. 146, 147.

41. Ibid., pp. 148–49, 165.

42. Ibid., pp. 155, 157.

43. Brian Jenkins, *Irish Nationalism and the British State: From Repeal to Revolutionary Nationalism* (Montreal and Kingston: McGill-Queens Press, 2006), pp. 54, 45.

44. Wilson, *United Irishmen, United States*, pp. 157, 160, 162.

45. Potter, *To the Golden Door*, p. 208.

46. See Thomas F. Moriarty, "The Irish American Response to Catholic Emancipation," *Catholic Historical Review* 66, no. 3 (July 1980): pp. 353–73.

47. Potter, *To the Golden Door*, p. 388.

48. Gilbert Osofsky, "Abolitionists, Irish Immigrants, and the Dilemma of Romantic Nationalism," *American Historical Review* 80, no. 4 (October 1975): pp. 890, 892.

49. Ibid., pp. 897, 898.

50. John T. McGreevy, *Catholicism and American Freedom: A History* (New York: W. W. Norton, 2003), pp. 56–57.

51. Osofsky, "Abolitionists, Irish Immigrants, and the Dilemma of Romantic Nationalism," p. 905.

52. Noel Ignatiev, *How the Irish Became White* (New York: Routledge, 1995), p. 97.

53. Ibid., p. 41.

54. Kevin Kenny, *The American Irish: A History* (New York: Longman, 2000), p. 67.

55. Ignatiev, *How the Irish Became White*, p. 111.

56. See Timothy J. Meagher, *The Columbia Guide to Irish American History* (New York: Columbia University Press, 2005), pp. 214–33, for a lengthy discussion of this issue of race and the Irish. Also see Bruce Nelson, *Divided We Stand: American Workers and the Struggle for Black Equality* (Princeton: Princeton University Press, 2001), pp. 12–18, where he discusses the issue of competition for work.

57. Patrick Carey, *An Immigrant Bishop: John England's Adaptation of Irish Catholicism to American Republicanism* (Yonkers, NY: U.S. Catholic Historical Society, 1982), p. 141.

58. Ibid.

59. Dolan, *Immigrant Church*, p. 9.

60. Ibid., p. 12; Peter Guilday, *The Life and Times of John England* (New York: America Press, 1927), 1:550.

61. James F. Connelly, *The History of the Archdiocese of Philadelphia* (Philadelphia: Archdiocese of Philadelphia, 1976), p. 145.

62. Jay P. Dolan, *Catholic Revivalism: The American Experience* (Notre Dame, IN: University of Notre Dame Press, 1978), p. 5.

63. Dolan, *Immigrant Church*, p. 57.

64. See Michael P. Carroll, *Irish Pilgrimage: Holy Wells and Popular Catholic Devotion* (Baltimore: Johns Hopkins University Press, 1999), for a discussion of this.

65. Ms. 2-15-1000, Michael McDermott Recollections, Library of Congress, Manuscript Division.

66. Jon Gjerde, ed., *Major Problems in American Immigration and Ethnic History* (New York: Houghton Mifflin, 1998), p. 137.

67. Ray Allen Billington, *The Protestant Crusade, 1800–1860* (Chicago: Quadrangle Books, 1964), p. 345.

68. Ibid., p. 181.

69. Francis Bowen, "The Irish in America," *North American Review* 52, no. 110, p. 221.

70. Ibid.

71. Anbinder, *Five Points*, pp. 30–31.

72. Billington, *Protestant Crusade*, p. 230.

73. Dale T. Knoebel, *Paddy and the Republic* (Middletown, CT: Wesleyan University Press, 1986), pp. 26, 57.

74. Ibid., p. 87.

75. Ibid., p. 103.

CHAPTER 3: THE GREAT HUNGER

1. John Killen, ed., *The Famine Decade: Contemporary Accounts, 1841–1851* (Belfast: Blackstaff Press, 1995), p. 33.

2. W. Steuart Trench, *Realities of Irish Life* (London: Longmans Green, 1870), pp. 102–3.

3. Jeremiah O'Donovan Rossa, *Rossa's Recollections* (New York: Mariners Harbor, 1894), p. 108.

4. Peter Gray, *The Irish Famine* (New York: Harry N. Abrams, 1995), p. 178.

5. R. F. Foster, *Modern Ireland, 1600–1972* (New York: Penguin Books, 1989), pp. 322, 327; and Timothy J. Meagher, *The Columbia Guide to Irish American History* (New York: Columbia University Press, 2005), p. 62.

6. Gearoid O Tuathaigh, *Ireland Before the Famine, 1798–1848* (Dublin: Gill and Macmillan, 1972), p. 207.

7. Trench, *Realities of Irish Life*, p. 386.

8. Ibid., p. 106.

9. James S. Donnelly Jr., "Mass Eviction and the Great Famine," in Cathal Pointeir, ed., *The Great Irish Famine* (Chester Springs, PA: Dufour Editions, 1995), p. 158.

10. Cecil Woodham-Smith, *The Great Hunger, 1845–49* (New York: New American Library, 1964), pp. 366, 362.

11. James S. Donnelly Jr., *The Great Irish Potato Famine* (Gloucestershire: Sutton Publishing, 2001), p. 20.

12. Gray, *Irish Famine*, p. 153.

13. Kevin Kenny, *The American Irish: A History* (New York: Longman, 2000), p. 95.

14. Gray, *Irish Famine*, p. 95.

15. Ibid., pp. 58–59.

16. Ibid., p. 65; and Donnelly, *Great Irish Potato Famine*, pp. 104, 109.

17. Donnelly, *Great Irish Potato Famine*, pp. 210, 215.

18. Gray, *Irish Famine*, p. 95.

19. Kerby A. Miller, *Emigrants and Exiles* (New York: Oxford University Press, 1985), pp. 291, 292; and Gray, *Irish Famine*, p. 100.

20. David Fitzpatrick, "Emigration, 1801–70," in W. E. Vaughan, ed., *A New History of Ireland*, vol. 5, *Ireland Under the Union, I: 1801–1870* (Oxford: Clarendon Press, 1989), p. 571.

21. Cormac O Grada, "The Famine, the New York Irish and Their Bank," in Cormac O Grada, *Ireland's Great Famine: Interdisciplinary Perspectives* (Dublin: University College Dublin Press, 2006), pp. 190–91.

22. Ibid., p. 575; and Miller, *Emigrants and Exiles*, pp. 296–97.

23. Fitzpatrick, "Emigration, 1801–70," p. 584.

24. Arnold Schrier, *Ireland and American Emigration, 1850–1900* (Chester Springs, PA: Dufour Editions, 1997), p. 18.

25. Ibid., pp. 43–44; and Fitzpatrick, "Emigration, 1801–70," p. 584.

26. Miller, *Emigrants and Exiles*, p. 558; and Schrier, *Ireland and American Emigration*, p. 90.

27. Fitzpatrick, "Emigration, 1801–70," pp. 600–602; and Gray, *Irish Famine*, p. 101.

28. Gray, *Irish Famine*, p. 106.

29. Donnelly, *Great Irish Potato Famine*, p. 181.

30. Fitzpatrick, "Emigration, 1801–70," p. 582.

31. Cormac O Grada and Kevin H. O'Rourke, "Mass Migration as Disaster Relief," in Cormac O Grada, *Ireland's Great Famine: Interdisciplinary Perspectives*, discusses this point on pp. 122–23.

32. Fitzpatrick, *Irish Emigration, 1801–1921*, p. 1; Miller, *Emigrants and Exiles*, pp. 346, 570–71; and Maldwyn A. Jones, "Scotch Irish," in Stephan Thernstrom, ed., *Harvard Encyclopedia of American Ethnic Groups* (Cambridge: Harvard University Press, 1980), p. 905.

33. Ibid., p. 353.

34. David Fitzpatrick, "Emigration, 1871–1921," in W. E. Vaughan, ed., *A New History of Ireland*, vol. 6, *Ireland Under the Union, II: 1870–1921* (Oxford: Clarendon Press, 1996), p. 606.

35. Fitzpatrick, *Irish Emigration, 1801–1921*, p. 44; and Miller, *Emigrants and Exiles*, p. 403.

36. Fitzpatrick, *Irish Emigration, 1801–1921*, p. 29.

37. Fitzpatrick, "Emigration, 1801–70," p. 606.

38. Grace Neville, " 'She Never Then After That Forgot Him': Irishwomen and Emigration to the United States in Irish Folklore," *Mid-America* 74, no. 1 (October 1992): p. 282.

39. Janet Nolan, *Servants of the Poor: Teachers and Mobility in Ireland and Irish America* (Notre Dame, IN: University of Notre Dame Press, 2004), p. 122.

40. Miller, *Emigrants and Exiles*, p. 357.

41. Kevin Whelan, "The Remaking of Irish America" (unpublished MS), p. 74. My thanks to Kevin Whelan for sharing this with me.

42. Sam Roberts, "A Great-Great-Great Day for Annie," *New York Times*, September 16, 2006, p. A15.

43. Patrick Blessing, "Irish," in *Harvard Ethnic Encyclopedia*, p. 530.

CHAPTER 4: FROM PADDIES TO PATRIOTS

1. Hamilton Holt, ed., *The Life Stories of Undistinguished Americans as Told by Themselves* (New York: Routledge, 2000), pp. 88–90.

2. Patrick Blessing, "Irish," in Stephan Thernstrom, ed., *Harvard Encyclopedia of American Ethnic Groups* (Cambridge: Harvard University Press, 1980), pp. 530, 540; and Patrick Blessing, "Irish in America," in Michael Glazier, ed., *The Encyclopedia of the Irish in America* (Notre Dame, IN: University of Notre Dame Press, 1999), pp. 460–62.

3. Jay P. Dolan, *The Immigrant Church: New York's Irish and German Catholics, 1815–1865* (Baltimore: Johns Hopkins University Press, 1975), p. 33.

4. Reverend Henry Lennon to Dr. Woodlock, October 22, 1849, All Hallows Seminary Archives, Dublin.

5. David T. Gleeson, *The Irish in the South, 1815–1877* (Chapel Hill: University of North Carolina Press, 2001), p. 48.

6. See Robert Ernst, *Immigrant Life in New York City* (Port Washington, NY: Ira J. Friedman, Inc., 1949), pp. 213–16; Oscar Handlin, *Boston's Immigrants* (Cambridge: Harvard University Press, 1959), pp. 250–51; R. A. Burchell, *The San Francisco Irish, 1848–1880* (Berkeley: University of California Press, 1980), p. 54; Gleeson, *Irish in the South*, p. 39; Dennis Clark, *The Irish in Philadelphia* (Philadelphia: Temple University Press, 1973), p. 76; and David M. Katzman, *Seven Days a Week: Women and Domestic Service in Industrializing America* (Champaign: University of Illinois Press, 1981), p. 66.

7. Ellen Roundtree to her brother Laurence, Philadelphia, August 26, 1857, Manuscript 8347, National Library of Ireland.

8. These figures are taken from the sources indicated in note 6.

9. Joseph P. Ferrie, *Yankeys Now* (New York: Oxford University Press, 1999), pp. 79, 98.

10. Kevin Kenny, *The American Irish: A History* (New York: Longman, 2000), p. 107.

11. Samuel Gompers, *Seventy Years of Life and Labor* (New York: E. P. Dutton, 1925), 1:24, 1:493–94.

12. Handlin, *Boston's Immigrants*, p. 113.

13. Clark, *Irish in Philadelphia*, p. 44.

14. Jay P. Dolan, *The American Catholic Experience: A History from Colonial Times to the Present* (Garden City, NY: Doubleday, 1985), p. 141.

15. Ibid.

16. Clark, *Irish in Philadelphia*, p. 54; and Stephan Thernstrom, *Poverty and Progress* (Cambridge: Harvard University Press, 1964), p. 156.

17. David N. Doyle, "Unestablished Irishmen: New Immigrants and Industrial America, 1870–1910," in Dirk Hoerder, ed., *American Labor and Immigration History, 1877–1920: Recent European Research* (Urbana: University of Illinois Press, 1983), p. 202; and Kerby A. Miller, *Emigrants and Exiles* (New York: Oxford University Press, 1985), pp. 351–52.

18. Timothy J. Meagher, *Inventing Irish America: Generation, Class, and Ethnic Identity in a New England City, 1880–1928* (Notre Dame, IN: University of Notre Dame Press, 2001), p. 50.

19. Ibid., p. 49.

20. Stephan Thernstrom, *The Other Bostonians: Poverty and Progress in the American Metropolis, 1880–1970* (Cambridge: Harvard University Press, 1973), p. 131; Dale B. Light Jr., "The Role of Irish-American Organisations in Assimilation and Community Formation," in P. J. Drudy, ed., *The Irish in America: Emigration, Assimilation and Impact* (Cambridge: Cambridge University Press, 1985), p. 118; Patricia Kelleher, "Young Irish Workers: Class Implications of Men's and Women's Experiences in Gilded Age Chicago," *Eire-Ireland* 36 (Spring/Summer 2001): p. 148; and Burchell, *San Francisco Irish*, p. 54.

21. Kelleher, "Young Irish Workers," 150.

22. Doyle, "Unestablished Irishmen," 195.

23. Kerby A. Miller, "Assimilation and Alienation: Irish Emigrants' Responses to Industrial America, 1871–1921," in Drudy, *Irish in America*, p. 96; and Doyle, "Unestablished Irishmen," 198–99.

24. Doyle, "Unestablished Irishmen," 202–3.

25. Blessing, "Irish," *Harvard Ethnic Encyclopedia*, p. 531.

26. Kenny, *American Irish*, p. 131.

27. Thernstrom, *Other Bostonians*, pp. 130–32; and Meagher, *Inventing Irish America*, pp. 100, 111–12.

28. Doyle, "Unestablished Irishmen," 202–3.

29. Charles Ffench, ed., *A Biographical History of the American Irish in Chicago* (Chicago: American Biographical Publishing Co., 1897). These findings were based on a sampling of 10 percent of the biographies.

30. Charles Fanning and Ellen Skerrett, "James T. Farrell and Washington Park: The Novel as Social History," *Chicago History* 80, no. 2 (Summer 1979): pp. 85–87.

31. Sam Bass Warner, *Streetcar Suburbs: The Process of Growth in Boston, 1870–1900* (Cambridge: Harvard University Press, 1962), p. 83.

32. Sam Bass Warner, *The Private City: Philadelphia in Three Periods of Its Growth* (Philadelphia: University of Pennsylvania Press, 1968), pp. 194–200.

33. Charles Fanning, *Finley Peter Dunne and Mr. Dooley: The Chicago Years* (Lexington: University Press of Kentucky, 1978), p. 94.

34. Daniel J. Casey and Robert E. Rhodes, eds., *Modern Irish-American Fiction: A Reader* (Syracuse: Syracuse University Press, 1989), p. 26.

35. Meagher, *Inventing Irish America*, p. 114.

36. Ibid., p. 102. See Kelleher, "Young Irish Workers," and Thernstrom, *Other Bostonians*, for discussion of the Irish being handicapped in their employment opportunities and consequently economic advancement. Richard Jensen argues that NO IRISH NEED APPLY signs or advertisements were extremely rare or nonexistent, suggesting that the Irish in America did not encounter discrimination in the workplace, a claim that the evidence just does not support. See his essay " 'No Irish Need Apply': A Myth of Victimization," *Journal of Social History* 36, no. 2 (2002): pp. 405–29.

37. See Tyler Anbinder, *Nativism and Slavery: The Northern Know Nothings and the Politics of the 1850s* (New York: Oxford University Press, 1992), pp. 103–26, for a discussion of their ideology.

38. Ibid., p. 127.

39. John R. Mulkern, *The Know-Nothing Party in Massachusetts* (Boston: Northeastern University Press, 1990), p. 76.

40. Anbinder, *Nativism and Slavery*, p. 266.

41. Ibid., pp. 277–78.

42. James M. McPherson, *Battle Cry of Freedom* (New York: Oxford University Press, 1988), pp. 606–7.

43. Ibid., p. 544.

44. Brendan O Cathaoir, *John Mitchel* (Dublin: Clothanna Teoranta, 1978), p. 18.

45. Thomas Keneally, *The Great Shame* (New York: Doubleday, 1999), p. 302.

46. Ibid., p. 374.

47. Ibid., p. 385.

48. McPherson, *Battle Cry of Freedom*, p. 609.

49. Kenny, *American Irish*, p. 124.

50. Michael A. Gordon, *The Orange Riots: Irish Political Violence in New York City, 1870 and 1871* (Ithaca: Cornell University Press, 1993), p. 33.

51. Ibid., p. 2.

52. L. Perry Curtis Jr., *Apes and Angels: The Irishman in Victorian Caricature* (Washington, DC: Smithsonian Institution Press, 1977), pp. 3, 5.

53. Ibid., p. 18.

54. Ibid., p. 21.

55. Ibid., p. 29.

56. Ibid., p. 58.

57. Both of these parades are described in Evelyn Savidge Sterne, *Ballots and Bibles: Ethnic Politics and the Catholic Church in Providence* (Ithaca: Cornell University Press, 2004), pp. 172, 150.

58. Meagher, *Inventing Irish America*, p. 120.

59. Miller, *Emigrants and Exiles*, p. 526.

CHAPTER 5: THE CATHOLIC IRISH

1. *New York Times*, May 26, 1879.
2. Margaret Carthy, O.S.U., *A Cathedral of Suitable Magnificence: St. Patrick's Cathedral New York* (Wilmington, DE: Michael Glazier, 1984), p. 43.
3. Jay P. Dolan, *The Immigrant Church: New York's Irish and German Catholics, 1815–1865* (Baltimore: Johns Hopkins University Press, 1975), p. 13; and Hugh McLeod, *Piety and Poverty: Working Class Religion in Berlin, London and New York, 1870–1914* (New York: Holmes and Meier, 1996), p. 58. Also Robert E. Sullivan and James M. O'Toole, eds., *Catholic Boston: Studies in Religion and Community, 1870–1970* (Boston: Roman Catholic Archbishop of Boston, 1985), p. 205; and Charles Shanabruch, *Chicago's Catholics: The Evolution of an American Identity* (Notre Dame, IN: University of Notre Dame Press, 1981), p. 237.
4. Michael P. Carroll, *Irish Pilgrimage: Holy Wells and Popular Catholic Devotion* (Baltimore: Johns Hopkins University Press, 1999), p. 19; and Emmet J. Larkin, "The Devotional Revolution in Ireland," *American Historical Review* 77 (June 1972): pp. 625–52.
5. See Patrick Corish, *The Irish Catholic Experience: A Historical Survey* (Dublin: Gill and Macmillan, 1985).
6. Dolan, *Immigrant Church*, pp. 45–67.
7. Jay P. Dolan, *Catholic Revivalism: The American Experience* (Notre Dame, IN: University of Notre Dame Press, 1978), p. 25.
8. Shanabruch, *Chicago's Catholics*, p. 233; and Dolan, *Immigrant Church*, p. 13.
9. Charles Morris, *American Catholic* (New York: Random House, 1997), p. 6.
10. McLeod, *Piety and Poverty*, p. 58.
11. Jay P. Dolan, *The American Catholic Experience: A History from Colonial Times to the Present* (Garden City, NY: Doubleday, 1985), p. 205.
12. Nick Salvatore, "Faith in Context: Three Catholic Parishes in Chicago, 1856–1930" (unpublished essay), p. 6. My thanks to Professor Salvatore for sharing this essay with me.
13. Thomas M. Mulkerins, S.J., *Holy Family Parish Chicago: Priests and People* (Chicago: Universal Press, 1923), p. 124.
14. Salvatore, "Faith in Context," pp. 7–8; and Ellen Skerrett, "The Irish of Chicago's Hull House Neighborhood," in Charles Fanning, ed., *New Perspectives on the Irish Diaspora* (Carbondale: Southern Illinois University Press, 2000), p. 189, for the quote about Farrell's grandmother.
15. Ellen Skerrett, "Sacred Space and Neighborhood in Chicago," in Ellen Skerrett, Edward R. Kantowicz, and Steven M. Avella, *Catholicism, Chicago Style* (Chicago: Loyola University Press, 1993), p. 145.
16. Salvatore, "Faith in Context," pp. 12–13.
17. Dolan, *American Catholic Experience*, p. 278; and Ellen Skerrett, "The Development of Catholic Identity Among Irish Americans in Chicago, 1880–1920," in Timothy Meagher, ed., *From Paddy to Studs: Irish American Communities in the Turn of the Century Era, 1880–1920* (Westport, CT: Greenwood Press, 1986), p. 118.
18. Dolan, *American Catholic Experience*, pp. 205–6; and Skerrett, "Irish of Chicago's Hull House Neighborhood," p. 195.

19. Jeffrey M. Burns, "*Qué Es Esto?* The Transformation of St. Peter's Parish, San Francisco, 1913–1990," in James P. Wind and James W. Lewis, eds., *American Congregations* (Chicago: University of Chicago Press, 1994), pp. 398, 400, 405.

20. Dolan, *American Catholic Experience*, p. 213; and Salvatore, "Faith in Context," pp. 10, 13.

21. Skerrett, "Irish of Chicago's Hull House Neighborhood," p. 196.

22. Dolan, *American Catholic Experience*, p. 216.

23. Ibid., p. 232; and Hugh McLeod, "The Golden Age of New York City Catholicism," in Jane Garnett and Colin Matthew, eds., *Revival and Religion Since 1700: Essays for John Walsh* (London: Hambledon Press, 1993), pp. 257, 258.

24. Salvatore, "Faith in Context," pp. 14–15.

25. James Rodechko, "Patrick Ford and His Search for America: A Case Study of Irish American Journalism, 1870–1913" (Ph.D. diss., University of Connecticut, 1967), p. 242.

26. McLeod, *Piety and Poverty*, p. 57.

27. Ibid., p. 56; Dolan, *Catholic Revivalism*, p. 55, 217m101; and Dolan, *American Catholic Experience*, pp. 207, 278, 397.

28. Dolan, *Catholic Revivalism*, p. 151; and Kevin Kenny, *The American Irish: A History* (New York: Longman, 2000), p. 136.

29. John F. Quinn, *Father Mathew's Crusade: Temperance in Nineteenth-Century Ireland and North America* (Amherst: University of Massachusetts Press, 2002), p. 168.

30. See Dolan, *Catholic Revivalism*, pp. 109–10.

31. Ibid., pp. 109, 156.

32. Leslie Woodcock Tentler, *Catholics and Contraception: An American History* (Ithaca: Cornell University Press, 2004), p. 20.

33. Dolan, *American Catholic Experience*, p. 227; Tentler, *Catholics and Contraception*, p. 14; and Reverend P. A. Von Doss, S.J., *Thoughts and Counsels for the Consideration of Catholic Young Men* (New York: Fr. Pustet, 1889), p. 214.

34. Right Reverend Augustine Egger, *The Catholic Young Man of the Present Day* (New York: Benziger Bros., 1890), pp. 59–60; and Reverend Bernard O'Reilly, *True Men as We Need Them* (New York: Peter F. Collier, 1878), p. 325.

35. Burns, *"Qué Es Esto?"* p. 403.

36. Kevin Condon, C.M., *The Missionary College of All Hallows, 1842–1891* (Dublin: All Hallows College, 1986), p. 116.

37. McLeod, *Piety and Poverty*, p. 61.

38. Skerrett, "Sacred Space and Neighborhood in Chicago," p. 150; and Eileen M. McMahon, *What Parish Are You From? A Chicago Irish Community and Race Relations* (Lexington: University Press of Kentucky, 1995), p. 21.

39. Sylvester L. Malone, *Dr. Edward McGlynn* (New York: Dr. McGlynn Monument Association, 1918), p. 8; see also Hugh McLeod, "Edward McGlynn: A Rebel Against the Archbishop of New York," in S. P. Menes, ed., *Modern Religious Rebels* (London: Epworth Press, 1993), pp. 166–83.

40. Patrick Carey, "Peter Christopher Yorke," *American National Biography*, www.anb .org; and Burns, *"Qué Es Esto?"* pp. 412, 402.

41. Suellen Hoy, *Good Hearts: Catholic Sisters in Chicago's Past* (Urbana: University of Illinois Press, 2006), pp. 49, 17.

42. Ibid., pp. 49, 24–25.

43. Maureen Fitzgerald, *Habits of Compassion: Irish Catholic Nuns and the Origins of New York's Welfare System, 1830–1920* (Urbana: University of Illinois Press, 2006), p. 58.

44. Hoy, *Good Hearts*, pp. 36–38.

45. Carol K. Coburn and Martha Smith, *Spirited Lives: How Nuns Shaped Catholic Culture and American Life, 1836–1920* (Chapel Hill: University of North Carolina Press, 1999), p. 192; and Barbra Mann Wall, *Unlikely Entrepreneurs: Catholic Sisters and the Hospital Marketplace, 1865–1925* (Columbus: Ohio University Press, 2005), p. 29.

46. Glenn Collins, "Glimpses of Heartache, and Stories of Survival," *New York Times*, September 3, 2007, p. 13.

47. Fitzgerald, *Habits of Compassion*, pp. 1–2; Collins, "Glimpses of Heartache"; and "Sister Irene's Funeral," *New York Times*, August 18, 1896, p. 1.

48. Hoy, *Good Hearts*, p. 6; and Mary J. Oates, "Organized Voluntarism: The Catholic Sisters in Massachusetts, 1870–1940," *American Quarterly* 30, no. 5 (Winter 1978): p. 654.

49. Archives of the Sacred Congregation for the Propagation of the Faith, ACTA 1883, *Relazio sullo stato della Chiesa Cattolica negli Stati Uniti D'America*, p. 2, v. 252, f.1132r–1138v.

50. Richard Shaw, *Dagger John: The Unquiet Life and Times of Archbishop John Hughes of New York* (New York: Paulist Press, 1977), pp. 194, 197.

51. John R. G. Hassard, *The Life of the Most Reverend John Hughes* (New York: D. Appleton and Company, 1866), p. 220.

52. Morris, *American Catholic*, p. 5; Dolan, *Immigrant Church*, p. 165; Shaw, *Dagger John*, p. 209; and Jay P. Dolan, *In Search of an American Catholicism: A History of Religion and Culture in Tension* (New York: Oxford University Press, 2002), p. 50.

53. John Tracy Ellis, *The Life of James Cardinal Gibbons, Archbishop of Baltimore, 1834–1921* (Milwaukee: Bruce Publishing Company, 1952), 2:500, 2:630.

CHAPTER 6: BORN TO RULE

1. James Michael Curley, *I'd Do It Again* (Englewood Cliffs, NJ: Prentice-Hall, 1957), p. 83.

2. Thomas H. O'Connor, *The Boston Irish: A Political History* (Boston: Northeastern University Press, 1995), p. 126; and William L. Riordan, *Plunkitt of Tammany Hall*, ed. Terrence J. McDonald (Boston: Bedford Books of St. Martin's Press, 1994), p. 65.

3. Perry R. Duis, *The Saloon: Public Drinking in Chicago and Boston, 1880–1920* (Urbana: University of Illinois Press, 1983), p. 126.

4. Edwin O'Connor, *The Last Hurrah* (Boston: Little, Brown, 1956), pp. 70, 75.

5. Steven P. Erie, *Rainbow's End: Irish-Americans and the Dilemmas of Urban Machine Politics, 1840–1985* (Berkeley: University of California Press, 1988), p. 33.

6. John Paul Bocock, "The Irish Conquest of Our Cities," *Forum* 17 (March–August 1894), pp. 186–87, 195; and Harold Zink, *City Bosses in the United States* (Durham: Duke University Press, 1930).

7. Kenneth D. Ackerman, *Boss Tweed* (New York: Carroll and Graf Publishers, 2005), pp. 48, 7–8, 2, 65.

8. William V. Shannon, *The American Irish* (New York: Macmillan, 1963), p. 69.

9. Ackerman, *Boss Tweed*, p. 340.

10. Alexander B. Callow Jr., *The Tweed Ring* (New York: Oxford University Press, 1965), pp. 202–3.

11. Ibid., pp. 125, 127.

12. Riordan, *Plunkitt of Tammany Hall*, p. 64.

13. Ibid., pp. 97–98.

14. Shannon, *American Irish*, p. 81.

15. Howard P. Chudacoff, *The Evolution of American Urban Society* (Englewood Cliffs, NJ: Prentice Hall, 1981), p. 153. For a biography of Croker, see Zink, *City Bosses*, pp. 128–46.

16. Nancy Joan Weiss, *Charles Francis Murphy, 1858–1924: Respectability and Responsibility in Tammany Politics* (Northampton, MA: Smith College, 1968), pp. 21–22, 88.

17. Christopher M. Finan, *Alfred E. Smith: The Happy Warrior* (New York: Hill and Wang, 2002), p. 74; and Shannon, *American Irish*, p. 82.

18. Finan, *Alfred E. Smith*, p. 74.

19. Daniel Czitrom, "Underworlds and Underdogs: Big Tim Sullivan and Metropolitan Politics in New York, 1889–1913," in Raymond Mohl, ed., *The Making of Urban America* (Wilmington, DE: Scholarly Resources, 1997), pp. 135–36.

20. Ibid., pp. 146–47.

21. Erie, *Rainbow's End*, pp. 79–91.

22. Ibid., pp. 89–90.

23. O'Connor, *Boston Irish*, pp. xv–xvi.

24. Ibid., p. 108.

25. Ibid., p. 162.

26. Lawrence W. Kennedy, "The Fateful Years: The Irish in Boston Politics" (unpublished mansucript), p. 81; and Jack Beatty, *The Rascal King: The Life and Times of James Michael Curley, 1874–1958* (New York: Addison-Wesley, 1992), p. 7.

27. O'Connor, *Boston Irish*, pp. 130–31.

28. Ibid., p. 156.

29. Kennedy, "The Fateful Years," p. 167.

30. James J. Connolly, *The Triumph of Ethnic Progressivism: Urban Political Culture in Boston, 1900–1925* (Cambridge: Harvard University Press, 1998), p. 23.

31. O'Connor, *Boston Irish*, pp. 147–48.

32. Leslie G. Ainley, *Boston Mahatma* (Boston: Bruce Humphries, 1949), pp. 13–14; Zink, *City Bosses*, p. 83; Thomas H. O'Connor, *Bibles, Brahmins, and Bosses: A Short History of Boston* (Boston: Public Library, 1976), p. 105.

33. John D. Buenker, "Martin Lomasney," *American National Biography*, www.anb.org.

34. O'Connor, *Boston Irish*, p. 167; Doris Kearns Goodwin, *The Fitzgeralds and the Kennedys: An American Saga* (New York: St. Martin's Press, 1987), p. 126; Connolly, *Triumph of Ethnic Progressivism*, pp. 82, 84.

35. Goodwin, *Fitzgeralds and the Kennedys*, p. 184.

36. O'Connor, *Boston Irish*, p. 178; Goodwin, *Fitzgeralds and the Kennedys*, pp. 226, 229–30; and Connolly, *Triumph of Ethnic Progressivism*, p. 103.

37. Goodwin, *Fitzgeralds and the Kennedys*, p. 289.
38. Ibid., p. 864.
39. O'Connor, *Boston Irish*, p. 180.
40. Beatty, *Rascal King*, p. 3.
41. Ibid., pp. 135, 152, 190.
42. Ibid., pp. 76–77, 491, 162.
43. Shannon, *American Irish*, p. 202.
44. Beatty, *Rascal King*, pp. 58, 320.
45. Connolly, *Triumph of Ethnic Progressivism*, p. 146.
46. O'Connor, *Boston Irish*, p. 189; and Connolly, *Triumph of Ethnic Progressivism*, pp. 134, 136.
47. Ibid., pp. 158–59.
48. Paul Michael Green, "Irish Chicago: The Multiethnic Road to Machine Success," in Peter d'A. Jones and Melvin G. Holli, eds., *Ethnic Chicago* (Grand Rapids: Wm. B. Eerdmans, 1981), p. 224.
49. Lloyd Wendt and Herman Kogan, *Lords of the Levee: The Story of Bath House John and Hinky Dink* (New York: Bobbs-Merrill, 1943), pp. 156, 318, 345.
50. Allen Davis, *American Heroine: The Life and Legend of Jane Addams* (Chicago: Ivan R. Dee, 2000), p. 121.
51. Jane Addams, "Why the Ward Boss Rules," in Riordan, *Plunkitt of Tammany Hall*, pp. 120–22.
52. John D. Buenker, "Edward F. Dunne: The Limits of Municipal Reform," in Paul M. Green and Melvin G. Holli, eds., *The Mayors: The Chicago Political Tradition* (Carbondale: Southern Illinois University Press, 1987), p. 34.
53. Ibid., pp. 48, 306n42.
54. Michael F. Funchion, "The Political and Nationalist Traditions," in Lawrence J. McCaffrey, Michael F. Funchion, Ellen Skerrett, and Charles Fanning, *The Irish in Chicago* (Urbana: University of Illinois Press, 1987), pp. 64–65.
55. Green, "Irish Chicago," p. 225.
56. Erie, *Rainbow's End*, p. 33.

CHAPTER 7: STRIKE

1. See Robert V. Bruce, *1877: Year of Violence* (Chicago: Ivan R. Dee, 1989); Milton Meltzer, *Bread and Roses: The Struggle of American Labor, 1865–1915* (New York: Alfred A. Knopf, 1967); and Philip S. Foner, *The Great Labor Uprising of 1877* (New York: Monad Press, 1977), for details on this strike.
2. Foner, *Great Labor Uprising*, p. 63; and Bruce, *1877*, p. 180.
3. Bruce, *1877*, pp. 314, 318.
4. Gary B. Nash et al., *The American People* (New York: Harper and Row, 1990), p. 633.
5. David Montgomery, *Beyond Equality: Labor and the Radical Republicans, 1862–1872* (New York: Alfred A. Knopf, 1967), p. 126; David Montgomery, "The Irish and the American Labor Movement," in David Noel Doyle and Owen Dudley Edwards, eds., *America and Ireland, 1776–1976: The American Identity and the Irish Connection* (Westport, CT: Greenwood Press, 1980), p. 206; and Gary M. Fink, ed., *Biographical Dictionary of American Labor Leaders* (Westport, CT: Greenwood Press, 1974).

6. Kevin Kenny, *The American Irish: A History* (New York: Longman, 2000), p. 175.

7. Melvyn Dubofsky and Warren Van Tine, eds., *Labor Leaders in America* (Urbana: University of Illinois Press, 1987), p. 45; and Leon Fink, *Workingmen's Democracy: The Knights of Labor and American Politics* (Urbana: University of Illinois Press, 1983), p. 228.

8. Dubofsky and Van Tine, *Labor Leaders*, p. 47; and quoted in Foster Rhea Dulles and Melvyn Dubofsky, *Labor in America: A History* (Arlington Heights, IL: Harlan Davidson, 1984), p. 134.

9. Harry J. Carman, Henry David, and Paul N. Guthrie, eds., *The Path I Trod: The Autobiography of Terence V. Powderly* (New York: AMS Press, 1968), p. 29.

10. Dubofsky and Van Tine, *Labor Leaders*, p. 44.

11. Craig Phelan, *Grand Master Workman: Terence Powderly and the Knights of Labor* (Westport, CT: Greenwood Press, 2000), pp. 1, 6, 150, 2; Dubofsky and Van Tine, *Labor Leaders*, p. 30.

12. Fink, *Workingmen's Democracy*, p. 12.

13. Carman et al., *Path I Trod*, p. 344.

14. Robert E. Weir, *Beyond the Veil: The Culture of the Knights of Labor* (University Park, PA: Pennsylvania State University Press, 1996), p. 12.

15. Ibid., p.186; and Sandra Opdycke, "Leonora Barry," *American National Biography*, www.anb.org.

16. Weir, *Beyond the Veil*, p. 185.

17. Robert E. Weir, "Elizabeth Rodgers," *American National Biography*, www.anb.org.

18. Quoted in Jay P. Dolan, *The American Catholic Experience: A History from Colonial Times to the Present* (Garden City, NY: Doubleday, 1985), p. 330; and Henry J. Browne, *The Catholic Church and the Knights of Labor* (Washington, DC: Catholic University of America Press, 1949), p. 55.

19. Dolan, *American Catholic Experience*, pp. 337–39; and David Brundage, *The Making of Western Labor Radicalism: Denver's Organized Workers, 1878–1905* (Urbana: University of Illinois Press, 1994), p. 130.

20. Kevin Kenny, *Making Sense of the Molly Maguires* (New York: Oxford University Press, 1998), pp. 186, 213.

21. Clark C. Spence, "Marcus Daly," *American National Biography*, www.anb.org.

22. Melvyn Dubofsky, "The Origins of Western Working Class Radicalism, 1890–1905," *Labor History* 7, no. 2 (Spring 1966): p. 134; and David M. Emmons, *The Butte Irish: Class and Ethnicity in an American Mining Town, 1875–1925* (Urbana: University of Illinois Press, 1989), p. 97.

23. Emmons, *Butte Irish*, pp. 248, 183, 184, 198.

24. Mark Wyman, *Hard Rock Epic: Western Miners and the Industrial Revolution, 1860–1910* (Berkeley: University of California Press, 1979), p. 172; Richard E. Lingenfelter, *The Hardrock Miners: A History of the Mining Labor Movement in the American West, 1863–1893* (Berkeley: University of California Press, 1974), p. 226; and Emmons, *Butte Irish*, p. 299.

25. Dubofsky, "Origins of Western Working Class Radicalism," pp. 142, 147.

26. Elliott Gorn, *Mother Jones: The Most Dangerous Woman in America* (New York: Hill and Wang, 2001), p. 151.

27. Elliott J. Gorn, "Mother Jones," *American National Biography*, www.anb.org.

28. Mary Harris Jones, *The Autobiography of Mother Jones* Mineola, NY: Dover Publications, 2004), p. 89.

29. Gorn, *Mother Jones*, pp. 180, 181, 189.

30. Ibid., pp. 73, 79.

31. L. A. O'Donnell, *Irish Voice and Organized Labor in America* (Westport, CT: Greenwood Press, 1997), pp. 49, 50.

32. Timothy J. Meagher, *The Columbia Guide to Irish American History* (New York: Columbia University Press, 2005), p. 272.

CHAPTER 8: NATION AMONG NATIONS

1. Alan J. Ward, *The Easter Rising: Revolution and Nationalism* (Arlington Heights, IL: Harlan Davidson, 1980), p. 10.

2. Wilfried Neidhardt, *Fenianism in North America* (University Park: Pennsylvania State University Press, 1975), p. 12.

3. Louis R. Bisceglia, "The Fenian Funeral of Terence Bellew McManus," in *Eire-Ireland* 14 (1979): p. 46.

4. Ibid., pp. 61–62.

5. Kerby A. Miller, *Emigrants and Exiles* (New York: Oxford University Press, 1985), p. 336.

6. Ibid., p. 276.

7. Ibid., p. 312.

8. Thomas N. Brown, *Irish-American Nationalism, 1870–1890* (Philadelphia: J. B. Lippincott Company, 1966), p. 24.

9. Brian Jenkins, *Irish Nationalism and the British State: From Repeal to Revolutionary Nationalism* (Montreal and Kingston: McGill-Queens Press, 2006), pp. 248, 311.

10. Brown, *Irish-American Nationalism*, p. 65.

11. Terry Golway, *Irish Rebel: John Devoy and America's Fight for Ireland's Freedom* (New York: St. Martin's Press, 1998), p. 319.

12. F. S. L. Lyons, *Charles Stewart Parnell* (London: Fontana/Collins, 1978), p. 114.

13. Golway, *Irish Rebel*, p. 107.

14. James J. Green, "American Catholics and the Irish Land League, 1879–1882," *Catholic Historical Review* 35 (1949): pp. 19–42.

15. Golway, *Irish Rebel*, p. 126.

16. Lyons, *Charles Parnell*, p. 111.

17. Eric Foner, "Class, Ethnicity, and Radicalism in the Gilded Age: The Land League and Irish-America," *Marxist Perspectives* 1 no. 2 (Summer 1978): p. 8.

18. Carla King, *Michael Davitt* (Historical Association of Ireland: Dundalgan Press, 1999), p. 33; Brown, *Irish-American Nationalism*, p. 122; and Joe Doyle, "Striking for Ireland on the New York Docks," in Ronald H. Bayor and Timothy J. Meagher, eds., *The New York Irish* (Baltimore: Johns Hopkins University Press, 1996), p. 358.

19. Foner, "Class, Ethnicity, and Radicalism," p. 21.

20. Ibid., p. 44.

21. Ibid., p. 14.

22. Patrick Ford, *Criminal History of the British Empire* (New York: Irish World, c. 1914), p. 1.

23. Foner, "Class, Ethnicity, and Radicalism," p. 14.

24. Ibid., p. 21.

25. David Montgomery, "Henry George," *American National Biography*, www.anb.org; Foner, "Class, Ethnicity, and Radicalism," p. 34; and T. W. Moody, *Davitt and the Irish Revolution, 1846–82* (Oxford: Clarendon Press, 1981), p. 413.

26. Moody, *Davitt and the Irish Revolution*, p. 414.

27. Foner, "Class, Ethnicity, and Radicalism," p. 1.

28. Lyons, *Charles Parnell*, p. 134.

29. Ibid., p. 476.

30. J. J. Lee, *Ireland, 1912–1985: Politics and Society* (New York: Cambridge University Press, 1989), p. 35.

31. Golway, *Irish Rebel*, p. 237.

32. Ibid., pp. 249–52.

33. Timothy J. Meagher, *Inventing Irish America: Generation, Class, and Ethnic Identity in a New England City, 1880–1928* (Notre Dame, IN: University of Notre Dame Press, 2001), p. 367.

34. Golway, *Irish Rebel*, p. 264; and Francis M. Carroll, "America and Irish Political Independence, 1910–1933," in P. J. Drudy, ed., *The Irish in America: Emigration, Assimilation and Impact* (Cambridge: Cambridge University Press, 1985), p. 284.

35. Lee, *Ireland*, p. 67.

36. Golway, *Irish Rebel*, p. 304.

37. Ibid.

38. Michael Collins, "Arguments for the Treaty," in Seamus Deane, ed., *The Field Day Anthology of Irish Writing* (Derry: Field Day Publications, 1991), 3:736, 3:738.

CHAPTER 9: UP FROM THE CITY STREETS

1. Alfred E. Smith, *Up to Now: An Autobiography* (New York: Viking, 1929), p. 3.

2. Ibid., pp. 58–59.

3. Christopher M. Finan, *Alfred E. Smith, the Happy Warrior* (New York: Hill and Wang, 2002), pp. 86, 85; and William V. Shannon, *The American Irish* (New York: Macmillan, 1963), p. 161.

4. Leonard J. Moore, *Citizen Klansmen: The Ku Klux Klan in Indiana, 1921–1928* (Chapel Hill: University of North Carolina Press, 1991), p. 20; and Kenneth T. Jackson, *The Ku Klux Klan in the City, 1915–1930* (New York: Oxford University Press, 1967), p. 21.

5. John F. Quinn, *Father Mathew's Crusade: Temperance in Nineteenth-Century Ireland and North America* (Amherst: University of Massachusetts Press), p. 190.

6. "Catholic and Patriot: Governor Smith Replies," *Atlantic Monthly* 139 (June 1927): p. 715.

7. Ibid., p. 722.

8. Ibid., pp. 726, 728; and Thomas J. Shelley, "What the Hell Is an Encyclical? Governor Alfred E. Smith, Charles C. Marshall, Esq., and Father Francis P. Duffy," *U.S. Catholic Historian* 15, no. 2 (Spring 1997): pp. 91, 98–99.

9. Finan, *Alfred E. Smith*, p. 210.

10. Timothy J. Meagher, *Inventing Irish America: Generation, Class, and Ethnic Identity*

in a New England City, 1880–1928 (Notre Dame, IN: University of Notre Dame Press, 2001), p. 319.

11. Matthew and Hannah Josephson, *Al Smith: Hero of the Cities* (Boston: Houghton Mifflin, 1969), p. 394.

12. Finan, *Alfred E. Smith*, p. 217; and Robert A. Slayton, *Empire Statesman: The Rise and Redemption of Al Smith* (New York: Free Press, 2001), p. xiv.

13. Finan, *Alfred E. Smith*, p. 221.

14. *Up from City Streets*, vol. 3 of *Long Journey Home*, video cassette (Burbank, CA: Buena Vista Home Entertainment, 1997).

15. Michael A. Lerner, *Dry Manhattan: Prohibition in New York City* (Cambridge, MA: Harvard University Press, 2007), p. 251.

16. Josephson, *Al Smith*, pp. 398–99; and Finan, *Alfred E. Smith*, p. 228.

17. Finan, *Alfred E. Smith*, pp. 227–28.

18. Ibid., pp. 229–30; and see also Slayton, *Empire Statesman*, pp. 322–24.

19. *Up from City Streets*; and Eileen M. McMahon, *What Parish Are You From? A Chicago Irish Community and Race Relations* (Lexington: University Press of Kentucky, 1995), p. 53.

20. Finan, *Alfred E. Smith*, p. 164.

21. Patrick Blessing, "Irish," in Stephan Thernstrom, ed., *Harvard Encyclopedia of American Ethnic Groups* (Cambridge: Harvard University Press, 1980), p. 528; J. J. Lee, "Emigration: 1922–1998," in Michael Glazier, ed., *The Encyclopedia of the Irish in America* (Notre Dame, IN: University of Notre Dame Press, 1999), pp. 263–66. See also Matthew J. O'Brien, "Transatlantic Connections and the Sharp Edge of the Great Depression," *Eire-Ireland* 37 (Spring-Summer 2002): pp. 38–57.

22. Matthew J. O'Brien, "Irishness in Great Britain and the United States: Transatlantic and Cross-Channel Migration Networks and Irish Ethnicity, 1920–1960" (Ph.D. diss., University of Wisconsin–Madison, 2001), pp. 50–54.

23. Linda Dowling Almeida, *Irish Immigrants in New York City, 1945–1995* (Bloomington: Indiana University Press, 2001), p. 29.

24. Matthew O'Brien, "Hibernians on the March: Irish America and Ethnic Patriotism in the Mid-twentieth Century," *Eire-Ireland* 40, no. 1 and 2 (2005): p. 173.

25. Christopher J. Kauffman, *Patriotism and Fraternalism in the Knights of Columbus* (New York: Crossroad Publishing, 2001), p. 3.

26. O'Brien, "Hibernians on the March," p. 179.

27. Ibid., p. 180.

28. Paul Blanshard, *The Irish and Catholic Power* (Boston: Beacon Press, 1953), p. 264.

29. O'Brien, "Irishness in Great Britain and the United States," pp. 393–94.

30. Marjorie R. Fallows, *Irish Americans: Identity and Assimilation* (Englewood Cliffs, NJ: Prentice Hall, 1979), p. 60; and Joel Perlmann, *Ethnic Differences: Schooling and Social Structure Among the Irish, Italians, Jews and Blacks in an American City, 1880–1935* (New York: Cambridge University Press, 1988), pp. 44–45.

31. W. Lloyd Warner and Leo Srole, *The Social Systems of American Ethnic Groups* (New Haven: Yale University Press, 1945), pp. 71–72, 40; Herbert Wallace Schneider, *Religion in 20th Century America* (New York: Atheneum, 1964), pp. 265–67; and E. P. Hutchinson, *Immigrants and Their Children, 1850–1950* (New York: John Wiley and Sons, 1956), p. 217.

32. Steven P. Erie, *Rainbow's End: Irish-Americans and the Dilemmas of Urban Machine Politics, 1840–1985* (Berkeley: University of California Press, 1988), p. 90.

33. Jeff Kisseloff, *You Must Remember This: An Oral History of Manhattan from the 1890s to World War II* (Baltimore: Johns Hopkins University Press, 1989), p. 512.

34. Robert W. Snyder, "The Neighborhood Changed: The Irish of Washington Heights and Inwood Since 1945," in Ronald H. Bayor and Timothy J. Meagher, eds., *The New York Irish* (Baltimore: Johns Hopkins University Press, 1996), p. 441.

35. McMahon, *What Parish Are You From?*, pp. 32–33.

36. Jeffrey M. Burns, "*Qué es esto?* The Transformation of St. Peter's Parish, San Francisco, 1913–1990," in James P. Wind and James W. Lewis, eds., *American Congregations* (Chicago: University of Chicago Press, 1994), p. 399.

37. Snyder, "The Neighborhood Changed," p. 442; and McMahon, *What Parish Are You From?*, p. 53.

38. Alan Ehrenhalt, *The Lost City: The Forgotten Virtues of Community in America* (New York: Basic Books, 1995), p. 97.

39. McMahon, *What Parish Are You From?*, p. 35.

40. Ehrenhalt, *Lost City*, p. 280.

41. Fallows, *Irish Americans*, p. 139; and see also Andrew M. Greeley, *The Irish Americans: The Rise to Money and Power* (New York: Warner Books, 1981), pp. 131–48, for a lengthy discussion of Irish achievement.

42. John T. McGreevy, *Parish Boundaries: The Catholic Encounter with Race in the Twentieth Century Urban North* (Chicago: University of Chicago Press, 1996), p. 84.

43. Snyder, "The Neighborhood Changed," p. 448.

44. McGreevy, *Parish Boundaries*, p. 96.

45. McMahon, *What Parish Are You From?*, p. 130.

CHAPTER 10: IRISH CATHOLICISM'S GOLDEN AGE

1. Charles Morris, *American Catholic* (New York: Random House, 1997), p. 171.

2. Ibid., pp. 170, 186; Edward R. Kantowicz, *Corporation Sole: Cardinal Mundelein and Chicago Catholicism* (Notre Dame, IN: University of Notre Dame Press, 1983), p. 2; and Hugh Nolan, "The Native Son," in James F. Connelly, ed., *The History of the Archdiocese of Philadelphia* (Philadelphia: Archdiocese of Philadelphia, 1976), p. 380.

3. James M. O'Toole, *Militant and Triumphant: William Henry O'Connell and the Catholic Church in Boston, 1859–1944* (Notre Dame, IN; University of Notre Dame Press, 1992), pp. 31, 87.

4. William L. Smith, *Irish Priests in the United States: A Vanishing Subculture* (Lanham, MD: University Press of America, 2004), pp. 27–37.

5. Les and Barbara Keyser, *Hollywood and the Catholic Church* (Chicago: Loyola University Press, 1984), p. 103.

6. Morris, *American Catholic*, pp. 196–209.

7. Kantowicz, *Corporation Sole*, p. 173.

8. John A. Ryan, *Social Doctrine in Action: A Personal History* (New York: Harper and Brothers Publishers, 1941), p. 8.

9. Jay P. Dolan, *The American Catholic Experience: A History from Colonial Times to the Present* (Garden City, NY: Doubleday, 1985), p. 342.

10. Francis L. Broderick, *Right Reverend New Dealer: John A. Ryan* (New York: Macmillan, 1963), p. 230.

11. Alan Brinkley, *Voices of Protest: Huey Long, Father Coughlin and the Great Depression* (New York: Vintage Books, 1983), p. 83.

12. Ronald H. Bayor, "Ethnic Relations: The Jews and the Irish," in Michael Glazier, ed., *The Encyclopedia of the Irish in America* (Notre Dame, IN: University of Notre Dame Press, 1999), p. 287.

13. Eileen M. McMahon, *What Parish Are You From? A Chicago Irish Community and Race Relations* (Lexington: University Press of Kentucky, 1995), p. 97.

14. Miss Mary Donahue, in her prize-winning essay, "A Home Art," in Archives of Sister of St. Joseph of Philadelphia, Chestnut Hill, PA, Sister Mary A. McEvoy Collection—my thanks to Kathleen Cummings for this information. Quoted in Jay P. Dolan, R. Scott Appleby, Patricia Byrne, and Debra Campbell, *Transforming Parish Ministry* (New York: Crossroad, 1989), p. 112.

15. Alan Ehrenhalt, *The Lost City: The Forgotten Virtues of Community in America* (New York: Basic Books, 1995), pp. 129–30.

16. McMahon, *What Parish Are You From?*, p. 68.

17. Maureen Waters, *Crossing Highbridge: A Memoir of Irish America* (Syracuse: Syracuse University Press, 2001), p. 44.

18. Ibid., p. 16.

19. Ehrenhalt, *Lost City*, p. 114.

20. Waters, *Crossing Highbridge*, p. 71.

21. Leslie Woodcock Tentler, *Catholics and Contraception: An American History* (Ithaca: Cornell University Press, 2004), pp. 162, 161, 146.

22. Ibid., p. 478.

23. Frank Walsh, *Sin and Censorship: The Catholic Church and the Motion Picture Industry* (New Haven: Yale University Press, 1996), p. 275.

24. Robert I. Gannon, *The Cardinal Spellman Story* (Garden City, NY: Doubleday, 1962), pp. 79, 287.

25. John Cooney, *The American Pope: The Life and Times of Francis Cardinal Spellman* (New York: Dell Publishing, 1984), p. 151.

26. Ehrenhalt, *Lost City*, p. 120.

CHAPTER II: CITY HALL AND THE UNION HALL

1. William V. Shannon, *The American Irish* (New York: Macmillan, 1963), p. 228.

2. Ibid., p. 216; and Thomas H. O'Connor, *The Boston Irish: A Political History* (Boston: Northeastern University Press, 1995), p. 217.

3. O'Connor, *Boston Irish*, p. 210; and Jack Beatty, *The Rascal King: The Life and Times of James Michael Curley, 1874–1958* (New York: Addison-Wesley, 1992), p. 440.

4. Beatty, *Rascal King*, p. 482.

5. Ibid., p. 456; and Tip O'Neill with William Novak, *Man of the House: The Life and Political Memoirs of Speaker Tip O'Neill* (New York: Random House, 1987), p. 73.

6. O'Neill with Novak, *Man of the House*, p. 73.

7. Paul Michael Green, "Irish Chicago: The Multiethnic Road to Machine Success," in Peter d'A. Jones and Melvin G. Holli, eds., *Ethnic Chicago* (Grand Rapids: Wm. B. Eerdmans, 1981), p. 254.

8. Roger Biles, *Big City Boss in Depression and War: Mayor Edward J. Kelly of Chicago* (De Kalb: Northern Illinois University Press, 1984), p. 47.

9. Ibid., pp. 20, 47.

10. Roger Biles, "Edward J. Kelly: New Deal Machine Builder," in Paul M. Green and Melvin G. Holli, eds., *The Mayors: The Chicago Political Tradition* (Carbondale: Southern Illinois University Press, 2005), p. 114.

11. Ibid., p. 135.

12. Biles, *Big City Boss*, p. 147.

13. Arnold R. Hirsch, "Martin H. Kennelly: The Mugwump and the Machine," in Green and Holli, *Mayors*, pp. 132, 139.

14. Michael P. Weber, *Don't Call Me Boss: David Lawrence, Pittsburgh's Renaissance Mayor* (Pittsburgh: University of Pittsburgh Press,1988), pp. 275, 388–89.

15. David McKean, *Tommy the Cork: Washington's Ultimate Insider from Roosevelt to Reagan* (South Royalton, VT: Steerforth Press, 2004), p. 2.

16. Shannon, *American Irish*, p. 348.

17. John Cooney, *The American Pope: The Life and Times of Francis Cardinal Spellman* (New York: Dell Publishing, 1984), p. 282.

18. Shannon, *American Irish*, p. 382.

19. David Brody, *Labor in Crisis: The Steel Strike of 1919* (New York: J. B. Lippincott, 1965), pp. 62, 136.

20. Robert H. Zieger, *American Workers, American Unions, 1920–1985* (Baltimore: Johns Hopkins University Press, 1986), p. 31.

21. David M. Kennedy, *Freedom from Fear: The American People in Depression and War, 1929–1945* (New York: Oxford University Press, 1999), p. 314; and Zieger, *American Workers*, p. 55.

22. Walter Licht and Hal Seth Barron, "Labor's Men: A Collective Biography of Union Officialdom During the New Deal Era," *Labor History*, Fall 1978, p. 536.

23. Melvyn Dubofsky and Warren Van Tine, *John L. Lewis: A Biography* (New York: Quadrangle, 1977), p. 111.

24. Ronald W. Schatz, "Philip Murray and the Subordination of the Industrial Unions to the United States Government," in Melvyn Dubofsky and Warren Van Tine, eds., *Labor Leaders in America* (Urbana: University of Illinois Press, 1987), p. 236; and Bruce Nelson, *Divided We Stand: American Workers and the Struggle for Black Equality* (Princeton: Princeton University Press, 2001), p. 187.

25. Schatz, "Philip Murray," p. 238.

26. Ibid.

27. Melvyn Dubofsky, "Labor's Odd Couple: Philip Murray and John L. Lewis," in Paul F. Clark, Peter Gottlieb, and Donald Kennedy, eds., *Forging a Union of Steel: Philip Murray, SWOC, and the United Steelworkers* (Ithaca: ILR Press, New York State School of Industrial and Labor Relations, Cornell, 1987), pp. 31–32.

28. Ibid., p. 44.

29. Ibid., p. 111; and David Brody, "The Origins of Modern Steel Unionism: The

SWOC Era," in Clark, Gottlieb, and Kennedy, *Forging a Union of Steel*, 26; Nelson, *Divided We Stand*, p. 187; and Zieger, *American Workers*, p. 101.

30. Schatz, "Philip Murray," pp. 244–45.
31. Ibid., p. 248; and Ronald W. Schatz, "Battling Over Government's Role," in Clark, Gottlieb, and Kennedy, *Forging a Union of Steel*, p. 92.
32. Zieger, *American Workers*, p. 131.
33. Nelson, *Divided We Stand*, pp. 190, 201, 212–13.
34. Archie Robinson, *George Meany and His Times: A Biography* (New York: Simon and Schuster, 1981), pp. 31–32.
35. Robert H. Zieger, "George Meany: Labor's Organization Man," in Dubofsky and Van Tine, *Labor Leaders*, p. 328.
36. Ibid., pp. 331, 333–34.
37. Ibid., p. 335.

CHAPTER 12: THE TRIUMPH OF THE IRISH

1. Adam Cohen and Elizabeth Taylor, *American Pharaoh: Mayor Richard J. Daley: His Battle for Chicago and the Nation* (Boston: Little, Brown, 2000), p. 265; and Kenneth P. O'Donnell and David F. Powers, *Johnny We Hardly Knew Ye: Memories of John Fitzgerald Kennedy* (Boston: Little, Brown, 1970), p. 223.
2. Theodore H. White, *The Making of the President 1960* (New York: Atheneum, 1961), pp. 330, 333.
3. O'Donnell and Powers, *Johnny We Hardly Knew Ye*, pp. 166–67.
4. White, *Making of the President 1960*, p. 259.
5. O'Donnell and Powers, *Johnny We Hardly Knew Ye*, pp. 206–7.
6. White, *Making of the President 1960*, pp. 391–93.
7. Theodore C. Sorensen, *Kennedy* (London: Hodder and Stoughton, 1965), p. 190; and O'Donnell and Powers, *Johnny We Hardly Knew Ye*, p. 210.
8. Sorensen, *Kennedy*, p. 219.
9. O'Donnell and Powers, *Johnny We Hardly Knew Ye*, p. 360.
10. Ian McCabe, "JFK in Ireland," *History Ireland*, Winter 1993, p. 38; O'Donnell and Powers, *Johnny We Hardly Knew Ye*, pp. 366, 363; and Richard Reeves, *President Kennedy: Profile of Power* (New York: Simon and Schuster, 1993), p. 537.
11. Arthur Mitchell, *JFK and His Irish Heritage* (Dublin: Moytura Press, 1993), p. 153; and Theodore C. Sorensen, *Kennedy* (New York: Bantam, 1966), p. 581.
12. William V. Shannon, *The American Irish* (New York: Macmillan, 1963), p. 393.
13. Pete Hamill, "Once We Were Kings," in J. J. Lee and Marion R. Casey, *Making the Irish American: History and Heritage of the Irish in the United States* (New York: New York University Press, 2006), pp. 526–27; and Christopher Finan, *Alfred E. Smith: The Happy Warrior* (New York: Hill and Wang, 2002), p. 230.
14. Matthew Frye Jacobson, *Roots Too: White Ethnic Revival in Post–Civil Rights America* (Cambridge: Harvard University Press, 2006), p. 12.
15. Nathan Glazer and Daniel Patrick Moynihan, *Beyond the Melting Pot: The Negroes, Puerto Ricans, Jews, Italians, and Irish of New York City* (Cambridge, MA: MIT Press, 1963), p. 287.
16. Andrew M. Greeley has documented the rise of the Irish in several of his books,

most notably *The Irish Americans: The Rise to Money and Power* (New York: Harper and Row, 1981).

17. Brian Sullivan, "The Triumph of Irish Power," *Improper Bostonian*, November 3, 1999, p. 229.

18. Dinita Smith, "The Irish Are Hot in the U.S. Again," *New York Times*, October 3, 1996, p. B4; and "The 400 Richest Americans," *Forbes*, September 21, 2006.

19. Michael Patrick MacDonald, *All Souls: A Family Story from Southie* (Boston: Beacon Press, 1999), pp. 6–7.

20. Morton D. Winsberg, "The Suburbanization of the Irish in Boston, Chicago and New York," *Eire Ireland* 21 (Fall 1986): p. 95; and Eileen M. McMahon, *What Parish Are You From? A Chicago Irish Community and Race Relations* (Lexington: University Press of Kentucky, 1995), pp. 157, 167.

21. McMahon, *What Parish Are You From?*, p. 166.

22. Cohen and Taylor, *American Pharaoh*, pp. 395–96.

23. Greeley, *Irish Americans*, p. 167; and see also John T. McGreevy, *Parish Boundaries: The Catholic Encounter with Race in the Twentieth Century Urban North* (Chicago: University of Chicago Press, 1996), for a discussion of Catholics and race in selected Northern cities.

24. Diarmaid Ferriter, *The Transformation of Ireland* (Woodstock and New York: Overlook Press, 2005), pp. 670–72.

25. John A. Barnes, "Across the Sea from Ireland Looking for Work," *Wall Street Journal*, September 30, 1987, p. 36.

26. Mary P. Corcoran, "Emigrants, *Eirepreneurs*, and Opportunists: A Social Profile of Recent Irish Immigrants in New York City," in Ronald H. Bayor and Timothy J. Meagher, eds., *The New York Irish* (Baltimore: Johns Hopkins University Press, 1996), p. 475.

27. Nina Bernstein, "Greener Pastures (on the Emerald Isle)," *New York Times*, November 10, 2004, p. A21.

28. Peter Steinfels, *A People Adrift* (New York: Simon and Schuster, 2003), p. 40.

29. Cohen and Taylor, *American Pharaoh*, p. 264.

30. Ibid., p. 278.

31. Ibid., p. 22.

32. Roger Biles, *Richard J. Daley: Politics, Race and the Governing of Chicago* (De Kalb: Northern Illinois University Press, 1995), p. 27.

33. Milton L. Rakove, *Don't Make No Waves . . . Don't Back No Losers: An Insider's Analysis of the Daley Machine* (Bloomington: Indiana University Press, 1975), pp. 34–35; and Cohen and Taylor, *American Pharaoh*, p. 160.

34. Cohen and Taylor, *American Pharaoh*, p. 526; and Rakove, *Don't Make No Waves*, pp. 52–53.

35. Dirk Johnson, "In Illinois, It's the Political Life for Riley, Gilhooley Et Al.," *New York Times*, March 14, 1999, sec. 4, p. 2; and Rakove, *Don't Make No Waves*, p. 53.

36. Rakove, *Don't Make No Waves*, p. 58.

37. Paul M. Green, "Richard M. Daley and the Politics of Addition," in Paul M. Green and Melvin G. Holli, eds., *The Mayors: The Chicago Political Tradition* (Carbondale: Southern Illinois University Press, 2005), pp. 264–65.

38. Shannon, *American Irish*, p. 412.

39. Kevin P. Phillps, *The Emerging Republican Majority* (New Rochelle, NY: Arlington House, 1969), pp. 69, 168; and Timothy J. Meagher, *The Columbia Guide to Irish American History* (New York: Columbia University Press, 2005), p. 163.

40. Jeff Manza and Clem Brooks, *Social Cleavages and Political Change* (Cambridge: Oxford University Press, 1999), p. 120.

41. Melvyn Dubofsky and Warren Van Tine, eds., *Labor Leaders in America* (Urbana: University of Illinois Press), p. 339.

42. Ibid., pp. 337, 344.

43. Joseph J. Fahey, "The Making of a Catholic Labor Leader," *America*, August 28–September 4, 2006, p. 17.

44. Ferriter, *Transformation of Ireland*, p. 626.

45. Andrew J. Wilson, *Irish America and the Ulster Conflict, 1968–1995* (Belfast: Blackstaff Press, 1995), p. 70.

46. Ibid., p. 289.

47. Ibid., pp. 86–89.

48. Ibid., p. 194.

49. Ibid., p. 131.

50. Mary Pat Kelly, "Peace Itself Is the Prize: A Nobel for John Hume," *Commonweal*, November 20, 1998, p. 236.

51. Conor O'Clery, *The Greening of the White House* (Dublin: Gill and Macmillan, 1996), p. 90.

52. Bill Clinton, *My Life* (New York: Alfred A. Knopf, 2004), p. 686.

53. O'Clery, *Greening of the White House*, p. 234.

54. Nigel Hamilton, *Bill Clinton: Mastering the Presidency* (New York: Public Affairs, 2007), p. 555.

55. Ibid., p. 557.

CHAPTER 13: IT'S CHIC TO BE IRISH

1. Peter Quinn, "An Interview: Tap Dancing into Reality," in William Kennedy, *Riding the Yellow Trolley Car* (New York: Viking, 1993), p. 54.

2. Nathan Glazer and Daniel Patrick Moynihan, *Beyond the Melting Pot* (Cambridge: MIT Press, 1963), p. 290.

3. Matthew Frye Jacobson, *Roots Too: White Ethnic Revival in Post–Civil Rights America* (Cambridge: Harvard University Press, 2006), pp. 7–8.

4. Dinitia Smith, "The Irish Are Hot in the U.S. Again," *New York Times*, October 3, 1996, p. B1.

5. Mary C. Waters, *Ethnic Options: Choosing Identities in America* (Berkeley: University of California Press, 1990), p. 151.

6. Dirk Johnson, "In Illinois, It's the Political Life for Riley, Gilhooley Et Al.," *New York Times*, March 14, 1999, sec. 4, p. 2. See also Hout's essay that explains this more scientifically: Michael Hout and Joshua R. Goldstein, "How 4.5 Million Irish Immigrants Became 40 Million Irish Americans: Demographic and Subjective Aspects of the Ethnic Composition of White Americans," *American Sociological Review* 59 (February 1994): pp. 64–82.

Index

Longshoremen's and Laborers United
    Benevolent Society, 165–66
Lord, Daniel, 233
loyalists, 22
Lynch, Peter, 278

MacDiarmada, Sean, 183
MacDonald, Michael Patrick, 279
Mackay, John, 174
Maclay Act (1842), 49
Madames of the Sacred Heart, 114
Maguire, Patrick, 148, 150
The Making of the President 1960
    (White), 271–72
Malone, Thomas H., 173, 181
Marian devotions, 239
Marshall, Charles C., 213–14
Maryknoll Society, 234
Maryland, Catholic Church in
    Baltimore, 133–34
Maryland colony, 9
    Carroll family, 10–15
    Catholicism in, 9–10, 12
Massachusetts. *See also* Boston
    Curley as governor and
        Congressman, 154–57
    economic mobility, 222
    immigrant home ownership, 89
    Know-Nothing Party, 97–98
    labor movement, 166
    Ursuline convent school incident
        (Charlestown), 60–61
    Worcester Irish, 90, 92–93, 96, 162,
        193
Mathew, Theobald, 122
McCarthy, Abigail, 217
McCarthy, Eugene, 292
McCarthy, Joseph, 257–58
McCarthy, Patrick J., 162
McCloskey, John, 107
McCloskey, Matthew, 275
McCoppin, Frank, 162
McCormack, John W., 247–48, 257
McCourt, Frank, 306
McDermott, Alice, 306
McDonald, Mike, 158

McDonough, "Big Joe," 288
McGivney, Michael, 219–20
McGlynn, Edward, 126–27, 180–81,
    196
McGowan, Raymond A., 235
McGreevy, John, 53, 226
McGuire, Peter J., 179
McKean, David, 256
McMahon, John, 228
McMahon, Thomas, 260
McManes, James, 162
McManus, Terence, 185–86
McNabb sisters, 84
Meagher, Thomas Francis, 99, 100
Meagher, Timothy, 90, 92, 105
Meany, George, 265–67, 294–95
Mellon, Richard K., 253
melting-pot ideology, 304
Mercy Hospital (Chicago), 129
middle class, 93–94, 104, 118–19, 147,
    222, 226, 278
Miller, Kerby, 9, 17, 106, 186
mine workers and mining industry,
    166, 173–79, 259, 260–61,
    262, 263
miraculous, belief in (devotional
    Catholicism), 120, 240
Mitchel, John, 68, 99–100, 187
Mitchell, George, 301
Mitchell, John, 173, 178–79
Molly Maguires, 173–74
Mooney, Edward, 236
Mooney, William, 28
Moore, Annie, 81–82
Morse, Samuel F. B., 60
Motion Picture Herald, 233
Motion Picture Production Code, 233
movies and Catholicism, 231–33, 242,
    279
Moylan, Stephen, 26, 27
Moynihan, Daniel Patrick, 278, 292,
    299, 304
Murphy, Charles, 143–44
Murphy, Frank, 257
Murray, John Courtney, 234
Murray, Philip, 259–60, 260–65

A Note on the Author

Jay P. Dolan is a professor emeritus of history at the University of Notre Dame. He retired from teaching in 2004 after thirty-five years. While at Notre Dame he founded the Cushwa Center for the Study of American Catholicism and served as its founding director from 1977 to 1993. The author of numerous books, he also served as president of both the American Society of Church History and the American Catholic Historical Association. His first book, *The Immigrant Church: New York's Irish and German Catholics, 1815–1865* (1975), is a groundbreaking study of an urban immigrant Catholic community. His history of American Catholicism, *The American Catholic Experience: A History from Colonial Times to the Present* (1985), is still regarded as the definitive account.